When should I travel to get the best airfare?
Where do I go for answers to my travel questions?
What's the best and easiest way to plan and book my trip?

frommers.travelocity.com

Frommer's, the travel guide leader, has teamed up with **Travelocity.com**, the leader in online travel, to bring you an in-depth, easy-to-use resource designed to help you plan and book your trip online.

At **frommers.travelocity.com**, you'll find free online updates about your destination from the experts at Frommer's plus the outstanding travel planning and purchasing features of Travelocity.com. Travelocity.com provides reservations capabilities for 95 percent of all airline seats sold, more than 47,000 hotels, and over 50 car rental companies. In addition, Travelocity.com offers more than 2,000 exciting vacation and cruise packages. Travelocity.com puts you in complete control of your travel planning with these and other great features:

> **Expert travel guidance from Frommer's** - over 150 writers reporting from around the world!
>
> **Best Fare Finder** - an interactive calendar tells you when to travel to get the best airfare
>
> **Fare Watcher** - we'll track airfare changes to your favorite destinations
>
> **Dream Maps** - a mapping feature that suggests travel opportunities based on your budget
>
> **Shop Safe Guarantee** - 24 hours a day / 7 days a week live customer service, and more!

Whether traveling on a tight budget, looking for a quick weekend getaway, or planning the trip of a lifetime, Frommer's guides and Travelocity.com will make your travel dreams a reality. You've bought the book, now book the trip!

Travelocity.com
A Sabre Company

Frommer's ™

Also available from Hungry Minds, Inc.:

Beyond Disney: The Unofficial Guide to Universal, Sea World, and the Best of Central Florida

Inside Disney: The Incredible Story of Walt Disney World and the Man Behind the Mouse

Mini Las Vegas: The Pocket-Sized Unofficial Guide to Las Vegas

Mini-Mickey: The Pocket-Sized Unofficial Guide to Walt Disney World

The Unofficial Guide to Bed & Breakfasts in California

The Unofficial Guide to Bed & Breakfasts in New England

The Unofficial Guide to Bed & Breakfasts in the Northwest

The Unofficial Guide to Bed & Breakfasts in the Southeast

The Unofficial Guide to Branson, Missouri

The Unofficial Guide to California with Kids

The Unofficial Guide to Chicago

The Unofficial Guide to Cruises

The Unofficial Guide to Disneyland

The Unofficial Guide to Florida with Kids

The Unofficial Guide to the Great Smoky and Blue Ridge Region

The Unofficial Guide to Golf Vacations in the Eastern U.S.

The Unofficial Guide to Hawaii

The Unofficial Guide to Las Vegas

The Unofficial Guide to London

The Unofficial Guide to Miami and the Keys

The Unofficial Guide to New Orleans

The Unofficial Guide to New York City

The Unofficial Guide to Paris

The Unofficial Guide to San Francisco

The Unofficial Guide to Skiing in the West

The Unofficial Guide to the Southeast with Kids

The Unofficial Guide to Walt Disney World

The Unofficial Guide to Walt Disney World for Grown-Ups

The Unofficial Guide to Walt Disney World with Kids

The Unofficial Guide to Washington, D.C.

the Unofficial Guide® to the Mid-Atlantic with Kids

1st Edition

Mitch Kaplan

To my children, Dan and Laina, for opening my eyes to wonderment, and to Penny, for her continued unending patience and love.

Every effort has been made to ensure the accuracy of information throughout this book. Bear in mind, however, that prices, schedules, etc., are constantly changing. Readers should always verify information before making final plans.

Hungry Minds, Inc.
An International Data Group Company
909 Third Avenue, 21st Floor
New York, New York 10022

Copyright © 2001 by Mitch Kaplan

All rights reserved. No part of this book may be reproduced or transmitted in any form or by any means, electronic or mechanical, including photocopying, recording, or by any information storage and retrieval system, without permission in writing from the publishers.

Produced by Menasha Ridge Press

UNOFFICIAL GUIDE is a registered trademark of Hungry Minds, Inc.

ISBN 0-7645-6221-5

ISSN 1531-7544

Manufactured in the United States of America

10 9 8 7 6 5 4 3 2 1

First edition

Contents

List of Maps

Acknowledgments

Thanks to Susan LaTempa, co-author of *The Unofficial Guide to California with Kids* and former editor at *Westways* and *LA Style*, for handling my panic-stricken phone calls—and for launching me into the ever-dazzling travel writing world in the first place. Thanks to the folks at Menasha Ridge Press—Molly Merkle and Holly Cross in particular—who kindly waited while I fussed and finished. And special thanks to Mindy Bianca for going above and beyond the call in helping to unveil Maryland's untold secrets and wonders.

About the Author

Mitch Kaplan has been covering adventure and family travel for more than ten years, with a special interest in skiing. Kaplan has written *52 New Jersey Weekends* and *535 Wonderful Things to Do This Weekend.* His work has appeared in *Skiing, Snow Country, Family Circle, Westways, Endless Vacation, LA Style,* and *Continental Airlines* magazines. Kaplan lives in suburban northern New Jersey with his non-skiing/non-golfing wife Penny, two college-age children who won't leave the nest, and a beautiful mutt named Callie.

Introduction

The Dynamics of Family Travel

Don't even think about planning a family trip until you answer this question: What does each member of the family want to get out of the vacation?

It seems like a simple question, but it'll take more time and thought to answer than you might realize. It means assessing your current relationship with your kids and your spouse. It means taking stock of your children's passions and fears, as well as your own. It means attaching a budget to everyone's wishes. And it invariably means compromise.

Start by asking yourself some questions. Is this vacation a time for togetherness, for time alone for you while the children are entertained, or for a little of each? Are you a single dad who doesn't get to see the kids much? Are you an at-home mom who never gets a break? Are you looking for exhilarating adventures or a laid-back getaway? Do you want intellectual stimulation for you and the kids? How well do your kids handle spontaneity?

Because your family's dynamics change with every birthday, the answers may surprise you. One child may be more ready for adventure than you've realized; another might be more ready for peace and quiet than you think.

THE PLEASURES OF PLANNING

It's best to decide what you want to do and come up with some options to start the ball rolling. Then call a family meeting and include your kids in the planning process. Let everyone ask questions. Show some brochures or books about the places you have in mind so they'll feel like they have enough information to be taken seriously. Pull out maps and a globe. Jump on the Internet. Teenagers in particular are quite vocal about expressing their choices, and they appreciate it when they can influence the planning process. The getaway is much more enjoyable when everyone wants to be there.

This shared planning time can be a great routine to continue as the trip itself gets under way. Remember, your kids may not be able to easily visualize your destination or the plane ride or cab ride you'll take on the way. And if you're traveling from place to place during your vacation, each new day dawns on the unknown. So keep the brochures and guidebooks handy, and break the itinerary down into manageable chunks. Offer an advance agenda every now and then, referring again to your original planning sessions ("Remember we thought that the Bubbling Brook motel sounded like a good one?") and letting the kids develop anticipation rather than anxiety.

It's essential to be realistic when you plan a family vacation. Parents of young children may have to concede that the days of romantic sunsets are over for a while if there's a toddler tugging at their shorts. With infants and toddlers, the best vacations are the simple ones. They don't much need to see the sights; the idea is to be somewhere comfortable and intriguing for the adults, with a pleasant environment in which to relax and enjoy your children. In the Mid-Atlantic region, simple beach resorts, self-contained mountain resorts, or approachable cities like Philadelphia, Baltimore, and Pittsburgh are ideal for parents of the youngest group of kids. School-age children revel in attractions created for their enjoyment—theme parks, amusement parks, arcades, rides. The metropolitan regions can also be a blast with elementary-age kids. Teens may seem reluctant, but if a pilgrimage to a special point of interest for them (a certain skateboard shop) is included, the whole trip becomes "worthwhile." And they thrive in safe, explore-it-on-your-own situations like Colonial Williamsburg or Ocean City (Maryland or New Jersey).

LESS IS MORE THAN ENOUGH

As you plan, we urge you to leave plenty of down time in the schedule. Some of our families' most memorable moments are simple breakfasts on the beach or early evening walks to nowhere, when the conversation naturally flows. Kids treasure moments, not places or days. Give your children plenty of room to run and play; a morning collecting seashells or an afternoon at the hotel pool can be more satisfying than standing in line at a crowded theme-park attraction.

A good rule of thumb may sound stringent: no more than two activities in a day. If you spend the morning at a museum, and plan to go to dinner in Georgetown, go back to the hotel in the afternoon to rest and swim. If you're driving from Washington, D.C., to Hershey, Pennsylvania, plan to visit the theme park the next day. Then you can stop on the way at the Gettysburg Battlefield or the funny little town that time forgot. Remember that travel itself is an activity.

Also, plan some activities that allow you to take a break from each other. The quarters get a little close after a week together in a hotel room, particularly if children are of significantly different ages. Schedule an afternoon where mom and dad split duties, giving each other a break; take advantage of child and teen programs offered in many resorts to make sure there's at least one evening alone with your spouse. Everyone benefits from a little elbow room.

Reconnections

Family vacations are a necessary indulgence in today's hurried-up world, a time for togetherness without the day-to-day distractions. Whether it's a car trip on a budget or a transcontinental flight, it's a time to reconnect with your family, especially teenagers. And the best times are the serendipitous moments—a heart-to-heart conversation on an evening hike, or silly "knock-knock" jokes while standing in line for the roller coaster. Roles are relaxed when schedules are flexible, and kids can have the opportunity to see their parents as interesting companions, not just bossy grown-ups. We all can learn from one another when there's time to listen and when we take the time to see the world through a loved one's eyes.

A seasoned traveler friend once scoffed at the notion of traveling with young children, "since they don't remember anything." I couldn't disagree more. On a trip to Huatulco, Mexico, our teenagers made fast friends, with whom they kept in contact for quite a while. They still talk with animation about the history they learned and the brilliant light show they saw more than ten years ago at Grand Coulee Dam in Washington. Side ventures on ski trips have exposed them to the ancient southwestern Anasazi culture, rural Vermont towns, and historic mining ghost towns in California. Given the open hearts and the innocence of childhood, new impressions may sink in even more deeply with kids than with adults.

Our children have a greater understanding of the rest of the world as a result of travel to new places and experiencing new ideas. And siblings have formed a special bond from traveling together, a bond less likely to be formed at home, where they have separate classrooms, separate friends, separate rooms. As parents, it's up to us to be sure there's some fun in a trip for each member of the family. As a family, we all need to remember to indulge our traveling companions from time to time. Remember, your responses to challenges on the road—delayed flights, long lines, unsatisfactory accommodations—will influence the way your children deal with frustrations. Be patient, be calm, and teach your children these important lifelong skills.

Vacations are times for adventure, relaxation, shared experiences, time alone—whatever your family decides. The goal of this book is to evaluate each destination with that in mind—recognizing that your family has needs based on ages, backgrounds, and interests, that are quite different from any other family's—and provide you with some structure to analyze your family's needs and create a vacation that works.

We have traveled extensively with our children, from Mexico and Canada to California, Florida, and the Rocky Mountains. Yet some of our most wondrous trips have been in our own backyard: a hotel weekend in Manhattan in Christmas season, a week spent with cousins at Nokamixon State Park in eastern Pennsylvania, or floating down the Delaware River in a tube. We can't imagine ever tiring of exploring our home region, whether we're stalking the newest amped-up amusement park or finding the next best beach.

This book is not meant to be a compendium of every family-priced hotel or every advertised attraction, though I strive to cover a variety of interests for a variety of ages. Instead of compiling a family-travel yellow pages, I've edited out the less worthy places to better draw attention to the destinations that will make your trip a hit.

Dozens of people have contributed their opinions to this book; it is evaluative and opinionated, and it offers advice for the best ways for families to have fun together and further their relationships.

Survival Guide for Little Kids

Think Small. Little ones love little pleasures: splashing in the hotel pool, playing hide-and-seek in the lobby, stacking up rocks on the beach. Don't overload them.

Seek Creative Transportation. For young children, getting there is often more fun than being there. When our daughter was 11, one of her greatest joys during a trip to Florida was the train that ran from the gates to the terminal at the airport. Seek out the ferries, trolleys, shuttles, trains, surreys, and double-decker buses, and you'll be rewarded with a cheap thrill that's as fun for little ones as a Disneyland ride.

Limit the Shopping. Our rule at attractions is a firm one: no shopping, not even looking, until we are leaving the place. Young children can get consumed by and panicky about choosing a souvenir, and they'll enjoy the museum or theme park more if they can focus on the activities, not the trinkets.

Give Them a Voice. Even four-year-olds will benefit from feeling like they have some control over their vacations. When possible, let them make simple choices for the family—like "Should we walk to the beach or ride the trolley?"

Allow for Lots of Down Time. Bring books or quiet hobbies to amuse yourself during nap times or play times. Remember, your children's ability to tackle the big world is much more limited than yours.

Accept Some Slowness. It's stressful enough to get a kindergartener out the door to school each morning, so don't keep up the stress on vacation. They need a break from being rushed, too. If they're happy playing in their pajamas for an extra half-hour, the museum can wait. Conversely, accept that the times you like to be more leisurely—like dinnertime—lead to impatience in children.

Survival Guide for School-Age Kids

Give Them Their Own Space. Whether it's a backpack, a carry-on train case, or one of those shoebag-like hanging pockets that fit over the car seat in front of them, each kid needs a portable room of his or her own in which to stow gum, cards, books, disposable cameras, and souvenirs.

Make a New Routine. At least until middle-school years, most kids do best with a certain amount of predictability, so it's a kindness to create little travel routines and rituals within your changed life. Knowing that their parents will always stop sight-seeing by 3 p.m. to swim (or will never check out without one last hour in the pool) is a comforting thought to many children. Knowing that they will have $5 spending money each day can do away with shopping anxiety. Having set turns as map reader can add some fun to a hundred-mile drive.

Avoid Eating Breakfast Out. Many savvy traveling parents never eat breakfast in a restaurant. School-age kids are at their brightest and best in the morning, and waiting for table service at a ho-hum restaurant can start the day on the wrong foot. We carry fruit, cereal, milk, and juices in coolers or to kitchenettes or pop for room service—it's the least expensive and most wonderfully indulgent time to do so.

Beware Befuddled Expectations. School-age kids are old enough to have some reference points, and young enough to have great gaping holes in their mental pictures of the world. Our kids have imagined that they'd have to sleep in the barn during a Pennsylvania Dutch Country farm stay; they've worried that the car would tumble down the cliff on a winding mountain road; they've expected to meet the president in person when visiting Washington, D.C. Ask what's going on in their minds. Listen. Don't overpromise.

Watch the Diet. It's fun to let vacation time be a time of special treats, but overindulgence in junk food, sweets, and caffeinated drinks may contribute to behavior changes in kids who aren't sleeping in their own beds and are full of adrenaline as it is.

Remember that Kids Hate Scenery. Drive them through it if you must, but don't make them actually look at too much of it.

Give Them a Ship's Log. A roll of tape and a blank book are all that's needed to turn ticket stubs, menus, brochures, and postcards from a clutter of trash into a wonderful scrapbook that's always ready to be shared and enjoyed.

Hotels and Motels Are Not Just for Sleeping. Allow time for getting ice, playing in the pool, reviewing all items and prices in the minibar, packing and unpacking, using the hairdryer, putting laundry into the laundry bags, trying out the vending machines, etc.

Hit the Playgrounds. Check your maps and ask ahead about public playgrounds with climbing and sliding equipment, and on days when you'll be sight-seeing, driving, or absorbing culture, allow for an hour's lunch or rest stop at the playground. Even on city vacations, try to set aside at least one day for pure physical fun at a beach or water park or ski slope.

Just Say Yes to Ranger Tours. These tours are often designed with schoolkids in mind. We'd never have learned the importance of sand dunes at Assateague National Seashore or learned the history of the Appalachian Trail if we hadn't checked the schedule at the state or national park information center and made a point to join the ranger walk.

Survival Guide for Teenagers

Don't Try to Fool Them. Don't try to tell them they'll have more fun with you than with their friends. They won't. But if you offer them the possibility of doing things they might want to tell their friends about later, they'll be interested.

Respect Their Culture. Let your teenagers play an active role in planning the vacation. Ask their opinions of your arrangements. Often teenagers will offer a great suggestion or an alternative that you may not have considered. And look for pop culture landmarks—movie locations, palaces of fashion or music or sport. Add a ball game to the itinerary.

Night Moves. A vacation is a great time to go with your teenager to a music club or a midnight movie, or on a moonlight hike. Go to the theater or the ballet; check out a jazz club. If you have other kids needing earlier bedtimes, let the parents switch-hit on going out at night with the older kids.

Give Them Options. You don't need to go everywhere with everyone. If your younger child wants to go see the dinosaurs at the museum, this is the time for a split plan: Dad and son see the dinosaurs, mother and daughter shop or take in a movie or a play. If you have teenagers who appreciate their sleep time, let them snooze late at least one morning. Slip out with younger siblings and take a walk or read a book. Also, set wake-up time before everyone says good night so that there are no grouchy morning risers (at least not because they've been awakened too early).

Give Them Freedom. Before age 12, kids are bound to parents, preferring to stay in your orbit; when adolescence hits, they're programmed to push away from you. Choose a vacation spot that is safe and controlled enough to allow them to wander or spend time with other teenagers. If you can't do that, look for an afternoon or evening at a controlled hangout place like a mall. Give them the night to themselves at Six Flags or Busch Gardens. Sign them up for an afternoon's surfing lesson at the Jersey Shore.

Compromise on the Headphone Thing. Headphones can allow teens to create their own space even when they're with others, and that can be a safety valve, but try to agree before the trip on some non-headphone parameters so you don't begin to feel as if they're being used to keep other family members and the trip itself at a distance. If you're traveling by car, take turns choosing the radio station or CD for part of the trip.

Don't Make Your Teenager the Built-in Baby-Sitter. It's a family vacation—a time for reconnecting, not for avoiding the kids. A special night out for parents also should be special for the children; let them order videos and room service, for example, or participate in age-appropriate hotel programs.

Make Peace with Shopping. Look for street markets and vintage stores; spend some time in surf shops and record stores. If you go with your teenager, you may find that the conversation in such an environment flows easily. Or hit the outlets—many a summer vacation has included a day of back-to-school shopping.

Just Say Yes to at Least One Big-Ticket Excursion. Teenagers will get a lot out of a half-day adventure. What look at first like expensive tours (often available through the hotel sports desk or concierge) have been memorable and important experiences for our kids that we, as parents, are simply not able to offer by ourselves. A raft ride, a desert jeep tour, a kayak and snorkel trip, a horseback trail ride—each took us far into the country we were exploring, and each was worth every cent. Or let the teenager sign up for a lesson: surfing, sailing, rock-climbing.

A Word on Homework

Both our elementary school and high school kids have faced a load of homework or a special project that had to be worked on during vacation time. If a surprise major assignment comes up, and plans can't be changed, there will be an unavoidable strain on the trip. Parents should consider strategies such as bringing along a laptop computer, scheduling vacation fun in half-day chunks so that the homeworked kid gets some work and some play, and/or a marathon session at a library at the vacation spot. You can also shamelessly beg the teacher for a reprieve, but make that a last resort.

The Secret to Visiting Art Museums

Room after room of paintings and sculptures are numbing to children. They need a focal point and a sense of adventure. Before your visit, find out what some of the major works on display are, and locate pictures of them (perhaps the museum will mail you a brochure with pictures, or you can look online or get an art book from the library). Let each child pick one or two works to sleuth out. They can learn a little about the artist and the work in question, and then when you visit the museum, they can go on a hunt for "their" artwork.

A Few Words for Single Parents

Because single parents generally are working parents, planning a special getaway with your children can be the best way to spend some quality time together. But remember, the vacation is not just for your child—it's for you, too. You might invite along a grandparent or a favorite aunt or uncle; the other adult provides nice company for you, and your child will benefit from the time with family members.

Don't try to spend every moment with your children on vacation. Instead, plan some activities for your children with other children. Look for hotels with supervised activities, or research the community you'll be visiting for school-vacation offerings at libraries, recreation centers, or temple or church day camps. Then take advantage of your free time to do what you want to do: read a book, have a massage, take a long walk or a catnap.

Tips for Grandparents

A vacation that involves generations can be the most enriching experience for everyone, but it is important to consider the needs of each family member, from the youngest to the oldest. Here are some things to consider.

- If you're planning to travel alone with your grandchildren, spend a little time getting to know them before the vacation. Be sure they're comfortable with the idea of traveling with you if their parents are not coming along.

- It's best to take one grandchild at a time, two at the most. Cousins can be better than siblings, because they don't fight as much.

- Let your grandchildren help plan the vacation, and keep the first one short. Be flexible and don't overplan.

- Discuss mealtimes and bedtimes. Fortunately, many grandparents are on an early dinner schedule, which works nicely with younger children. Also, if you want to plan a special evening out, be sure to make the reservation ahead of time. Stash some crayons and paper in your bag to keep kids occupied.

- Gear plans to your grandchildren's age levels, because if they're not happy, you're not happy.

- Choose a vacation that offers some supervised activities for children in case you need a rest.

- If you're traveling by car, this is the one time we highly recommend headphones. Teenagers' musical tastes are vastly different from most grandparents', and it's simply more enjoyable when everyone can listen to their own style of music.

- Take along a nightlight.

- Carry a notarized statement from parents for permission for medical care in case of an emergency. Also, be sure you have insurance information.

- Tell your grandchildren about any medical problems you may have so that they can be prepared if there's an emergency.

- Many attractions and hotels offer discounts for seniors, so be sure you check ahead of time for bargains.

- A cruise may be the perfect compromise—plenty of daily activities for everyone, but shared mealtimes.

If planning a child-friendly trip seems overwhelming, try Grandtravel (800) 247-7651, a tour operator/travel agent aimed at kids and their grandparents.

For Travelers with Disabilities

Facilities for the disabled are plentiful throughout the Mid-Atlantic. Most public buildings have some form of access for those who use wheelchairs. In addition, many public buses are equipped with wheelchair lifts. Most of the states' attractions offer facilities and services for those with physical challenges, and many hotels have specially equipped rooms.

Almost every major city in each state has guides for the disabled. Visit state and city web sites or call ahead for specific information.

How the *Unofficial Guide* Works

ORGANIZATION

Our informal polls show that most families tend to choose a vacation spot based on geography—a place that's new and different, or familiar and comfortable. So we've divided the Mid-Atlantic first by states, and then each state into general geographic regions (either north to south or east to west), with family-friendly information in each region. For great places to stay within those regions—resorts, hotels, campgrounds—see the Family Lodging sections within each chapter; kid- and parent-pleasing restaurants are recommended in the Family-Friendly Restaurants sections found in each chapter.

The states include New Jersey, Pennsylvania, Delaware, Maryland, Washington, D.C., Virginia, and West Virginia.

Each regional chapter reviews outdoor adventures and attractions ranging from theme parks to science museums. We've also included serendipitous sidebars on offbeat places that you'll want to know about, from performing arts theaters in northern New Jersey to a great place for ice cream in the Pennsylvania Dutch Country.

If you're looking for some healthy family bonding, stretch beyond the man-made attractions. Have a sense of adventure and plan some activities that are new and exciting—not necessarily strenuous, but memorable. Each region has specific spots for the following activities:

Biking. Cycling is one of the best ways to experience an area firsthand and can be enjoyed year-round in much of the Mid-Atlantic. For beginners, we recommend miles of paved bicycle trails; older kids will like the mountain biking spots we've found. You don't even have to bring your own bike; you can rent one at many resorts and bike shops. Many shops rent trailers for small children (age five and younger) to travel safely behind you—they're much safer than bicycle seats. Know that helmets are the law for children in many states, and it is strongly advised that all cyclists wear helmets.

Camping. We've selected a few choice family-friendly campgrounds throughout the states. If it's your family's first experience, you might opt for a cabin; we list them in many state parks.

Hiking. Great hiking is found throughout the Mid-Atlantic; we've concentrated on the easiest spots suitable for kids, from urban nature hikes to the Appalachian Trail.

Kayaking, Tubing, Canoeing, and White-Water Rafting. Excellent venues for all these adventurous (and not so adventurous, too) pastimes can be found on the ocean, lakes, and rivers in all the states we cover. These are wonderful bonding adventures for families with kids over ages five or six.

Surfing. Most folks don't think of surfing when they think of the East Coast, but it is practiced from North Jersey to Virginia. So, we've recommended some surfing resources, as well as good beaches for wave riders of all kinds, including body boarders.

Whale-Watching. Whales migrate up the East Coast in spring and autumn, and many sites along their route offer whale-watching. Even if you don't spot one of the great whales, you'll surely enjoy whatever sea life you encounter and an exhilarating ride on the Atlantic Ocean.

The *Unofficial Guide* Rating System for Attractions

Our system includes an Appeal by Age Group category, indicating a range of appeal from one star ★ (don't bother) up to five stars ★★★★★ (not to be missed).

WHAT'S "UNOFFICIAL" ABOUT THIS BOOK?

The material in this guide originated with the authors and researchers and has not been reviewed, edited, or in any way approved by the attractions, restaurants, and hotels we describe. Our goal is to help families plan a vacation that's right for them by providing important details and honest opinions. If we've found a family-oriented destination to be dreary or a rip-off, we simply don't include it.

Readers care about the author's opinion. The author, after all, is supposed to know what he or she is talking about. This, coupled with the fact that the traveler wants quick answers (as opposed to endless alternatives), dictates that authors should be explicit, prescriptive, and, above all, direct. The *Unofficial Guide* tries to do just that—it spells out alternatives and recommends specific courses of action. It simplifies complicated destinations and attractions and allows the traveler to feel in control in the most unfamiliar environments. The objective of the *Unofficial Guide* is not to have the most information or all of the information, but to have the most accessible, useful information, unbiased by affiliation with any organization or industry.

This guide is directed at value-conscious, consumer-oriented families who seek a cost-effective, though not spartan, travel style.

Letters and Comments from Readers

We expect to learn from our mistakes, as well as from the input of our readers, and to improve with each book and edition. Many of those who use the *Unofficial Guides* write to us asking questions, making comments, or sharing their own discoveries and lessons learned. We appreciate all of the input, both positive and critical, and encourage our readers to continue

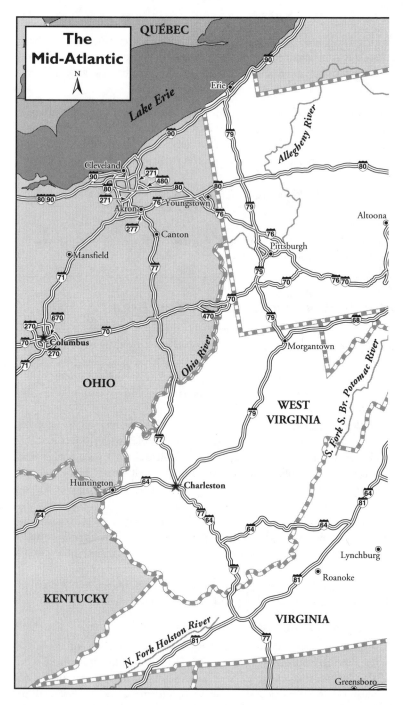

The Mid-Atlantic

N

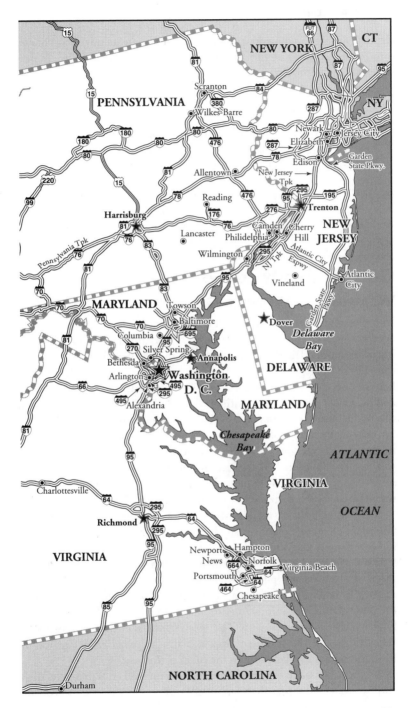

writing. Readers' comments and observations are frequently incorporated into revised editions of the *Unofficial Guide* and will contribute immeasurably to its improvement.

How to Write the Author

Mitch Kaplan
The Unofficial Guide to the Mid-Atlantic with Kids
P.O. Box 43673
Birmingham, AL 35243

When you write, be sure to put your return address on your letter as well as on the envelope—sometimes envelopes and letters get separated. And remember, our work takes us out of the office for long periods of time, so forgive us if our response is delayed.

Getting Ready to Go

WEATHER AND WHEN TO GO

The climate varies tremendously throughout the Mid-Atlantic region, and experiencing a destination in winter can be very different from experiencing it in summer. Travel during autumn, with the colorful foliage displayed throughout the region (from mid-September in northern New Jersey until late October in southern Virginia and West Virginia), adds an eye-dazzling and delightful dynamic. The entire region can be wiltingly hot and humid during the height of summer, especially in its more southerly reaches, and can be equally bitter cold in winter, particularly to the far north. Within these extreme margins, however, the region generally offers moderate weather, and travelers benefit from excellent outdoor activities in all seasons—from world-class skiing and hiking in the mountains to excellent water-based activities on the coast, lakes, and rivers.

We're most fond of visiting Mid-Atlantic cities in late spring or early fall, when there's still plenty of sun but not too much extreme heat or cold. However, in summer the cities do offer an endless parade of special events, festivals, and outdoor concerts, which means more outdoor activities for those who don't mind potentially high temperatures. If you're staying at the beach, note that during May and June the water remains quite cold; the peak of summer—July, August, and September—is best, as days are long and the water warms up. The mountains, from the Poconos to the Blue Ridge and the southern Appalachians, are wonderful year-round, from the ski days of February to the hikes of August.

In general, popular tourist sights are busier on weekends than weekdays, and Saturdays are busier than Sundays. Locals say the least crowded time to visit theme parks is on a rainy weekday in the winter.

Of course, family travel schedules often center around school holidays, which tend to be the busiest times to travel. But consider taking your children out of school for special family trips—a well-planned week of family travel is just as enriching as five days in a classroom. Make it clear that traveling is a privilege and agree that all missed work must be made up upon return. Talk with teachers ahead of time.

PACK LIGHT

We limit ourselves to one carry-on bag each and a backpack, no matter what the duration of the trip or how we are traveling. (The exception is a ski or snow trip, which demands bulky clothes.) If you have small children, stashing an extra T-shirt and pair of shorts in your backpack comes in handy in emergencies. Dress is generally casual, but when visiting Philadelphia, Washington, D.C., or another city in the region, everyone should pack one nice outfit for a special evening out.

Make a list of necessities and let the kids pack their own bags (subject to your inspection). T-shirts, shorts, and bathing suits are perfect in the warmer regions, but never travel without a jacket or sturdy sweatshirt. The weather is fickle, and you may be surprised with extreme cold or heat. Take along a small bottle of detergent for hand-washing. The vacation is much more enjoyable if you don't have a bunch of bags to haul around busy airports or hotel lobbies.

Let your children pack their own backpack, then ask them to wear it around the house to test how comfortable it will be on a long trip. Our children have become savvy packers, aware that each piece counts. Of course, you should check their bags before departing, just to be sure the essentials are all there.

Finally, you may want to take along a "surprise bag" for young travelers. Sticker books, a card game, or a new book are perfect, lightweight diversions to bring out when everyone's patience is wearing thin.

WHAT TO TAKE WITH YOU: A CHECKLIST

No matter what your means of transportation, be sure you take along (and have handy at all times):

- Sunglasses and hats to protect you from the sun.
- Sunscreen, at least 15 SPF.
- Emergency information—who to contact at home in case of an accident or emergency, medical insurance cards, and your pediatrician's telephone number (they can often diagnose and call in a prescription by phone).
- A travel-size bottle of antibacterial gel (the kind that doesn't require water).

- Basic first-aid kit—children's aspirin and aspirin substitute, allergy medication, Dramamine for motion sickness, insect repellent, bandages, gauze pads, thermometer, cough syrup, decongestant, medication for diarrhea, antibiotic cream, tweezers, and fingernail scissors.
- Prescription medications.
- Unscented baby wipes that can be used for any clean-up.
- A small sewing kit with scissors.
- A small nightlight to ease fear of darkness.
- A couple of extra paperback books, especially for teenagers.
- A folding cooler. Perfect for carrying fruit, drinks, even sandwiches to theme parks, on walks, or in the car.
- Lightweight windbreakers for cool evenings at the beach.
- Inexpensive rain ponchos for surprise rainstorms.
- Comfortable walking shoes for nature trails, botanical gardens, and beachside strolls (as well as theme parks).
- Each child should bring along some cash of her own, even just a few dollars. Tell them it is theirs to spend on souvenirs or whatever they choose. When it's their money, they're much more judicious shoppers.
- A sense of humor. Traveling with children can be trying at times.

REMEMBERING YOUR TRIP

When you choose a destination, write or call for information (listed at the end of each chapter). The travel brochures can later be used as part of a scrapbook commemorating your trip.

Purchase a notebook for each child and spend time each evening recording the events of the day. If your children have trouble getting motivated or don't know what to write about, start a discussion; otherwise, let them write, or draw, whatever they want to remember the day's events.

Collect mementos along the way and create a treasure box in a small tin or cigar box. Months or years later, it's fun to look at postcards, seashells, or ticket stubs to jump-start a memory. One of my kids collected ski resort pins on a hat; the other created a collage of vacation photos that we hung on the rec room wall.

Add inexpensive postcards to your photographs to create an album, then write a few words on each page to accompany the images.

Give children a disposable camera to record their versions of the trip. One five-year-old snapped an entire series of photos that never showed anyone above the waist—his view of the world (and the photos are priceless).

Nowadays, many families travel with a camcorder, though we don't recommend using one—parents end up viewing the trip through the lens rather than enjoying the sights. If you must take it along, only record a few moments of major sights (too much is boring anyway). Let the kids tape and narrate.

Even better, because it's more compact, carry a palm-sized tape recorder and let your family members describe their experiences. Hearing a small child's voice years later is so endearing, and those recorded descriptions will trigger an album's worth of memories, far more focused than what most novices capture with a camcorder.

GETTING THERE

By Car

Driving is certainly the most economical way to travel, but if you're covering a lot of miles, it's time-consuming and can try the patience of every passenger. For starters, don't pull any punches with your kids about just how long you'll be in the car.

If it's a long trip, leave before daylight. Take along small pillows and blankets (we use our children's baby blankets), and let the kids snooze. When they're fully awake a few hours down the road, stop for breakfast and teeth brushing.

Be sure there are books, crayons and paper, and a couple of laptop games (though not the electronic kind with annoying beeps). Parents can stash a few surprises to dole out along the way: sticker books, action figures, magazines. We take along a beach ball to blow up, a Frisbee, or a Koosh ball for impromptu play times at rest stops.

Be sure you have maps, and chart your trip before you leave home. Share the maps with the children so that they'll understand the distance to be covered.

Traffic is a force to be reckoned with in all urban areas, and you should plan around it. Don't even think about driving across Washington, D.C., at 5:30 p.m.

Seat belts for front seat drivers and passengers are the law in most Mid-Atlantic states. Child car safety seats are mandatory for children under four years of age or 40 pounds.

Snacks are great, but leave the drinks (preferably water, since it doesn't stain or get sticky when spilled) until the last moment, or frequent rest room stops will prolong the journey. Rest areas can be found along all major highways, and the ones on the toll roads (NJ Turnpike, etc.) are open around the clock. Pack a picnic for mealtimes, and everyone can take a walk or stretch.

Small pillows and your own CDs or tapes make the journey peaceful. Take turns and let everyone choose a favorite. If kids fight over music, make them take turns choosing. To solve the seat fights, we rotate turns, either weekly or daily, for who gets to choose a seat first.

Always lock your car, and never leave wallets or luggage in sight. Keep valuables locked in the trunk.

By Train

Amtrak runs trains up and down the northeast corridor from Boston to Washington. You can use Amtrak to reach Philadelphia, Lancaster, Harrisburg, and Pittsburgh, PA; Baltimore and Hagerstown, MD; Charlottesville, Richmond, Williamsburg, Newport News, Virginia Beach, and Charlottesville, VA; and Wheeling and Charleston, WV. New Jersey Transit operates commuter service that can be used to reach certain shore spots.

For youngsters, train trips are interesting for about the first hour. But with books, games, and activities to occupy the time, it's a leisurely and relatively inexpensive way to travel, with time to unwind and spend quality moments with your family. The train can be an excellent way to travel between East Coast cities—from Washington, D.C., to Philadelphia or Baltimore, for example. You can stand up and stretch or go for a walk, and there's more legroom than in an airplane or car (and no traffic jams). Many trains offer dining cars. But remember, trips on local trains making many stops can be mighty long, and the fare is not much less than cut-rate airfares.

Amtrak offers a children's discount—kids ages 2–15 ride for half-price when accompanied by a full-fare-paying adult. Each adult can bring two children for the discount; children under age 2 ride free.

For reservations and information, call (800) USA-RAIL or visit www.amtrak.com.

By Plane

Almost every part of the Mid-Atlantic region is served by major airlines. However, more remote areas of Virginia, Pennsylvania, and West Virginia can be reached only by smaller carriers. Still, choosing a flight is primarily a matter of time and economics. Booking as far in advance as possible can save hundreds of dollars for a family. When you book your tickets, be sure to get your seat assignments. Request bulkhead for small kids who won't be entertained by a movie but might be able to move around a bit. Although far-front seats are preferred for the most part, be sure to inquire as to how the movie is shown; if you're more than a few rows back from a small screen, it can be hard to enjoy the film.

Take-off and landing bother some children's ears, particularly if they have a cold. Look for plastic earplugs designed to ease ear-pressure pain. They come in children's sizes and are available at travel stores, drug stores, and airport sundry stores. We've found them to be highly effective. One pair lasts for two plane flights at least; they cost two or three dollars per pair. You can also take along gum for older children or a bottle or sipper cup for babies and toddlers. A washcloth heated with hot water from a thermos and held to ears will also help the younger ones who can't tolerate earplugs. Most of your fellow passengers would agree that the best babies on airplanes are sleeping babies, so, if possible, book your flights around nap times, which assures a peaceful flight for you and a happy child as you land.

Pack a few nutritious snacks, like pretzels, dried fruit, crackers, and a small bottle of water. Food and beverage service takes a while on a packed flight (and food isn't always served). If you and your children want or need a special meal, be sure to call the airlines at least 48 hours in advance to request.

Bring your own child-safety seat. Though airlines allow children under age two to fly free on a parent's lap, it's much safer if they're strapped in a safety seat (and they're much more likely to nap, giving you a break). A car seat must have a visible label stating it is approved for air travel.

IF YOU RENT A CAR

A car is necessary anywhere outside the heart of big cities. Rental rates are generally competitive, and every major company is located at most airports, as well as at downtown city locations and scattered throughout the suburbs. In general you will save money by renting at airport locations rather than at in-town or suburban spots. Recreational vehicles, four-wheel-drives, and convertibles also can be rented, though they are considerably more expensive. To rent a car, you will need a valid driver's license, proof of insurance, and a major credit card. Some companies have minimum age requirements.

Ask about extras. Many companies offer cellular phones, ski racks, area maps, and child-safety seats.

If there are more than four in your family, consider renting a minivan. They cost a little more to rent, but the comfort is worth it.

Family Lodging

HOTELS, MOTELS, AND RESORTS

In each regional chapter you'll find our favorite family-friendly hotels, motels, and resorts. Note that we said favorite *family-friendly* hotels, not favorite hotels—many wonderful retreats were excluded because they're aimed at romantics or businesspeople, and they'd make parents of an energetic four-year-old feel like lepers. We've reviewed only places that particularly catch our fancy or seem suitable for families, and we've strived to find places with character. If you don't see an accommodation in the region you wish to visit, call the 800 number of your favorite chain to find out what they can offer.

Tips on Hotels, Motels, and Resorts with Kids

First, there has to be a pool. After that, you get some choices.

One room or two? Large or small? Upscale hotel or basic motel? Old or new? There are pros and cons with each of these overnight options, and we've found that on different days on the same vacation, we might make different choices.

Overall, one of the hardest things for some of us parents to adjust to is being awake when the kids are asleep but not wanting to leave them alone in the room. Although adjoining rooms are a good option in some hotels, they're not offered everywhere, and the choice between one or more rooms for a family always seems to come up.

So we try, on an extended family vacation during which we're moving from place to place, to book ourselves into several different kinds of facilities and have different solutions. In a hub city where we're not expecting to be in a picturesque setting, we look for a business-suite chain, especially on the weekends, when discounts are often offered (but check to see that all amenities, like breakfasts, continue). The price for a spacious suite may be the same as for a cramped room at the motel down the street, and it's great to be able to watch the late show while the little ones snooze.

Big landmark hotels or luxury hotels with character are worth the splurge for us if the location is workable, and they might come at the end of a road trip, when the only choices in small-town stops on the way have been inexpensive roadside motels. Our kids tell us they like the excitement of big hotels (it's almost like a theme park, they say) and even enjoy "the neat old stuff" in some establishments. And room service is God's gift to traveling parents. But we also always ask about the executive, concierge, or butler floor of this kind of establishment, because the lounge areas often offer breakfast, coffee, snacks, and wine at various hours. For one thing, it's convenient for grabbing a muffin for a kid in the room; for another, it's a place for parents to escape to, like a living room, without being far away.

The all-American motel is, of course, a favorite with families. No need to find a bellman—you park in front of your room and unload only what you need. Kids love roaming the corridors for ice, soda from the machines, and the spotting of other children. Lack of towel service poolside may be compensated for by the existence of a coin laundry. At this kind of hostelry, we might opt for one room, but we'd request a room near the pool with a patio or veranda. Proximity to the pool allows kids of a certain age to come and go; the patio extends the living space nicely.

CAMPING

We've included a small but choice collection of campgrounds—ones that are easily accessible, fun for children, and not too demanding of parents (we consider bathrooms and running water, for instance, to be essential). Camping can be a wonderful family experience, slowing down the pace so you can all take pleasure in the small things, from fishing in a stream to chasing butterflies. And, of course, camping takes you to the region's most beautiful places for very little money.

Nearly all the campgrounds we list are state or national park properties, and all are popular; for those that take reservations, make them early. For state campgrounds, call the tourism division of the state in which you intend to camp (see How to Get More Information for the state or region). To reserve a federal campground, call (800) 365-2267.

Tips on Camping with Children

We've had wonderful family camping trips—and horrible ones. Basically, if you are regular campers and your children are used to it from birth, you'll be happy at any of the campgrounds we recommend. If you are not regular campers, we'd recommend the motel option while your children are between infancy and the age of at least three, maybe four. Truth be told, our family never took well to sleeping on the ground, but we've loved the cabin camping we've done. Be realistic about yourselves.

Camping is a superb opportunity to teach children independence and self-reliance. If they're all expected to pitch in, and the adventure aspect is played up, they'll help prepare food, pitch tents, and do all the camp chores.

Adopt some basic rules to maximize safety and comfort, such as:

- No one is allowed to leave the campsite (even to go to the bathroom) without a whistle. Children wear the whistle around their necks; adults can carry it as they like. The whistle is blown only in an emergency, which can range from a twisted ankle to getting lost.
- Hats and sunscreen must be worn on all outings.
- Water must be carried on all outings.
- No playing, exploring, or hiking until the morning campsites are tidied and breakfast dishes are done.

Finally, recognize that camping is tiring, and after a few days of sleeping on the ground, tempers of both children and adults can get frayed. After two or three nights of roughing it, nothing cheers a family up like clean hotel sheets, a swimming pool, and a restaurant hamburger.

WHAT TO LOOK FOR IN A HOTEL

Some families want every moment planned; others just want advice on interesting hotels that other families recommend. Many of our recommendations are suites or apartments, since the best vacations give everyone space of their own. Four in a hotel room may be economical, but adjoining rooms or an apartment or condominium may save your sanity and be worth the extra dollars.

Here are some important questions you might want to ask before booking a reservation:

- Do kids stay free?
- Is there a discount for adjoining rooms? How much?
- Can you rent cribs and rollaway beds?
- Does the room have a refrigerator? A microwave?
- Is the room on the ground floor? (Particularly important if you have small children.)
- How many beds are in the room?
- Is there a swimming pool? Is there a lifeguard? Is the pool fenced?
- How close is the room to the pool?
- Are there laundry facilities on the premises?
- Is there a kid-friendly restaurant? A breakfast buffet? Other kid-friendly restaurants nearby?
- Is there a supervised children's program? What are the qualifications of the staff? How much does it cost? How do you make a reservation?
- Is there in-room baby-sitting? What are the qualifications of the caregivers? How much does it cost per hour? How do you make a reservation?
- Are the rooms childproofed? Can patio or balcony doors be securely locked and bolted?
- Is there an on-site doctor or clinic nearby that the hotel recommends?

WHAT'S IN A ROOM?

Except for cleanliness, state of repair, and decor, travelers pay little attention to hotel rooms. There is, of course, a clear standard of quality and luxury that differentiates Motel 6 from Holiday Inn, Holiday Inn from Marriott,

---

Childproof Your Room

When you arrive at the hotel, some childproofing may be in order. Be sure that both the front door and any patio or balcony doors and windows can be securely locked and bolted. Some hotels offer electrical outlet coverings if you have toddlers, and protective covers for sharp furniture corners. They will also remove glass objects or other knick-knacks that might be easy for a toddler to break. And if the minibar is stocked with junk food and alcoholic beverages, it should be locked.

and so on. Many hotel guests, however, fail to appreciate that some rooms are better engineered than others. Making the room usable to its occupants is an art, a planning discipline that combines both form and function.

Decor and taste are important, certainly. No one wants to stay in a room that is dated, garish, or ugly. But beyond decor, how "livable" is the room? In Washington, D.C., for example, we have seen some beautifully appointed rooms that simply aren't well designed for human habitation. The next time you stay in a hotel, note the details and design elements of your room. Even more than decor, these are the things that will make you feel comfortable and at home.

CHILDREN'S PROGRAMS

Many large hotels offer supervised programs for children, some complimentary, some with fees. We've included several throughout the Mid-Atlantic region that offer exemplary activities.

If you decide to take advantage of the kids' programs, call ahead for specific children's events that are scheduled during your vacation. Ask about cost and the ages that can participate; the best programs divide children into age groups. Make reservations for activities your child might enjoy (you can always cancel after arrival).

After check-in, stop by and visit with the kids' program staff. Ask about counselor-child ratio and whether the counselors are trained in first aid and CPR. Briefly introduce your children to the staff and setting, which typically will leave them wanting more, thereby easing the separation anxiety when they return to stay.

Some hotels offer in-room baby-sitting, but if your hotel does not, there is a national, not-for-profit referral program called Child Care Aware that will help you locate a good, high-quality sitter. You can call (800) 424-2246, Monday–Friday, 8:30 a.m.–4:30 p.m.

Be sure to ask if the sitter is licensed, bonded, and insured. To ease your children's anxiety, tell them how long you plan to be away, and be sure they feel good about the person who will be caring for them. Finally, trust your own instincts.

Family-Friendly Restaurants

We love food and love to eat out, and our kids love to eat out, too, but rarely do we agree on what constitutes a good restaurant. We like comfort, good service, creative cooking, and a nice glass of wine. They like noise, cups with lids, and as much fried food as possible. Hence the challenge: to put together a roster of restaurants that make both parents and children happy. We had more success in some areas than others; some parts of the region don't have much more than coffee shops and chain restaurants, so you'll have to make do. Other areas, however (especially Washington, D.C., Philadelphia, and Baltimore), are rich in kid- and parent-friendly dining.

You'll note that most major chain restaurants and all the chain fast-food restaurants are not found in the listings that follow. We encourage you to skip McDonald's whenever possible and make the effort to patronize local places—not only is it better for your health, but you're more likely to get a feel for an area when you sit with the locals and eat a burrito or dim sum or pancakes. As for the big chain restaurants, we find most of them to be soulless and dull. There are exceptions, especially in such smaller, regional chains such as Eat 'n Park Family Restaurants and The 94th Aero Squadron.

Major tourist areas all seem to have Hard Rock Cafes and Planet Hollywoods, but we cover those rarely—after all, if you've been to one Hard Rock, you've been to them all. Your hotel can steer you to one of them.

Tips on Dining Out with Children

Be Realistic about Age Limits. We ate at elegant restaurants when our children were sleeping infants in car seats. By the time toddlerhood hit, we restricted ourselves to quality fast food, child-friendly ethnic restaurants (Chinese, Cuban, Mexican, etc.), and takeout food enjoyed in park picnic areas. We began restaurant-training in earnest at about age four, the dawn of a years-long process of gentle reminding about napkins on laps, feet off chairs, and proper butter-knife etiquette. We expect to have achieved success around the junior year of college.

Don't Battle a Picky Eater. You'll never win this one. If everything looks yucky, get them some plain rice and plain bread. Enjoy your food with gusto, and if the kids get hungry enough, they'll break down and ask to try some.

Look Beyond the Children's Menu. The vast majority of children's menus are monotonous and unhealthy, consisting mostly of burgers, deep-fried chicken, and french fries. Encourage experimentation in the grown-up menu, and ask if it's possible to order smaller portions of the "adult" food.

Remember the Tailgate. We had more fun eating on a tailgating vacation than perhaps any other. Grocery stores, delis, upscale gourmet shops, and mini-marts are all stocked with foods that seem almost too decadent to buy at home—but if you're tailgating, you have to go for the convenience foods. So we'd get takeout salads and chicken, made-to-order sandwiches, sushi, poached salmon, fresh baguettes, imported cheeses, and exotic fruits. The price was still less than a bad meal at a roadside coffee shop.

Watch the In-Betweeners. When they feel too old for (or don't like) the children's menu but can't really eat a big meal, some parental diplomacy is in order, or the in-betweener will be taking one bite from a huge order of whatever and then stopping, overwhelmed. Some kids will agree to splitting or sharing a meal, but let them choose most of it. Sometimes it's just a matter of ordering three meals for four people, so you avoid huge quantities of leftovers (which you can't take home when traveling) and yet allow for some tasting of different things.

Soup, Soup, Soup. Not only is it comforting and homey, but it's also often a tasty, nutritious, affordable basis for a kid's meal that needs only an appetizer to complete it.

Let Them Be Weird. One man we know is still grateful to his parents for letting him order hamburgers at breakfast, and conversely, how many people aren't cheered up by a nice breakfast at 7 p.m.? As much as possible, let your kids enjoy the get-what-you-want pleasure of restaurant eating as part of their vacation. Remember, they're also missing home, routine, and the certainty of their daily meal rituals.

Special Challenges to a Mid-Atlantic Vacation

Most families with children travel during the summer months, when school is out—and much of the region can get seriously hot, particularly in August and early September. But a number of sites make terrific winter vacation spots as well. So before starting off on a day of touring, a visit to the beach, or a day of skiing, parents should keep some things in mind.

Overheating, Sunburn, and Dehydration. Due to the tendency toward high humidity and high temperatures in the Mid-Atlantic climate, parents with young children on a day's outing need to pay close attention to their kids. The most common problems of smaller children are overheating, sunburn, and dehydration. A small bottle of sunscreen carried in a pocket or fanny pack will help you take precautions against overexposure to the powerful sun. Be sure to put some on children in strollers, even if the stroller has a canopy. Some of the worst cases of sunburn we have seen were on the exposed foreheads and feet of toddlers and infants in strollers. To avoid overheating, rest at regular intervals in the shade or in an air-conditioned museum, hotel lobby, restaurant, or public building.

Don't count on keeping small children properly hydrated with soft drinks and water fountain stops. Long lines at popular attractions often make buying refreshments problematic, and water fountains are not always handy. What's more, excited children may not inform you or even realize that they're thirsty or overheated. We recommend renting a stroller for children six years old and under, and carrying plastic water bottles.

Blisters. Blisters and sore feet are common for visitors of all ages, so wear comfortable, well-broken-in shoes or sandals. If you or your children are usually susceptible to blisters, carry some precut "moleskin" bandages; they offer the best possible protection, stick great, and won't sweat off. When you feel a hot spot, stop, air out your foot, and place a moleskin over the area before a blister forms. Moleskin is available by name at all drugstores. Sometimes small children won't tell their parents about a developing blister until it's too late. We recommend inspecting the feet of preschoolers two or more times a day.

Sunglasses. If you want your smaller children to wear sunglasses, it's a good idea to affix a strap or string to the frames so the glasses won't get lost and can hang from the children's necks while they're indoors.

Beach Safety. To avoid a severe sunburn that can ruin a child's—and your—vacation, dress your children in hats and T-shirts and gob the sunscreen on exposed skin. Be particularly careful on windy days, because kids don't feel the sun burning.

More advice: Don't let kids swim alone and don't leave your children alone on the beach—it's easy for them to get disoriented. Mark your street number so you don't get lost.

Dress in Layers for Winter Activities. In the mountains of Pennsylvania and even West Virginia, Old Man Winter can be mean. The best way to dress for skiing or other winter activities is in layers. Warm air is trapped between the layers, helping to keep the body warm. Try not to wear cotton next to your skin, but use thermal underwear made from one of the new "wicking" fabrics, which will help prevent over-heating during activities. The outer layer should be windproof and waterproof. On very cold, and especially windy, days frostbite can be a danger; be sure to keep faces covered and wear warm gloves. Always use lip balm.

SAFETY

- Discuss safety with your family before you leave home.

- Discuss what to do if someone gets lost. If you are going to a crowded theme park or anywhere that there's a possibility you and your child could get separated, write the child's name on adhesive tape and tape it inside his or her shirt. Be sure that young children know their full name, address, and phone number (with area code).

- Carry photos of your kids for quick ID.

- Travelers' checks are the easiest way to protect your money.

- In emergencies, call 911 for assistance in reaching paramedics, law enforcement, or the fire department.

- Teach your children to find the proper authorities if they are lost. Tell them to approach a security guard, a store clerk, or a grown-up who is working in the area.

- If you are unsure about the safety of an area, ask the front-desk manager or concierge in your hotel before heading out for a stroll.

- Always lock your car when it is parked.

- Always try to keep your gas tank full.

- At night, try to park your car under a street light or in a hotel parking garage. Never leave wallets, checkbooks, purses, or luggage in the car. It's best to lock any of your belongings out of sight in the trunk.

- Keep your wallet, purse, and camera safe from pickpockets. A fanny pack worn around the waist is the most convenient way to stash small items safely.

- Leave your valuables at home, and if you must bring them along, check with your hotel to see if there is a safe.

- Be sure you lock sliding doors that lead to your hotel balcony or porch while you are in your room and always when you leave. Never open the hotel room door if you are unsure about who is at the door.

- Keep medicine out of reach of small children; it's easy to forget and leave it out in hotel rooms.

- Check with the front desk, hotel security, or guest services at attractions for lost property. Report lost or stolen travelers' checks and credit cards to the issuing companies and to the police.

- Crime can happen anywhere, so use common sense and take necessary precautions.

Part One

New Jersey

New Jersey will surprise you. Despite its reputation for being small, over-crowded (it *is* the most densely populated state), and industrial, the truth is you'll find nearly every kind of environment here except desert—from mountains to flatlands, and from backwater lakes and streams to popular beach resorts. You'll also find a lot of history: Washington crossed and recrossed the state during the Revolution, and it was an industrial hub for early America. We've divided the state loosely into **Northern New Jersey, Southern New Jersey,** and the **Shore.** The latter region—nearly 130 miles long—has itself been subdivided into north and south. There's a lot to do, and most of it's within easy driving distance of either New York City or Philadelphia.

How to Get Information before You Go

New Jersey Commerce and Economic Growth Commission, P.O. Box 820, 20 West State Street, Trenton, NJ 08625; (800) 847-4865 or (609) 777-0885; www.visitnj.org

An Invaluable Resource for Bike Riders

The State of New Jersey publishes a series of map/route guides to themed and/or long-distance cycling routes. To obtain them, contact Pedestrian/Bicycle Advocate, New Jersey Department of Transportation, 1035 Parkway Avenue, P.O. Box 600, Trenton, NJ 08625; or, for general information and other New Jersey cycling resources, visit www.state.nj.us/njcommuter/html/bikewalk.htm.

New Jersey's Not-to-Be-Missed Attractions

North Jersey

High Point State Park
Liberty Science Center
Newark Museum
Mountain Creek
Delaware Water Gap National
   Recreation Area

Delaware River Region/South Jersey

Wharton and Bass River State
   Forests
Cowtown Rodeo
New Jersey State Museum
New Jersey State Aquarium
Wheaton Village

Northern Shore

Gateway National Recreation Area
Island Beach State Park
Six Flags Great Adventure and Wild
   Safari
Jenkinson's Aquarium
Jenkinson's Pavilion Boardwalk and
   Amusement Park

Southern Shore

Cape May Point State Park
Cape May Historic District/
   Mid-Atlantic Center for the Arts
Historic Cold Spring Village
Long Beach Island
Ocean City

Calendar of Festivals and Events

January

Super Science Weekend, New Jersey State Museum, Trenton. The museum experiments with wild and wacky science; (609) 292-6330.

February

New Jersey Flower and Garden Show, Garden State Exhibition Center, Somerset. A whiff of spring in midwinter, and the next best thing to the big flower show in Philadelphia; (732) 919-7660.

March

The Passion Play, Park Theater, Union City. A marvelous production of the Easter story with professional and amateur actors that's been produced for more than 85 years; (201) 865-6980.

April

Essex County Cherry Blossom Festival, Branch Brook Park, Newark. The annual blooming of the East's largest collection of Japanese cherry trees; (973) 268-3500.

Shad Festival, Lambertville. This tiny town on the Delaware River celebrates the return of the shad with lots of food, booths, performances, and even a professional shad-net-fishing demonstration; (609) 397-0110.

May

New Jersey Audubon's Cape May Spring Weekend, Cape May Point State Park, Cape May. An amazing array of migrating birds, butterflies, and egg-laying horseshoe crabs; (609) 884-2159.

Wildwood International Kite Festival, Wildwood. Billed as the world's largest kite fest, it includes stunt flying, indoor flying, and kite-building lessons; (609) 523-0100.

Juried American Indian Arts Festival, Rankokus Indian Reservation, Westhampton. One of the best juried exhibitions, augmented by spectacular performances, storytelling, and food; (609) 261-4747. Repeated again in October over Columbus Day weekend.

June

New Jersey Fresh Seafood Festival, Atlantic City. An astounding amount of seafood to sample, plus entertainment, games, rides, etc.; (609) 347-4386.

Beach Fest, Atlantic City. Claims to be the largest free family festival on the Eastern Seaboard. It's big, that's for sure; (609) 484-9020.

July

St. Anne's Italian Festival, Hoboken. A classic urban street fair with tons of entertainment and Italian food; (201) 659-1116.

QuickChek New Jersey Festival of Ballooning, Readington. The largest summertime balloon fest on the East Coast, with more than 100 balloons in flight; (800) 468-2479.

Whitesbog Blueberry Festival, Whitesbog. A Pinelands tradition in the place where blueberries were first commercially cultivated; (609) 893-4646.

August

The Magic of Alexandria Balloon Festival, Pittstown. Smaller than the Quick-Chek, but easier to handle, especially with younger children; (908) 735-0870.

Sussex County Horse and Farm Show, Augusta. The state's largest livestock and horse show, it hearkens back to New Jersey's agricultural days, with good old-fashioned ag contests, entertainment, and exhibits; (973) 948-5500.

September

Miss America Week and Miss America Pageant, Atlantic City. The big one; (609) 344-5278.

Wings 'n' Water Festival, Wetlands Institute, Stone Harbor. A huge family-oriented celebration of Southern New Jersey life; (609) 368-1211.

Clownfest, Seaside Heights. Pro clowns from all over perform and teach everyone to clown; (732) 793-1510.

Old Time Barnegat Bay Duck and Decoy Show, Tuckerton. Some 400 vendors at three sites celebrate the heritage of Barnegat Bay; (609) 971-3085.

October

Victorian Week, Cape May. Guided tours, vaudeville shows, entertainment, and special food as the whole town celebrates its past; (609) 884-5404.

Chatsworth Cranberry Festival, Chatsworth. Pinelands traditions at their best, and be sure to take the cranberry bog tour; (609) 859-9701.

December

Washington Crossing the Delaware and the Battles of Trenton, Christmas Day and December 26, Titusville and Trenton. You've got to see him standing up in that boat to believe it; (609) 737-0623.

Cool Web Sites for New Jersey–Bound Kids

New Jersey Hangout—the state Web site kids' page:
www.state.nj.us/hangout

New Jersey Pinelands Commission Kids Corner—all about the
Pines: www.state.nj.us/pinelands/kidskrnr.htm

Endangered New Jersey, including places to see wildlife:
tqjunior.thinkquest.org/5736

KidsGuide, New Jersey's Guide to Places and Events for Children
and Families: www.kidsguide.com

Shorecam.com has live views from Cape May and Ocean City:
www.shorecam.com

Hadrosaurus, all about where the first dinosaur skeleton was
found in Haddonfield: www.levins.com/dinosaur.html

George Washington and the Crossing, a site about the Battle of
Trenton and the Revolutionary War designed by eighth-grade
students: www.jwjhs.reg4.k12.ct.us/tc

The Colonies during the Revolutionary War, a clickable map
with information on the Battles of Trenton and Monmouth.
Among others: www.ilt.columbia.edu/text_version/k12/history/
aha/ARMain.html

Mainstage Center for the Arts lists South Jersey performances
and events: www.mainstage.org

Yucky for Kids, from New Jersey Online: www.yucky.com

North Jersey: Gateway and Skylands

Folks arrive in Northern New Jersey primarily through Newark Airport or via the New Jersey Turnpike, and all they see is heavy industry. But the truth is, while much of the area is heavily built up, there's much to see and do that's worthwhile and fun. The Gateway region covers Newark, Jersey City, and the nearest New York City suburban communities, some of which are quite old and culturally rich. The **Jersey City Museum** (call (201) 547-4514) is a small art museum with an eclectic collection and hands-on children's events. In **West Orange,** the **Turtle Back Zoo** (call (973) 731-5800) is a small zoo that features a train ride and petting zoo. **Lyndhurst,** about five miles directly east of midtown Manhattan, is home to the **Meadowlands Environment Center and Trash Museum** (call (201) 460-8300), an ecology center with walking trails in the shadow of the Jersey Turnpike. In adjacent **East Rutherford,** you'll find the **Meadowlands Sports Complex** (call (201) 935-8500), home to football's New York Giants and Jets, hockey's New Jersey Devils, basketball's New Jersey Nets, and the Meadowlands Racetrack. A bit farther east, **Teterboro** has the **Aviation Hall of Fame and Museum of New Jersey** (call (201) 288-6345), a small but enjoyable spot beside the Teterboro Airport's single runway. Nearby, in **Hackensack,** the **New Jersey Naval Museum** (call (201) 342-3268) offers guided tours of the World War II submarine USS *Ling,* and the **Bergen Museum of Art and Science** (call (201) 968-1001) features a mastodon skeleton, science wing, and youth gallery. In the heart of suburban **Paramus** sits the **New Jersey Children's Museum** (call (201) 262-5151), which houses more than 65 hands-on and other exhibits for preschoolers and toddlers. The **Paterson Museum** (call (973) 881-3874) in **Paterson** depicts that city's role as the nation's first planned industrial city and houses the world's first practical submarine. Moving about half an hour south, you'll find **New Brunswick,** home to **Rutgers University,** the

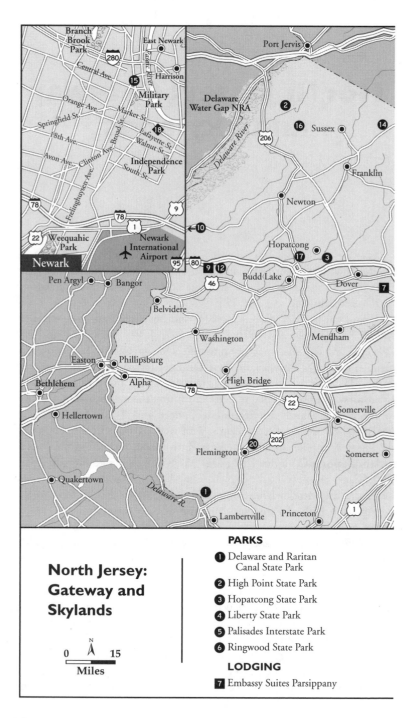

North Jersey: Gateway and Skylands

0 ⟨N⟩ 15
Miles

PARKS

1 Delaware and Raritan Canal State Park
2 High Point State Park
3 Hopatcong State Park
4 Liberty State Park
5 Palisades Interstate Park
6 Ringwood State Park

LODGING

7 Embassy Suites Parsippany

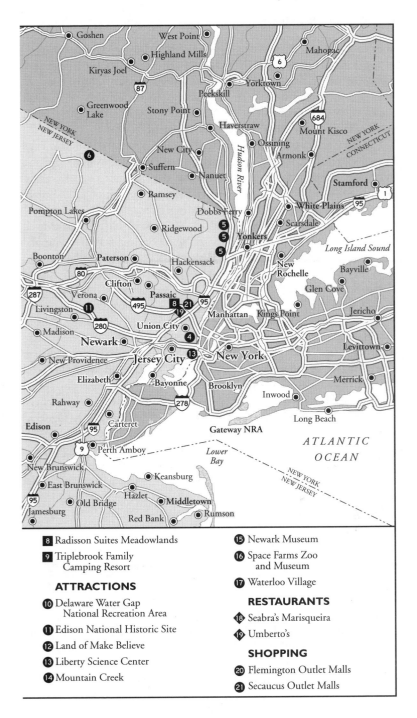

8 Radisson Suites Meadowlands

9 Triplebrook Family
Camping Resort

ATTRACTIONS

10 Delaware Water Gap
National Recreation Area

11 Edison National Historic Site

12 Land of Make Believe

13 Liberty Science Center

14 Mountain Creek

15 Newark Museum

16 Space Farms Zoo
and Museum

17 Waterloo Village

RESTAURANTS

18 Seabra's Marisqueira

19 Umberto's

SHOPPING

20 Flemington Outlet Malls

21 Secaucus Outlet Malls

major college in the state system. There, the **New Jersey Museum of Agriculture** (call (732) 249-2077), **Rutgers Gardens at Cook College** (call (732) 932-8451), and the **Rutgers University Geology Museum** (call (732) 932-7243) provide more than a day's worth of activity. In **Oak Ridge, Fairy Tale Forest** (call (973) 697-5656) is a children's storyland theme park based on classic fairy tales.

The **Skylands** cover the northwestern section of the state and hold large tracts of woodlands, the highest elevations, the **Delaware Water Gap,** and abundant outdoor activity, as well as some nifty commercial attractions. **Morristown** is famous for having housed George Washington several times during the Revolution and is rich in wartime history. The area's historical highlights include **Acorn Hall** (call (973) 267-3465); **Historic Speedwell** (call (973) 540-0211), where Samuel F. B. Morse first publicly demonstrated the telegraph; **Morristown National Historical Park** (call (973) 543-4030), site of the Continental Army's 1779–80 winter encampment; and **Schuyler Hamilton House** (call (973) 267-4039). Nearby, in **Morris Township, Fosterfields Living Historical Farm** (call (973) 326-7645) offers a living history look at farming circa 1890–1910. Golfers should stop in **Far Hills** at the **USGA Golf House and Museum** (call (908) 234-2300) not only to see golf artifacts and memorabilia but also to see how golf balls and clubs are tested. Moving farther north, in **Netcong** you'll find **Wild West City** (call (973) 347-8900), where the Old West comes to life with live action shows and rides on stagecoaches, trains, and ponies. The **Pequest Trout Hatchery and Natural Resource Education Center** (call (908) 637-4125) in **Ogdensburg** offers a wonderful look at trout being raised and the state's ecology issues. Toward the southern part of the region and center of the state, the **Black River and Western Railroad** (call (908) 782-6600) runs scenic rides out of **Ringoes** through rural Hunterdon County. **Flemington** has **Northlandz** (call (908) 782-4022), home of the largest miniature railway in the world, a 2,000-pipe theater organ, and a 94-room dollhouse.

How to Get There

By Car. The New Jersey Turnpike (I-95) is the main thoroughfare for northbound arrivals from Pennsylvania, Delaware, and so on. It skirts Newark and Jersey City, terminating at I-80, the main east-west access to the more northerly areas of the region. I-78 parallels I-80 in the more southerly areas. The Garden State Parkway runs north-south parallel to the shore for the state's full length. I-287 skirts the westernmost edge of the area in a loop from Edison (near New Brunswick) up through Morristown and finally all the way to the New York state line in the northeast corner of the state. To reach the northwest corners of the region, follow I-80 to State Route 23 north and County 511, or U.S. 206.

By Plane. Newark International Airport is actually the New York metro area's busiest airport and is served by all major carriers; it's located at New Jersey Turnpike exits 14-A and 15; (973) 961-6000.

By Train. Amtrak operates frequent service to Newark's downtown Penn Station; (800) 872-7245. New Jersey Transit operates commuter trains from Hoboken and Newark to most of the region; (800) 772-2222 or (800) 626-7433.

How to Get Information before You Go

Skylands of New Jersey Tourism Council, 2 Locust Street, P.O. Box 329, Columbia, NJ 07832; (800)-475-9526 or (908) 496-8598; www.njskylands.com.

Historic Morris Visitor Center, 6 Court Street, Morristown, NJ 07960; (973) 631-5151.

Gateway Regional Tourism Council, P.O. Box 602, Little Ferry, NJ 07643; (201) 641-7632.

The Best Parks

Delaware and Raritan Canal State Park. Serving the central part of the state, this 70-mile linear park and towpath are great for canoeing, jogging, hiking, bicycling, fishing, and horseback riding. The canal and towpath are part of the National Recreational Trail System. The 26-acre Cook Natural Area and the 3,000-acre Six Mile Run Reservoir Site combine to be one of Central New Jersey's least crowded resources for hiking, biking, and horseback riding. 625 Canal Road, Somerset, NJ 08873; (732) 873-3050.

Delaware Water Gap National Recreation Area. (See Attractions below.)

High Point State Park. Encompassing 14,193 acres, this is the site of New Jersey's highest point—1,803 feet above sea level—which is marked by a 220-foot obelisk-type monument. A 20-acre natural lake has a swimming beach, bathhouse, and food concession. In addition to numerous hiking trails, the park's Cross-Country Ski Center maintains 15 kilometers of groomed trails, half of which are serviced with artificial snow, and rents skis and other winter sports equipment. 1480 Route 23 Sussex, NJ 07461; (973) 875-4800.

Hopatcong State Park. The park is set at the southwest end of 2,500-acre Lake Hopatcong. You can swim here, visit the Hopatcong Historical Museum, fish, and boat. Several marinas are located in the adjacent town; P.O. Box 8519, Landing, NJ 07850; (973) 398-7010.

Liberty State Park. A surprising 1,122-acre park in an urban waterfront setting, Liberty yields great Manhattan views from its riverside promenade. The park also offers swimming, fishing, crabbing, tennis, a nature reserve, picnicking, numerous special events, and access to the historic nineteenth-century Central Railroad of New Jersey Terminal, Liberty Science Center (see Attractions below), and ferries to the Statue of Liberty and Ellis Island. Morris Pesin Drive, Jersey City, NJ 07305; (201) 915-3400; www.liberty statepark.com.

Palisades Interstate Park. Located at Exit 2 of the Palisades Interstate Parkway, it has picnic areas, a boat-launching ramp, cross-country ski trails, a nature sanctuary, and hiking trails along the Hudson River with some terrific New York City views; P.O. Box 155, Alpine, NJ 07620, (201) 768-1360.

Ringwood State Park. Covering 5,237 acres, the park centers on the state botanical garden and Shepherd's Lake, a spring-fed lake that offers swimming, boating, canoeing, and fishing. A network of trails surrounds the lake for horseback riding, hiking, and mountain biking. Winter sports include ice skating, cross-country skiing, snowmobiling, ice fishing, and sledding. 1304 Sloatsburg Road, Ringwood, NJ 07456; (973) 962-7031.

Family Outdoor Adventures

Biking. Freeman's Bicycle Shop. Rents bikes with daily, weekly, and hourly rates for rides on bike paths along the Delaware River; 52 Bridle Street, Frenchtown, NJ 08825, (908) 996-7712.

Cross-Country Skiing. High Point State Park (see The Best Parks above). Also, Fairview Lake Cross-County Ski Center offers a full variety of trails, a lodge, rentals, and instruction; 1035 Fairview Lake Road, Newton, NJ 07860, (973) 983-9282.

Hiking. Delaware Water Gap National Recreation Area (see Attractions below). Also, the New Jersey Audubon Society's Weis Ecology Center is a 160-acre, private, nonprofit environmental education facility offering family and adult weekend programs, camping, and hiking trail access to Norvin Green State Forest; 150 Snake Den Road, Ringwood, NJ 07456, (973) 835-2160.

Horseback Riding. Watchung Stable rents horses and offers trail rides and lessons; 1160 Summit Lane, Mountainside, NJ 07092, (908) 789-3665. Washington Riding Stables offers trail rides, pony rides, lessons, beginner horsemanship clinics, and public riding every Saturday and Sunday; 1707 South Washington Avenue, Perth Amboy, NJ 08854, (732) 249-2471.

Lord Stirling Stables offers rentals, lessons, moonlight rides, and special events near the home of the U.S. Equestrian Team; 256 South Maple Avenue, Basking Ridge, NJ 07920; (908) 766-5955.

Mountain Biking. Cheesequake State Park. A variety of trails for all ability levels; 300 Gordon Road, Matawan, NJ 07747, (732) 566-2161. Mountain Creek (see Attractions below).

Paddling. Delaware Water Gap National Recreation Area (see Attractions below). T&W Canoe Rental stages canoe trips on the Delaware River; Box 571, Route 46, Columbia, NJ 07832, (908) 475-4608. Indian Head Canoes rents canoes, rafts, kayaks, and tubes for trips on the Delaware River; 8 Hampton Downs, Newton, NJ 07860, (800) 874-2628.

Skiing. Mountain Creek (see Attractions below). Also, Hidden Valley Resort has two dozen trails. Breakneck Road, Box 433, Vernon, NJ 07462, (973) 764-4200.

Family Lodging

Embassy Suites Parsippany
An all-suites property in a suburban location that's central to the region— near to the Morristown historical attractions, and within reasonable driving distance of the region's outdoor activities and summertime attractions. There's a pool and on-site restaurant, and the property participates in Embassy Suites' Family Fun Pack Program.

909 Parsippany Boulevard, Parsippany, NJ 07054; (973) 334-1440. Rates $99–179.

Radisson Suites Meadowlands
A 151-room, all-suite hotel right in the heart of things, about five miles from New York City, near outlet shopping in Secaucus, and a 15-minute drive from Newark Airport. Indoor pool, fitness center, nearby restaurants, refrigerators in all rooms, pets permitted, and nearby bus service to New York City.

350 Route 3 West, Secaucus, NJ 07094; (201) 863-8700. Rates $159–219; $169 for family of four with full breakfast. Kids under 19 stay free.

Triplebrook Family Camping Resort
In the Western New Jersey hills, a 250-acre, 200-site campground with RV and "wilderness" tent sites, as well as trailer rentals. There are many activities and organized events on site, and it's within driving distance to the Delaware Water Gap and northwestern New Jersey attractions.

58 Honey Run Road, Blairstown, NJ 07852; (888) 343-2267 or (908) 459-4079. Rates $25–50.

Attractions

Delaware Water Gap National Recreation Area

(See also the Pennsylvania chapter.)
Kittatinny Point Visitor Center, I-80, Columbia, NJ 07832;
   (908) 496-4458; www.nps.gov/dewa

Hours: Visitors center open April–October, daily 9 a.m.–5 p.m.;
   November–March, Saturday–Sunday 9 a.m.–5 p.m.

Admission: Free; fee for camping and some services

Appeal by Age Groups:

Pre-school	Grade School	Teens	Young Adults	Over 30	Seniors
★★★★★	★★★★★	★★★★★	★★★★★	★★★★★	★★★★★

Description and Comments   While the facilities on the Jersey side of the gap aren't as extensive as those on the Pennsylvania side, it's still a magnificent outdoor wonderland where you can swim, fish, canoe, tube, hike, camp, bike, cross-country ski, picnic, and indulge in all manner of outdoor activities. The Kittatinny Ranger Station offers information, an audiovisual program, and displays, and rangers present impromptu "Terrace Talks" on weekends. Make the trip to Millbrook Village, located about 12 miles north of I-80 on Old Mine Road. You've got to hike a bit to reach this nineteenth-century settlement, but it's an ongoing process of restoration, which in itself is fascinating. Selected buildings are staffed Thursday–Sunday, 9 a.m.–5 p.m., from spring through late October, and traditional trades such as blacksmithing and woodworking are demonstrated. (For exact craft demonstration hours, call (908) 841-9531.)

Edison National Historic Site

Main Street and Lakeside Avenue, West Orange, NJ 07052;
   (973) 736-0550; www.nps.gov/edis/home.htm

Hours: Variable

Admission: $2 adults age 17 and up

Appeal by Age Groups:

Pre-school	Grade School	Teens	Young Adults	Over 30	Seniors
★	★★★★	★★★★★	★★★★★	★★★★★	★★★★★

Touring Time: Average 3 hours, minimum 2 hours

Rainy-Day Touring: Yes

Services and Facilities:

Restaurants No	Baby stroller rental No
Alcoholic beverages No	Lockers No
Disabled access Yes, laboratory;	Pet kennels No
no, house	Rain check No
Wheelchair rental Yes	Private tours No

Description and Comments The site comprises Edison's invention factory, his laboratory, the workshops where he developed the phonograph and the motion picture camera, and his home, Glenmont Mansion. To say this is a fascinating place would be to drastically understate it. We retain vivid memories of visiting here more than 40 years ago. And why not? The guy was ingenious and fascinating; and he was granted more than 1,000 patents during his lifetime.

Note: The site is closed during 2000 for renovations. Call ahead to make sure it has reopened and for new visiting hours.

Land of Make Believe

Great Meadows Road, Route 611, Hope, NJ 07844; (908) 459-5100; www.lomb.com

Hours: Memorial Day–mid-June, Saturday–Sunday 10 a.m.–6 p.m.; mid-June–Labor Day plus the weekend after Labor Day, daily 10 a.m.–6 p.m.

Admission: $12.50 adults, $11.50 seniors 62+, $15.50 children ages 2–18, free for children under 2

Appeal by Age Groups:

Pre-school	Grade School	Teens	Young Adults	Over 30	Seniors
★★★★	★★★★★	★★★	★★★	★★★★	★★★★

Touring Time: Average 6 hours, minimum 4 hours

Rainy-Day Touring: No

Services and Facilities:

Restaurants Yes	Lockers Yes
Alcoholic beverages No	Pet kennels No
Disabled access Yes	Rain check No
Wheelchair rental No	Private tours No
Baby stroller rental No	

Description and Comments One of the best amusement and water parks around for younger children. The rides and water park are scaled to little kids, who just have a ball here. Tame rides include a miniature steam train and a hay wagon ride, and Santa's Summer Home is always a hit. Less tame rides include a small roller coaster and the Black Hole water slide, but all are suitable for ages 8 to 12. Arcades, games, and ongoing shows round out the activity. A huge picnic grove makes bring-your-own easy.

Liberty Science Center

Liberty State Park, 251 Phillip Street, Jersey City, NJ 07305;
  (201) 200-1000; www.lsc.org

Hours: Daily 9:30 a.m.–5:30 p.m.; closed Thanksgiving and Christmas
  days

Admission: Museum only: $9.50 adults, $7.50 seniors 62+ and children
  ages 2–18; free for children under 2. Exhibits plus IMAX plus 3-D
  Theater: $15.50 adults, $13.50 seniors 62+ and children ages 2–18,
  $10 children under 2; other combination tickets also available

Appeal by Age Groups:

Pre-school	Grade School	Teens	Young Adults	Over 30	Seniors
★★★★	★★★★★	★★★★★	★★★★★	★★★★★	★★★★★

Touring Time: Average 3 hours, minimum 2 hours

Rainy-Day Touring: Yes

Services and Facilities:

Restaurants Yes	Lockers Yes
Alcoholic beverages No	Pet kennels No
Disabled access Yes	Rain check No
Wheelchair rental Yes; free	Private tours No
Baby stroller rental Yes; free	

Description and Comments   A state-of-the-art interactive science museum, this place is usually crowded, noisy, and fun. The three floors are divided by theme: invention, health, and environment. The Touch Tunnel, on the health floor, is a big hit—100 feet long and completely dark, so you have to feel your way through. On the environment floor, our kids loved the Bug Zoo. The Solar Telescope beams down real images of the sun's surface. And from the museum roof, you get great views of Manhattan. The IMAX Theater ranks with the best, and the 3-D Laser Shows are worth the extra cost.

If you're coming from Manhattan or Newark, the new Bergen-Hudson Light Rail System can make the trip a fun one. Take the PATH train to Exchange Place in Jersey City, or the ferry from the World Financial Center to the Colgate Center in Jersey City. The light rail regularly runs here from Exchange Place.

Mountain Creek

200 Route 94, Vernon, NJ 07462; (973) 827-2000;
www.mountaincreek.com

Hours: Vary by day and season

Admission: Varies by season

Appeal by Age Groups:

Pre-school	Grade School	Teens	Young Adults	Over 30	Seniors
★★★★★	★★★★★	★★★★★	★★★★★	★★★★★	★★★★★

Touring Time: Average 6 hours, minimum 4 hours

Rainy-Day Touring: Yes, winter; no, summer

Services and Facilities:

Restaurants Yes	Lockers Yes
Alcoholic beverages Yes	Pet kennels No
Disabled access Yes; partial	Rain check No
Wheelchair rental No	Private tours No
Baby stroller rental Yes	

Description and Comments   It's hard for some to imagine that New Jersey houses a major ski area, but it does. There are 46 trails here, with more than 1,000 feet of vertical drop, serviced by 11 lifts and tows, including two high-speed chairlifts and one unique gondola. The ski season generally runs from mid-December to mid-March, and it's nicely augmented by one of the most powerful snowmaking operations in the industry. Snowboarders love this place for its two huge half-pipes, giant terrain park, and boarder-x course. And the ski/snowboard school is excellent.

The activity continues nonstop for summertime with a major water park, lift-assisted mountain biking, an in-line/skateboard skate park, BMX biking, a rock-climbing wall, and something they call "Extreme Golf" that's played on the ski trails. The water park features some heart-stopping slides, a River Rapid Ride, a large wave pool, and for those not thrill-ready, a special area for toddlers and little ones. A full-day Kids Kamp program is open to ages 4–12 and includes both outdoor learning and adventure, from lake canoeing and learning about the local flora and fauna to playing in the water park.

Newark Museum

49 Washington Street, Newark, NJ 07101, (973) 596-6550;
www.newarkmuseum.org

Hours: Wednesday–Sunday noon–5 p.m., Thursday noon–8:30 p.m.; closed Mondays, Tuesdays, the Fourth of July, and Thanksgiving, Christmas, and New Year's days

Admission: Free. Planetarium: $3 adults, $1 seniors and students, $2 children

Appeal by Age Groups:

Pre-school	Grade School	Teens	Young Adults	Over 30	Seniors
★★	★★★★	★★★★	★★★★	★★★★★	★★★★★

Touring Time: Average 2 hours, minimum 1 hour

Rainy-Day Touring: Yes

Services and Facilities:

Restaurants Yes	Lockers Yes (coatroom)
Alcoholic beverages Yes	Pet kennels No
Disabled access Yes	Rain check No
Wheelchair rental Yes; free	Private tours No
Baby stroller rental No	

Description and Comments One of the most surprising museums in the metro New York area, it's a treasure trove of Tibetan, American, Oriental, and classical works. But there's also a planetarium, a firefighter museum, a mini-zoo, a sculpture garden, and the Victorian Ballantine House, a National Historic Landmark once home to the Ballantine Beer family. Hands-on workshops are offered on weekend afternoons in art and science explorations, mini-zoo "Reptile Rap," science demonstrations, and other topics. Summertime brings jazz concerts and other performances.

Space Farms Zoo and Museum

218 Route 519, Beemerville, NJ 07461; (973) 875-5800; www.spacefarms.com

Hours: May 1–October 31, daily 9 a.m.–5 p.m.

Admission: $8.95 adults, $7.95 seniors, $4.50 children

Appeal by Age Groups:

Pre-school	Grade School	Teens	Young Adults	Over 30	Seniors
★★★★★	★★★★★	★★★★	★★★★★	★★★★★	★★★★★

Touring Time: Average 3 hours, minimum 2 hours

Rainy-Day Touring: Yes

Services and Facilities:

Restaurants Yes	Lockers No
Alcoholic beverages No	Pet kennels No
Disabled access Yes	Rain check No

Wheelchair rental No   Private tours No
Baby stroller rental Yes

Description and Comments   This incredible place started in 1927 as a rural general store/gas station/repair shop. Today it's a 100-acre complex that holds the world's largest private collection of North American wildlife: more than 500 animals from more than 100 species. Despite the name, it has nothing to do with outer space. (Space was the original owners' family name.) The store has grown into 11 buildings that hold more than 100,000 items collected with no single theme: rare autos, carriages, wagons, farm tools, antique firearms, and any old, wonderful artifacts of American rural heritage. The daily animal shows, demonstrations, and informational talks make a visit educational and lots of fun.

Waterloo Village

525 Waterloo Road, Stanhope, NJ 07874; (973) 347-0900;
www.waterloovillage.org

Hours: April, Wednesday–Friday 10 a.m.–3 p.m.; May–October, Wednesday–Friday 10 a.m.–4 p.m., Saturday–Sunday 11 a.m.–5 p.m.; November, Wednesday–Friday 10 a.m.–4 p.m.

Admission: $9 adults, $8 seniors, $7 children ages 6–15, free for children 5 and under

Appeal by Age Groups:

Pre-school	Grade School	Teens	Young Adults	Over 30	Seniors
★★★	★★★★	★★★★	★★★★★	★★★★★	★★★★★

Touring Time: Average 3 hours, minimum 2 hours

Rainy-Day Touring: Yes

Services and Facilities:

Restaurants Yes   Lockers No
Alcoholic beverages Yes   Pet kennels No
Disabled access No   Rain check No
Wheelchair rental No   Private tours No
Baby stroller rental No

Description and Comments   In the 1760s, the Andover Iron Works opened here. In 1831, the town became an important lock site and stop along the Morris Canal. Waterloo Village re-creates those eras in 28 buildings that house artifacts and working artisans who practice the skills of the time. You can also see one of the locks from the old canal, and for a small extra fee, you can tour the site by hay wagon. Waterloo also contains a re-created Lenape Indian village circa 1625, and a variety of jazz, classical, rock, pop, and country music concerts are staged throughout the summer.

Family-Friendly Restaurants

SEABRA'S MARISQUEIRA

87 Madison Street, Newark; (973) 465-1250

Meals served: Dinner
Cuisine: Portugese
Entree range: $11.95–26.95
Children's menu: No, but small-portion menu
Reservations: Yes
Payment: Major credit cards

The Ironbound section of Newark (near the NJ-PAC performing arts center) has long been famous for its Portugese and Spanish cuisine. Seabra's has a very local/neighborhood feel—the specials on the board by the bar are listed only in Portuguese—and the place is bustling and family-run, so kids won't feel constrained. The dishes favor seafood and meats—and they're good.

UMBERTO'S

425 Route 3 East, Secaucus; (201) 864-4001

Meals served: Lunch and dinner
Cuisine: Italian
Entree range: $7.99–12.99 (lunch), $11.95–25.95 (dinner)
Children's menu: No
Reservations: Yes
Payment: Major credit cards

In a region overflowing with Italian restaurants, this one stands out. Good, authentic, homemade food in an atmosphere that's, well, maybe a bit over-whelmingly kitschy. But North Jerseyans love their Italian, and this one is highly recommended.

North Jersey Outlet Shopping

The Garden State has become famous for its manufacturers' outlet shopping. Clothes makers have long warehoused goods in Secaucus. One day they realized they could sell leftovers right from the warehouse. It's not all repositories anymore, nor is it limited to clothes, but you can find some great bargains, particularly in Secaucus and Flemington.

Flemington

Circle Outlet Center, Routes 202 and 31, (908) 782-4100

Feed Mill Plaza Factory Outlet Center, Route 12, (908) 788-0386

Liberty Village Factory Outlets, 1 Church Street, (908) 782-8550

Secaucus

Lenox Factory Outlet, Harmon Cove Outlet Center, (201) 319-1980

Outlets at the Cove, 45 Meadowlands Parkway, (800) 358-2373

Secaucus Outlets/Harmon Cove Outlets, 20 Enterprise Avenue North (800) 877-688-5382

The Arts Are Alive and Well in Northern New Jersey

Used to be you had to go into the Big Apple to see top-quality performances. No more. Some choice venues:

Englewood   John Harms Theater presents headline performers from all disciplines, including a range of family entertainments and children's productions; (201) 567-3600.

Madison   New Jersey Shakespeare Festival beautifully stages the Bard and other classics; (973) 408-3278.

Millburn   Paper Mill Playhouse, the official state theater, produces musicals, plays, and concerts; (973) 376-4343.

New Brunswick   The American Repertory Ballet Company is in residence at the New Brunswick Cultural Center; (732) 249-1254. Crossroads Theater Company is one of the country's top African American troupes; (732) 249-5560. George Street Playhouse stages premiers and Broadway-bound productions; (732) 846-2895. Shoestring Players, part of Rutgers University/Douglass College, produces unique children's theater; (732) 932-9772. State Theater produces major concerts, children's theater, musicals, and dance; (732) 246-7469.

Newark   New Jersey Performing Arts Center (NJ-PAC) is Newark's newest attraction, a world-class center that hosts nationally and internationally celebrated performing artists. It's home to the New Jersey State

Opera and the New Jersey Symphony Orchestra and offers some terrific shows for kids in its two theaters; (888) 466- 6572.

Princeton   McCarter Theater Center for the Performing Arts mounts more than 140 performances annually in all disciplines and was the 1994 Tony Award winner for outstanding regional theater; (856) 683-8000.

Teaneck   American Stage Company stages original productions and revivals in its own 290-seat theater; (201) 692-7744 or (201) 692-7720.

Delaware River Region/South Jersey

This region presents a mix of environments, from the old industrial cities of Trenton and Camden, to sprawling suburbs like Cherry Hill, to the Ivy League gentility of Princeton, to an almost southern ruralness in places like Bivalve along the Delaware Bay or Millville and Vineland in the state's southern heart. Taking up a major portion of the state—indeed, nearly one-quarter of New Jersey's total land area—is the famous Pinelands. The Pines (or, as it's also called, the Pine Barrens) encompasses four state forests and some 338,000 wild acres. It's created from a unique combination of sandy soil, abundant rainfall, frequent wildfires, and a 17-trillion-gallon subterranean aquifer, all combining to establish an outdoorsman's paradise, rife with streams, ponds, lakes, dirt roads, and trails. It's also history-rich, having served as a mainstay for bog iron production in the country's early years and as a longtime glassmaking center.

Starting in the northern reaches of the area, one should go to **Princeton** just to wander around the **Princeton University** campus and soak up the Ivy League ambience. The college is home to the **McCarter Theater** and an excellent art museum, and downtown has a very attractive and active shopping district. History is rich here, too. **Princeton Battlefield State Park** (call (609) 921-0074), set on 80 acres outside town, has the Thomas Clark House museum, a Quaker Meeting House, and a Revolutionary War firearms and sword display. **Rockingham Historic Site** (call (609) 921-8835) was George Washington's last wartime headquarters and has a children's museum. **Trenton,** the state capital, is an important historic locale, where you can visit the **Old Barracks Museum** (call (609) 396-1776), the only original French and Indian War barracks still standing in the United States, and site of the first Battle of Trenton. In **Cherry Hill,** a Philadelphia suburb, the **Garden State Discovery Museum** (call (856) 424-6516) has hands-on, interactive exhibits for young children.

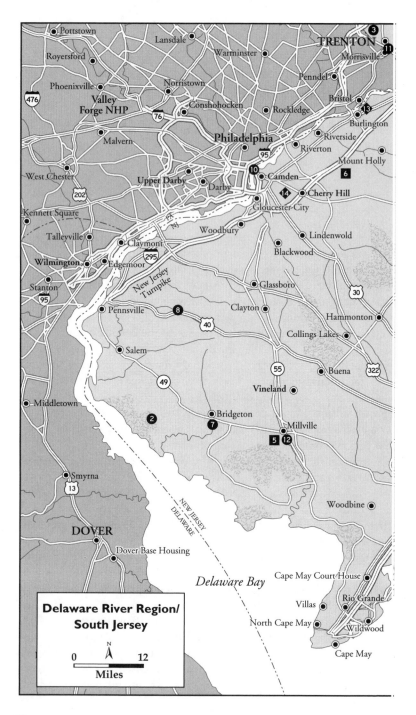

Delaware River Region/
South Jersey

0   ^N   12

Miles

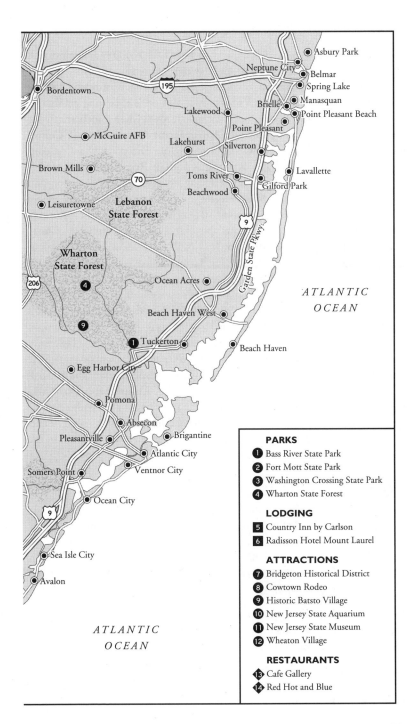

ATLANTIC
OCEAN

ATLANTIC
OCEAN

PARKS

1 Bass River State Park
2 Fort Mott State Park
3 Washington Crossing State Park
4 Wharton State Forest

LODGING

5 Country Inn by Carlson
6 Radisson Hotel Mount Laurel

ATTRACTIONS

7 Bridgeton Historical District
8 Cowtown Rodeo
9 Historic Batsto Village
10 New Jersey State Aquarium
11 New Jersey State Museum
12 Wheaton Village

RESTAURANTS

13 Cafe Gallery
14 Red Hot and Blue

Fort Dix is a major military base, and its **Fort Dix Military Museum** (call (609) 562-2334) holds a trove of military memorabilia.

Moving south, hidden in Lebanon State Forest is **Whitesbog Village** (call (609) 893-4646), almost a ghost town, but once a thriving cranberry- and blueberry-producing community, the first town where blueberries were commercially grown and processed. **Appel Farms Arts and Music Center** (call (856) 358-2472) in **Elmer** stages many folk and country music concerts and kids' programs. The **Rankokus Indian Reservation** (call (609) 261-4747) in **Rancocas** is the home of the Powhatan Lenape Nation and offers a **Native American Indian Heritage Museum** with historical gallery and nature trails, and the reservation stages two of the state's best festivals (see Calendar of Festivals and Events above) in May and October. In **Glassboro,** the **Heritage Glass Museum** (call (856) 881-7468) offers a look at glassblowing, modern and antique. The **Grounds for Sculpture** (call (609) 586-0616) in **Hamilton Township** has 22 acres of outdoor art, a park, and a museum. Dads can take a trip back to their own childhoods at the **Matchbox Road Museum** (call (856) 697-2800) in **Newfield,** home to 20,000 Matchbox cars and trucks. **Bivalve** is an interesting place—a tiny town on Delaware Bay, it was long an oyster-producing mainstay. Now, the **Delaware Bay Schooner Project** (call (609) 785-2060), a restored schooner and the state's "official tall ship," shows how it was with sailing trips and a small museum. **Clementon** holds **Clementon Lake Amusement Park and Splashworld** (call (856) 783-0263), a sizable amusement park with a petting zoo. In **Titusville, Howell Living History Farm** (call (609) 737-3299) is one of the state's best living history installations, and visitors can join in the chores during special programs on many Saturdays.

How to Get There

By Car. The region's main north-south through roads are the New Jersey Turnpike (I-95) and I-295, which parallels the Turnpike from Trenton to the Delaware Memorial Bridge. East-west, the Atlantic City Expressway runs through the center of the region, while State Route 70 is the main route from the northern Jersey shore to Camden/Philadelphia, and U.S. 40 runs through the southern section.

By Plane. Philadelphia International Airport is the nearest major airport; (215) 492-3181. Newark International Airport is located about an hour north of the Trenton/Princeton area; (973) 961-6000.

By Train. Amtrak services Philadelphia; (800) 872-7245. New Jersey Transit services Trenton, Princeton, and the outlying Philadelphia suburbs like Cherry Hill; (800) 626-7433.

How to Get Information before You Go

Delaware River Regional Tourism Council, c/o New Jersey State Aquarium, One Riverside Drive, Camden, NJ 08103; (609) 365-3300 ext. 230.

Trenton Convention and Visitors Bureau, Lafayette at Barrack Streets, P.O. Box 206, Trenton, NJ 08625; (609) 777-1770.

Pinelands Commission, P.O. Box 7, New Lisbon, NJ 08064; (609) 894-9342.

The Best Parks

Bass River State Forest. While you can camp, fish, canoe, swim, and hike in this natural area, the highlight is walking through the 3,800-plus acres of the West Pine Plains Natural Area, known as the Pygmy Forest. A globally rare place, it supports an extensive area of pine and oak trees that grow to just four feet at maturity. The Batona Trail runs through Bass River, too. 762 State Road, New Gretna, NJ 08224; (609) 296-1114.

Fort Mott State Park. This small park (104 acres) is noteworthy because of its location and fortifications. Fort Mott was part of a coastal defense system designed for the Delaware River in the late 1800s. Its fortifications were built in 1896 for the Spanish-American War. The Delaware River shoreline offers good walking and picnicking. The New Jersey Coastal Heritage Trail Welcome Center has displays on Fort Mott and the environment. 454 Fort Mott Road, Pennsville, NJ 08070; (856) 935-3218.

Washington Crossing State Park. The New Jersey side of this two-state park contains Swan Historical Foundation Collection, an assemblage of more than 700 objects dating from 1745 to 1789. The Johnson Ferry House was probably used by General Washington as he staged the crossing of the Delaware. You can picnic here along the river, and there are hiking, horseback riding, and mountain biking trails. On Christmas Day, Washington's crossing is reenacted. 355 Washington Crossing–Pennington Road, Titusville, NJ 08560-1517; (609) 737-0623.

Wharton State Forest. Wharton exemplifies the Pinelands. Crisscrossed by rivers and streams, trails, some 500 miles of unpaved roads, and numerous lakes, it's great for canoeing, mountain biking, horseback riding, and hiking; it even includes a large section of the 50-mile Batona Trail. In addition to a campground, there are six furnished cabins. This is also the home of Batsto Village (see Attractions below). 4110 Nesco Road, Hammonton, NJ 08037; (609) 561-0024.

Family Outdoor Adventures

Hiking. The 50-mile Batona Trail starts at Lebanon State Forest and runs through Batsto and Lebanon State Forests to Bass River State Forest. Lebanon State Forest, (609) 726-1191; Bass River State Forest, (609) 296-1114.

Horseback Riding. Winslow Timber Creek Ranch offers horseback riding, pony rentals, and trail riding; (856) 262-3800.

Paddling. Princeton Canoe Rental rents canoes for use on the Delaware and Raritan Canal. 483 Alexander Road, Turning Basin Park, Princeton, NJ 08540, (609) 452-2403.

Skiing. Belle Mountain is a small ski area with rentals and lessons; (609) 397-0043.

Paddling the Pines

Rivers, streams, lakes, and ponds are found throughout the Pinelands, making for some great paddling in nearly all seasons. It's easy to get lost in there, however, so be cautious or hire a guide. Among the places to rent equipment, get maps, and hire guides:

Paint Island Canoe and Kayak, 350 Farnsworth Avenue, Bordentown; (609) 324-8200.

Pine Barrens Canoe and Kayak Rental, 3260 Route 563, Chatsworth; (800) 732-0793 or (609) 726-1515.

Mick's Canoe Rental Inc., 3107 Route 563, Jenkins; (800) 281-1380 or (609) 726-1380.

Kayak King Rentals, P.O. Box 171, Route 679 and Chatsworth Road, New Gretna; (609) 296-8002.

Al and Sam's Canoe and Boat Rentals, 4775 North Delsea Drive, Newfield; (856) 692-8440.

Clark's Canoe Rental, P.O. Box 19, 156 Birmingham Road, Pemberton; (609) 894-4448.

Pinelands Preservation Alliance, 114 Hanover Street, Pemberton; (609) 894-8000.

Adams Canoe Rentals, Inc., 1005 Atsion Road, Shamong; (609) 268-0189.

Family Lodging

Country Inn by Carlson

Next door to Wheaton Village, a 100-room facility with regular rooms and suites, a pool, and an on-site restaurant.

1125 Village Drive, Millville, NJ 08332; (856) 825-3100. Rates $75–130.

Radisson Hotel Mount Laurel

A 283-room high-rise hotel with pool and on-site restaurant. It's off Exit 4 of the Turnpike—a convenient and central location, within reasonable driving distance of Princeton, Trenton, Camden, Six Flags/Great Adventure, Philadelphia, Sesame Place, and much of eastern Pennsylvania. Special offers have been available with Sesame Place and Six Flags.

915 Route 73, Mount Laurel, NJ 08054; (609) 234-7300. Rates $79–149; B&B rates plus second-room discounts available.

Attractions

Bridgeton Historical District

50 East Broad Street, Bridgeton, NJ 08302; (800) 319-3379 or
    (609) 451-4802

Hours: Variable

Admission: Nominal to some sites

Appeal by Age Groups:

Pre- school	Grade School	Teens	Young Adults	Over 30	Seniors
★★★★	★★★★★	★★★★	★★★★★	★★★★★	★★★★★

Touring Time: Average 3 hours, minimum 2 hours

Rainy-Day Touring: Yes

Services and Facilities:

Restaurants Yes	Lockers No
Alcoholic beverages Yes	Pet kennels No
Disabled access Yes	Rain check No
Wheelchair rental No	Private tours No
Baby stroller rental No	

Description and Comments   Bridgeton, hidden in the belly of the state, is something of a forgotten place for most New Jerseyans. But it holds New Jersey's largest historical district, some 2,200 Colonial, Victorian, and Federalist buildings. The downtown is lined with brick walkways; a scenic promenade fronts the river and offers good shopping. A 1,100-acre city park has four museums, a zoo, canoe rentals, swimming, and picnicking. The Nail House Museum, (609) 455-4100, displays early iron tools, glass, and local history. New Sweden Farmstead Museum, (800) 319-3379 or (609) 455-9785, is a re-created seventeenth-century Swedish settler's farmstead, with log cabins, a blacksmith shop, and a threshing barn, where reenactments and other special events are often staged. Potter's Tavern, (609) 451-4802, is a restored 1776 building. Call for exact museum hours and event festival information.

Cowtown Rodeo

780 Route 40, Pilesgrove, NJ 08098, (856) 769-3200;
www.cowtownrodeo.com/rodeo/html

Hours: May 27–September, Saturday 7:30 p.m.

Admission: $10 adults, $5 children 12 and under

Appeal by Age Groups:

Pre-school	Grade School	Teens	Young Adults	Over 30	Seniors
★★★	★★★★★	★★★★★	★★★★★	★★★★★	★★★★★

Touring Time: Average 4 hours, minimum 3 hours

Rainy-Day Touring: No

Services and Facilities:

Restaurants Yes	Lockers No
Alcoholic beverages Yes	Pet kennels No
Disabled access Yes	Rain check No
Wheelchair rental No	Private tours No
Baby stroller rental No	

Description and Comments Okay, this is a bit hard to fathom, but not only can you watch real professional rodeo every summer Saturday night just 15 minutes from Philadelphia, but it's also the longest-running regularly scheduled rodeo in the whole darned country. This is so unexpected and so much fun that we drive more than two hours to see it. Come early, bring a picnic, and then, if you've got the stamina, stay late. Seems that more contestants want to compete than one show can handle, so there's a second show. Who competes in which show is decided by lot. You just might see a national champion contestant in the second show. You can also come down much earlier in the day and, right on the grounds, visit one of the state's biggest flea markets.

Historic Batsto Village

Wharton State Forest, Route 542, Batsto, NJ 08037; (609) 561-3262 or (609) 561-0024

Hours: Daily 9 a.m.–4 p.m.; closed Thanksgiving, Christmas, and New Year's days

Admission: Free admission to village; mansion tour: $2 adults, $1 children ages 6–11

Appeal by Age Groups:

Pre-school	Grade School	Teens	Young Adults	Over 30	Seniors
★★	★★★★	★★★★	★★★★★	★★★★★	★★★★

Touring Time: Average 2 hours, minimum 1 hour

Rainy-Day Touring: Yes

Services and Facilities:

Restaurants No	Lockers No
Alcoholic beverages No	Pet kennels No
Disabled access Yes	Rain check No
Wheelchair rental No	Private tours No
Baby stroller rental No	

Description and Comments Batsto was a nineteenth-century ironworks (supplying munitions for the American Revolution and the War of 1812) and glassmaking center. The restored village consists of 33 buildings and structures. The mansion, which looks like something from a Hitchcock movie, is worth touring. Other buildings include a carriage shed, a store, a mill, and a series of workers' houses, some of which are occupied today by working craftspeople. There's a small nature center as well, and plenty of picnic space, plus an annotated nature trail and, if you're up for it, all of Wharton State Forest to explore by foot, mountain bike, or canoe.

New Jersey State Aquarium

1 Riverside Drive, Camden, NJ 08103; (800) 616-5297 or
(856) 365-3300; www.njaquarium.org.

Hours: Mid-September–mid-April, Monday–Friday 9:30 a.m.–4:30 p.m., Saturday–Sunday 10 a.m.–5 p.m.; mid-April–mid-September, daily 9:30 a.m–5:30 p.m.; closed Thanksgiving, Christmas, and New Year's days

Admission: $12.95 adults, $11.45 seniors 65+ and students, $9.95 children ages 3–11, free for children 2 and under; RiverPass, a combined ticket to the New Jersey State Aquarium and the Independence Seaport Museum at Penn's Landing, Philadelphia, with transportation on the RiverLink Ferry: $21.50 adults, $21 seniors, $15.50 children

Appeal by Age Groups:

Pre-school	Grade School	Teens	Young Adults	Over 30	Seniors
★★★★★	★★★★★	★★★★★	★★★★★	★★★★★	★★★★★

Touring Time: Average 3 hours, minimum 2 hours

Rainy-Day Touring: Yes

Services and Facilities:

Restaurants Yes	backpackpacks available
Alcoholic beverages No	Lockers Yes (coatroom)
Disabled access Yes	Pet kennels No
Wheelchair rental Yes; free	Rain check No
Baby stroller rental No; baby	Private tours No

Description and Comments This first-rate aquarium features a 760,000-gallon Open Ocean Tank, a New Inguza Island–Rare South African Penguin Exhibit, a Children's Garden horticultural playground, an Aquatic Nursery, a very cool Water Colors exhibit with a camouflage wall, Jewels of the Rainforest, and something they call "WOW! Weird? Or Wonderful?" a unique collection of freaky-looking fish from all over the world. Seal shows, dive shows, films, and animal talks and presentations are scheduled daily. Look for the Drama Gills shows, interactive performances by a resident theater troupe that emphasizes the funny side of things aquatic.

New Jersey State Museum

205 West State Street, Trenton, NJ 08625; (609) 292-6333; planetarium information, (609) 292-6303; www.state.nj.us/state/museum

Hours: Tuesday–Saturday 9 a.m.–4:45 p.m., Sunday 12–5 p.m.; closed Mondays and all state holidays

Admission: Museum, free; planetarium, $1 per person

Appeal by Age Groups:

Pre-school	Grade School	Teens	Young Adults	Over 30	Seniors
★★	★★★★	★★★★	★★★★★	★★★★★	★★★★★

Touring Time: Average 2 hours, minimum 1 hour

Rainy-Day Touring: Yes

Services and Facilities:

Restaurants Yes	Baby stroller rental No
Alcoholic beverages No	Lockers No
Disabled access Yes	Pet kennels No
Wheelchair rental Yes, free;	Rain check No
reserve ahead, (609) 292-6307	Private tours No

Description and Comments A major museum with significant collections and exhibitions in archaeology and ethnology, fine and decorative arts, and natural history. The planetarium offers shows on Saturday and Sunday at 1 p.m., 2 p.m., and 3 p.m. that are always a favorite with kids. Kaleidoscope Kids, a program of hands-on workshops that explore specific themes, meets on Sunday afternoons. Sessions cost $2 per child, and parents may participate for free.

Wheaton Village

1501 Glasstown Road, Millville, NJ 08332-1566; (800) 998-4552; www.wheatonvillage.org

Hours: April–December, daily 10 a.m.–5 p.m.; January–March, Wednesday–Sunday 10 a.m.–5 p.m.; closed Easter Sunday, Thanksgiving, Christmas, and New Year's days

Admission: April–December: $7 adults, $6 seniors 62+, $3.50 students; January–March: $6 adults, $5 seniors 62+, $2.50 students; children 5 and under always free

Appeal by Age Groups:

Pre-school	Grade School	Teens	Young Adults	Over 30	Seniors
★★★★	★★★★★	★★★★★	★★★★★	★★★★★	★★★★★

Touring Time: Average 3 hours, minimum 2 hours

Rainy-Day Touring: Yes

Services and Facilities:

Restaurants Yes; adjacent	Lockers No
Alcoholic beverages Yes	Pet kennels No
Disabled access Yes	Rain check No
Wheelchair rental Yes; free	Private tours No
Baby stroller rental No	

Description and Comments   Millville was once an international glassmaking capitol. Wheaton Village pays homage to that heritage with the Museum of American Glass, one of the finest collections we've seen. But the village also encompasses many other elements, including the T. J. Wheaton Glass Factory and the Crafts and Traders' Row, where you can see glassmaking and craftmaking demonstrations, and the Down Jersey Folklife Center. There are also many stores, a miniature train ride, and a long list of special events.

Family-Friendly Restaurants

CAFE GALLERY

219 High Street, Burlington; (609) 386-6150

Meals served: Lunch and dinner
Cuisine: Continental
Entree range: $5.75–19.75 (lunch and dinner)

Children's menu: Yes
Reservations: Yes
Payment: Major credit cards

A beautiful setting in a restored Colonial building overlooking the Delaware River. The specialty is seafood, but there's good food for everybody here.

RED HOT AND BLUE

Route 70, Sayer Avenue, Cherry Hill; (856) 665-7427

Meals served: Lunch and dinner
Cuisine: Southern barbecue
Entree range: $5.95–15.95
Children's menu: Yes
Reservations: Yes
Payment: Major credit cards

A bustling, noisy place with a southern atmosphere, where the specialties are ribs, pulled pork, and chicken. Loud live blues on the weekends.

Northern Shore

"Goin' down da shore" has long been New Jersey's favorite pastime, dating back a century and a half or more. It's no wonder—the state borders the sea for 127 miles. Today, at least five dozen hamlets can be considered "shore towns," ranging from the internationally known, like Atlantic City, to the little-known, like Spray Beach. We've divided the shore into two sections: Northern, the area from Sandy Hook at the mouth of New York Harbor down to greater Atlantic City; and Southern, running from Atlantic City to Cape May.

The Northern Shore offers a plethora of worthwhile sites. **Popcorn Park Zoo** (call (609) 693-1900) in **Forked River** is operated by the Humane Society and houses a collection of abandoned wildlife. The **Haluwasa Shoreline Railroad** (call (609) 561-3081) in **Hammonton** is, at two miles, New Jersey's longest 24-inch-gauge railroad. **Keansburg** is home to **Keansburg Amusement Park and Runaway Rapids** (call (800) 805-4386), which has a 2,500-foot fishing pier and a free beach. In **Middletown,** kids up to ten will enjoy **Imagine That** (call (732) 706-9000), a hands-on museum with 50 activities. The **U.S. Army Communications Electronics Museum** (call (732) 532-4390) in **Fort Monmouth** features communications electronics dating back to 1917. **The Metz Bicycle Museum** (call (732) 462-7363) in **Freehold** claims to have the world's best collection of antique bicycles, plus an extensive collection of children's riding toys, kitchen and household gadgets, hand tools, farm implements, and antique cars. For summertime entertainment, few places can rival the **PNC Bank Arts Center** (call (732) 335-0400) in **Holmdel,** where big-name acts and ethnic festivals run all summer. **Longstreet Farm** (call (732) 946-3758) presents living history circa 1890. One of our favorite small museums is the **Barnegat Bay Decoy and Baymen's Museum** (call (609) 296-8868) in **Tuckerton,** which preserves the heritage and lifestyle of baymen and the Jersey shore. For local musical flavor, **Albert Music Hall** (call

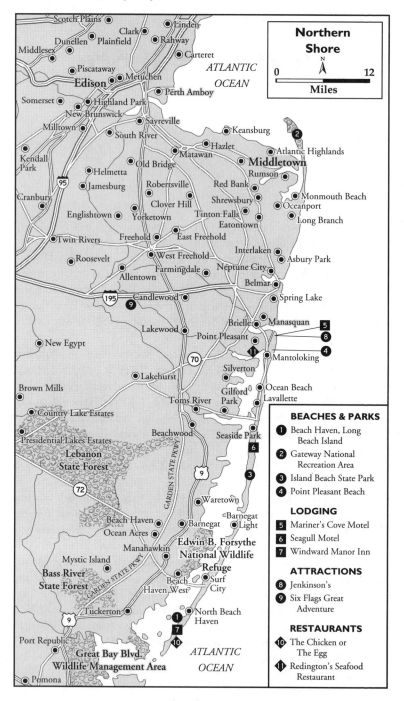

Scotch Plains ●
Linden ●
Clark ●
Dunellen ● Plainfield ● Rahway ●
Middlesex ●
Carteret ●
Piscataway ●
ATLANTIC
Metuchen ●
Edison ●
Perth Amboy ●
OCEAN
Somerset ●
Highland Park ●
New Brunswick ●
Sayreville ●
Keansburg ●
Milltown ●
South River ●
Hazlet ● **2**
Atlantic Highlands ●
Kendall Park ●
Matawan ●
Middletown
Helmetta ●
Old Bridge ●
Rumson ●
95
Jamesburg ●
Robertsville ●
Red Bank ●
Monmouth Beach ●
Cranbury ●
Clover Hill ●
Shrewsbury ●
Oceanport ●
Englishtown ● Yorketown ●
Tinton Falls ●
Long Branch ●
Eatontown ●
Twin Rivers ●
Freehold ● East Freehold ●
Roosevelt ●
West Freehold ●
Interlaken ●
Asbury Park ●
Farmingdale ●
Neptune City ●
Allentown ●
195
Candlewood ● **9**
Belmar ●
Spring Lake ●
Brielle ● Manasquan ● **5**
Lakewood ●
Point Pleasant ● **8**
New Egypt ●
70
11
4
Mantoloking ●
Silverton ●
Lakehurst ●
Ocean Beach ●
Brown Mills ●
Toms River ●
Gilford Park ●
Lavallette ●
Country Lake Estates ●
Presidential Lakes Estates ●
Beachwood ●
Lebanon
Seaside Park ●
State Forest
6
GARDEN STATE PKWY
72
9
3
Waretown ●
Barnegat Light ●
Beach Haven ●
Barnegat ●
Ocean Acres ●
Manahawkin ●
Edwin B. Forsythe
National Wildlife
Mystic Island ●
Refuge
Bass River
Beach ● Surf City
State Forest
Haven West ●
Tuckerton ●
9
1
North Beach Haven ●
7
Port Republic ●
10
ATLANTIC
Great Bay Blvd
Wildlife Management Area
OCEAN
Pomona ●

Northern Shore

N

0 ———————— 12

Miles

BEACHES & PARKS

1 Beach Haven, Long Beach Island
2 Gateway National Recreation Area
3 Island Beach State Park
4 Point Pleasant Beach

LODGING

5 Mariner's Cove Motel
6 Seagull Motel
7 Windward Manor Inn

ATTRACTIONS

8 Jenkinson's
9 Six Flags Great Adventure

RESTAURANTS

10 The Chicken or The Egg
11 Redington's Seafood Restaurant

(609) 971-1593) in **Waretown** presents live music of the Pinelands on Saturday nights. In **Fair Haven,** regional history is nicely depicted at **Allaire State Park** (call (732) 938-2253), site of a restored nineteenth-century village and the **Pine Creek Railroad.** Near **Sandy Hook,** in **Highlands,** the **Navesink Light Station at Twin Lights Historic Site** (call (732) 872-1814) is one of the cooler lighthouses you'll ever visit—its twin beacons sit on a hill 256 feet above the water. Horse lovers should check the show and competition schedule at **The Horse Park of New Jersey** (call (609) 259-0170) in **Allentown,** the state's first major horse show grounds.

How to Get There

By Car. Most people get to the shore on the Garden State Parkway, which can become a veritable parking lot southbound on Friday evenings and northbound on Sunday. Northern Shore exits run from Exit 117 to Exit 63. I-195 runs east-west, intersecting the Parkway at Exit 98 and merging at its eastern end with State 138, which continues on to the Belmar area. State Route 70 also runs east-west, crossing the Parkway at Exit 88 and continuing to Point Pleasant and Bay Head. To reach Seaside Heights, Seaside Park, and Island Beach State Park, use Parkway Exit 88. Access to Long Beach Island is via Route 37, at Parkway Exit 63.

By Plane. Newark International Airport is about two hours from the heart of the region; (973) 961-6000. Atlantic City International Airport is half an hour south of the area, in the Southern Shore region; (609) 645-7895.

By Train. New Jersey Transit's New Jersey Coast Line, (800) 772-2222, operates trains serving New York, Newark, Red Bank, Long Branch, Monmouth Park, and Shore locations to Point Pleasant Beach/Bay Head. Some hotels offer transportation from local stations.

How to Get More Information before You Go

Shore Regional Tourism Council, 700 Hope Road, Tinton Falls, NJ 07724; (732) 544-9300 ext. 708.

Monmouth County Economic Development/Tourism, Main Street, Freehold, NJ 07728; (732) 431-7476.

Ocean County Public Affairs and Tourism, 101 Hooper Avenue, #109, P.O. Box 2191, Toms River, NJ 08754; (732) 929-2138.

The Best Parks and Beaches

Beach Haven, Long Beach Island. Long Beach Island, or LBI, attracts folks from north and south. The island holds some nine towns or more, but it's

Beach Haven, the second to southernmost on the island, that gets our nod because it somehow manages to maintain a quiet, accessible, and perfectly kept beach within walking distance to a downtown that includes some decent shopping, good restaurants, and kid-friendly amusements and water park.

Gateway National Recreation Area. The park actually comprises several installations in New York City and Highlands, New Jersey, and the latter offers one of the most interesting beach reserves in the state (at Sandy Hook). In addition to several miles of open beach with views of Manhattan in the distance, the park has a visitors center; a former 1894 U.S. Life-Saving Station, with exhibits, a bookstore, and information on programs; a mile-long walking trail through the dunes; the Sandy Hook Lighthouse; and Fort Hancock, first built in 1895 and shored up during World War II, with a museum, buildings, and fortifications to explore. Special programs are offered daily during the summer, ranging from nature walks and history talks to concerts by the New York Philharmonic Orchestra and the Metropolitan Opera. The food concessions also offer live rock bands on weekend afternoons. The park parking lots often fill up early in peak beach season. Sandy Hook and Highlands; (732) 872-5970.

Island Beach State Park. If you like your beaches pure and uncluttered, this is the place to be. One of the few remaining undeveloped barrier beaches on the North Atlantic coast, the park holds more than 3,000 acres and has ten miles of coastal dunes and one mile of life-guarded swimming beach. The bathhouses are clean and modern, with snack bars, and the park offers historic buildings, trails, naturalist programs, bike paths, and excellent facilities for people with disabilities. During the summer months, check out the naturalist-led, guided canoe and kayak trips through the bayside tidal marsh. For boardwalk addicts, the arcades of Seaside Park and Seaside Heights loom just to the north. P.O. Box 37, Seaside Park, NJ 08752; (732) 793-0506.

Point Pleasant Beach. Point Pleasant is just all-round great for families with kids up to age 12. The beach is wide, the boardwalk is amiable and not too honky-tonk, the Jenkinson's attractions (see Attractions, below) are old-timey and wonderful, and the overall atmosphere is family-friendly at its best. Chamber of Commerce, 517-A Arnold Avenues, Point Pleasant Beach, NJ 08742; (732) 295-2820.

Family Outdoor Adventures

Biking. Henry Hudson Trail runs nine miles from Aberdeen to Atlantic Highlands on a paved, former railroad right-of-way; (732) 842-4000.

Boating. Beach Haven Watersports rents waverunners and boats; 2702 Long Beach Boulevard, Beach Haven, NJ 08008, (609) 492-0375. Beachwood Yacht Club offers family-oriented sailing instruction for kids; Compass Avenue, Beachwood, NJ 08722, (732) 349-9604. Horizon Sailing Center rents sailboats and kayaks and offers tours and lessons; 3206 Long Beach Boulevard, Brant Beach, NJ 08008, (609) 494-9393; Island Surf and Sail rents windsurfers, kayaks, and wakeboards; 3304 Long Beach Boulevard, Brant Beach, NJ 08008, (609) 494-5553. Watersports rents Jet-Skis; 3100 Long Beach Boulevard, Brant Beach, NJ 08008, (609) 494-2727.

Hiking. Henry Hudson Trail (see Biking just above). Hartshorne Woods Park, a 736-acre park with 15 miles of trails; Navesink Road, Locust Section, Middletown, NJ 07752, (732) 842-4000. Huber Woods Park has six miles of multiuse trails; Brown's Dock Road, Locust Section, Middletown, NJ 07748, (732) 872-2670.

Horseback Riding. Circle A Riding Academy, 116 Herbertsville Road, Howell, NJ 07731, (732) 938-2004. Quiet Season Stables, Vanderveer Road, Howell, NJ 07731, (732) 431-0457. Tall Oaks Farm, 151 Oak Glen Road, Howell, NJ 07731, (732) 938-5445.

Paddling. Triple T Canoes Inc. rents canoes and kayaks and sells supplies; 1034 Locust Road, Beachwood, NJ 08722, (732) 349-9510. Jersey Paddler offers canoe and kayak sales, rentals, and lessons; 1756 Route 88 West, Brick Township, NJ 08724, (732) 458-5777. Mohawk Canoe Livery rents canoes and kayaks; Squankum Yellow Brook Road, Farmingdale, NJ 07727, (732) 938-7755. Pineland Canoes Inc. offers canoe and kayak rentals and overnight trips; 26 Whitesville Road, Route 527, Jackson, NJ 08527, (800) 281-0383 or (732) 364-0389.

Scuba. Underwater Discovery offers diving instruction, sales, service, and rentals; 2722 Route 37 East, Toms River, NJ 08753, (732) 270-9100.

Family Lodging

Mariner's Cove Motel

Two blocks from the beach, a comfortable motel with refrigerators in the rooms and restaurants nearby.

50 Broadway, Point Pleasant Beach, NJ 08742; (732) 899-0060. Rates $100–125.

Seagull Motel

An oceanside motel not far from Island Beach State Park, with local beach privileges, cable TV with several movie channels, and personal refrigerators.

Portacribs are available. One-bedroom, two-bedroom, and efficiency units.

1401 North Ocean Avenue, Seaside Park, NJ 08752; (732) 793-0815.
Rates $105–149.

Windward Manor Inn

Located one block from the beach and three blocks from the amusements,
restaurants, and shops in town, this is a historic old house converted into a
ten-room, friendly, family-managed B&B. Rooms range from studios to
two-room efficiencies. All rooms have refrigerators and cable TV. Portacribs
are available for a small fee, and beach privileges are included.

Amber and Atlantic Avenues, Beach Haven, NJ 08008; (609) 492-
5216; www.windardmanorinn.com. Rates $120–268.

Attractions

Jenkinson's Aquarium
Jenkinson's Pavilion Boardwalk and Amusement Park

3 Broadway, Point Pleasant Beach, NJ 08742; (732) 892-0600;
www.jenkinsons.com

Hours: Aquarium: daily 10 a.m.–5 p.m. Boardwalk attractions:
June–Labor Day, daily noon–midnight; variable weekend hours in
spring and fall

Admission: Aquarium: $7 adults, $4.50 children, free for children under
3; rides: $10

Appeal by Age Groups:

Pre- school	Grade School	Teens	Young Adults	Over 30	Seniors
★★★★★	★★★★★	★★★★	★★★	★★★★★	★★★★★

Touring Time: Average 4 hours, minimum 2 hours

Rainy-Day Touring: Yes

Services and Facilities:

Restaurants Yes		Lockers Yes
Alcoholic beverages Yes		Pet kennels No
Disabled access Yes		Rain check No
Wheelchair rental No		Private tours Yes
Baby stroller rental No		

Description and Comments Jenkinson's is a long-standing Point Pleasant
Beach institution. While you'll find many of the usual arcades, rides, a fun-
house, games of chance, restaurants, and novelty shops, it's all presented in
a kind of squeaky-clean wholesome way that puts a parent at ease. The

aquarium is among the best small aquariums in the land, with a wonderful flock of penguins and all the requisite attractions—exotic fish, mammals, birds, touch tank, fossil room, seals, alligators, and nature programs throughout the summer—but on a scale that's perfect for younger kids. The mini-beach train is always a fun novelty ride (and beats walking in the hot sun). You'll also find three miniature golf courses and several batting cages. The facility is served by four private parking lots (fees are around $8.50 per day).

Six Flags Great Adventure and Wild Safari

Route 537, Jackson, NJ 08527; (732) 928-1821; www.sixflags.com

Hours: May–October, park opens at 10 a.m.; closing times vary; Wild Safari: 9 a.m.–4 p.m.

Admission: Theme park (plus 6% tax): $43.96 adults, $27.97 seniors 55+, $21.98 children 48 inches and shorter; theme park and safari: $45.94 adults, $28.96 seniors, $22.97 children; safari only: $15 per person; parking $8

Appeal by Age Groups:

Pre-school	Grade School	Teens	Young Adults	Over 30	Seniors
★★★★★	★★★★★	★★★★★	★★★★★	★★★★★	★★★★★

Touring Time: Average 7 hours, minimum 5 hours

Rainy-Day Touring: Yes

Services and Facilities:

Restaurants Yes	Lockers Yes
Alcoholic beverages Yes	Pet kennels Yes
Disabled access Yes	Rain check No
Wheelchair rental Yes	Private tours No
Baby stroller rental Yes	

Description and Comments   This is one big place. The theme park has 75 rides, including 11 roller coasters, and a water park, new in summer 2000 and also gargantuan. Come early and plan to spend the entire day and on into the night. In addition to rides and water, there's also a huge selection of ongoing shows, Looney Tunes characters roaming around, and live concerts by national names. And then there's the Wild Safari, a 350-acre drive-through wildlife preserve that's home to more than 1,200 animals from six continents. They roam free as you drive the 4.5-mile roadway at about five miles per hour, listening to a narration on your car radio. The Safari is divided into 13 sections, from Baboons and Elephant/Rhinos to birds and animals from Australia. Kids love it when the baboons climb on the car. For an extra fee, an air-conditioned, guided safari tour bus is an option.

As with most major theme parks, lines can be long and food expensive, so plan on making this a major outing. Some nice touches include baby-changing stations in all women's and most men's restrooms, a designated nursing area, and excellent facilities for disabled people. Note that Wild Safari opens an hour before the theme park, which is usually the best time to drive through; it closes at 4 p.m.

Family-Friendly Restaurants

THE CHICKEN OR THE EGG

207 North Bay Avenue, Beach Haven; (609) 492-3695

Meals served: Breakfast, lunch, and dinner
Cuisine: American
Entree range: $5.25–15.50
Children's menu: Yes
Reservations: No
Payment: Major credit cards

They serve probably the best breakfast on Long Beach Island and specialize in wings, burgers, sandwiches, and fried seafood the rest of the day.

REDINGTON'S SEAFOOD RESTAURANT

816 Arnold Avenue, Point Pleasant; (732) 892-4343

Meals served: Lunch and dinner
Cuisine: Seafood
Entree range: $6.95–10.95 (lunch), $16.95–20.95 (dinner)
Children's menu: Yes
Reservations: Yes, for 6 or more
Payment: AE, MC, V

A small local favorite (15 tables) with surprisingly good gourmet food.

Southern Shore

A word about **Atlantic City.** We are not gamblers, nor are we fans of gambling, and like it or not, Atlantic City today is primarily about gambling. Once that's understood, a trip to Atlantic City can be approached intelligently. The area thrives with restaurants, and its boardwalk is certainly alive with all manner of amusements, food both fast and slow, and lots of kitschy shops. The beach is clean. We prefer Atlantic City for a day visit, but for those who want to stay over, most of the casino hotels will give you a decent room for a reasonable price. For families the best casino is probably the **Hilton** (call (800) 257-8677). Why? Because it's on the boardwalk, has organized on-beach activities, and offers a child-care center. **Trump Plaza,** too, has a children's activity center (call (800) 677-7378). Atlantic City does offer a variety of worthwhile family-friendly attractions. **The Atlantic City Historical Museum and Cultural Center** (call (609) 347-5839) does an excellent job of depicting Atlantic City's storied past. The **Steel Pier** (call (609) 345-4893) is an A.C. landmark laden with classic boardwalk amusements and rides. For rainy days, check out the bowling center at the **Showboat** (call (609) 343-4040). The **Absecon Lighthouse** (call (609) 449-1360) is New Jersey's tallest. And just south of A.C., in **Margate, Lucy the Elephant** (call (609) 823-6473), the world's only 65-foot-high elephant that you can walk through, has been delighting all ages since the late 1800s.

Just north of A.C., in **Brigantine,** the **Sea Life Museum–Marine Mammal Stranding Center** (call (609) 266-0538) houses life-size replicas of much sea life, and you can learn of their important work in saving stranded marine mammals. **Oceanville** is home to the **Noyes Museum of Art** (call (609) 652-8848), a surprisingly fine, very modern facility set seemingly in the middle of nowhere. In **Egg Harbor Township, Story Book Land** (call (609) 641-7847), a theme park based on children's stories, is great for little ones. Moving south, the **Wetlands Institute and**

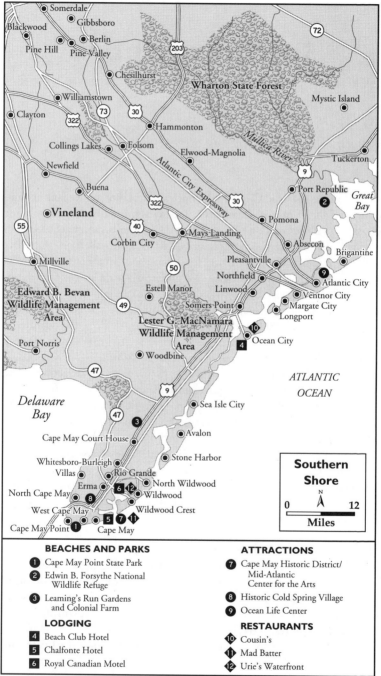

Southern
Shore

N

0   12

Miles

BEACHES AND PARKS

1 Cape May Point State Park

2 Edwin B. Forsythe National
Wildlife Refuge

3 Leaming's Run Gardens
and Colonial Farm

LODGING

4 Beach Club Hotel

5 Chalfonte Hotel

6 Royal Canadian Motel

ATTRACTIONS

7 Cape May Historic District/
Mid-Atlantic
Center for the Arts

8 Historic Cold Spring Village

9 Ocean Life Center

RESTAURANTS

10 Cousin's

11 Mad Batter

12 Urie's Waterfront

Museum (call (609) 368-1211) in **Stone Harbor** is one of the finer ecological installations around, offering exhibits and nature walks.

HOW TO GET THERE

By Car. Southern Shore exits from the Garden State Parkway range from Exit 40, just north of Atlantic City, to Exit 1 at Cape May, the state's southernmost point. East-west traffic moves into Atlantic City on the Atlantic City Expressway, a toll road, and via U.S. 40. State 50 cuts southeast from U.S. 40 to the Parkway at Exit 20, while State Route 47 is the main east-west route serving Cape May. U.S. 9 parallels the Parkway, while Ocean Boulevard, a local street, runs north-south along the sea from Ocean City to North Wildwood, crossing some nifty drawbridges.

By Plane. Atlantic City International Airport is the primary access to this part of the state; (609) 645-7895. Philadelphia International Airport is within two hours of most of the area; (215) 492-3181.

HOW TO GET INFORMATION BEFORE YOU GO

> *Greater Atlantic City Regional Tourism Council, Towne of Historic Smithville, One North New York Road, Smithville, NJ 08201; (609) 652-7777.*

> *Greater Wildwoods Tourism Improvement and Development Authority, P.O. Box 217, Wildwood, NJ 08260; (800) 992-9732.*

> *Cape May County Tourism Department, P.O. Box 365, Cape May Court House, NJ 08210; (609) 463-6415.*

> *Ocean County Public Affairs and Tourism, 101 Hooper Avenue, #109, P.O. Box 2191, Toms River, NJ 08754; (732) 929-2138.*

The Best Parks and Beaches

Cape May Point State Park. The state's southernmost tip (which is actually at a more southerly latitude than Washington, D.C.) is preserved by this park, ranked among the world's great bird-watching sites. In addition to a fine, clean beach, the park has an environmental museum; the 157-foot-high Cape May Lighthouse, still in use today; and the Cape May Point Natural Area, where several trails allow exploration of the park's pond, coastal dune, marsh, and forest habitats. Located off the southern end of the Garden State Parkway. P.O. Box 107, Cape May Point, NJ 08212; (609) 884-2159.

Edwin B. Forsythe National Wildlife Refuge. Covering 40,000 acres, the refuge comprises tidal salt meadow and marsh interspersed with shallow coves and bays. About 6,000 acres are designated as Wilderness Area. Some 275 species of migratory birds pass through here. People are welcome at the Brigantine Division, where the highlight is an eight-mile wildlife automobile trail that reveals beautiful marshland views plus, with some irony, the overdeveloped Atlantic City skyline views in the background. There are two foot trails, one annotated. Great Creek Road, Oceanville, NJ 08231; (609) 652-1665.

Leaming's Run Gardens and Colonial Farm. We don't usually recommend gardens as great escapes with children, but this is different. You follow a path through the woods that keeps leading you into a series of magnificent small gardens, each with a color theme. There are 25 gardens in all, plus a huge vegetable garden, and tobacco and cotton plants. Weekly tours of seashore colonial life are also offered, but it's those color bursts as you walk that make the day. 1849 Route 9 North, Swainton, NJ 08210; (609) 465-5871.

Family Outdoor Adventures

Boating. Cape May Water Sports rents waverunners, boats, and kayaks; 1286 Wilson Drive, Cape May, NJ 08204; (609) 884-8646.

Camping. Belleplain State Forest, set a few miles northwest of the Wildwoods, offers 169 tent and trailer sites with fire rings and picnic tables. Flush toilets, showers, and laundry facilities; County Route 550, P.O. Box 450, Woodbine, NJ 08270; (609) 861-2404. Route 9, north of Cape May. Uniquely, this area has developed into a favorite for Quebec residents, and a number of commercial campgrounds set along Route 9 greet you with signs saying "Nous parlons Français!" Camping in this area, therefore, can become an international experience.

Horseback Riding. Hidden Valley Ranch offers riding lessons and special summer riding programs; 4070 Bayshore Road, West Cape May, NJ 08204; (609) 884-8205. Triple R Ranch has trail riding and lessons; 210 Stagecoach Road, Cape May Court House, NJ 08210; (609) 465-4673.

Paddling. Bel Haven Canoe and Kayak rents and sells canoes and kayaks, rents tubes, and offers canoe, kayak, and tube trips on Pine Barrens rivers; 1227 Route 542, Egg Harbor City, NJ 08215; (609) 965-2205. Mullica River Boat Basin and Canoe Rentals rents canoes and kayaks and functions as a full-service sport shop on the Mullica River; 1118 Route 542, Green

Bank, NJ 08215; (609) 965-2120. Canal Side Boat and Kayak Rental, 1710 Delaware Avenue, North Wildwood, NJ 08260; (609) 522-7676.

Whale-Watching. Cape May Whale Watcher, *Miss Chris 2,* sails on whale, dolphin, and history cruises; Wilson Drive, Cape May, NJ 08204; (800) 786-5445 or (609) 884-5445. Captain Mey's Inn can arrange dolphin and whale cruises; 202 Ocean Street, Cape May, NJ 08204; (800) 981-3702. Delta Lady–Silver Bullet Sightseeing specializes in intercoastal waterway sight-seeing and dolphin-watching cruises; 508 West Rio Grande Avenue, Wildwood, NJ 08260; (609) 522-1919. Cape May Whale Watch and Research Center stages whale-watching cruises; 1286 Wilson Drive, Cape May, NJ 08204; (609) 898-0055. Captain Sinn's Marine Center offers dinner, sight-seeing, and whale-watching cruises; 6006 Park Boulevard, Wildwood Crest, NJ 08260; (609) 522-3934.

Family Lodging

Beach Club Hotel

One of several good hotels along the boardwalk, the Beach Club features a pool and wading pool, private balconies, and in-room refrigerators.

13th Street and Boardwalk, P.O. Box 929, Ocean City, NJ 08226; (609) 399-8555. Rates $90–230.

Chalfonte Hotel

For a true taste of old-time Cape May, the Chalfonte is the oldest Victorian hotel in town, having been in continual operation since 1876. It's old-fashioned—the rooms are basic and are not heated or air-conditioned, but the big verandas make terrific places to catch ocean breezes. The dining room features southern-style cooking, and there's a separate dining room for kids six and under. Open seasonally from Memorial Day to Columbus Day, the hotel also features special family accommodations.

301 Howard Street, Cape May, NJ 08204; (609) 884-8409. Rates $109–209 Modified American Plan.

Royal Canadian Motel

One of innumerable Wildwood offerings, the Royal Canadian is half a block from the beach and boardwalk. It has a pool and 86 rooms: half are two-bedroom suites, and all have refrigerators.

3300 Atlantic Avenue, Wildwood, NJ 08260; (800) 957-6925 or (609) 522-0950. Rates $85–125.

Attractions

Cape May Historic District/Mid-Atlantic Center for the Arts

1048 Washington Street, P.O. Box 340, Cape May, NJ 08204;
  (609) 884-5404; www.capemaymac.org

Hours: Vary

Admission: Physick Estate and Trolley Tour combination: $11 adults,
  $5.50 children ages 3–12; trolley only: $5.50 adults, $2.75 children;
  Physick Estate only: $7 adults, $3.50 children

Appeal by Age Groups:

Pre-school	Grade School	Teens	Young Adults	Over 30	Seniors
★	★★★★	★★★★	★★★★★	★★★★★	★★★★★

Touring Time: Trolley, 90 minutes; estate, 45 minutes

Rainy-Day Touring: Yes

Services and Facilities:

Restaurants No	Baby stroller rental No
Alcoholic beverages No	Lockers No
Disabled access Yes, to some	Pet kennels No
trolleys	Rain check No
Wheelchair rental No	Private tours No

Description and Comments   You could say that the Emlen Physick Estate, a
classic 1879 Victorian home, saved Cape May. Slated many years back to be
razed, it was saved, renovated, and put on display. Soon, much the same
thing began to happen to the town's entire remarkable collection of Victorian architecture. Now the town is listed on the National Historic Register
and has become renowned for its Victoriana. The 18-room Emlen Physick
Estate serves as a Victorian house museum, and tour guides do an excellent
job of explaining how life was lived at a time when Cape May was a favorite
retreat of the Washington and Philadelphia elite. As to the trolley tours,
three are offered: East End, West End, and Beachfront. We like the West
End best, which includes massive Congress Hall, the Pink House, and
Decatur Street, where the porches all line up. Many kids, however, may go
for the Beachfront, just because it's, well, on the beach. Trolley tours begin
at the Washington Street Mall Information Booth at Ocean Street.

The Mid-Atlantic Center for the Arts sponsors a huge range of special
events, from a spring music festival, October Victorian Week, and Victorian Christmas to an increasingly significant jazz festival and a potpourri of
specialty tours (like a Sherlock Holmes Tour or a Victorian Murder Mystery Dinner).

Historic Cold Spring Village

720 Route 9, Cape May, NJ 08204; (609) 898-2300; www.hcsv.org

Hours: Memorial Day–late June and Labor Day–mid-September,
Saturday–Sunday 10 a.m.–4:30 p.m.; late June–Labor Day
Weekend, daily 10 a.m.–4:30 p.m.

Admission: Free

Appeal by Age Groups:

Pre-school	Grade School	Teens	Young Adults	Over 30	Seniors
★★★	★★★★★	★★★★	★★★★★	★★★★★	★★★★★

Touring Time: Average 3 hours, minimum 1½ hours

Rainy-Day Touring: Yes

Services and Facilities:

Restaurants No	Lockers No
Alcoholic beverages No	Pet kennels No
Disabled access Partial	Rain check No
Wheelchair rental No	Private tours No
Baby stroller rental No	

Description and Comments   Of New Jersey's many living history and historical re-creations, this is one of our favorites. The "residents" of the village are really into their roles, and they love to tell tales of life during their times—that of a small South Jersey rural community 150 years ago. The village includes many working craftspeople—potters, blacksmiths, wheelwrights, etc.—and a variety of hands-on things to do (we had a great time making rope). The bakery, by the way, sells their goods, and they are just that—good. Very good. To get a great perspective on how life has changed, visit the school outhouse—a five-holer. Special events are staged most weekends, and free Saturday evening concerts feature brass bands, jazz, R&B, and Pinelands (or "Piney") music. Just by the entrance, you can take a most pleasant walk along the Nature Trail at Bradner's Run. And one of the newest features is round-trip passage on the train to the Cape May County Zoo.

Ocean Life Center

New Hampshire Avenue and The Bay, Atlantic City, NJ 08401;
(609) 348-2880; www.oceanlifecenter.com

Hours: Daily 10 a.m.–5 p.m.

Admission: $7 adults, $5 seniors, $4 students and children 4 and up, free
for children 3 and under

Appeal by Age Groups:

Pre-school	Grade School	Teens	Young Adults	Over 30	Seniors
★★★★	★★★★★	★★★★	★★★★	★★★★★	★★★★★

Touring Time: Average 2 hours, minimum 1 hour
Rainy-Day Touring: Yes
Services and Facilities:

Restaurants No	Lockers No
Alcoholic beverages No	Pet kennels No
Disabled access Yes	Rain check No
Wheelchair rental No	Private tours No
Baby stroller rental No	

Description and Comments A refreshing small aquarium in Atlantic City's Gardner's Basin section. It features small aquariums, a touch tank, a series of interactive and computer exhibits, and an interesting room devoted to the Coast Guard. The second- and third-floor indoor/outdoor observation decks allow you to view the ocean and the bay and also have an operating weather station.

Family-Friendly Restaurants

COUSIN'S

104 Asbury Avenue (at First Avenue), Ocean City; (609) 399-9462; www.cousins-ocnj.com

Meals served: Lunch and dinner
Cuisine: Italian
Entree range: $10 early-bird specials; $6.95–24.95 (dinner)
Children's menu: Yes
Reservations: Yes
Payment: V, MC, DC

A fine little Italian restaurant set in the basement of an old house or outdoors, and family-style take-out is also available. Home cooking with lots of flavor, and a congenial atmosphere.

MAD BATTER

19 Jackson Street, Cape May; (609) 884-5970

Meals served: Breakfast, lunch, and dinner
Cuisine: American

Entree range: $16–23 (dinner)
Children's menu: Yes
Reservations: Yes, for dinner
Payment: Major credit cards

Set in a Victorian B&B, this is a long-standing Cape May tradition. The food is creative and delicious, and the portions are sizable. Try breakfast on the veranda.

URIE'S WATERFRONT

588 West Rio Grande Avenue (at Susquehanna Street), Wildwood; (609) 522-4189

Meals served: Lunch and dinner
Cuisine: Seafood
Entree range: $7.95–24.95
Children's menu: Yes
Reservations: No
Payment: Major credit cards

Good seafood by the sea.

The Best of the Jersey Shore Towns

While kids will find fun at almost any of the shore's towns—kids, sand, and water equal happiness—a few stand out.

Best for Families with Young Kids

Cape May. The queen of Victoriana at the bottom of the state, the town has more ambience than you can shake a stick at, and the nearby attractions—both man-made and natural—offer excellent variety. There is a beach fee; (609) 884-5508.

Ocean City. A dry town, so you have to go back to the mainland if you want to buy beer—that's how family-oriented this place is. Along the boardwalk you'll find unique activities, like brass band concerts, and an endless array of special events, including the inimitable Miss Crustacean Hermit Crab Beauty Contest, in which a shellfish is crowned as a beauty queen. The boardwalk is clean, with just the right amount of hokeyness. Among the highlights are Gillian's Island at Plymouth Place, offering family rides, water slides, and a water-spraying playground, or its sister, Gillian's Wonderland Pier, at Sixth Street. Tee Time Golf is also near Sixth Street on the boardwalk. The Ocean City Aquarium is in town on Asbury Avenue, and the Discovery Sea Shell Museum stands a few blocks away. Beach fees required; (609) 399-6111.

Point Pleasant Beach. Highlighted by Jenkinson's Pavilion and Aquarium. Here you'll find an impeccable beach, affordable accommodations, a boardwalk that's not overbearing, small-child amusements, and accessible parking. There is a beach fee; (732) 899-2424.

Seaside Park. Seaside Park better suits small children than Seaside Heights next door. While the boardwalk has the requisite entertainment, it's less honky-tonk and intense than the Heights' more garish version. The highlight is Funtown Pier at Porter Avenue and the boardwalk. There is a beach fee; (732) 793-0234.

The Wildwoods. Three towns make up the Wildwoods—North Wildwood, Wildwood itself, and, to the south, Wildwood Crest. Everyone has their favorite. The three towns hold what one preservationist professional once told us was "the best collection of 1950s motel architecture in the country." Motels of every size, shape, and quality fill the towns, so do some research before making a lodging choice. But there are plenty of good ones. The beach here is, if anything, too wide, but it's immaculate and certainly plenty roomy. Special events here include the World Marble Championships and the world's largest beach kite-flying festival. Morey's Pier, at 25th Avenue, is the biggest attraction, with two water parks in addition to rides, etc. Nickel's Midway Pier at 3500 Boardwalk features kiddie rides. Wyland's Whaling Wall is a huge mural (220 feet by 30 feet) depicting life-size whales and dolphins. Beach fees are enforced. Wildwood Crest information, (800) 524-2776; Wildwoods information, (800) 992-9732.

Best for Families with Teens

Seaside Heights. The Heights is, among other things, a surfing spot, but it's the 1.5-mile wild-and-crazy boardwalk scene that teens love, including New Jersey's only beach skyride. MTV chose this spot for its summer house in 1999, so you know it's teen-land. The Big Top Arcade at 1020 North Boardwalk has the latest in video games, as do Casino Arcade at Sherman Avenue and Central Arcade, at Hamilton Avenue. Casino Pier and Water Works, 800 Ocean Terrace, offers the gamut of rides, water park, arcades, and games, while Floyd Moreland's, at Sherman Street, takes you back in time, with an original, historic Dentzel/Looffe carousel, accompanied by a genuine 1920 Wurlitzer organ. Still other arcades include Lucky Leo's at 315 Boardwalk, Lucky's at 1215 Boardwalk, and Pleasure Island Arcade and Miniature Golf at 1415 Ocean Terrace, where indoor miniature golf and batting cages are part of the scene. Beach fees are required; (800) 732-7467.

The Wildwoods. As good as it is for little ones, Wildwoods—with its massive beach, fun piers, and special events—also appeals to teens.

Best for Young Adults

Belmar. This is the kind of place where 20-somethings get together to rent a beach house for the summer. Activities run the gamut from sunbathing to fishing, scuba diving, and surfing, and, while Belmar Casino, at 1400 Ocean Avenue, has the requisite video games, skeeball, miniature golf, batting cages, and carnival rides, the boardwalk scene falls somewhere in the middle ground as far as action is concerned. There is a beach fee; (732) 681-3700.

Appeals to Everybody

Long Beach Island. This is where most North Jerseyans go when they want to spend a week or a long weekend. It's clean and isolated, funky in places and serene in others, and generally offers something for everyone. We like Beach Haven best—at the island's south end—but almost any one of the island's "towns" (some are only a few blocks long) is okay—particularly Harvey Cedars, Lavellette, Ship Bottom, and Loveladies. Why do we like Beach Haven? In addition to the quiet beach and easy access to the northern section of the Forsythe Preserve, there's the Surflight Theatre, which stages full musical productions and children's theater; Fantasy Island Amusement Park, one of the cleaner, more pleasant amusement areas we've seen; Show Place Ice Cream Parlour, where the service comes with a song; and a nice bike path running for several miles from the island's southern tip. Each town invokes a beach fee; Beach Haven general information, (609) 494-7211.

Part Two

Pennsylvania

Pennsylvania is big, book-ended east and west by major cities with ridged mountains streaking north-south through its center. We've divided the state in workable sections, starting with the **Pocono and Endless Mountains** in northeast corner, then dropping down into greater **Philadelphia** and the **Lehigh and Brandywine Valleys.** We move west from there into **Hershey** and the **Pennsylvania Dutch Country,** after which we travel north to the state's middle with the **Valleys of the Susquehanna** and the **Southern Alleghenies** and the **Laurel Highlands.** Next comes the **Northern Tier,** ranging from the forested north-central region to Lake Erie, and last we look at **Greater Pittsburgh.** It's a substantial state, filled with railroading, coal mining, oil drilling, and Revolutionary War and Civil War history. Have fun.

HOW TO GET INFORMATION BEFORE YOU GO

Department of Community & Economic Development, Office of Travel, Tourism & Film Production, Room 404, Forum Building, Harrisburg, PA 17120; (800) 847-4872 or (717) 787-5453; www.experiencepa.com.

Pennsylvania Bureau of State Parks, P.O. Box 8551, Harrisburg, PA 17105-8551; (888) 727-2757; www.dcnr.state.pa.us.

Pennsylvania's Not-to-Be-Missed Attractions
Pocono Mountains and Endless Mountains Delaware Water Gap National Recreation Area Ricketts Glen State Park

Pennsylvania's Not-to-Be-Missed Attractions (continued)

Pocono Mountains and Endless Mountains (continued)

Steamtown National Historic Site
Camelback Ski Area/
    Camelbeach Water Park

Philadelphia

Fairmount Park
Independence National Historic
    Park/Lights of Liberty
Franklin Institute Science Museum
Philadelphia Museum of Art
Eastern State Penitentiary
Philadelphia Zoo
Reading Terminal Market

Lehigh and Brandywine Valleys

Sesame Place
The Crayola Factory
Valley Forge National
    Historical Park

Hershey, Harrisburg, and Pennsylvania Dutch Country

Stay Overnight on a Working Farm
The Amish Experience/
    Amish Country Homestead/
    Amish Farmlands Tours
HersheyPark/Zoo America
Gettysburg National Military Park

Valleys of the Susquehanna Region

Little League Museum
Penn's Cave
Eat Ice Cream at The Creamery

The Southern Alleghenies and Laurel Highlands

Raystown Lake/Seven Points Marina
Johnstown Flood Museum and
    National Memorial
Ohiopyle State Park
Seven Springs Resort

Pennsylvania's Not-to-Be-Missed Attractions (continued)

Lake Erie Region   Waldameer Park and Water World

Allegheny National Forest Region
                          Allegheny National Forest
                          Zippo Case Visitors Center
                          Cook Forest State Park

Greater Pittsburgh   Highland Park
                          Carnegie Science Center
                          Carnegie Museums of Art and
                              Natural Science
                          National Aviary in Pittsburgh
                          Mattress Factory
                          Ride the Incline from Station Square
                          Grab Something to Eat in the
                              Strip District

Calendar of Festivals and Events

February

Endless Mountains: Winterfest at Alparon Park, Alparon Park, Troy. Ice-sculpting, snow-mobiling runs, vintage sleds, cross-country skiing, food, and camping; (570) 673-4100.

Northern Tier: Winter Family Festival, Parker Dam Day Use Area, Penfield. Skating, sledding, skiing, ice-fishing, blizzard volleyball, and more; (814) 765-0630.

March

Philadelphia: Philadelphia Flower Show. The country's most celebrated flower show; (215) 988-8899; www.libertynet.org/flowrsho.

April

Endless Mountains: National Park Week, Steamtown National Historic Site, Scranton. Special exhibits, demonstrations, and expanded historic interpretive programs; (888) 693-9391.

May

Lehigh Valley: Mayfair, Allentown. A huge festival with six stages for live performances and lots of events like the Parent/Child Look-Alike Contest; (610) 437-6900; www.mayfairfestival.org.

Philadelphia: Philadelphia International Theatre Festival for Children. The Annenberg Center at University of Pennsylvania. A wonderful collection of live performances for kids; (215) 898- 6791.

June

Dutch Country: Pennsylvania Dutch Folk Festival, Summit Station. A huge festival with everything from polka bands and flintlock firings to quilt making and broom-winding. Plus an Amish wedding and a mock execution; (610) 683-8707; www.dutchfest.com.

Dutch Country: Gettysburg Civil War Heritage Days, Gettysburg. Living history encampments, Civil War battle re-enactments, collectors show, band concerts, and a fireman's festival; (717) 334-6274.

Northern Tier: Forest Fest, Allegheny National Forest, Bradford and Kane. All things natural and forest-oriented; (814) 723-5150.

Pittsburgh: Three Rivers Festival. Seventeen days of non-stop performance, food, and fun throughout downtown; (412) 281-8723.

July

Northern Tier: Bark Peelers Convention, Pennsylvania Lumber Museum, Galeton. Milling, cutting, crafting, fiddling, distance tobacco spitting, birling, and frog jumping; (814) 435- 2652.

Philadelphia: Welcome America! For the ten days preceding and through July Fourth weekend, the city stages more than 50 free events and neighborhood arts fairs; (800) 770-5883; www.americasbirthday.com.

Valleys of the Susquehanna: Central Pennsylvania Festival of the Arts, State College. A week is given over to the arts, both visual and performing; (814) 238-3682; www.arts-festival.com.

August

Laurel Highlands: Fayette County Fair. New Stanton; (724) 628-3360.

Lehigh Valley: Musikfest, Bethlehem. Ten days of 650 free music and street-theater performances of all kinds; (610) 861-0678; www.musikfest.org.

Northern Tier: Sawmill Summerfest & Quilt Show, Cook Forest Sawmill Center for the Arts, Cooksburg. Arts, crafts, performances, food; (814) 927-6655; www.sawmill.org.

Northern Tier: Erie Days Festival, Erie. Four days of nationally known performers, sporting events, boat races, ethnic performances, food and craft booths, and a giant fireworks display; (814) 833-7343.

September

Lehigh Valley: Great Allentown Fair, Allentown. A huge fair with nationally known performers and a little something for everyone; (610) 435-7469; www.Allentownfairpa.org.

Pittsburgh: Allegheny County Fair & Exposition & Rib Cook-Off. At the South Park Fairgrounds; (412) 678-1727.

Southern Alleghenies: Johnstown Folkfest, Johnstown. For Labor Day weekend, they pull out all the stops; (888) 221-1889 or (814) 539-1889; www.ctcnet.net/jaha/pages/folkfest.htm.

October

Laurel Highlands: Fall Foliage Festival, Bedford. Antique cars, apple-cider making, crafts, entertainment; (800) 765-3331 or (814) 623-1771.

November

Dutch Country: International Gift Festival, Fairfield Mennonite Church, Fairfield. Just in time for Christmas shopping, the proceeds go to Ten Thousand Villages, an organization that helps Third World artisans; (717) 334-6274.

Hershey: HersheyPark Christmas Candylane. This place goes nuts through the New Year with characters, performances, and millions of lights; (800) 437-7439; www.800hershey.com/calendar.

December

Lehigh Valley: Christkindlmarkt Bethlehem. A family holiday market of handmade crafts, entertainment, antique toys, and a children's shopping area; (610) 861-0678; www.fest.org/markt/home.htm.

PENNSYLVANIA COAL MINING ATTRACTIONS

At one time Pennsylvania coal powered the world. Between 1830 and 1960, more than four billion tons of hard coal were mined in the Lackawanna and Wyoming Valleys alone, and even today 80 percent of the world's anthracite coal is found in the state. It was coal that fired the great railroad steam locomotives and massive Bessemer ovens that brought on the age of steel. But mining was a dirty and dangerous job. A visit to Pennsylvania's various coal mine attractions offers kids a chance to see how it was done in the old days, as well as how it's done now, and affords a first-hand trip into the earth for a look at American labor history.

Ashland. Museum of Anthracite Mining at Ashland, 17th and Pine Streets, (717) 875-4708; Pioneer Tunnel Coal Mine, (717) 875- 3850.

Eckley. Eckley Miners Village, Weatherly; (717) 636-2070.

Patton. Seldom Seen Valley Tourist Coal Mine; (814) 247-6305.

Robertsville. Broad Top Area Coal Miners Museum & Entertainment Center, Main Street; (814) 635-3807.

PENNSYLVANIA RAILROADING ATTRACTIONS

Railroading is such an integral part of Pennsylvania history that railroading sites abound. Among them:

Poconos and Endless Mountains

Stourbridge Line Rail Excursion. 50-mile scenic ride; Honesdale; (717) 253-1960.

Steamtown National Historic Site. Scranton (see Attractions page 99).

Rail Tours, Inc. Scenic and seasonal special rides in the Poconos; Jim Thorpe; (570) 325-4606; www.railtours-inc.com.

Philadelphia and Lehigh and Brandywine Valleys

New Hope and Ivyland Railroad. 1920s railroading site; New Hope; (215) 862-2332.

Wanamaker, Kempton & Southern Railroad. Scenic steam-train rides; Kempton; (610) 756-6469.

Hershey and Dutch Country

Strasburg Railroad Co. Turn-of-the-century wooden-coach rides through Amish Country; Strasburg; (717) 687-7522.

National Toy Train Museum. Large layouts of toy trains; Strasburg; (717) 687-8976.

Railroad Museum of Pennsylvania. 100 locomotives and cars on display; City; (717) 687-8628.

Gettysburg Scenic Railway. Operates scenic rides April–December; Gettysburg; (888) 948-7246 or (717) 334-6932.

Middletown & Hummelstown Railroad. Vintage 1920s trains take passengers on an 11-mile journey; Middletown; (717) 944-4435.

Liberty Limited/Northern Central Railway. Rides and dining trips on circa 1940s and 1950s trains; New Freedom; (800) 948-7246.

Southern Alleghenies and Laurel Highlands

Tunnels Park & Museum. Where today's trains pass through a modified 1854 tunnel; Gallitzin; (814) 886-8871.

Horseshoe Curve National Historic Landmark. Built in 1854, the curve that opened the gateway to the west; Altoona; (888) 425-8666.

East Broadtop Railroad. Rockhill Furnace (see Attractions page 154).

Allegheny Portage Railroad National Historic Site. Series of incline planes that preceded Horseshoe Curve; Cresson; (814) 886-6150.

Northern Tier: Allegheny National Forest and Lake Erie Regions

Oil Creek & Titusville Railroad. A 2½-hour ride; Titusville; (814) 676-1733.

Bellefonte Historical Railroad. Operates a 60-mile route from this classic Victorian town; Bellefonte; (814) 355-0311.

Knox, Kane, Kinzua Railroad. Sends a steam train through northern Pennsylvania forests; Marienville; (814) 927-6621.

Tioga Central Railroad. Offers scenic rides through Pennsylvania's canyon country; Wellsboro; (717) 724-0990.

Greater Pittsburgh

Pennsylvania Trolley Museum. A three-mile antique trolley ride with car barn and shop tour; Washington; (724) 228-9256.

Cool Web Sites for Pennsylvania-Bound Kids

State of Pennsylvania Kids Page: www.state.pa.us/kids

Carnegie Museum of Natural History Discovery Room Online: www.clpgh.org/cmnh/discovery

The Amish, the Mennonites, and the "Plain People": www.800padutch.com/amish

Virtual tour of Historic Philadelphia: www.ushistory.org/tour

Sturgis Pretzel Factory: www.sturgispretzel.com

The Liberty Bell Story: www.ushistory.org/libertybell

Camp Life at Gettysburg (for older kids): www.cr.nps.gov/csd/gettex

Discover Pittsburgh!: trfn.clpgh.org/pgh

Pocono Mountains and Endless Mountains Region

In the Pocono Mountains, located within an hour's drive of greater Philadelphia and 90 minutes of the New York City suburbs, some spots are isolated and beautiful, some are highly commercial and developed. You can, therefore, choose your preference. In **Bushkill,** in addition to the Delaware Water Gap and Bushkill Falls (see The Best Parks and Attractions, below), the **Pocono Indian Museum** (call (570) 588-9338) reviews the history of human habitation in the region, and the **Mary Stoltz Doll Museum** (call (570) 588-7566) houses a large collection of dolls, including many Barbies. **Lake Wallenpaupack** (call (717) 424-6050) offers fishing, cruising, and other lake recreation. Nearby, the **Claws 'n' Paws Wild Animal Park** (call (570) 698-6154) holds more than 100 species and two petting zoos. **Lackawaxen** is home to the **Zane Grey Museum** (call (570) 685-4871), a National Park Service facility that covers the novelist's life and work, plus the Wild West. **Jim Thorpe,** a town named after a person, is a major recreational center, but it also is the site of the **Mauch Chunk Museum and Cultural Center** (call (570) 325-9190; www.mauch chunkmuseum.org), a place that features a tribute to Thorpe and a history of the area. The **Old Jail Museum** (call (570) 325-5259) is an old jail that's creepy-cool. Model railroad buffs will go for the **Old Mauch Chunk H-O Scale Model Train Display** (call (570) 386-2297) and, in nearby **Leighton,** the **Pocono Museum Unlimited** (call (570) 386-3117). In **Ashland,** the **Pioneer Tunnel Mine & Steam Train** (call (570) 875-3850) offers an excellent underground tour and above-ground, narrow-gauge train ride. For special treats, check out these sites: **Callie's Candy Kitchen & Pretzel Factory** (call (570) 595-2280) in **Mountain Home,** and **Pocono Cheesecake Factory** (call (570) 839-6844) in **Swiftwater. Apple-Tree Farm** in **Mount Pocono** (call (570) 839-7680) entertains little ones with a petting zoo and pony rides.

Scranton informally separates the more northerly **Endless Mountains** from the southerly Poconos. The largest city in the region, it houses the **Houdini Museum** (call (717) 342-5555), which is a bit hokey but fun, and the **Everhart Museum** (call (717) 346-8370), where the focus is on science, history, and fine/visual arts. The **Olde Mill Village Museum** (call (570) 465-3448) in **New Milford** depicts nineteenth-century life. **Honesdale**, with its quaint homes and period architecture, presents a trip to Victorian times. There, the **Wayne County Historical Society Museum** (call (717) 253-3240) displays railroading, canal, and Native American histories.

How to Get There

By Car. I-80 runs east-west through the heart of the Poconos. To head north from there, follow I-380, which connects with I-81 in Scranton. I-81 cuts right through Scranton and the Endless Mountains, but only skirts the western edge of the Poconos. Coming from the south and Philadelphia, the best route utilizes the Pennsylvania Turnpike's Northern Extension, a.k.a. I-476. Use I-84 if you're entering the region from northwestern New Jersey; it terminates just south of Scranton.

By Plane. Philadelphia International Airport is the closest major airport to the region; (215) 492-3181.

How to Get Information before You Go

Endless Mountain Visitors Bureau, 712 SR East, Tunkhannock, PA 18657; (800) 769-8999 or (717)836-5431; www.endlessmountains.org.

Pocono Mountains Vacation Bureau, 1004 Main Street, Stroudsburg, PA 18360; (800) 762-6667 or (717)424-6050; www.poconos.org.

The Best Parks

Delaware Water Gap National Recreation Area. Covering nearly 70,000 acres, the preserve includes about 40 miles of the Delaware River, one of the longest free-flowing rivers in the United States, in both Pennsylvania and New Jersey. Activities include canoeing, tubing, swimming, fishing, hiking, water skiing, and boating, plus a variety of nature programs and fantastic scenery. Lifeguards staff two beaches during the summer months. At Dingman's Ferry, the Pocono Environmental Education Center, (570) 828-2319, offers weekend and weeklong family environmental learning

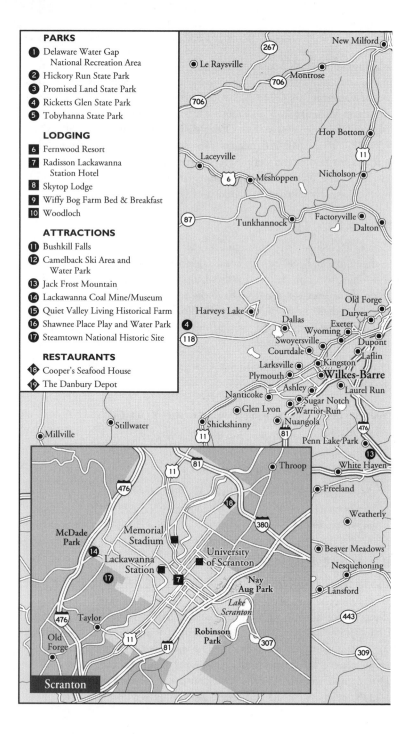

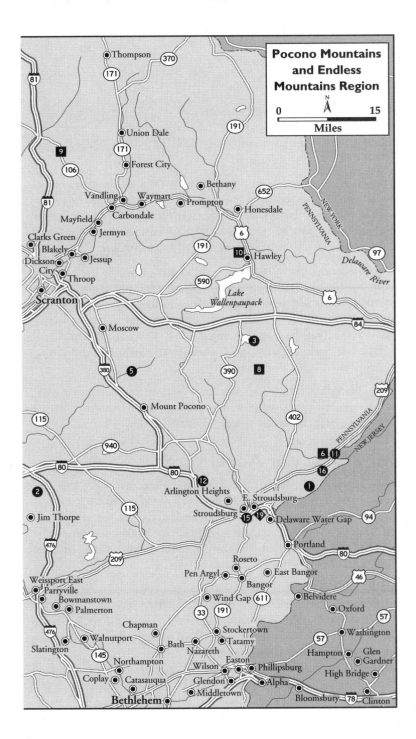

Pocono Mountains and Endless Mountains Region

0 N 15
Miles

programs for very reasonable prices. River Road, Bushkill; (570) 588-2451; www.nps.gov/dewa/home.htm.

Hickory Run State Park. Covering more than 15,000 acres, this park is home to the amazing Boulder Field (literally a huge field of boulders), three natural areas, miles of streams, and Hawk Falls. RR 1, White Haven; (570) 443-0400.

Promised Land State Park. Covers more than 3,000 acres, with two lakes, two swimming beaches, campgrounds, several small streams, and extensive hiking trails. The Civilian Conservation Corps (CCC) did much of the work to create this park in the 1930s, and an on-site museum, open seasonally, highlights CCC contributions, as well as area wildlife.

Ricketts Glen State Park. You'll find one of the most beautiful hiking trails anywhere on the Falls Trail in the Glens Natural Area, a National Natural Landmark. It passes 22 free-flowing waterfalls, 94-foot Ganoga Falls being the highest. The park covers 13,050 acres in three counties, offering camping, cabin camping, fishing and boating on a 245-acre lake. Ricketts Glen is truly among the most strikingly beautiful parks in the Mid-Atlantic states. RR 2, Benton; (570) 477-5675.

Tobyhanna State Park. This park holds 5,440 acres of land area plus a 170-acre lake, a swimming pool, and primitive campsites. Hiking, snow-mobiling, ice fishing, and boat rentals. Tobyhanna; (570) 894-8336.

Family Outdoor Adventures

Biking. The region has four major rails-to-trails routes. The Lehigh Gorge Trail follows the Lehigh River for 25 miles. The D&H Trail has 10 miles of paved path from Simpson to Unionville and another 22 miles of cinder surface; (717) 785-7245. Switchback Trail travels 18 miles between Summit Hill and Jim Thorpe. And the O&W Trail runs 6 miles from just outside Hancock; (717) 785-7245.

Camping. Lackawanna State Park has a 96-site campground with modern wash houses, hot showers, and rest rooms. It is within walking distance of a lake and swimming area and features children's play areas, small fishing ponds, and a self-guiding nature trail; RR 1, Dalton; (570) 945-3239 or (570) 563-9995 for campground office.

Promised Land State Park has some 487 campsites in four tent and trailer camping areas. One, Pickerel Point Campground, is open year-round, and all are near swimming, boating, fishing, and hiking. Bear Wallow Cabin Colony contains 12 rustic rental cabins constructed by the

Civilian Conservation Corps, equipped with a fireplace, electricity, and an adjacent private bath; (570) 676-3428.

Hiking. You'll find 25 miles of trails in the Delaware Water Gap National Recreation Area, 28 miles at Tobyhanna State Park, and another 30 at Promised Land State Park (see The Best Parks, pages 89 and 92).

Horseback Riding. More than a half-dozen stables operate in the area. Deer Path Riding Stable runs one- and two-hour trail rides; Route 940, White Haven, (570) 443-7047. Triple W Riding Stable rides on 183 acres and also offers pony rides, camping, a bed-and-breakfast inn, and all-day rides. RR 2, Box 1543 (off Route 6), Honesdale; (800) 540-2620 or (570) 226-2620, www.triplewstable.com.

Mountain Biking. Two shops in Jim Thorpe rent bikes and provide maps and shuttle service to Lehigh Gorge State Park and other area trails. Blue Mountain Sports, (800) 599-4421 or (570) 325-4421; and Lehigh Gorge Outdoor Sports, (800) 424-7238 or (570) 325-4960.

Paddling. The region's two primary paddling rivers are the Delaware and the Lehigh. Both are served by commercial guiding services. Kittatinny Canoes, (800) 356-2852, rents canoes, kayaks, and rafts at several spots along the Delaware River, guides rafting trips, and operates two campgrounds. Pocono Whitewater Adventures, (717) 325-3655, runs one-day whitewater rafting trips out of Jim Thorpe.

Skiing. This region is rich in skiing areas. We like the following: Camelback Ski Resort (see Attractions, page 96); Big Boulder/Jack Frost Ski Areas (see Attractions, page 96); Blue Mountain Ski Area, with 27 runs and seven lifts, (610) 826-7700, www.skibluemt.com; Elk Mountain Ski Resort, 27 trails with nifty terrain and an old-fashioned ambience, Union Dale, (570) 679-4400, www.elkskier.com; Montage Mountain, with 22 trails, including the outrageous White Lightning run with 70 percent pitch, and tubing. Montage Mountain Road, Scranton, (570) 969-7669, www.skimontage.com.

Family Lodging

Radisson Lackawanna Station Hotel

A 146-room historic hotel (it was once the showpiece train station in the Lackawanna system) within ten minutes' walk or two minutes' drive of the Steamtown National Historic Site and the Steamtown Mall in downtown Scranton. The architecture is grand French Renaissance. The two-and-a-half-story lobby has a leaded-glass ceiling and walls decorated with faience panels depicting scenes of sites along the Lackawanna routes. Unfortunately, it has no swimming pool, but does feature a fitness room, sauna, and game room. Rooms have in-room coffee makers and iron/ironing board. (Check out the old vault safe, now converted into a public telephone room.) Rates: $109–149; participates in Radisson's "Family Magic" program at $109 per room with 25 percent off for a connecting room, free breakfast, and kids' welcome pack (coloring books, crayons, puzzles, etc.) for ages 12 and under. 700 Lackawanna Avenue, Scranton; (570) 342-8300.

Wiffy Bog Farm Bed & Breakfast

Wiffy Bog is a bed-and-breakfast inn that's family run and welcomes families. It's in a beautiful foothills setting, just across the road from a buffalo farm and five miles from skiing. It has a game room, fitness room, hot tub, and on-site ice skating—plus good breakfasts. Rates: $25–65 per person. Routes 374 and 106, Union Dale; (570) 222-7777.

FAMILY RESORTS

The Poconos are second only to New York's Catskills for seemingly innumerable all-inclusive resorts. Some are pretty hokey honeymoon retreats, others are designed for golf and adult getaways, but there are a few that are recommended for families.

Fernwood Resort & Conference Center

Fernwood is a full-service resort with a full list of activities, including supervised kids programs, golf, mini-golf, par-3 golf, indoor and outdoor pools, an arcade, fishing, paddle boating, hiking, tennis, volleyball, skiing, sledding, and snowtubing. On-site restaurants include family-style Italian dining, a classic diner, a pub, and a food court with Dunkin' Donuts, TCBY, and Pizza Hut. Rates: $99–189; paddle boats, bumper boats, horseback riding, golf, miniature golf, bicycles, skiing, snow tubing, video arcade, and live entertainment at extra cost. Route 209, Bushkill; (888) 337-6966 or (570) 588-9500.

Skytop Lodge

Housing 150 guest rooms and 16 suites, the resort opened as a private club in 1928 and sits amid 5,500 acres of wilderness. On-site activities include biking, hiking, fishing, croquet, golf, paddle tennis, archery, lawn bowling, Nordic and alpine skiing, tobogganing, and ice-skating. In the warm months there are wildlife weekends, guided by a resident naturalist, and interactive programs are offered about reptiles, amphibians, birds, and native wildlife. The Camp-in-the-Clouds program provides daily supervised day camp for kids ages 4–12. Rates: $290–520 per room, including all meals; children ages 16 and under stay free in their parents' room. One Skytop, Skytop; (800) 345-7759 or (717) 595-7401.

Woodloch

This summer camp for families offers a variety of housing options from lodge rooms to four-bedroom houses. Families find a plethora of activities, group and individual, from golf to weekly tournaments in (among others) volleyball, trivia, basketball, softball, and shuffleboard, plus races of various kinds and contests. You can ski, skate, toboggan, snowtube, waterslide, swim, play racketball, water ski, etc. Weekend and weeklong packages are available. Rates: $230–650 per person for weekends, plus $45–300 per child (depending on age); $300–810 five days, plus $30–375 per child; children 3 and under stay free; $15 crib charge. RR 1, Hawley; (800) 572-6658 or (570) 685-7121.

Attractions

Bushkill Falls

P.O. Box 151, Bushkill; (888) 628-7454 or (570) 588-6682;
 www.visitbushkillfalls.com

Hours: April–October, daily 9 a.m.–6 p.m. or 8 p.m. (closing time varies with time of year)

Admission: $8 adults, $7 seniors, $2 children ages 4–10, free for children 3 and under

Appeal by Age Groups:

Pre-school	Grade School	Teens	Young Adults	Over 30	Seniors
★★★	★★★★★	★★★★	★★★★	★★★★	★★★★

Touring Time: Average 2½ hours, minimum 1 hour

Rainy-Day Touring: Yes

Services and Facilities:

Restaurants Yes	Baby stroller rental No
Alcoholic beverages Yes	Lockers No
Disabled access Yes, buildings; no, trails	Pet kennels No
	Rain check No
Wheelchair rental No	Private tours No

Description and Comments   At Bushkill Falls, Bushkill Creek drops in a series of eight waterfalls, including the 100-foot Main Falls. The walk to the Main Falls and observation deck requires about 45 minutes to one hour, out and back, at a leisurely pace. Three additional hiking trails allow viewing of all eight waterfalls with hikes up to two miles long requiring two hours. At the entrance to the park stand the Pennsylvania Wildlife Exhibit and the Native American Exhibit, a snack bar, a gift shop, an ice cream parlor, and a fudge shop. Fishing can be done on Twin Lakes. Altogether, it's a bit of a hokey/commercial enterprise, but it's all rather fun.

Camelback Ski Area & Camelbeach Water Park

I-80, Exit 45, P.O. Box 168, Tannersville; (570) 629-1661;
   www.skicamelback.com

Hours: Vary by date and season
Admission: Varies by season and activity
Appeal by Age Groups:

Pre-school	Grade School	Teens	Young Adults	Over 30	Seniors
★★★★★	★★★★★	★★★★★	★★★★★	★★★★★	★★★★★

Touring Time: Average 5 hours, minimum 3 hours
Rainy-Day Touring: Yes, winter; No, summer
Services and Facilities:

Restaurants Yes	Lockers Yes
Alcoholic beverages Yes	Pet kennels No
Disabled access Yes	Rain check Yes; summer
Wheelchair rental No	Private tours No
Baby stroller rental No	

Description and Comments   The premier ski area in the Poconos, Camelback has developed into a very popular summer play place. The skiing is on 33 runs, 26 of which are lit for night skiing. There's a lit halfpipe, a terrain park, and a huge snow-tubing park, which requires an extra fee. Summertime features a large but not overwhelming water park with water slides large and small, a river ride, bumper boats, and a large swimming pool. Younger kids love Camel Cove, an interactive activity pool. Dry-land activities include an alpine slide and miniature golf.

Jack Frost Mountain

Route 903 South, P.O. Box 707, Blakeslee; (800) 468-2442 or
   (570) 443-8425; www.big2resorts.com

Hours: Vary by season and activity
Admission: Varies by activity
Appeal by Age Groups:

Pre-school	Grade School	Teens	Young Adults	Over 30	Seniors
★★★	★★★★★	★★★★★	★★★★★	★★★★★	★★★★★

Touring Time: Average 4 hours, minimum 2 hours
Rainy-Day Touring: Yes
Services and Facilities:

Restaurants Yes	Lockers Yes
Alcoholic beverages Yes	Pet kennels No
Disabled access Partial	Rain check No
Wheelchair rental No	Private tours No
Baby stroller rental No	

Description and Comments This is a ski area—two ski areas, actually—that has gone to year-round action sports. What was once a small ski area has expanded into a multi-use, year-round playground. In winter, skiing is on 27 runs at Jack Frost and another 14 at adjacent Big Boulder. There are also a snow-tubing hill, snowmobile rentals, and Nordic skiing trails. In summer, the resort offers mountain biking, ATV driving, an in-line skate park, and a paintball facility. Nearby you'll find horseback riding and hiking. Special festivals are staged throughout the summer with families in mind. On-site lodging and dining is available.

Lackawanna Coal Mine Tour and The Pennsylvania Anthracite Museum

RR 1, Bald Mountain Road, Scranton; (717) 963-4804

Hours: Tour: daily 10 a.m.–4:30 p.m., leaves hourly or when enough people are present. Museum: Monday–Saturday 9 a.m.–5 p.m., Sunday noon–5 p.m.

Admission: Tour: $6 adults, $5.75 seniors 65 and older, $4 children ages 3–12, free for children under age 3; museum: $3.50 adults, $3 seniors 60 and older, $2 children, $12 families

Appeal by Age Groups:

Pre-school	Grade School	Teens	Young Adults	Over 30	Seniors
★	★★★	★★★	★★★	★★★★	★★★★

Touring Time: Average 2 hours, tour; 1 hour, museum; minimum 1 hour, tour; 30 minutes, museum

Rainy-Day Touring: Yes
Services and Facilities:

Restaurants Yes; snack bar	Baby stroller rental Yes; free for
Alcoholic beverages No	mine tour
Disabled access Yes	Lockers No
Wheelchair rental Yes, free for	Pet kennels No
mine tour	Rain check No
	Private tours No

Description and Comments While these two attractions require separate entry fees, they are next to each other and are logically visited together. If you're pressed for time, or must choose only one, take the tour—it's more dynamic and lively. Visitors descend 255 feet underground via coal-mine train to the mine's fourth level. The guides, former miners, then lead a walking tour, revealing the hardships experienced by the miners and pointing out changes over time in mining technology and techniques. Mannequin tableaux are encountered to illustrate how the miners worked.

The museum is small and somewhat staid, but it does contain some interesting content on mining, silk milling (which came to the area in 1880), and, in particular, the region's people.

Quiet Valley Living Historical Farm

1000 Turkey Hill Road, Stroudsburg; (570) 992-6161

Hours: Late June–Labor Day, Tuesday–Saturday 10 a.m.–5:30 p.m. and Sunday 1–5:30 p.m.

Admission: $6 adults, $3.50 children ages 3–12

Appeal by Age Groups:

Pre-school	Grade School	Teens	Young Adults	Over 30	Seniors
★★	★★★★	★★★★	★★★★	★★★★★	★★★★★

Touring Time: Average 2½ hours, minimum 1½ hours

Rainy-Day Touring: Yes

Services and Facilities:

Restaurants No	Lockers No
Alcoholic beverages No	Pet kennels No
Disabled access Yes, but difficult	Rain check No
Wheelchair rental No	Private tours No
Baby stroller rental No	

Description and Comments This living history museum depicts life with the Zepper family, German immigrants who settled here in 1765. Costumed interpreters take you through the various rooms of the main house and through the outbuildings depicting life in the late 1700s and early 1800s. There are lots of farm animals and antique farm equipment to see, plus special events like the Farm Animal Frolic in May and, outside the regular season, the October Harvest Festival and Old Time Christmas.

Shawnee Place Play and Water Park

Hollow Road, Shawnee-on-Delaware; (570) 421-7231; www.shawneemt.com

Hours: Mid-June–Labor Day, daily 10 a.m.–5 p.m.; mid-May–mid-June, Saturday and Sunday 10 a.m.–5 p.m.

Admission: $10 adults, $8 seniors 60 and older, $14 children, $8 toddlers 40 inches tall or less, free for children age 1 year and under

Appeal by Age Groups:

Pre-school	Grade School	Teens	Young Adults	Over 30	Seniors
★★★★	★★★★★	★★★	★★★	★★★★	★★★★

Touring Time: Average 5 hours, minimum 3 hours

Rainy-Day Touring: No

Services and Facilities:

Restaurants Yes	Baby stroller rental No
Alcoholic beverages Yes; beer and wine	Lockers Yes
	Pet kennels No
Disabled access Yes	Rain check Yes
Wheelchair rental No	Private tours No

Description and Comments   A combination wet and dry park, Shawnee is aimed at kids ages 2–12 and is a great place for families with little ones. More than 15 play elements include ball crawls, cloud bounces, and climbing nets. There's a large sand box area and a special section for toddlers. Three times daily the park stages magic shows indoors at its air-conditioned theater. The park also offers supervised activities like juggling workshops and water-balloon tosses throughout the day. You can ride the ski lift to the top of the mountain.

Steamtown National Historic Site

Lackawanna and Cliff Avenues, Scranton; (888) 693-9391 or (570) 340-5204, TDD (570) 340-5207; www.nps.gov/stea

Hours: January 2–June 30 and after Labor Day–December 31, daily 9 a.m.–5 p.m.; June 1–Labor Day, daily 9 a.m.–6 p.m.

Admission: Museum: $7 adults, $6 seniors 62 and older, $2 children ages 6–12, free for children 5 and under; Train Excursion: $10 adults, $8 seniors, $5 children; Combination: $15 adults, $13 seniors, $6 children ages 6–12, $5 children 5 and under

Appeal by Age Groups:

Pre-school	Grade School	Teens	Young Adults	Over 30	Seniors
★★★	★★★★	★★★	★★★★	★★★★	★★★★

Touring Time: Average 3 hours, minimum 1½ hours

Rainy-Day Touring: Yes
Services and Facilities:

Restaurants No, adjacent shopping mall has food court	Baby stroller rental No
	Lockers No
Alcoholic beverages No	Pet kennels No
Disabled access Yes	Rain check No
Wheelchair rental Yes; free	Private tours No

Description and Comments   Once the heart and hometown of the Lackawanna Railroad, Scranton has a long railroading tradition. The museum centers on a working railroad yard and a renovated roundhouse. Hour-long excursions are offered in the spring, summer, and autumn; short, narrated excursions within the rail yard are offered several times a day when long excursions are not. The display space is divided into History and Technology. Both sides feature video presentations and annotated artifact exhibitions. History focuses on the people who made the railroads go and who rode them. Technology exhibits use multiple video presentations to show how steam engines work, what the engineer and fireman did, and how some of the large bridges and viaducts were constructed. A 15-minute introductory film tells the story of steam railroading in America in the twentieth century. Guided tours are led through the locomotive shop, where an actual engine has been "cutaway" (it's essential parts cut open and color-coded). Often, a massive locomotive is being rebuilt in the shop and can be viewed.

Family-Friendly Restaurants

COOPER'S SEAFOOD HOUSE

701 North Washington Avenue, Scranton; (570) 346-6883

Meals served: Lunch and dinner
Cuisine: Seafood/American
Entree range: $6.50–29 (lunch and dinner)
Children's menu: Yes
Reservations: Yes
Payment: V, MC, D

Locally owned, Cooper's is one of those places that hides good food behind a wall of kitsch. The building's roof resembles an old sailing ship, populated by ruffians-of-the-sea figures. Taped dialogue of seamen exchanging seafaring barbs plays continuously outside. The interior overflows with memorabilia, seafaring artifacts, antique newspaper front pages, and period photographs. Meanwhile, the food's good. The breads, pastas, and sauces are homemade. In addition to seafood, the menu offers steaks, chicken, and sandwiches. A choice of 220 beers, friendly service, and tables with built-in video games will please the whole family. And it's not far from the Steamtown National Historic Site.

THE DANBURY DEPOT

50 Crystal Street, East Stroudsburg; (570) 476-0500

Meals served: Lunch and dinner
Cuisine: Continental, steak, and seafood
Entree range: $6–15 (lunch and dinner)
Children's menu: Yes
Reservations: Yes
Payment: Major credit cards

Set in an 1864 railroad depot, this is a pleasant place with solid if not remarkable food. Kids love the railroading decor and the model train that travels from room to room. This is one of the few non-chain restaurants in the area, and it's conveniently located near I-80.

Philadelphia

Philadelphia is a marvelous city. History-rich, filled with child-friendly attractions, and blessed with abundant, delicious dining options, it's not too big, not too small, but just right. When you visit, it's best to park your car and forget about it until you decide to venture out to the nearby countryside. The central city is laid out in a grid, with numbered streets (with the exception of Broad Street) running north-south, starting with easternmost Second Street alongside the Delaware River. Named streets run east-west. When Broad meets Market Street, you're right smack in the middle. The neighborhoods? **Center City** is, well the center of things downtown, from South Street up to Benjamin Franklin Parkway and out to the Delaware River. **Fairmount Park** is found just northwest of downtown along the Schuylkill River and is home to the Philadelphia Zoo. Logically enough, **West Philadelphia** is directly west of downtown, **North Philly** directly north, and **South Philly** directly south of South Street. You'll find **Chinatown** just to the northeast of Center City, and the **Olde City** at the far eastern end, running from the Delaware River out to Fifth Street and from Chestnut Street up to Race Street.

Center City contains a lot to see and do, and perhaps one of the best place to go first (after you've stopped in the **Visitors Center** on 16th Street, (800) 537-7676 or (215) 636-1666) is **City Hall** (call (215) 686-2840), where the observation deck atop the 548-foot tower reveals terrific city views. The **Academy of Fine Arts** (call (215) 972-7600) is just a block away. There, the Family Inform audio tour tells kids about the various artworks. The **U.S. Mint** (call (215) 597-7350) offers a self-guided tour to see coins being made. Two blocks over, you'll find **Betsy Ross House** (call (215) 627-5343), where Ms. Ross actually lived. The Olde City is found just a block or two from there. So, too, is **Firemans' Hall** (call (215) 923-1438), where firefighting equipment dating to 1730 is displayed (Philly was home to the country's first fire department).

North Philadelphia houses some off-beat museums, namely the **Temple University Dental Museum** (call (215) 707 2816) and the **Foot Museum** (call (215) 629-0300), the latter of which displays, among other things, famous people's shoes. The **University of Pennsylvania Museum of Archeology & Anthropology** (call (215) 898-4015) contains cool African, Roman, Polynesian, and Mayan artifacts, including real mummies. Also at the university, the **Annenberg Center** for performing arts (call (215) 898-6791) mounts one of the country's best children's theater festivals and presents other live entertainment. In the northeast part of town, the **Insectarium** (call (215) 338-3000) displays live and mounted bugs of all descriptions, and the **Afro-American Historical & Cultural Center** (call (215) 574-0380) offers a fascinating look at black culture.

How to Get There

By Car. Arriving from the south, I-95 leads right up the city's east side. From the north, use the New Jersey Turnpike to Exit 4. Coming from western Pennsylvania, take the Pennsylvania Turnpike Exit 24 to I-76, the Schuylkill Expressway. I-95 and I-76 connect to I-676 to reach Center City.

By Plane. Philadelphia International Airport, (215) 492-3181, is at the city's far southwest perimeter; it's a US Airways hub and is served by most major airlines. SEPTA trains (Southeastern Pennsylvania Transportation Authority) can take you into Center City.

By Train. The city's 30th Street Station is a major stop on Amtrak's system, (800) 872-7245, and is well-served by SEPTA's subways, buses, and trolley lines, (215) 580-7800. Coming from suburban New Jersey, take commuter trains operated by New Jersey Transit, (800) 626-7433; two kids age 11 and under ride free with each adult on weekends and holidays. PATCO, the high-speed line, presents another option from certain Jersey suburbs.

Getting around the City

The heart of Philadelphia really isn't that big, and much of it is walkable. SEPTA subways, buses, and trolleys serve all segments of the city, and special children's and family fares are offered; two kids up to 42 inches tall ride free with a fare-paying passenger. PHLASH is a minibus that runs a circular route from City Hall down to the South Street area, out to the river, past Independence Mall, along the Avenue of the Arts, and out to the Art Museum and back at a cost of $3 for all-day use—and kids under age six ride free. Pick up a ticket at many hotels, restaurants, and attractions.

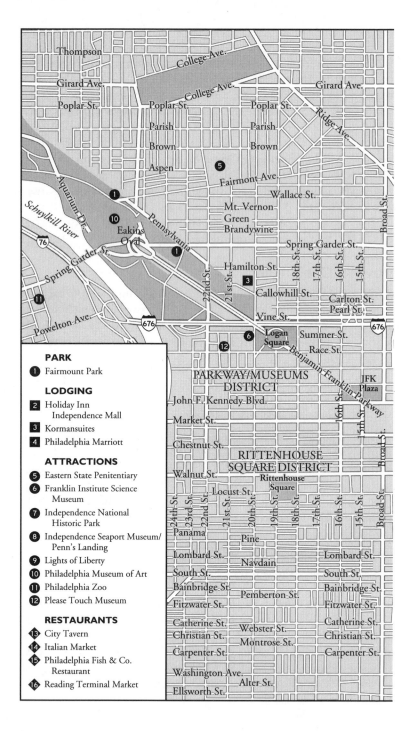

PARK

1 Fairmount Park

LODGING

2 Holiday Inn
Independence Mall

3 Kormansuites

4 Philadelphia Marriott

ATTRACTIONS

5 Eastern State Penitentiary

6 Franklin Institute Science
Museum

7 Independence National
Historic Park

8 Independence Seaport Museum/
Penn's Landing

9 Lights of Liberty

10 Philadelphia Museum of Art

11 Philadelphia Zoo

12 Please Touch Museum

RESTAURANTS

13 City Tavern

14 Italian Market

15 Philadelphia Fish & Co.
Restaurant

16 Reading Terminal Market

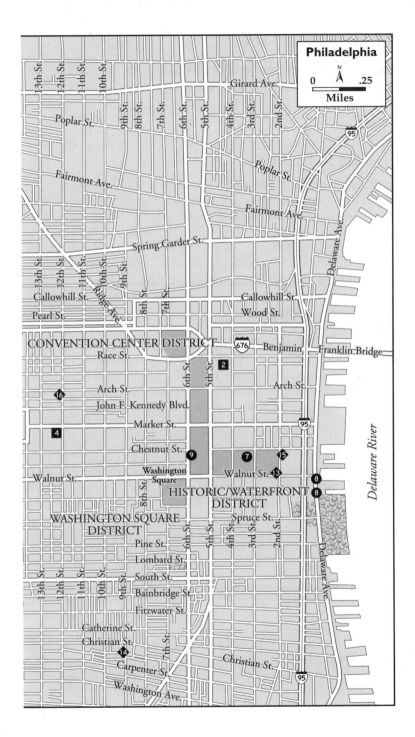

HOW TO GET INFORMATION BEFORE YOU GO

Philadelphia Convention & Visitors Bureau, 1515 Market Street, Suite 2020 Philadelphia, PA 19102; (800) 225-5745 or (215) 636-3300, fax (215) 636-3415; www.pcvb.org.

The Best Park

Fairmount Park. This is one of the world's largest urban parks at 8,700 acres. The park is a treasure trove of sites, including the zoo. The Andorra Natural Area has trails and the hands-on Treehouse Visitors Center, where special activities often happen. The Smith Playground and Playhouse features a giant slide wide enough for ten kids and nifty play elements like a miniature train and kid-sized cars to drive. You can rent sailboats, canoes, and bikes, play tennis, go for a swim, or attend free concerts.

Family Lodging

Holiday Inn Independence Mall

Located just a half-block from the Liberty Bell and other attractions, the hotel has an outdoor pool and a kids' game and reading library. Complimentary in-room refrigerators and cribs are available, and you get a check-in gift. Rates $139–159; Weekender rates with breakfast are available; kids stay and eat free. 400 Arch Street, Philadelphia; (800) 843-2355 or (215) 923-8660.

Kormansuites

This luxury hotel is near Fairmount Park and the art museums. All rooms have a refrigerator, microwave, coffee maker, and a washer/dryer. Amenities include free garage parking, complimentary shuttle throughout the city, a fitness center, a salon, a Jacuzzi, a restaurant, and complimentary coffee and newspapers. Rates: $149–209. 2001 Hamilton, Philadelphia; (215) 569-7000.

Philadelphia Marriott

This downtown hotel has 23 floors with more than 1,400 rooms, including 76 suites. The on-site restaurant has a children's menu. An indoor pool and in-room movies appeal to kids; baby sitting and cribs available. Rates: $138–350; kids stay free; special weekend rates are available. 1201 Market Street, Philadelphia; (215) 972-6700.

Attractions

Eastern State Penitentiary

2124 Fairmount Avenue, Philadelphia; (215) 236-3300;
  www.easternstate.org

Hours: May, September, and October, Saturday and Sunday 10 a.m.–
  5 p.m.; June–August, Wednesday–Sunday 10 a.m.–5 p.m.; last tour
  leaves at 4 p.m.

Admission: $7 adults, $5 seniors and students, $3 children ages 7–17

Appeal by Age Groups:

Pre-school	Grade School	Teens	Young Adults	Over 30	Seniors
*N/A	★★★★★	★★★★★	★★★★★	★★★★★	★★★★★

Note: children under seven are not permitted into the prison

Touring Time: Average 2 hours, minimum 1 hour

Rainy-Day Touring: Yes

Services and Facilities:

Restaurants No	Lockers No
Alcoholic beverages No	Pet kennels No
Disabled access Yes, but difficult	Rain check No
Wheelchair rental No	Private tours No
Baby stroller rental No	

Description and Comments This castle-like building with a wagon-wheel, or radial, floor plan opened in 1829 as a model prison designed to change prisoners' behavior through "confinement in solitude with labor." It became the most copied building in the country, and some 300 prisons worldwide have been based on its design. It was abandoned in 1971, and now stands as a crumbling semi-ruin. It's creepy in here, and you must don a hard hat to tour, but it's really unique—Alcatraz being the only comparable tour that comes to mind. The guided tours last an hour and cover the central rotunda, solitary-confinement yards, baseball diamond, and death row. Exhibits and art installations add an extra dynamic to the overall experience. And, by the way, the Halloween ghost tours are a big hit.

Franklin Institute Science Museum

20th Street and Benjamin Franklin Parkway, Philadelphia;
  (215) 448-1200; www.fi.edu

Hours: Science Center: Sunday–Saturday 9:30 a.m.–5 p.m. Mandell Center: Sunday–Thursday 9:30 a.m.–5 p.m., Friday and Saturday 9:30 a.m.–9 p.m.; closed Thanksgiving, Christmas Eve, Christmas, and New Year's days

Admission: Museum only: $9.75 adults, $8.50 seniors 62 and older and children ages 4–11; museum plus IMAX: $12.75 adults, $10.50 seniors and children; museum plus planetarium: $12.75 adults, $10.50 seniors and children; museum plus IMAX and planetarium: $14.75 adults, $12.50 seniors and children; IMAX only: $7.50 per person

Appeal by Age Groups:

Pre-school	Grade School	Teens	Young Adults	Over 30	Seniors
★★	★★★★★	★★★★★	★★★★★	★★★★★	★★★★★

Touring Time: Average 3 hours, minimum 2 hours

Rainy-Day Touring: Yes

Services and Facilities:

Restaurants Yes	Lockers Yes; coatroom
Alcoholic beverages No	Pet kennels No
Disabled access Yes	Rain check No
Wheelchair rental Yes; free	Private tours No
Baby stroller rental No	

Description and Comments   One of the great science museums anywhere, the Franklin covers trains, ship-making, electricity, bioscience, communications, aviation, and astronomy. Two longstanding highlights are the walk-through heart and the climb-aboard 1926 Baldwin steam locomotive. The Mandel Center devotes itself to technologies that will shape the twenty-first century, and the Tuttleman Ominverse Theater shows IMAX films on a four-story screen.

The newest addition, completed in cooperation with The Please Touch Museum, is the First Union Science Park. Open May–September daily in good weather from 10 a.m.–3:30 p.m., this is a 25,000-square-foot interactive science-leaning playground outfitted with sundials, sand pendulums, hide-and-seek tunnels, and mini-periscopes.

Independence National Historic Park/Lights of Liberty

Park: Third Street at Chestnut Street, Philadelphia; (215) 597-8974; www.nps.gov/inde

Lights: Peco Energy Center, Sixth Street at Chestnut Street, Philadelphia; (877) 462- 1776; www.lightsofliberty.org

Hours: Daily 9 a.m.–5 p.m.

Admission: Historical Park: free; $2 fee for some buildings; Lights of

Liberty: $18 adults, $16 seniors, $12 children ages 6–12; $50 Family-4-Pack (two adults and two children under age 12)

Appeal by Age Groups:

Pre-school	Grade School	Teens	Young Adults	Over 30	Seniors
★	★★★★	★★★★	★★★★★	★★★★★	★★★★★

Touring Time: Average 3 hours, minimum 1½ hours

Rainy-Day Touring: Yes

Services and Facilities:

Restaurants No	Lockers No
Alcoholic beverages No	Pet kennels No
Disabled access Yes	Rain check No
Wheelchair rental No	Private tours No
Baby stroller rental No	

Description and Comments The park comprises more than 18 buildings, but you'll want to focus on the Liberty Bell/Independence Hall, plus perhaps the Second Bank of the United States, Franklin Court (home to a Ben Franklin–style printing press), and the Bishop White and Todd Houses. Whatever you do, start at the Visitors Center, where the 28-minute film *Independence* sets the scene and the interactive touch screens provide more background information. Special events are staged frequently, and town criers, park rangers, and actors dressed in period costumes offer glimpses into life in the Colonial and Revolutionary periods. Consider taking The Liberty Tale Tour, a 50-minute guided walking tour of the area that tells the story of William Penn and the founding of Philadelphia ($3 adults, $1 children).

The *Lights of Liberty* show bills itself as "the world's only portable light and sound show." Staged after dark on summer evenings in groups of 50 people, you don a unique 3-D headset and are led back to eighteenth-century Philadelphia. The tour makes five stops on the grounds of Independence National Historical Park; at each stop the sky is lit with huge projections, six times larger than life. Narration for adults is by Walter Cronkite, Charlton Heston, and Ossie Davis. Kids get their own version narrated by Whoopi Goldberg.

Independence Seaport Museum/Penn's Landing

211 South Columbus Boulevard, Philadelphia; (215) 925-5439; www.libertynet.org/seaport

Hours: Daily 10 a.m.–5 p.m.; closed Thanksgiving, Christmas, and New Year's days

Admission: Museum only or ships only: $5 adults, $4 seniors, $2.50

children ages 5–12; Museum and Historic Ship Zone: $7.50 adults, $6 seniors, $3.50 children ages 5–12

Appeal by Age Groups:

Pre-school	Grade School	Teens	Young Adults	Over 30	Seniors
★★★★	★★★★★	★★★★★	★★★★★	★★★★★	★★★★★

Touring Time: Average 3 hours, minimum 2 hours

Rainy-Day Touring: Yes

Services and Facilities:

Restaurants No; plenty nearby	Lockers Yes
Alcoholic beverages No	Pet kennels No
Disabled access Yes	Rain check No
Wheelchair rental Yes, free	Private tours No
Baby stroller rental No	

Description and Comments   Penn's Landing marks the site where William Penn came ashore to found Pennsylvania Colony. In addition to housing the museum and historic ships, many concerts, special events (like July Fourth fireworks), and festivals are staged here. The museum houses a fascinating collection of nautical artifacts, ranging from "Coming to America" and "Delaware River Boats" to "Home Port Philadelphia," an exhibit in which kids can navigate a vessel beneath a three-story replica of the Ben Franklin Bridge. Many exhibits are interactive, like operating a miniature crane to unload a cargo ship, fishing from a re-created pier, or simulated rowing on the Schuylkill River. The historic ships are the *Olympia,* circa 1892, one of the first steel warships, and the World War II submarine *Becuna.*

Note that you can purchase RiverPass tickets that give you entrance to the Independence Seaport Museum, the Historic Ship Zone, and the New Jersey State Aquarium at Camden, including round-trip passage on the Penn's Landing RiverLink Ferry.

Philadelphia Museum of Art

Benjamin Franklin Parkway and 26th Street, Philadelphia; (215) 763-8100, TDD (215) 684-7600; www.philamuseum.org

Hours: Tuesday–Sunday 10 a.m.–5 p.m., Wednesday 10 a.m.–8:45 p.m.; closed Mondays and legal holidays

Admission: $8 adults, $5 seniors, children under age 18, and students, free for children 5 and under; free on Sunday until 1 p.m.

Appeal by Age Groups:

Pre-school	Grade School	Teens	Young Adults	Over 30	Seniors
★	★★★	★★★★	★★★★★	★★★★★	★★★★★

Touring Time: Average 2½ hours, minimum 1½ hours

Rainy-Day Touring: Yes

Services and Facilities:

Restaurants Yes	Lockers Yes
Alcoholic beverages Yes	Pet kennels No
Disabled access Yes	Rain check No
Wheelchair rental Yes; free	Private tours Yes
Baby stroller rental Yes; free	

Description and Comments   Before you go, rent the movie *Rocky.* Then, when you arrive, the whole family runs up the steps and raises arms in victory. Good. Now you can visit the museum. There are more than 40,000 artworks here, and they cover a wealth of cultures worldwide: American Art, Costume and Textiles, East Asian and Middle Eastern Art, European Decorative Arts and Sculpture Before 1700 (including little-boy favorites Arms and Armor), European Painting Before 1900, Indian and Himalayan Art, and Modern and Contemporary Art. Plus, there are special exhibitions. As with any grand art museum don't try to see it all in one visit. Pick up a gallery guide and make a plan. Perhaps start with a free highlight tour. Tours are given Tuesday through Sunday, hourly from 10 a.m. until 3 p.m., and on Wednesday evenings. Wednesday evenings are also devoted to special themed performances and films, and Sundays feature family programs ranging from storytelling to art-making aimed at kids ages 3–12.

Philadelphia Zoo

3400 West Girard Avenue, Philadelphia; (215) 243-1100;
www.phillyzoo.org

Hours: April–October, Monday–Friday 9:30 a.m.–5 p.m., Saturday–Sunday 9:30 a.m.–6 p.m.; November and March, daily 9:30 a.m.–5 p.m.; December–February, daily 10 a.m.–4 p.m.; closed Thanksgiving, Christmas Eve, Christmas, New Year's Eve, and New Year's days

Admission: $10.50 adults, $8 seniors 65 and older and children ages 5–11, $6 children ages 2–4; free for children under age 2

Appeal by Age Groups:

Pre-school	Grade School	Teens	Young Adults	Over 30	Seniors
★★★★★	★★★★★	★★★★	★★★★	★★★★★	★★★★★

Touring Time: Average 4 hours, minimum 2½ hours

Rainy-Day Touring: Yes

Services and Facilities:

Restaurants Yes	Lockers No
Alcoholic beverages Yes	Pet kennels No
Disabled access Yes	Rain check No
Wheelchair rental Yes	Private tours No
Baby stroller rental Yes	

Description and Comments   The Philly Zoo—America's first—has improved significantly in the past few years. New Reptile and Primate Houses have been built, and the 2.5-acre Peco Primate Reserve is a model of modern zoo creation and animal preservation. Little ones love the Children's Zoo, where they can ride camels, elephants, and ponies during the warmer months or pet barnyard animals. The Treehouse consists of seven indoor fiberglass habitats that allow kids to "become" animals and explore animal homes using all their senses; hourly shows are performed there as well. Other nifty zoo features: Just Ask carts, filled with interpretive materials and staffed by docents; Zone Guides, docents who welcome visitors to exhibit areas and answer questions; and Meet the Keepers, a chance to chat with animal keepers.

Please Touch Museum

210 North 21st Street, Philadelphia; (215) 963-0067;
www.pleasetouchmuseum.org

Hours: Labor Day–July 1, daily 9 a.m.–4:30 p.m.; July 1–Labor Day, daily 9 a.m.–6 p.m.; closed Thanksgiving, Christmas, and New Year's days

Admission: $6.50 per person, free for children under age 1

Appeal by Age Groups:

Pre-school	Grade School	Teens	Young Adults	Over 30	Seniors
★★★★	★★★★★	★★	★★★	★★★★	★★★★

Touring Time: Average 3 hours, minimum 1½ hours

Rainy-Day Touring: Yes

Services and Facilities:

Restaurants No	Lockers No
Alcoholic beverages No	Pet kennels No
Disabled access Yes	Rain check No
Wheelchair rental No	Private tours No
Baby stroller rental No	

Description and Comments   A hands-on place for kids ages two to eight, Please Touch may be a better alternative for the little ones than the Franklin Museum. The highlight here is the landscape derived from Maurice Sendak's books *(Where the Wild Things Are*, etc.) in which the walls turn into wild things before your very eyes. After exploring indoors, head across the street to the First Union Science Park (see Franklin Museum above) for outdoor fun. Please Touch also stages a variety of live performances of music, dance, magic, and more.

CityPass

CityPass offers admission to multiple attractions (six, in this case) at a discounted rate. Included are the Philadelphia Zoo, Philadelphia Museum of Art, the Franklin Institute, the Academy of Natural Sciences Museum, Independence Seaport Museum, and the New Jersey State Aquarium in Camden, New Jersey (ferry ride extra). The pass is valid for nine days; cost is $27.50 adults, $23.75 seniors 65 and older, $20 children ages 3–11.

PHILADELPHIA SPECTATOR SPORTS

All the big leagues play here. Major League Baseball's Phillies (call (215) 463-6000) can be seen at Veterans Stadium, as can the National Football League's Eagles (call (215) 463-2500); the stadium is located at the south end of Broad Street. The CoreStates Center, right next door, is home to the National Basketball Association's 76ers (call (215) 339-7600) and the National Hockey League's Flyers (call (215) 465-4500). Tickets can usually be obtained without too much difficulty.

Family-Friendly Restaurants

CITY TAVERN

138 South Second Street, Philadelphia; (215) 413-1443

Meals served: Lunch and dinner
Cuisine: American
Entree range: $10–38.50
Children's menu: Yes, all entrees $8.95
Reservations: Yes
Payment: Major credit cards

A tavern much as it would have been during the American Revolution, City Tavern first opened in 1773, and was a social gathering place for the men of the First Continental Congress. Come 1786, the Constitutional Convention's closing banquet was held here. Here's a chance to eat where guys like George Washington and Thomas Jefferson hung out. How cool is that? Kids can choose from the traditional fare listed on the children's menu.

PHILADELPHIA FISH & CO. RESTAURANT

207 Chestnut Street, Philadelphia; (215) 625-8605

Meals served: Lunch and dinner
Cuisine: Seafood
Entree range: $7.95–19.95
Children's menu: No
Reservations: Yes
Payment: Major credit cards

An excellent fish place in the heart of downtown. If you're not a seafood fan, choose from the landlubber options.

Dining Alternative: Two Markets

Take your kids back to the good old days when mothers used to shop every day for fresh foods.

Reading Terminal Market, at 12th and Arch streets, (215) 922-2317, is a beehive of activity. You'll see sticky buns and pretzels being baked plus all the pizzazz and clamor that one of the country's great fresh food/farmers markets would be expected to produce. It's open Monday–Saturday for breakfast and lunch.

The Italian Market, on Ninth Street between Christian and Wharton streets, (215) 922-2317, is another fun spot. It's an outdoor food mall with clothing and cookware outlets, too, and it presents a variety of stand-up or sit-down eating options.

Lehigh and Brandywine Valleys

The countryside surrosunding Philadelphia contains a wealth of historical, natural, industrial, and recreational opportunities. Starting northernmost with the **Lehigh Valley,** the small city of **Easton,** near the New Jersey line, is home not only to the **Crayola Crayon Factory** (see Attractions), but features the **National Canal Museum** (call (610) 515-8000), where you can take a mule-drawn boat ride on a canal. **Bethlehem,** home to the once-mighty steel company, offers a look at the history and lifestyle of the Moravians, a German sect who founded the town, at the **Moravian Museum of Bethlehem** (call (610) 867-0173). Bethlehem also offers walking tours of the **18th Century Industrial Area** (call (610) 868-1513) and an eighteenth-century farmstead, **Burnside Plantation** (call (610) 868-5044). During December, the **Christkindlmarkt Bethlehem** (call (610) 861-0678, ext. 222) features handmade crafts, specialty foods, and musical performances. Nearby, Allentown is home to the **Museum of Indian Culture** (call (610) 797-2121); **Lost River Caverns** (call (610) 838-8767), which features guided walking tours; and the unique **Lehigh Valley Velodrome** (call (610) 967-7587), site of professional bicycle races on summer Friday nights. The **Mennonite Heritage Center** (call (215) 256-3020) in **Harleyville,** located just north of the Philadelphia suburbs, covers that group's Pennsylvania history. And two unique industrial facilities offer tours: **Mack Trucks, Inc. Museum** (call (610) 266-6767) in Allentown, and the **Martin Guitar Company** (call (610) 759-2837) in **Nazareth.**

Bucks County sits between the Lehigh Valley and Philadelphia. It's famous for arts and crafts. In **Doylestown,** the **Moravian Pottery & Tile Works** (call (215) 345-6722) has been producing decorative tiles and pottery for hundreds of years. Additional unique tile work can be seen, along with other collectible oddities, in the **Fonthill Museum** (call (215) 348-9461), a castle made of concrete. In **Lahaska, Peddler's Village** (call (215)

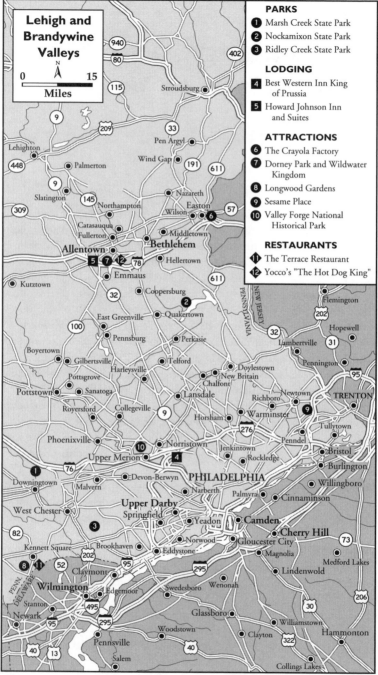

Lehigh and Brandywine Valleys

N

0 — 15 Miles

PARKS

1. Marsh Creek State Park
2. Nockamixon State Park
3. Ridley Creek State Park

LODGING

4. Best Western Inn King of Prussia
5. Howard Johnson Inn and Suites

ATTRACTIONS

6. The Crayola Factory
7. Dorney Park and Wildwater Kingdom
8. Longwood Gardens
9. Sesame Place
10. Valley Forge National Historical Park

RESTAURANTS

11. The Terrace Restaurant
12. Yocco's "The Hot Dog King"

794-4000) is a 42-acre shopping/dining/entertaining complex that features Carousel World. On the Delaware River's shores, **New Hope** is replete with shops, antiques stores, art and craft galleries, and restaurants. New Hope also offers antique transportation opportunities at the **New Hope Mule Barge** (call (215) 862-2842) on the Delaware Canal, the scenic **New Hope and Ivyland Railroad** (call (215) 862-2332), and on the Delaware River at the **Boat Rides at Wells Ferry** (call (215) 862-5965). **Washington Crossing National Historic Park** (call (215) 493-4076) in **Washington Crossing** is the site from which George crossed the Delaware to begin his famous Christmas attack on Trenton.

South of Philadelphia, in the Brandywine Valley, **Chadds Ford** puts you in the holiday spirit year-round at the **American Christmas Museum** (call (610) 388-0600). This town also has George Washington's headquarters for the Battle of Brandywine at **Brandywine Battlefield** (call (610) 459-3342). In **West Chester,** the Brandywine Airport features everything whirlybird at the **American Helicopter Museum & Education Center** (call (610) 701-9312). The eighteenth and nineteenth centuries are re-created at **Historic Yellow Springs** (call (610) 827-7414) in **Chester Springs.** Everything mushroom is depicted at the **Phillips Mushroom Museum** (call (610) 388- 6082) in **Kennett Square,** which is also home to the **Brandywine River Museum** (call (610) 388-2700), largest holder of the Wyeth family's artworks. More art can be found in **Merion** at **The Barns Foundation** (call (610) 667-0290), one of the largest private collections of Impressionist and Post-Impressionist works.

How to Get There

By Car. To reach the Lehigh Valley coming from Philadelphia, take the northbound Pennsylvania Turnpike's Northern Extension (I-476) towards Allentown. I-76 takes you due east out of Philly to Valley Forge, and U.S. 1, although prone to congestion, heads southeast to Kennett Square. Coming into the Lehigh Valley from New Jersey or central Pennsylvania, I-78/U.S. 22 is the way to go.

By Plane. To get to this region, air travelers first fly into Philadelphia (see How to Get There by Plane on page 103).

How to Get Information before You Go

Chester County Tourist Bureau, 601 Westtown Road, Suite 170, West Chester, PA 19382; (800) 228-9933 or (610) 344-6365, fax (610) 334-6999; www.brandywinevalley.com.

Bucks County Conference & Visitors Bureau, 152 Swamp Road, Doylestown, PA 18901; (800) 836-2825 or (215) 345-4552, fax (215) 345-4967; www.bctc.org.

Delaware County Convention & Visitors Bureau, 200 East State Street, Suite 100, Media, PA 19063; (800) 343-3983 or (610) 565-3679, fax (610) 565-0833; www.delcocvb.org.

Lehigh Valley Convention & Visitors Bureau, P.O. Box 20785, Lehigh Valley, PA 18002; (800) 747-0561 or (610) 882-9200, fax (610) 882-0343; www.lehighvalleypa.org.

Valley Forge Convention & Visitors Bureau, 600 West German-town Pike, Suite 130, Plymouth Meeting, PA 19462; (888) 847-4883 or (610) 834-1550, fax (610) 834-0202; www.valleyforge.org.

The Best Parks

Marsh Creek State Park. At 1,705 acres with a 535-acre lake, this site is popular for sailing and windsurfing. There's a marina and boat launch, plenty of fishing, a six-mile hiking trail, a swimming pool and, in winter, sledding and tobogganing. 675 Park Road, Downingtown; (610) 458-5119.

Nockamixon State Park. This park offers multiple places to picnic, a 2.8-mile bicycle trail, and 20 miles of equestrian trails, with a nearby private horse-rental establishment (call (215) 257-6271). There's a lot of fishing and boating to be done in the lake, and a fishing pier and boat-rental facility are on site. If you'd like to stay over, rent one of the camping cabins. 1542 Mountain View Drive, Quakertown; (215) 529-7300.

Ridley Creek State Park. You'll find equestrian, hiking, and bicycling trails through woods and meadows at Ridley Creek. Hiking trails connect with Tyler Arboretum trails. A five-mile paved multi-use trail along Sycamore Mills and Forge Roads is designated for biking, jogging, walking, and cross-country skiing. The 4.7-mile equestrian trail is serviced by a stable that offers lessons, pony rides, and other horse-related services. Colonial Pennsylvania Plantation depicts a Delaware County Quaker farm prior to the American Revolution. The park also has 14 picnic areas and about 12 miles of hiking. Sycamore Mills Road, Media; (610) 892-3900.

Family Outdoor Adventures

Boating. Lake Nockamixon State Park has two boat launches for sailboats and boats with motors up to ten horsepower. The boat concession rents canoes, motorboats, rowboats, sailboats, paddleboats, and pontoon boats; 1542 Mountain View Drive, Quakertown; (215) 529-7300.

Camping. Lake Nockamixon State Park features ten modern family cabins, available throughout the year. Each cabin contains a furnished living area, kitchen/dining area, toilet/shower room, and two or three bedrooms. Cabins are equipped with electric heat; 1542 Mountain View Drive, Quakertown; (215) 529-7300.

Paddling. See the Poconos section for river outfitters (page 93).

Scuba Diving. Dutch Springs offers freshwater diving with visibility up to 40 feet; 4733 Hanoverville Road, Bethlehem; (610) 759-2270, www.dutch springs.com.

Skiing. Blue Mountain Ski Area features 27 trails and the state's highest vertical drop, plus a snow-tubing park; Palmerton; (877) 754-2583 or (610) 826-7700, www.skibluemt.com.

Family Lodging

Best Western Inn at King of Prussia

Located in northwestern suburban Philadelphia, this moderate property has an outdoor pool, offers a free continental breakfast, and is conveniently located to Valley Forge and many other attractions. Rates: $95–129 per night. 127 South Gulph Road, King of Prussia; (610) 265-4500.

Howard Johnson Inn & Suites

In the heart of everything just off I-78, the Howard Johnson doesn't offer pretty country living, but the 58-room property has an indoor pool plus in-room coffee makers, microwaves and refrigerators. It offers free continental breakfasts. Rates: $39–199 per night. 3220 Hamilton Boulevard, Allentown; (800) 446-4656 or (610) 439-4000.

Attractions

The Crayola Factory

Two Rivers Landing, 30 Centre Square, Easton; (610) 515-8000; www.crayola.com

Hours: Memorial Day–Labor Day, Monday–Saturday 9 a.m.–6 p.m. and Sunday 11 a.m.–6 p.m.; Labor Day–Memorial Day, Tuesday–Saturday 9:30 a.m.–5 p.m. and Sunday noon–5 p.m.; open Mondays in summer and on Labor Day, Columbus Day, the Monday after Christmas, Martin Luther King Jr. Day, President's Day, Easter Monday, and Memorial Day; closed New Year's, Thanksgiving, Christmas Eve and Christmas days, and Easter Sunday

Admission: $7 adults and children, $6.50 seniors 65 and older, free for children 2 and under; includes admission to the National Canal Museum

Appeal by Age Groups:

Pre-school	Grade School	Teens	Young Adults	Over 30	Seniors
★★★★★	★★★★★	★★★	★★★★	★★★★★	★★★★★

Touring Time: Average 4 hours, minimum 3 hours

Rainy-Day Touring: Yes

Services and Facilities:

Restaurants Yes; McDonald's on site	Baby stroller rental No
Alcoholic beverages No	Lockers No; coatroom
Disabled access Yes	Pet kennels No
Wheelchair rental Yes, free	Rain check No
	Private tours No

Description and Comments Everybody loves this place. Admission is on a first-come, first-served basis, so it pays to arrive early. You get to see how crayons and markers are made, to bring home free souvenirs from the assembly line, and do just about anything you can think of with coloring. Different rooms offer the history of Crayola products, the Crayola Hall of Fame, a Creative Studio for just coloring, a Chalk Walk giant sidewalk, Inside Out for coloring on glass walls, plus several other elements that explore coloring, lighting effects, computer-generated art, and sculpturing with modeling compound, foam blocks, and other materials. You may think of crayons as a children's pastime, but the factory will wow any age.

Dorney Park and Wildwater Kingdom

3700 Hamilton Boulevard, Allentown; (800) 386-8463 or (610) 395-3724; www.dorneypark.com

Hours: Mid-June–mid-August, Sunday–Friday 10 a.m.–10 p.m. and Saturday 10 a.m.–11 p.m.; hours vary from May–mid-June and mid-August–October

Admission: $31 ages 4–59 and 48 inches and taller in shoes; $7 ages 4–59 and less than 48 inches in shoes; $7 age 60 and older; free for children under age 3 or less than 48 inches in shoes; reduced prices during early and late season when water park is closed

Appeal by Age Groups:

Pre-school	Grade School	Teens	Young Adults	Over 30	Seniors
★★★★★	★★★★★	★★★★★	★★★★★	★★★★	★★★

Touring Time: Average 6 hours, minimum 4 hours

Rainy-Day Touring: Yes

Services and Facilities:

Restaurants Yes	Lockers Yes
Alcoholic beverages No	Pet kennels No
Disabled access Yes	Rain check No
Wheelchair rental Yes	Private tours No
Baby stroller rental Yes	

Description and Comments   One whopper of an amusement and water park, with one of the country's largest steel-frame roller coasters. There's plenty for little ones, including Camp Snoopy, a theme park within the park that uses Peanuts characters for rides and entertainment. Dorney regularly stages shows and laser-light spectaculars.

Longwood Gardens

Route 1, Kennett Square; (610) 388-1000; www.longwoodgardens.org

Hours: January–March and November 1–Thanksgiving, daily 9 a.m.–5 p.m.; April, May, September, and October, daily 9 a.m.–6 p.m.; Thanksgiving–New Year's Day, daily 9 a.m.–9 p.m. Summer: Monday, Wednesday, Friday, and Sunday 9 a.m.–6 p.m.; Tuesday, Thursday, Saturday, Memorial Day, and Labor Day weekends 9 a.m.–1 hour after dusk

Admission: $12 adults ($8 on Tuesdays), $6 ages 16–20, $2 children ages 6–15, free for children under age 6

Appeal by Age Groups:

Pre-school	Grade School	Teens	Young Adults	Over 30	Seniors
★★	★★★★	★★★	★★★★★	★★★★★	★★★★★

Touring Time: Average 4 hours, minimum 2 hours

Rainy-Day Touring: Yes

Services and Facilities:

Restaurants Yes	Baby stroller rental No
Alcoholic beverages Yes	Lockers No
Disabled access Yes; some limitations	Pet kennels No
	Rain check No
Wheelchair rental Yes; free	Private tours No

Description and Comments   This is one of the largest formal gardens anywhere, and it has developed many elements to keep kids happy. The Children's Garden has a ruin, a maze, and mushroom-shaped fountains. The larger-than-life topiary rabbits are a hit, as are the three small pools with interactive fountains. An indoor Children's Garden is open year-round. Also popular are a kid-oriented, A–Z vegetable garden, a scarecrow, and other elements. On summer weekends, the Kids Corner Clubhouse stages scavenger hunts and arts and crafts workshops. Periodically, storytimes are offered for three- to five-year-olds. Longwood also presents performances and concerts for children, including the Winter Fabulous Fun Days and Summer Ice Cream Concert series. And then there are the fountains. Longwood has more fountains than any other garden in United States, and its Festival of Fountains, from late May to early September, is highlighted by the half-hour-long, illuminated shows on Tuesday, Thursday, and Saturday evenings.

Sesame Place

100 Sesame Road, Langhorne; (215) 752-7070; www.sesameplace.com

Hours: Vary from mid-May–late October

Admission: $31.95 adults and children over age 2; several local lodging properties offer "play-and-stay" packages

Appeal by Age Groups:

Pre-school	Grade School	Teens	Young Adults	Over 30	Seniors
★★★★★	★★★★★	★★★★	★★★★★	★★★★★	★★★

Touring Time: Average 6 hours, minimum 4 hours

Rainy-Day Touring: Yes

Services and Facilities:

Restaurants Yes	Baby stroller rental Yes
Alcoholic beverages No	Lockers Yes
Disabled access Yes; not all	Pet kennels No
attractions	Rain check No
Wheelchair rental Yes	Private tours No

Description and Comments   They say this park is aimed at ages 3 to 15, but we defy anyone to come here and not have fun. Set next door to a shopping mall, the park has 15 water elements and some 50 play elements. There's also a roller coaster, a Sesame Street TV studio, and lots of live performances with Sesame Street characters. So many things to do and places to climb, splash, and bounce. The food is good and reasonably priced by theme-park standards. Recent seasons have seen the development of more attractions and events aimed at teens, but older teens might look askance at a park aimed so strongly at little ones. Seniors may find it all a bit overwhelming—it can get crowded and hectic. Still, this place is a true winner for children.

Valley Forge National Historical Park

Valley Forge; (610) 783-1077; www.nps.gov/vafo

Hours: Park grounds open daily, sunup to sundown; Visitor Center and Washington's Headquarters: daily 9 a.m.–5 p.m.; closed Christmas Day

Admission: $2 adults, free for children under age 17

Appeal by Age Groups:

Pre-school	Grade School	Teens	Young Adults	Over 30	Seniors
★★	★★★★	★★★★	★★★★★	★★★★★	★★★★★

Touring Time: Average 3 hours, minimum 2 hours

Rainy-Day Touring: Yes

Services and Facilities:

Restaurants No	Lockers No
Alcoholic beverages No	Pet kennels No
Disabled access Yes	Rain check No
Wheelchair rental No	Private tours No
Baby stroller rental No	

Description and Comments   This is the country's best-known Revolutionary War site. Start at the Visitors Center by viewing the 18-minute film, *Valley Forge: A Winter Encampment,* shown every half-hour from 9:30 a.m. to 4:30 p.m. You can tour the park in your own car or by bus. If you go it alone, buy or rent the two-hour cassette-tape tour and take a free map of the tour route. The bus tours operate daily from May through October; you can get on and off the bus en-route to explore, then catch the next one that comes by. Highlights include Washington's Headquarters, the Memorial Chapel, and the Artillery Park. The park also offers terrific recreational opportunities: 12 miles of multi-purpose trails (six of which are paved), segments of the Horse-Shoe hiking trail, the 22-mile Philadelphia-to-Valley Forge Bikeway, and 22 miles of designated equestrian trails.

Family-Friendly Restaurants

THE TERRACE RESTAURANT

Longwood Gardens, Route 1, Kennett Square; (610) 388-6771

Meals served: Lunch and dinner
Cuisine: Continental
Entree range: $6.95–21.95
Children's menu: Yes
Reservations: Yes
Payment: Major credit cards

The restaurant at Longwood Gardens offers fine dining in a kid-friendly manner. It has a large salad bar and the option of eating next door in the cafeteria. Weekend brunch buffets are served, and many special events (like breakfast with Santa) are staged. Try the mushroom strudel appetizer.

YOCCO'S "THE HOT DOG KING"

625 Liberty Street and 2128 Hamilton Street, Allentown, plus other locations in Emmaus and Fogelsville; (610) 433-7563

Meals served: Lunch and dinner
Cuisine: Hot dogs, burgers, pierogi, and sausages
Entree range: $9.95–15.95
Children's menu: No
Reservations: No
Payment: Major credit cards

A local landmark since 1922, this is old-time fast food the way grandma and grandpa might remember it. The big deal here is homemade chili sauce on homemade dogs. Or, you can opt for pierogi or a steak sandwich. It's dining down, but it's fun.

Hershey, Harrisburg, and Pennsylvania Dutch Country

This region lies in the lower half of the state on the eastern side, running from roughly an hour east of Philadelphia to about mid-state. Harrisburg, the state capital, sits right in the area's center. There are few places to compare with this one to take you back in time. The Amish still farm the way people did 200 years ago, with horses and hand tools, and the surrounding countryside is as about as bucolic as things can get. There's a strong German heritage in the region and a Mennonite influence, too. Then there's Hershey, historically home to the famous candy company and today home to a major destination theme park and Gettysburg, site of the Civil War's pivotal battle.

In **Harrisburg,** the **State Museum of Pennsylvania** (call (717) 787-4978) covers a variety of disciplines, **City Island** is a unique mid-river park, the **Pride of the Susquehanna Riverboat** (call (717) 234- 6500) offers on-river tours, and **Fort Hunter Mansion** (call (717) 599- 5751) looks at nineteenth-century life. The **Lancaster** area represents the heart of Amish country. The **Heritage Center of Lancaster** (call (717) 299-6440) highlights local art and history. **Dutch Wonderland** (call (717) 291-1888) is a family-oriented amusement park, and the **Hands-on-House Children's Museum** (call (717) 569-5437) is popular with kids up to age ten. Beyond the battlefield in **Gettysburg,** the **Lincoln Room Museum** (call (717) 334-8188) preserves the room where Lincoln lodged and wrote the Gettysburg address; the **Lincoln Train Museum** (call (717) 334-5678) simulates a train trip and holds a huge model train collection; the **Gettysburg Scenic Rail Tour** (call (717) 334-6932) offers 16- and 50-mile trips into the countryside; **The National Civil War Wax Museum** (call (717) 334-6245) depicts famous figures; and, for something different, the **Land of Little Horses** (call (717) 334-7259) features performing and riding miniature horses.

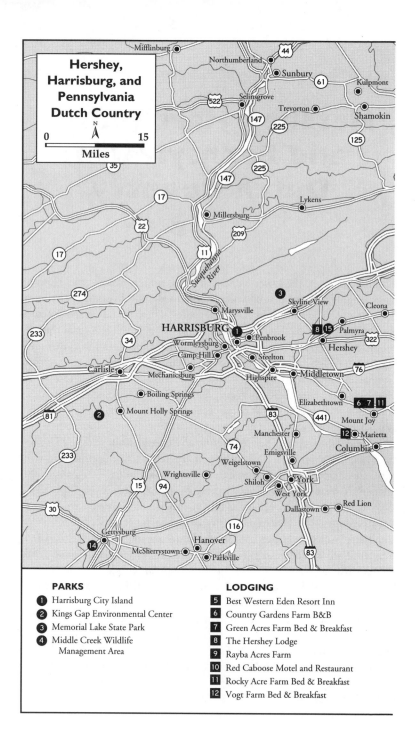

Hershey, Harrisburg, and Pennsylvania Dutch Country

N

0 — 15

Miles

Mifflinburg

Northumberland

Sunbury

Kulpmont

Selinsgrove

Trevorton

Shamokin

HARRISBURG

Millersburg

Lykens

Skyline View

Cleona

Marysville

Palmyra

Hershey

Penbrook

Wormleysburg

Camp Hill

Steelton

Carlisle

Mechanicsburg

Highspire

Middletown

Boiling Springs

Mount Holly Springs

Elizabethtown

Mount Joy

Manchester

Marietta

Emigsville

Columbia

Weigelstown

York

Wrightsville

Shiloh

West York

Red Lion

Dallastown

Gettysburg

Hanover

McSherrystown

Parkville

PARKS

1 Harrisburg City Island

2 Kings Gap Environmental Center

3 Memorial Lake State Park

4 Middle Creek Wildlife
   Management Area

LODGING

5 Best Western Eden Resort Inn

6 Country Gardens Farm B&B

7 Green Acres Farm Bed & Breakfast

8 The Hershey Lodge

9 Rayba Acres Farm

10 Red Caboose Motel and Restaurant

11 Rocky Acre Farm Bed & Breakfast

12 Vogt Farm Bed & Breakfast

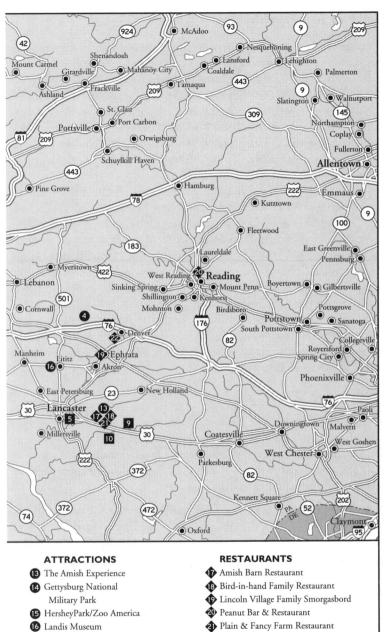

ATTRACTIONS

13 The Amish Experience

14 Gettysburg National
    Military Park

15 HersheyPark/Zoo America

16 Landis Museum

RESTAURANTS

17 Amish Barn Restaurant

18 Bird-in-hand Family Restaurant

19 Lincoln Village Family Smorgasbord

20 Peanut Bar & Restaurant

21 Plain & Fancy Farm Restaurant

22 Zinn's Diner

Strasburg is a busy little city with shopping malls and much railroading, including the **Railroad Museum of Pennsylvania** (call (717) 687-8628); scenic rides on the **Strasburg Railroad** (call (717) 687-7522); the **Choo-Choo Barn** (call (717) 687-7911), which exhibits 17 miniature trains traveling through animated scenes plus a *Thomas the Tank Engine* shop; and the **National Toy Train Museum** (call (717) 687-8976), where the focus is on metal electric trains. **Strasburg** also has the **Gast Classic Motorcars Exhibit** (call (717) 687-9500) and a tour of an Amish home at **Amish Village** (call (717) 687-8511).

Other family-friendly attractions in the region include the **National Association of Watch & Clock Collectors Museum** (call (717) 684-8261) in **Columbia;** the **Crystal Cave** (call (610) 683-6765) tour in Kutztown; the **Mary Merritt Doll Museum & Merritt's Museum of Early Childhood** (call (610) 385-3408) in **Douglassville; Daniel Boone Homestead** (call (610) 582-4900), the site of his birth, in **Birdsboro;** a nonstop holiday season at **Kozar's Christmas Village** (call (610) 488- 1110) in **Bernville;** the historic **Cornwall Iron Furnace** (call (717) 272- 9711) in **Cornwall;** and the kitschy but almost irresistible **Roadside America** (call (610) 488-6241), the "world's largest miniature village" in **Shartlesville.** For something more natural, visit the **Hawk Mountain Sanctuary** (call (610) 756-6961) in **Kempton.**

HOW TO GET THERE

By Car. The Pennsylvania Turnpike, I-76, travels east-west through the heart of the region. Also traveling northeast-southwest as far as Harrisburg are I-78 and I-81, both of which converge at Harrisburg. Coming from Maryland and the south, I-83 is the main thoroughfare, passing through York before terminating at Harrisburg.

By Plane. Harrisburg International Airport is served by a dozen airlines. It's easily accessible from the Pennsylvania Turnpike and State Route 230, and most of the region is within an hour's drive. 135 York Drive, Middletown; (717) 948-3510.

HOW TO GET INFORMATION BEFORE YOU GO

Harrisburg-Hershey-Carlisle Tourism & Convention Bureau, 4211 Trindle Road, Camp Hill, PA 17011; (800) 995-0969 or (717) 975-8161; www.visithc.com.

Gettysburg Convention & Visitors Bureau, 35 Carlisle Street, Gettysburg, PA 17325; (717) 334-6274; www.gettysburg.com.

Pennsylvania Dutch Convention & Visitor Bureau, 501 Green-field Road, Lancaster, PA 17601; (800) 723-8824 or (717) 299-8901; www.800padutch.com.

York County Convention & Visitors Bureau, One Market Way East, York, PA 17401; (800) 673-2429 or (717) 848-4000; www.yorkpa.org.

The Best Parks

Harrisburg City Island. An urban island park in the Susquehanna River, this one has ball fields, a river-swimming beach, a bathhouse, and playgrounds. It hosts numerous special events; (717) 865-6470.

Kings Gap Environmental Center & Education Center. Sixteen miles of hiking trails, including two that are disabled-accessible and annotated in Braille. 500 Kings Gap Road, Carlisle; (717) 486-5031.

Memorial Lake State Park. An 85-acre lake is the mainstay here. You can canoe, wind surf, fish, hike, picnic, ice skate, ice fish, and cross-country ski. RR 1, Grantville; (717) 865-6470.

Middle Creek Wildlife Management Area. A 1.4-million-acre reserve that's terrific for bird-watching. Tundra swans come by the thousands in February and March. Eight hiking trails and some excellent fishing streams round out the recreational opportunities. Hopeland Road, Kleinfeltersville; (717) 733-1512.

Family Outdoor Adventures

Biking. Cumberland County Biker/Hiker Trail leads to relics of an old iron-making community; Pine Grove Furnace State Park, RR 2, Box 399B, Gardners; (717) 486-7174. Stony Valley Railroad Grade has an underground stream running under part of it. It runs past the Rausch Gap Cemetery and is disabled-accessible. The ghost of the "headless railroad worker" is said to prowl the old railroad bed; 2001 Elmerton Avenue, Harrisburg; (717) 787-9612.

Camping. Gifford Pinchot State Park has 340 campsites and ten modern camping cabins, making it one of the largest state park campgrounds in Pennsylvania. Features include a swimming beach, outdoor amphitheater, hiking trails, boat launch and mooring area, staffed contact station, and modern bathhouses. The cabins have boat mooring areas on the lakeshore; 2200 Rosstown Road, Lewisberry; (717) 432-5011.

Hiking. Kings Gap Environmental Center & Education Center (see The Best Parks, page 129). Caledonia State Park, holds a portion of the Appalachian Trail and more than ten miles of other maintained hiking, scenic, historic, and nature trails; 40 Rocky Mountain Road, Fayetteville; (717) 352-2161.

Horseback Riding. Susquehannock State Park has many trails, as does the adjacent Muddy Run Recreation Area; contact Gifford Pinchot State Park, 2200 Rosstown Road, Lewisberry; (717) 432-5011.

Mountain Biking. Whitetail Ski Resort offers lift-assisted and trail riding; 13805 Blairs Valley Road, Mercersburg; (717) 329-9400. Swatara State Park has a ten-mile loop trail; contact Memorial Lake State Park, RR 1, Grantville; (717) 865-6470.

Paddling. Blue Mountain Canoe & Kayak Rentals offers scenic, family-style canoe or kayak float trips on the Susquehanna River; 103 South State Road, Routes 11 and 15, Marysville; (717) 957-2413.

Skiing. Ski Liberty, a nifty little ski area near the Maryland state line, has 16 trails on two sides of the mountain and a base-area hotel; Country Club Road, Carroll Valley; (717) 642-8282. Ski Roundtop is a small, very family-friendly hill just minutes from downtown Harrisburg; 925 Roundtop Road, Lewisberry; (717) 432-7000. Whitetail Ski Resort is a thoroughly modern resort that features three high-speed lifts; 13805 Blairs Valley Road, Mercersburg; (717) 329-9400.

Family Lodging

Best Western Eden Resort Inn

This Best Western is a 275-room property with some apartment-style suites, three pools, a health club, tennis courts, a playground, two restaurants, and in-room movies and coffee makers. Rates: $59–249; ask about seasonal specials. Kids under age 18 stay free with parents. 222 Eden Road, Routes 30 and 272, Lancaster; (717) 569-6444.

The Hershey Lodge

The Hershey Lodge is a full-service resort hotel with 457 rooms and suites, free shuttle service to HersheyPark, organized sports, storytime and crafts activities, two pools, miniature golf, movies, a ropes course, a fitness center, three restaurants, and babysitting. Rates: $136–163 per night in summer; children under age 18 stay free. Rates are lower in off-peak season. A variety of packages are available seasonally with combined admission to HersheyPark. Chocolate Avenue, Hershey; (800) 533-3131 or (717) 533-3311.

Red Caboose Motel and Restaurant

You sleep in real caboose or a farmhouse. There's no pool, but you'll find a petting zoo, buggy rides, a game room, country music, and on-site eating in a railroad dining car. Rates: $50–95 per night. P.O. Box 175, Paradise Lane and Route 741, Strasburg; (888) 687-5005 or (717) 687-5000.

WORKING FARM LODGING

Overnighting at a working farm is one of best ways to experience Dutch Country. One of our most successful vacations took place at such a farm, highlighted with the birth of a calf on our first morning there. You get to see farming in action, and sometimes you can help. Prices range from $45 to $125 a night, usually including breakfast. Some farms offer efficiencies, others just have rooms in the house. Most, but not all, have private baths, so ask.

Country Gardens Farm B&B, 86 Rock Point Road, Mount Joy; (717) 426-3316

Green Acres Farm Bed & Breakfast, 1382 Pinkerton Road, Mount Joy; (717) 653-4028

Rayba Acres Farm, 183 Black Horse Road, Paradise; (717) 687-6729

Rocky Acre Farm Bed & Breakfast, 1020 Pinkerton Road, Mount Joy; (717) 653-4449

Vogt Farm Bed & Breakfast, 1225 Colebrook Road, Marietta; (800) 854-0399

Attractions

The Amish Experience/Amish Country Homestead/ Amish Farmlands Tours

3121 Old Philadelphia Pike, Bird-in-Hand; (717) 768-8400; www.amishexperience.com

Hours: Homestead hours vary widely according to season; call ahead. Tours: April–November, Monday–Saturday 10:30 a.m. and 2 p.m. and Sunday 11:30 a.m.; December–March, daily 11:30 a.m.

Admission: Film: $6.95 adults, $3.75 children ages 4–12; Homestead: $5.25 adults, $3.25 children; Tour: $19.95 adults, $10.95 children; Film/Homestead combination: $10.50 adults, $6.50 children; Film/Homestead/Tour combination: $25.95 adults, $15.95 children

Appeal by Age Groups:

Pre-school	Grade School	Teens	Young Adults	Over 30	Seniors
★★	★★★★	★★★★★	★★★★★	★★★★★	★★★★★

Touring Time: Average 2½ hours (add 2 hours for bus tour), minimum 1½ hours without tour

Rainy-Day Touring: Yes

Services and Facilities:

Restaurants Yes	Lockers No
Alcoholic beverages No	Pet kennels No
Disabled access No	Rain check No
Wheelchair rental No	Private tours No
Baby stroller rental No	

Description and Comments   This is a multifaceted, albeit rather commercial, look at Amish life. Start with "The Amish Experience," which begins with an "experiential" film entitled *Jacob's Choice.* The show is projected on multiple screens in one of only three such theaters in North America. It tells the story of a fictional Amish family as they fight to preserve their lifestyle and culture. The Homestead, continuing the theme, represents the home of the film's fictional Old Order Amish family. Guides teach Amish traditions and practices as you tour the house. The tour has won awards for its authenticity and high-quality interpretive value. The Amish Farmlands Tour is a two-hour bus tour that explores the area's Amish farms, shops, roadside stands, schoolhouses, and other sites. Aaron and Jessica's Buggy Tours leave from nearby, offering three-hour buggy tours of the area (see Buggy Rides, page 136).

Gettysburg National Military Park

97 Taneytown Pike, Gettysburg; (717) 334-1124; www.nps.gov/gett

Hours: Park grounds and roads: daily 6 a.m.–10 p.m.; Visitor Center: daily 8 a.m.–5 p.m., 8 a.m.–6 p.m. in summer; Cyclorama Center: daily 9 a.m.–5 p.m.; buildings are closed Thanksgiving, Christmas, and New Year's days; National Cemetery opens at dawn and closes at sunset

Admission: Park: free; Electric Map and Cyclorama programs: $3 adults, $2.50 senior citizens age 62 and older, $2 children ages 6–16, free for children under 6

Appeal by Age Groups:

Pre-school	Grade School	Teens	Young Adults	Over 30	Seniors
★★★	★★★★★	★★★★★	★★★★★	★★★★★	★★★★★

Touring Time: Average 3½ hours, minimum 2 hours

Rainy-Day Touring: Yes

Services and Facilities:

Restaurants No	**Baby stroller rental** No
Alcoholic beverages No	**Lockers** No
Disabled access Yes; in main	**Pet kennels** No
buildings	**Rain check** No
Wheelchair rental Yes; free	**Private tours** No

Description and Comments   The Battle of Gettysburg took place from July 1 to July 3, 1863, finishing with the infamous "Pickett's Charge." The Union Army won, turning back the second northern invasion by General Robert E. Lee. More than 51,000 soldiers were killed, wounded, or captured, making it the Civil War's bloodiest battle and a major turning point. The Visitor Center contains the Gettysburg Museum of the Civil War, featuring a huge collection of Civil War and Gettysburg memorabilia, and the Electric Map, the park's orientation program to the battle. The Gettysburg Cyclorama is a 360-foot-long, circular, oil-on-canvas painting depicting Pickett's Charge. It's one of the country's last surviving cycloramas, and it's accompanied by a 20-minute sound and light show. A free 20-minute film is also shown.

Gettysburg Tours

One of the best ways to see the battlefield is by guided tour. The Gettysburg Convention and Visitors Bureau (35 Carlisle Street, (717) 334-6274) offers a guide of tour operators. Among them:

The Association of Licensed Battlefield Guides. A licensed guide accompanies you in your own car. 97 Taneytown Road, Gettysburg; (717) 334-4474.

CCInc Auto Tape Tours. Tapes with facts, music, and sound effects to play in your car as you drive through. National Civil War Wax Museum, 297 Steinwehr Avenue, Gettysburg; (717) 334-6245.

Gettysburg Battlefield Tape Tour. Tapes from the Emmy Award-winning producers of *Civil War Journal.* Greystone's American History Store, 461 Baltimore Street, Gettysburg; (717) 338-0631.

Licensed Battlefield Guide Tapes. Written and recorded by licensed guides. Available for rent or purchase at Farnsworth House Bookstore, campgrounds, and other lodgings; (717) 337-1217.

Historic Battlefield Bus Tours. Two-hour tours in a restored, classic 1930s, open-top, Yellowstone Park bus. 55 Steinwehr Avenue, Gettysburg; (717) 334-8000.

Gettysburg Battlefield Bus Tours. Two-hour tours in which actors re-create the battle in stereo as you ride in an air-conditioned, double-decker bus. Gettysburg Tour Center; (717) 334-6296.

HersheyPark/Zoo America

100 HersheyPark Drive, Hershey; (800) 437-7439 or (717) 534-3090; www.hersheypark.com

Hours: Mid-April–December, operating hours vary

Admission: $32.95 ages 9–54, $17.95 ages 3–8 and ages 55–69, $13.95 ages 70 and older, free for children age 2 and under; purchase a regular full-day admission ticket for the next day 2½ hours prior to park closing and enter the park free that evening; two-day and three-day tickets are available

Appeal by Age Groups:

Pre-school	Grade School	Teens	Young Adults	Over 30	Seniors
★★★★★	★★★★★	★★★★★	★★★★★	★★★★★	★★★★★

Touring Time: Full day

Rainy-Day Touring: Yes

Services and Facilities:

Restaurants Yes	Lockers Yes
Alcoholic beverages Yes	Pet kennels No
Disabled access Yes	Rain check No
Wheelchair rental Yes	Private tours No
Baby stroller rental Yes	

Description and Comments   We once knew a kid whose cousin lived in Hershey and was allergic to chocolate. That's somebody's definition of cruel. Luckily for him, and for the rest of us, Hershey has grown way beyond chocolate. This is a major destination theme park with all the trappings you'd expect: huge rides for big people, small rides for little people, water rides, old-fashioned rides like the Ferris wheel and carousel, plus games, shows, and roving entertainment. Kids step right up to the "measure-up" signs to discern if they're tall enough to get aboard the rides. Holidays present reasons for special goings-on, especially Christmas (starting here in mid-November), when the entire place transforms into Christmas Candylane, illuminated by more than a million lights.

Adjacent is Zoo America (included with admission), an 11-acre wildlife park that is open year-round. More than 200 animals from 75 species live here, representing five distinct North American regions, Canada's evergreen forest, the Great Plains and Rocky Mountains, Florida's Everglades, the eastern woodlands, and the Arizona desert. In addition, although not a part of HersheyPark, Hershey's Chocolate World, (717) 534-4900, is the official visitors center of Hershey Foods Corporation; open year-round, it's free and a worthwhile addition to your visit. While you can't actually tour the factory floor anymore (like we did as kids), the simulated factory ride yields an idea of how it's all made, and samples are handed out at the end.

There's more, each with separate admissions. The Hershey Trolley, (717) 533-300, features singing conductors who lead an anecdotal tour through the town. The Hershey Museum, (717) 534-3439, tells the town's history and shows original candy-making machinery and early Hershey products. Hershey Gardens, (717) 534-3492, is a 23-acre botanical garden, which also houses a terrific Butterfly House. Plan to spend two or three days, if you can, to get it all in without making yourself crazy.

Landis Museum

2451 Kissel Hill Road, Lancaster; (717) 569-0401;
    www.landisvalleymuseum.org

Hours: March 1–December 31, Monday–Saturday 9 a.m.–5 p.m. and
    Sunday noon–5 p.m.; closed major holidays

Admission: $7 adults, $6.50 seniors, $5 children ages 6–12, $19 per
    family, free for children under 6

Appeal by Age Groups:

Pre-school	Grade School	Teens	Young Adults	Over 30	Seniors
★★★	★★★★	★★★	★★★★	★★★★★	★★★★★

Touring Time: Average 1½ hours, minimum 1 hour

Rainy-Day Touring: Yes

Services and Facilities:

Restaurants No	Lockers No
Alcoholic beverages No	Pet kennels No
Disabled access Yes	Rain check No
Wheelchair rental Yes; free	Private tours No
Baby stroller rental No	

Description and Comments   This is a Pennsylvania German living history village with several buildings, a tavern, an eighteenth-century Log Farmstead, a nineteenth-century Brick Farmstead, an eighteenth-century Country Store, and a Gun Shop (Lancaster County was the home of the famous Pennsylvania Long Rifle, developed in the 1700s, and museum houses a large display of flintlock and long rifles). The visitor center starts you out with an exhibit area and audio-visual presentations. The farmstead is home to plenty of animals as well. Guided tours are available.

FACTORY TOURS

The Daniel Weaver Company. The oldest commercial bologna maker in the country. Weavertown Road, Lebanon; (717) 274-6100.

Harley Davidson Inc. Antique Motorcycle Museum & Factory Tour. The museum is open to everyone, but you must be at least 12 years old to tour the factory. 1425 Eden Road, York; (717) 848-1177.

Herr Goods, Inc. See potato chips being made. Routes 272 and 131, Nottingham; (800) 284-7488.

Julius Sturgis Pretzel House. Watch pretzels being made, then twist your own. Costs $2 per person. 219 East Main Street, Lititz; (717) 626-4354.

BUGGY RIDES

When in Amish country, why not travel like the locals? These two- to three-hour tours give you an Amish-eye view of things.

Aaron & Jessica's Buggy Rides. At Plain and Fancy Farms/Amish Country Homestead; (717) 768-4400.

Abe's Buggy Rides. 2596 Old Philadelphia Pike, Bird-in-Hand; (717) 392-1794.

Ed's Buggy Rides. Route 896, Strasburg; (717) 687- 0360.

Family-Friendly Restaurants

PEANUT BAR & RESTAURANT

332 Penn Street, Reading; (610) 376-8500

Meals served: Lunch and dinner
Cuisine: American
Entree range: $6.95–19.95
Children's menu: Yes
Reservations: Yes
Payment: Major credit cards

Stop at this longstanding Reading landmark, and you've entered an old-time bar room just like your grandfather might have frequented. The food is basic but good, ranging from deli sandwiches and fried seafood to staples like Southern fried chicken and baby-back ribs. They still offer Blue Plate Specials, like sweet-and-sour cabbage borsht. Feel free to toss your peanut shells on the floor.

ZINN'S DINER

Route 272, Denver; (717) 336-2210

Meals served: Breakfast, lunch, and dinner
Cuisine: American and Pennsylvania Dutch
Entree range: $6.79–13.49 (dinner)
Children's menu: Yes
Reservations: No
Payment: V, MC, D

This local institution offers all-American comfort foods, plus Pennsylvania Dutch specialties (smoked sausage, hasenpfeffer, shoo-fly pie, and potato fritters) and homemade pies to die for. Next door is Zinn's Recreational Park, which features hoops shooting, batting cages, and two miniature golf courses, plus (in case you've not gotten enough to eat) a snack bar and ice cream stand.

Eating Amish Style

At some point when in Pennsylvania Dutch County, you must eat in the local tradition—huge portions of basic wholesome foods. Many places serve it up family-style, which can be fun and an interesting way to meet new folks. Some spots to look out for:

Amish Barn Restaurant, Route 340, Bird-in-Hand; (717) 768-8886. Breakfast, lunch, and dinner; menu dining or family style.

Bird-in-Hand Family Restaurant, 2760 Old Philadelphia Pike, Bird-in-Hand; (717) 768-8266. Breakfast, lunch, and dinner; menu dining or all-you-can-eat buffets.

Plain & Fancy Farm Restaurant, Route 340, Bird-in-Hand; (717) 768-8281. Family-style lunch and dinner.

The Lincoln Village Family Smorgasbord, 1737 West Main Street, Route 322, Ephrata; (717) 738-4231. Lunch and dinner.

Valleys of the
Susquehanna Region

Stretching west from the Poconos and Endless Mountains through the north-central heart of the state, the Valleys of the Susquehanna encompasses some of the state's wildest and most beautiful countryside wilderness, state forest reserve lands in its northern section, and hog-back ridges running north-south through the center and southern sections. It's a land that offers great outdoor recreation—camping, fishing, hiking, paddling, mountain biking, and more—and it also holds two of the state's better known small cities—Williamsport, home of the Little League World Series, to the north, and State College, site of Penn State University, in the southwestern section. Either makes a good spot from which to center your activities.

While in **Williamsport,** consider a historic Susquehanna River cruise on the **Hiawatha Paddler** (call (800) 358-9000), an afternoon at the **Children's Discovery Workshop** (call (717) 322-5437), or a visit to **Clyde Peeling's Reptileland** (call (717) 538-1869), an accredited reptile zoo. In **State College,** the **Penn State University** campus is an attraction, offering productions in all the performing arts, varsity sports events, the **Palmer Museum of Art** (call (814) 865-7672), the **Earth & Mineral Sciences Museum** (call (814) 865-6427), the **Frost Entomological Museum** (call (814) 863-2865), the **Jerome K. Agricultural Museum** (call (814) 865-2081), and, a few miles down the road, the **Millbrook Marsh Nature Center** (call (814) 863-2000) and **Tussey Mountain Ski Area** (call (800) 733-2754), which has a fun park in summer.

Bellefonte is a Victorian town located about 12 miles north of State College. Here you can visit the **Bellefonte Museum of Centre County** (call (814) 353-1473) to explore the area's heritage and see some fascinating old-time toys, then ride the **Bellefonte Historical Railroad** (call (814) 355-0311). Heading back east to **Mifflinburg,** the **Mifflinburg Buggy Museum** (call (717) 966-1355) displays Amish and Mennonite carriages plus an antique sleigh collection. And during summer in **Elysburg, Knoebels Amusement Park** (call (800) 487- 4386), is a throwback to the amusement parks of another time; they also operate an excellent commercial campground.

How to Get There

By Car. Auto is the best way access to the area. You can fly into Harrisburg (see page 128), but you'll need to rent a car. Coming from east or west, I-80 bisects the region, with the I-180 spur running up to Williamsport. To get to State College, exit at U.S. 220 (soon to be I-99), following it south to U.S. 322 east. From the south, I-99 comes from the Pennsylvania Turnpike to U.S. 322 through Altoona. From Harrisburg, follow U.S. 22/322 west. State Route 45 runs east-west between State College and Lewisburg, passing through Mifflinburg along the way.

How to Get Information before You Go

Susquehanna Valley Visitors Bureau, RR 3, 219D Hafer Road, Lewisburg, PA 17837; (800) 525-7320 or (717) 524-7282, fax (717) 524-7282; www.svvb.com.

Centre County Convention & Visitors Bureau Penn State Country, 1402 S. Ahterton Street, State College, PA 16801; (800) 358-5466 or (814) 231-1400; www.visitpennstate.org.

The Best Parks

Black Moshannon State Park. This park encompasses 3,394 acres of forests and wetlands and is surrounded by 43,000 acres of the Moshannon State Forest. A special feature is the Black Moshannon Bog Natural Area that can be explored via a boardwalk. The 250-acre Black Moshannon Lake has a sandy beach and is good for swimming, boating, and fishing. The campground offers 80 sites and 13 rustic cabins. Hiking trails range from 0.8 miles to more than 10 miles, and there are trails for mountain biking, cross-country skiing, and snowmobiling. RR 1, Philipsburg; (814) 342-5960.

Sproul State Forest. This state forest encompasses about 450 square miles of true primitive backwoods, offering fishing, hiking, mountain biking, snowmobiling, cross-country skiing, canoeing, and wilderness camping as available activities. Hyner State Park, (570) 923-6000, which holds a swimming pool and playground area, is found within Sproul's boundaries. HCR 62; (570) 923-6011.

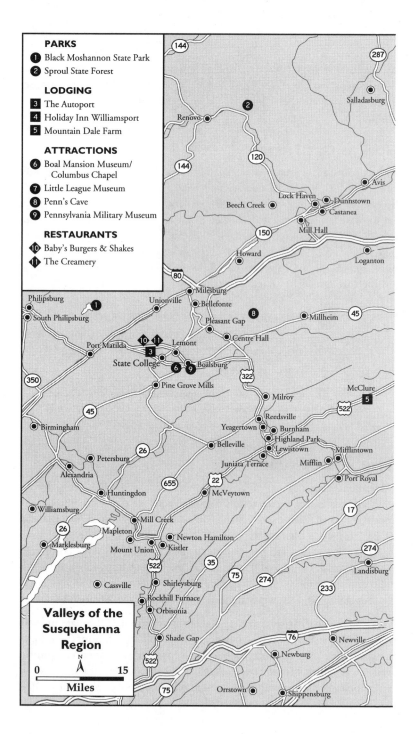

PARKS
1 Black Moshannon State Park
2 Sproul State Forest

LODGING
3 The Autoport
4 Holiday Inn Williamsport
5 Mountain Dale Farm

ATTRACTIONS
6 Boal Mansion Museum/
  Columbus Chapel
7 Little League Museum
8 Penn's Cave
9 Pennsylvania Military Museum

RESTAURANTS
10 Baby's Burgers & Shakes
11 The Creamery

Valleys of the Susquehanna Region

N

0   15
Miles

144
287
Salladasburg
2
Renovo
Avis
120
Lock Haven   Dunnstown
Beech Creek   Castanea
144
Mill Hall
150
Howard
Loganton
80
Milesburg
Philipsburg   Unionville   Bellefonte
1   Pleasant Gap
South Philipsburg   8   Millheim   45
10 11   Lemont   Centre Hall
Port Matilda   3
State College   6   9   Boalsburg
322
Pine Grove Mills   McClure
350   Milroy   522
45   Reedsville   5
Birmingham   Yeagertown   Burnham
26   Belleville   Highland Park
Petersburg   Lewistown   Mifflintown
Alexandria   Juniata Terrace   Mifflin
655   22   Port Royal
Williamsburg   Huntingdon   McVeytown
17
26   Mill Creek
Mapleton   Newton Hamilton   274
Marklesburg   Mount Union   Kistler   Landisburg
522
Cassville   35
Shirleysburg   75   274
Rockhill Furnace   233
Orbisonia
76   Newville
Shade Gap   Newburg
522
75   Orrstown   Shippensburg

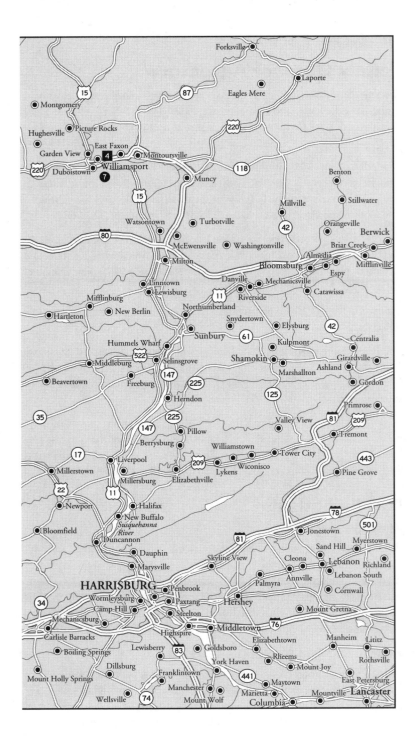

Forksville

Laporte

Montgomery

15

87

Eagles Mere

220

Hughesville

Picture Rocks

Garden View

East Faxon

4

Montoursville

Williamsport

118

Benton

220

Duboistown

7

Muncy

15

Stillwater

Millville

Watsontown

Turbotville

42

Orangeville

Berwick

80

McEwensville

Washingtonville

Briar Creek

Almedia

Bloomsburg

Mifflinville

Espy

Milton

Danville

Mechanicsville

Linntown

Mifflinburg

Lewisburg

11

Riverside

Catawissa

Hartleton

New Berlin

Northumberland

Snydertown

Elysburg

42

Sunbury

61

Kulpmont

Centralia

Hummels Wharf

522

Selinsgrove

Shamokin

Girardville

Middleburg

Marshallton

Ashland

Freeburg

147

225

125

Gordon

Beavertown

Herndon

35

147

225

Pillow

Valley View

81

Primrose

209

Berrysburg

Williamstown

Tower City

Tremont

17

Liverpool

209

Lykens

Wiconisco

443

Millerstown

Millersburg

Elizabethville

Pine Grove

22

11

Newport

Halifax

78

New Buffalo

Susquehanna River

501

Bloomfield

Duncannon

81

Jonestown

Myerstown

Dauphin

Sand Hill

Skyline View

Cleona

Lebanon

Richland

Marysville

Palmyra

Annville

Lebanon South

HARRISBURG

Penbrook

Cornwall

Wormleysburg

34

Camp Hill

Paxtang

Hershey

Mount Gretna

Steelton

Mechanicsburg

Highspire

Middletown

76

Carlisle Barracks

Elizabethtown

Manheim

Lititz

Lewisberry

83

Goldsboro

Rheems

Rothsville

Boiling Springs

Dillsburg

York Haven

Mount Joy

East Petersburg

Mount Holly Springs

Franklintown

441

Maytown

Wellsville

74

Manchester

Marietta

Mountville

Lancaster

Mount Wolf

Columbia

Family Outdoor Adventures

Boating. Stone Valley Recreation Area, near State College, rents rowboats, canoes, paddleboats, and sailboats; State College; (814) 863-9762. Black Moshannon State Park's marina rents power and other boats; (814) 342-5960.

Camping. Black Moshannon State Park (see The Best Parks, page 139). Knoebels Amusement Resort, a 500-site commercial campground adjacent to a classic amusement park, has sites for tents, and RVs and has cabins for rent; 149 Main Park Road, Howard; (800) 487-4386 or (717) 672-2572.

Hiking. Black Moshannon State Park (see The Best Parks, page 139). Reeds Gap State Park offers kid-friendly, creekside hiking on loops of 1.8 miles and 1.3 miles, plus a self-guided 1.1-mile interpretive trail; 1405 New Lancaster Valley Road, Milroy; (717) 667-3622.

Mountain Biking. Black Moshannon State Park (see The Best Parks, page 139).

Paddling. Bubb's Outdoor Rentals rents and shuttles canoes and kayaks on 150 miles of the West Branch Susquehanna River and on 50 miles of Pine Creek. Hughesville; (570) 584-4547. Canoe Susquehanna offers canoe touring; RR 2, Lewisburg; (570) 524-7692.

Swimming. Reeds Gap State Park (see Hiking, above) has two swimming pools. Cowaneque Lake and Tioga-Hammond Lakes are three man-made lakes near the New York state line. They offers grassy beaches with bathhouses and concession stands; RD #1, Tioga; (570) 835-5281.

Family Lodging

The Autoport

Pennsylvania's first motel, The Autoport opened in the 1930s and was recently completely renovated. You can stay in a cottage, apartment, family room that sleeps six, or a suite. On-site you'll find a heated pool, two eateries, live entertainment, and plenty of modernized 1930s–1950s atmosphere. Rates $65–90. Business Route 322, 1405 South Atherton Street, State College; (814) 237-7666 or (800) 932-7678 (reservations only).

Holiday Inn/T.G.I.Fridays Complex

This 159-room hotel has a variety of room choices, including some with a refrigerator, microwave, and sofa bed. Room amenities include cable TV with HBO, in-room coffee maker, iron and ironing board, and hair dryer. The hotel has an outdoor pool and offers a kids-eat-free program at on-site restaurants. Rates: $69–139. Kids under age 18 stay free with parents. Rates are higher during the Little League World Series. 1840 East Third Street, Williamsport; (800) 369-4572 or (570) 326-1981.

Mountain Dale Farm

At this working farm in the eastern reaches of the region lodging can be in an efficiency cottage, dorm-style cabins, rustic cabins, or in the farmhouse. There are plenty of animals to feed, and you can hike, cross-country ski, paddleboat, and pond fish on the property. Rates: $55–75 per person, half-price for children age 12 and under; meals extra, $4/$6/$8 for breakfast/lunch/dinner, kids $1 or $2 less depending on age. RR 02, McClure; (570) 658-3536.

Attractions

Boal Mansion Museum and Columbus Chapel

Route 322 Business, Boalsburg; (814) 946-0048;
www.vicon.net/~boalmus

Hours: May 1–Memorial Day and Labor Day–October 31, daily 1:30–5 p.m.; Memorial Day–Labor Day, Monday–Saturday 10 a.m.–5 p.m. and Sunday noon–5 p.m.

Admission: $10 adults, $6 children ages 7–11, free for children under age 7

Appeal by Age Groups:

Pre-school	Grade School	Teens	Young Adults	Over 30	Seniors
★	★★★	★★★★	★★★★	★★★★★	★★★★★

Touring Time: 1 hour

Rainy-Day Touring: Yes

Services and Facilities:

Restaurants No	Lockers No
Alcoholic beverages No	Pet kennels No
Disabled access No	Rain check No
Wheelchair rental No	Private tours No
Baby stroller rental No	

Description and Comments   The mansion is suitable only for children from about age 11 and up. While the mansion and family history are fascinating (the Boal and Lee families connect to Robert E. Lee and Christopher Columbus, among other notables), the major attractions for kids are an incredible collection of Christopher Columbus artifacts (the most significant in the world), a notable collection of guns and swords dating from Colonial America, and a delightful pair of nineteenth-century carriages.

That the Lee family still lives in the house makes this a living connection to the history.

Little League Museum

Route 15, South Williamsport; (570) 326-3607; www.littleleague.org

Hours: Memorial Day–Labor Day, Monday–Saturday 9 a.m.–7 p.m. and Sunday noon–7 p.m.; Labor Day–Memorial Day, Monday–Saturday 9 a.m.–5 p.m. and Sunday noon–5 p.m.

Admission: $5 adults, $3 seniors 62 and older, $1.50 children ages 13 and under, $13 family

Appeal by Age Groups:

Pre-school	Grade School	Teens	Young Adults	Over 30	Seniors
★	★★★★	★★★	★★★★	★★★★	★★★★

Touring Time: Average 1 hour, minimum 30 minutes

Rainy-Day Touring: Yes

Services and Facilities:

Restaurants No	Lockers No
Alcoholic beverages No	Pet kennels No
Disabled access Yes	Rain check No
Wheelchair rental No	Private tours No
Baby stroller rental No	

Description and Comments   This is where Little League started in 1939 and where its world championships are played annually. The museum covers the league's history, with some interesting audiovisual displays and such esoterica as how balls, gloves, and bats are made and how proper nutrition affects an athlete's play. Most kids will like the Play Ball Room, where they can be videotaped as they hit off a tee, pitch and run, and get electronic pointers. You'll find lots of memorabilia, and you can wander out back to see the Little League stadium where the championship games take place.

Penn's Cave

R.D. #2, Route 192, Centre Hall; (814) 364-1664; www.pennscave.com

Hours: February 15–March 31, daily 9 a.m.–4 p.m.; April 1–May 31 and September 1–November 30, daily 9 a.m.–5 p.m.; June 1–August 1, daily 9 a.m.–8 p.m.; December, Saturday and Sunday 11 a.m.–5 p.m.; closed in January; call for exact time of last tour of the day

Admission: Cave tour: $10 adults, $9 seniors, $4.75 children ages 2–12, free for children under age 2 (children under 1 not permitted in cave); Wildlife Sanctuary tour: $12 adults, $11 seniors, $5.75 children ages 2–12, free for children under age 2

Appeal by Age Groups:

Pre-school	Grade School	Teens	Young Adults	Over 30	Seniors
★★★	★★★★★	★★★★	★★★★★	★★★★★	★★★★★

Touring Time: Average 3 hours, minimum 1½ hours

Rainy-Day Touring: Yes

Services and Facilities:

Restaurants Yes; snack bar	Lockers No
Alcoholic beverages No	Pet kennels No
Disabled access No	Rain check No
Wheelchair rental No	Private tours No
Baby stroller rental No	

Description and Comments These are the largest water-bound caverns in the state, and the boat tour is worthwhile. The guides are knowledgeable and have a sense of humor, although some of the "figures" they see in the stalactite and stalagmite formations are a bit hokey. Bring a sweater or light jacket even on the hottest of days. The safari tour's worthiness is a tougher call. It's conducted in a converted school bus, and you do see some fine animals (from bison and longhorn cattle to deer and wild turkeys) up-close, but the narration is minimally informative and the environment (although covering large acreage) hardly natural. Suitability is best for kids ages eight and under. Maybe it's the strange mix of fauna, or the rattling bus that bothered us, but adults are likely to be less than enthralled, as we were.

Pennsylvania Military Museum

Route 322 Business, Boalsburg; (814) 466-6263;
www.psu.edu/dept/aerospace/museum

Hours: April–October, Tuesday–Saturday 9 a.m.–5 p.m. and Sunday noon–5 p.m.; closed Mondays but open Memorial Day, July Fourth, and Labor Day; November and March, Wednesday–Saturday 10 a.m.–4 p.m. and Sunday noon–4 p.m.; December–February, Friday and Saturday 10 a.m.–4 p.m. and Sunday noon–4 p.m.

Admission: $3.50 adults, $3 seniors 60 and older, $1.50 children ages 6–12, $8.50 families, free for children under age 6

Appeal by Age Groups:

Pre-school	Grade School	Teens	Young Adults	Over 30	Seniors
★	★★★★	★★★★	★★★★	★★★★★	★★★★★

Touring Time: Average 1 hour, minimum 30 minutes

Rainy-Day Touring: Yes

Services and Facilities:

Restaurants No	Lockers No
Alcoholic beverages No	Pet kennels No
Disabled access Yes	Rain check No
Wheelchair rental Yes; free	Private tours Yes; give one-week
Baby stroller rental No	notice

Description and Comments   Set in a 65-acre park, the museum's highlight is its walk-through diorama of a French Army World War I trench, complete with battle sounds, light effects, and antique vehicles (check out the tank). The building contains things military with Pennsylvania connections dating from 1747. Outside stands the huge and moving 28th Division Shrine, plus a number of tanks that kids will love to climb on.

Family-Friendly Restaurants

BABY'S BURGERS & SHAKES

131 South Garner Street, State College; (814) 234-4776

Meals served: Breakfast, lunch, and dinner
Cuisine: American
Entree range: $2.49–9.50
Children's menu: Yes, including kid-sized desserts
Reservations: No
Payment: V, MC, D

A 1950s diner with an old-fashioned soda fountain and the kind of comfort food that, well, you could get at the old malt shop. Burgers and fries, meat loaf with mashed potatoes, and heavenly shakes are the standard fare. The portions are large, and the prices small. Try the Teeny-Weeny hot fudge sundae for 50¢.

THE CREAMERY

Penn State University, State College; (814) 865-7535

Meals served: Snacks
Cuisine: Ice cream, snacks, and other dairy products
Entree range: $1.75–3.50
Children's menu: No
Reservations: No
Payment: Cash

The Creamery, operated by the Department of Food Science, is Penn State's ice cream/dairy store. How good is this ice cream? Well, Ben and Jerry came here to learn how to make the stuff. Creamery ice cream is so fresh that only four days, on the average, elapse between the cow and your newly dipped cone. Try the Peachy Paterno, named after football coach Joe Paterno. You can also buy fresh cheese, milk, and other picnic supplies.

The Southern Alleghenies and Laurel Highlands

The Southern Alleghenies

The land west of Harrisburg and State College that covers the center of the state is rugged country, lined with the long mountain ridges and deep valleys that long made east-west travel problematic. It's country steeped in industrial and labor history, for it was here in places like Johnstown and Altoona that much coal was mined, that the American steelmaking industry first rolled out Bessemer process product, and that the Pennsylvania Railroad, once the country's mightiest, based its operations and solved the most difficult railroading engineering enigma of its dayVhow to cross the seemingly unpassable Allegheny Mountain.

Johnstown remains most famous for the flood that swept the city away in 1889, and its museums to the memory of that event are must-dos for everyone. But while you're there, be sure to take a ride on the **Inclined Plane** (call (814) 536-1816), said to be the world's steepest. A few miles east of town on Route 56 lies the town of **Windber,** home to the **Windber Coal Heritage Center** (call (877) 826-3933 or (814) 467-6680, or visit www.allegheny.org/windber), which paints a poignant portrait of life in a company coal town and elicits the feel of being in a coal mine without actually descending into the earth. Near Altoona, in the tiny town of **Patton,** you can descend underground at the **Seldom Seen Tourist Coal Mine** (call (800) 235-8590), where you'll see how mining was done in the 1950s and 1960s. Altoona's railroading history is legion, and outside town two of the great railroading engineering achievements can be seen: **Horseshoe Curve National Monument** (call (814) 946-0834 or visit www.rail roadcity.com), which explains the building of this 1854 wonder and provides an overlook to see it, and the nearby **Gallitzin Tunnels** (call (814) 886-8871), a modern railroading marvel worthy of a look.

In **Gallitzin,** the **Allegheny Portage Railroad National Historic Site** (call (814) 886-6100; www.nps.gove/alpo) shows how a series of incline railroads took people, cargo, and canal boats over the mountain before Horseshoe Curve was built; it also provides excellent hiking and cross-country skiing. In **Altoona,** the **Quaint Corner Children's Museum** (call (814) 944-6830), set in an old house complete with "grandma's attic," will keep kids under age ten wonderfully entertained for hours. You can see pretzels being made (and sample them, too) at **Benzel's Pretzel Factory** (call (814) 942-5062 or visit www.benzels.com). Roller coaster fans will want to check out **Lakemont Park** (call (800) 434-8006), home to the world's oldest coaster.

West of Altoona and south of State College, where U.S. 22 and State Route 26 meet, stands **Huntingdon,** gateway to **Raystown Lake.** The **Swigart Antique Auto Museum** (call (814) 643-0885 or visit www.swigart museum.com) is small but holds an international reputation for displaying unique cars, from Hollywood's famous Herbie the Volkswagen to a proto-type Tucker; the museum also has an incredible collection of license plates, car company emblems, and other auto paraphernalia. Just outside town you'll find the **1,000 Steps** (it's not well marked, so ask in town how to find it), literally more than 1,000 stone steps (count them as you climb) laid into a mountainside to be used by nineteenth-century stone quarry workers.

HOW TO GET THERE

By Car. From the east or west, leave the Pennsylvania Turnpike at Exit 11 and follow U.S. 220/I-99 north and U.S. 22 west. From the northeast, follow I-80 to Milesburg, then U.S. 200/I-99 south.

By Plane. See Pittsburgh International Airport (page 180).

By Train. Amtrak service goes to Altoona; (800)-872-7245.

HOW TO GET INFORMATION BEFORE YOU GO

Allegheny Mountains Convention & Visitors Bureau, Logan Valley Mall, Route 200 and Goods Lane, Altoona, PA 16602; (800) 842-5766 or (814) 943-4183; www.amcvb.com.

Greater Johnstown/Cambria County Convention & Visitors Bureau, 111 Market Street, Johnstown, PA 15901; (800) 237-8590 or (814) 536-7993; www.visitjohnstownpa.com.

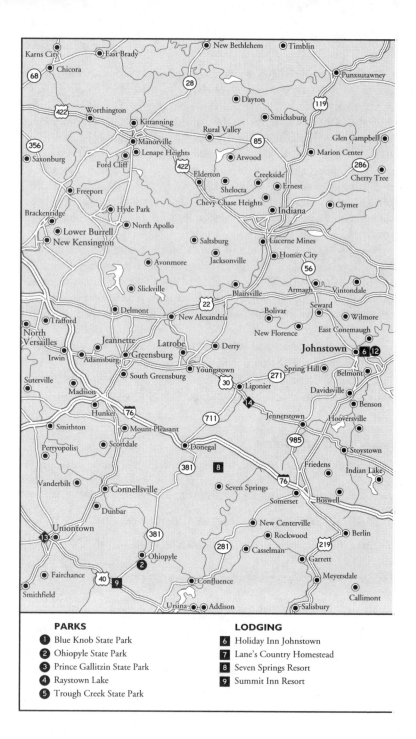

PARKS

1. Blue Knob State Park
2. Ohiopyle State Park
3. Prince Gallitzin State Park
4. Raystown Lake
5. Trough Creek State Park

LODGING

6. Holiday Inn Johnstown
7. Lane's Country Homestead
8. Seven Springs Resort
9. Summit Inn Resort

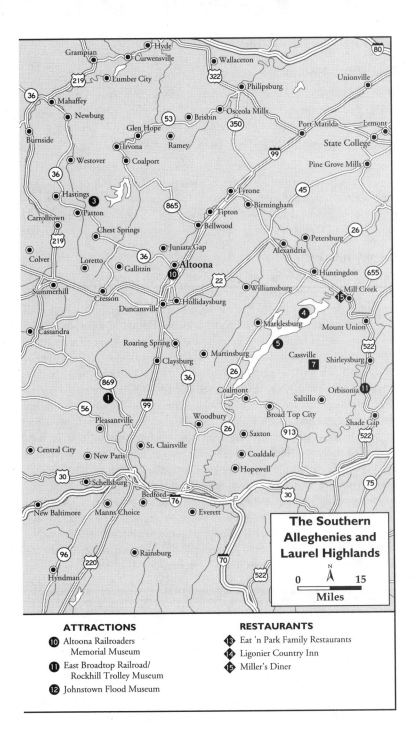

The Southern Alleghenies and Laurel Highlands

N
0   15
Miles

ATTRACTIONS

10 Altoona Railroaders Memorial Museum

11 East Broadtop Railroad/ Rockhill Trolley Museum

12 Johnstown Flood Museum

RESTAURANTS

13 Eat 'n Park Family Restaurants

14 Ligonier Country Inn

15 Miller's Diner

THE BEST PARKS

Prince Gallitzin State Park. This park has magnificent vistas, nine miles of hiking and interpretive trails, swimming, 400-plus camping sites, ten camping cabins, fishing, many picnicking spots, and cross-country skiing in winter; 966 Marina Road, Patton; (814) 674-1000.

Trough Creek State Park. Excellent scenery in a gorge created where Great Trough Creek cuts through Terrace Mountain. Good hiking, although some is definitely challenging, with one nice ramble across a suspension bridge to Rainbow Falls. Nice picnicking, and some campsites; RR 1, James Creek; (814) 658-3847.

Raystown Lake

The largest (albeit man-made) lake in Pennsylvania, Raystown is a complete outdoor activity wonderland, offering everything from a simple picnic to camping or from an easy hike to high-speed water skiing. Boat rentals and ski and fishing equipment are available at **Seven Points Marina** (call (814) 658-3074), as are tour boat rides and three eateries. Own your own boat? Seven launch sites are situated around the lake. Also at Seven Points Marina is a sandy beach with a snack bar, lockers, showers, and playgrounds. The park has more than 500 campsites for tents or RVs. Hikers can follow a variety of terrain, including an 18-mile trek on the Terrace Mountain Trail that offers spectacular lake views. Fishing can be done from shore or from boats; the lake hides many quiet coves and rocky points from which to fish. Finally, for those not inclined to rough it, at the **Lake Raystown Resort** (call (814) 658-3500), you can camp or lodge in a cabin or lakeside inn, plus play mini-golf, cruise in a showboat, and play in the waterpark. For something different, rent a houseboat from **Lake Cruises & Charters** at the marina (call (814) 658-3074 or visit www.7pointsmarina.com) for three or four nights ($600–1,800). Some houseboats come with on-board hot tubs. A number of professional guide services can lead you to top-notch lake fishing spots. Try Trophy Guide Service (RD 3, Box 50, Huntingdon, PA 16652; (814) 627-5231, www.trophyguide.com); Lunker Guide Service, (RR 1, Box 96, River Road, Alexandria, PA 16611; (814) 669-8887, www.lunkerguide.com); or Tim Grace Striper Service, P.O. Box 78, Hesston, PA 16647; (814) 658-2088, www.striper-guide.com).

FAMILY OUTDOOR ADVENTURES

Biking. Cycle Southern Alleghenies offers numerous self-guided cycling tour routes in the region for all ability levels, plus help in finding lodging, food, and other adventures; 541 58th Street, Altoona; (800) 458-3433; www.cyclesa.com.

Paddling. The Juniata River offers a variety of gentle paddling and float opportunities. Adventure Marine Canoe & Kayak organizes float and canoe trips; Bedford; (814) 623-1821; www.bedford.net/canoe. Miller's Canoe Rentals can set you up with a canoe as well as direct you to primitive camping, full-service campgrounds, or area motels; RD 2, Millerstown; (717) 589-3159.

FAMILY LODGING

Holiday Inn Johnstown

Set in the heart of downtown, this hotel is a block from the Inclined Plane and two blocks from the Johnstown Flood Museum. It has a fitness center, an indoor pool, and an on-site restaurant. Suites are available. Rates: $109–250 per night; children under 18 stay free with parents. 250 Market Street, Johnstown; (800) 433-5663 or (814) 535-7777.

Lane's Country Homestead

A 1789 restored country home with four bedrooms, 2.5 baths, and a full kitchen, Lane's is set five miles east of Raystown Lake. There's a pool on the property, hiking trails nearby, and a pond for fishing. Run by friendly local folks, this is something different. Rate: $75 for four people, $10 per extra person, to rent the entire house. No meals are served. HCR-1, Cassville; (814) 448-3351.

ATTRACTIONS

Altoona Railroaders Memorial Museum

1300 Ninth Avenue, Altoona; (888) 425-8666; www.railroadcity.com

Hours: Daily 9 a.m.–5 p.m.; closed Thanksgiving, Christmas, and New Year's days

Admission: $8.50 adults, $7.75 seniors 62 and older, $5 children ages 5–15; combination ticket with Horseshoe Curve National Historic Landmark: $10 adults, $9 seniors, $5.50 children

Appeal by Age Groups:

Pre-school	Grade School	Teens	Young Adults	Over 30	Seniors
★★	★★★★★	★★★★	★★★★	★★★★★	★★★★★

Touring Time: Average 2 hours, minimum 1 hour

Rainy-Day Touring: Yes

Services and Facilities:

Restaurants No	Lockers No; coat check room
Alcoholic beverages No	Pet kennels No

Disabled access Yes	Rain check No
Wheelchair rental No	Private tours No
Baby stroller rental No	

Description and Comments   Unlike other railroading museums, this one is dedicated to the people who worked in the industry, especially those who worked the gigantic Pennsylvania Railroad works in Altoona, once the largest railroad yard and locomotive/rail car fabrication complex in the country. Start with the introductory film, which ably depicts life in those sooty, bustling times, and then visit the interactive exhibits that draw you into the railroad life. Hard to believe these days, but Altoona was once a major stop for barnstorming baseball teams, vaudeville acts, theater troupes, and politicians and VIPs of all sorts.

East Broadtop Railroad and Rockhill Trolley Museum

Meadow Street, Route 994, Rockhill Furnace; Railroad: (814) 447-3011, Trolley: (814) 447-9576 or (717) 263-3943

Hours: Train: June–October, Saturday and Sunday 11 a.m., 1 p.m., and 3 p.m.; Trolley: Memorial Day–October, Saturday, Sunday, and holidays, 11:30 a.m. and 4:30 p.m.

Admission: Train: $9 adults, $6 children ages 2–11; Trolley: $3 adults, $2 children ages 2–12

Appeal by Age Groups:

Pre-school	Grade School	Teens	Young Adults	Over 30	Seniors
★★★	★★★★★	★★★★	★★★★	★★★★★	★★★★★

Touring Time: Train: average 2 hours, minimum 1 hour; Trolley: average 1½ hours, minimum 1 hour

Rainy-Day Touring: Yes

Services and Facilities:

Restaurants No	Baby stroller rental No
Alcoholic beverages No	Lockers No
Disabled access Yes; for train and trolley	Pet kennels No
	Rain check No
Wheelchair rental No	Private tours No

Description and Comments   These are two separate attractions situated adjacent to each other. The railroad is one of only a few remaining narrow-gauge steam trains. Once a self-sufficient operation, making and maintaining all its own rolling stock, the line closed in 1956. What you see today is just as it was left the day it closed (much of it still functions). The site is now des-ignated a National Historic Landmark. You can peek into the roundhouse and the repair shops, and then take the 50-minute excursion through the hills. The trolley museum features half-hour rides on vintage trolleys from around the world, plus tours of the restoration shop and trolley barns. Together the two offer a day of prime railroading experience and history.

Johnstown Flood Museum

304 Washington Street, Johnstown; (888) 222-1889 or (814) 539-1889; www.jaha.org

Hours: November 1–April 30, daily 10 a.m.–5 p.m.; May 1–October 31, Sunday–Thursday 10 a.m.–5 p.m. and Friday–Saturday 10 a.m.–7 p.m.

Admission: $4 adults, $3.25 seniors 62 and older, $2.50 students ages 6–19, free for children under 6

Appeal by Age Groups:

Pre-school	Grade School	Teens	Young Adults	Over 30	Seniors
★★	★★★★	★★★★★	★★★★★	★★★★★	★★★★★

Touring Time: Average 1½ hours, minimum 1 hour

Rainy-Day Touring: Yes

Services and Facilities:

Restaurants No	Lockers No
Alcoholic beverages No	Pet kennels No
Disabled access Yes	Rain check No
Wheelchair rental No	Private tours Yes; call ahead
Baby stroller rental No	

Description and Comments   It took ten minutes for the Great Johnstown Flood to kill more than 2,000 people. The date was May 31, 1889, and the calamity became an instant piece of American folklore. This museum, designed by the same folks who gave us the Ellis Island museum in New York City, beautifully and poignantly describes the events that led to the flood, and the disaster's aftermath. The introductory film, *The Johnstown Flood,* won a 1989 Academy Award. The lobby's three-dimensional, electric, topographic map illustrates the sequence of events. Other fascinating displays include 3-D viewers with period photos and a description of the physics that drove the flood waters. If possible, combine your visit with a stop at the National Park Service's **Johnstown Flood National Memorial,** (814) 495-4643), in nearby St. Michael, set at the site of the failed dam that sparked the flood; they, too, show a mesmerizing film and offer the opportunity to walk right out to the dam site.

FAMILY-FRIENDLY RESTAURANTS

Johnstown and Altoona offer a full range of chain restaurants, including an Eat 'n Park (a regional chain we like) in each city (Plank Road at Route

220, Altoona, (814) 943-4070; Westwood Plaza, 1900 Minno Drive, Johnstown, (814) 255-7711); Olive Garden (3315 Pleasant Valley Boulevard, Altoona, (814) 949-9540); and Ponderosa Steak House (406 Galleria Drive, Johnstown, (814) 269-1331).

For local flavor in the Raystown Lake area, we liked the following place:

MILLER'S DINER

Route 22 East, Mill Creek; (814) 643-3418

Meals served: Breakfast, lunch, and dinner
Cuisine: American homestyle
Entree range: $6.95–10.95
Children's menu: Yes
Reservations: No
Payment: Major credit cards

A locals' favorite, Miller's offers entrees like smoked ham and breaded veal cutlets. You can get "regular" dinners or smaller-sized portions. The homemade pies are to die for. You'll find Miller's just a few miles east of Huntingdon.

The Laurel Highlands

So close to Pittsburgh, yet light years away in atmosphere, the Highlands is southwestern Pennsylvania's outdoor playground. While **Ohiopyle State Park** is the outdoor adventurer's centerpiece, the region has much to offer. In **Laughlintown,** the **Compass Inn Museum** (call (724) 238-4983) illustrates what a roadside inn was like circa 1800. **Idlewild Park** (call (412) 238-3666) is a theme park that features Mr. Rogers' Neighborhood of Make Believe, as well as a bounty of attractions for the 12-and-under set and a few for older kids. In **Mill Run** stands Frank Lloyd Wright's **Fallingwater** (call (724) 329-8501), one of his most famous house designs, into which a waterfall has been integrally included; house tours are appropriate for age nine and older. **Uniontown** is the site of **Fort Necessity National Battlefield** (call (412) 329-5512), commemorating George Washington's first battle, and the **National Road Heritage Park** (call (412) 329-1560), which honors the country's first national highway.

How to Get There

By Car. The Laurel Highlands is accessed from the north or south by I-79. Coming from the east or west, use the Pennsylvania Turnpike Exits 7 or 10 or, farther south, I-70. U.S. 30, U.S. 22, and U.S. 40 are other main highways in the region.

By Plane. See Pittsburgh International Airport (page 180).

By Train. Amtrak provides service to Johnstown, Greensburg, Latrobe, and Connellsville; (800)-872-7245.

How to Get Information before You Go

Laurel Highlands Visitors Bureau, 120 East Main Street, Ligonier, PA 15658; (800) 952-7669 or (412) 238-5661; www.laurelhighlands.org.

The Best Parks

Blue Knob State Park. With the state's second highest peak, Blue Knob, this park's views are great. The park has a swimming pool, 17 miles of hiking trails, a small campground, mountain biking trails, and 200 picnic tables; 124 Park Road, Imler; (814) 276-3576.

Ohiopyle

Ohiopyle is the region's epicenter for outdoor activity. Here you can bike, hike, river raft, swim, fish, horseback ride, camp, mountain bike, snowmobile, cross-country ski, or just ogle the magnificent scenery created by the Youghiogheny River. Much of the action is accessible to disabled persons. At the heart of it all is Ohiopyle State Park, one the state's most popular action-sports gathering spots; P.O. Box 105, Ohiopyle, PA 15470; (412) 329-8591.

Ohiopyle adventures include:

Biking/Walking/Jogging/Cross-Country Skiing. A 28- mile, paved, disabled-accessible rails-to-trails path runs through Ohiopyle State Park. Several local outfitters rent bikes and ski equipment. Mountain Streams and Wilderness Voyageurs Inc. (see Paddling, below) offers guided family biking trips and rents bikes.

Camping. The park has 226 campsites, open from late April–December. Scarlett Knob Campground, a private facility, offers campsites and cabins adjoining the park; Route 382 North, Ohiopyle; (412) 329-5200.

Fishing. The Youghiogheny is trout-stocked, while Meadow Brook is good for smaller stream fish. Contact the Laurel Highlands Visitors Bureau at (412) 238-5661 for more information.

Hiking. Terrific hiking is found just to the north at Laurel Ridge State Park, which contains the Laurel Highlands Hiking Trail. One end of the Laurel Highlands Trail is set in Ohiopyle Park, and it travels 70 miles through Laurel Ridge State Park. Ohiopyle Park holds more than 40 miles of its own trails for all abilities, revealing fantastic panoramas. The Fern-cliff Natural Area within the park has interpretive trails and programs. Mountain Streams Paddling offers guided family hiking trips; RD 3, Rockwood; (412) 455-3744.

Horseback Riding. Nemacolin Woodlands, an upscale, full-service resort a few miles south of Ohiopyle, offers trail, pony, and sleigh rides at its Equestrian Center; 1001 LaFayette Drive, Farmington; (800) 422-2736 or (724) 329-8555.

Mountain Biking. Wilderness Voyageurs, Inc. (see Paddling, below) rents mountain bikes and leads guided adventures.

Paddling. The Youghiogheny River, fondly called the Yough, has become an eastern rafting mecca, offering a range of whitewater experiences from relatively mild to outlandishly challenging. Ohiopyle area outfitters offer guided tours, or they'll rent you a ducky, raft, kayak, or canoe to go it on your own (only if you know what you're doing, please). Single-day trips generally cost $30–60 per person, depending on the day of the week and time of year; overnight trips and advanced rafting on the Cheat River can also be arranged. Local outfitters include:

Laurel Highlands River Tours, P.O. Box 107, Ohiopyle, PA 15470; (800) 472-3846 or (724) 329-8531

Mountain Streams, P.O. Box 106, Ohiopyle, PA 15470; (800) 723-8669 or (724) 329-8810

Ohiopyle Trading Post Inc., P.O. Box 94, Ohiopyle, PA 15470; (888) 644-6795 or (724) 329-1450

Riversport, 355 River Road, P.O. Box 95, Confluence, PA 15424; (800)-216-6991 or (814) 395-5744

Wilderness Voyageurs Inc., P.O. Box 97, Ohiopyle, PA 15470; (800) 272-4141 or (724) 329-1000

White Water Adventurers Inc., P.O. Box 31, Ohiopyle, PA 15470; (800) 992-7238 or (724) 329-8850

FAMILY OUTDOOR ADVENTURES

Caving. Laurel Caverns offers one-hour guided tours of the catacomb caves, reputed to be the largest in Pennsylvania. Also offered are staff-directed adventure tours to undeveloped parts of the cavern; RD 1, Farmington; (800) 515-4150 or (724) 438-3003.

Rails-to-Trails. The Highlands offers no fewer than nine rails-to-trails for hiking and cycling. Some allow cross-country skiing and/or horseback riding. The Allegheny Highlands Trail, with a compacted stone surface, runs 19.5 miles along the Maryland state line; call (814) 445-6431. The Ghost Town Trails runs 16 miles on a stone surface north of U.S. 22 through three counties; call (724) 463-8636. The PW&S Trail covers 34 miles on varying surfaces, with interconnecting loops, in Forbes State Forest and along the Laurel Ridge.

Skiing. Seven Springs Resort (see Attractions, below). Hidden Valley Four Seasons Resort, has 25 trails, cross-country skiing, snowshoeing, and snowtubing; One Craighead Drive, Hidden Valley; (800) 458-0175 or (814) 443-8000; www.hiddenvalleyresort.com. Laurel Mountain Ski Company, located in Laurel Mountain State Park, has 20 slopes (including "the steepest trail in Pennsylvania"), plus snowtubing and cross-country skiing; 201 Summit Ski Road, Boswell; (877) 754-5287 or (724) 238-9816; www.skilaurelmountain.com.

FAMILY LODGING

Seven Springs Resort

Seven Springs is a large ski/golf/summer resort complex with a hotel and condominiums (see Attractions, below). Hotel rates: $160–420 per night, including complimentary breakfast buffet and certain activities; children age 17 and under stay free in parents' room. Condominium rates: $340–700 for two-nights with one to four bedrooms; weekly rates and package rates are available. RD 1, Champion; (800) 452-2223 or (814) 352-7777; www.7springs.com

Summit Inn Resort

A grand resort on the Victorian scale, this hotel opened in 1907. It sits on 1,200 acres just south of Ohiopyle State Park and offers full amenities, including indoor and outdoor pools, a nine-hole golf course, tennis courts, hiking, game and fitness rooms, and a full-service restaurant. Rates: $75–124 European plan; $89–138 B&B plan; $125–174 Modified American plan; children age 12 and under room stay free in parents room but are charged for dining; children's menus available. Two Skyline Drive, Farmington; (724) 438-8594 or (800) 433-8594 (regional toll-free number).

ATTRACTION

Seven Springs Resort

RD 1, Champion; (800) 452-2223 or (814) 352-7777;
  www.7springs.com
Hours: Vary by activity

Admission: Varies by activity

Appeal by Age Groups:

Pre-school	Grade School	Teens	Young Adults	Over 30	Seniors
★★★★★	★★★★★	★★★★★	★★★★★	★★★★★	★★★★★

Touring Time: Average full day to several days, minimum half-day

Rainy-Day Touring: Yes

Services and Facilities:

Restaurants Yes	Lockers Yes
Alcoholic beverages Yes	Pet kennels No
Disabled access Yes	Rain check No
Wheelchair rental Yes; free	Private tours No
Baby stroller rental No	

Description and Comments   Seven Springs is a fantasy. A major ski area for the region, it houses a base lodge hotel that functions as shopping mall, entertainment center, restaurant row, arcade emporium, and aquatic facility. In winter, skiing takes place on 30 runs served by ten chairlifts and eight tows. You can also ice skate, go on sleigh rides, and have fun in the snow-tubing park. In summer, the activity menu includes an alpine slide, horseback riding, mountain biking, hiking, hayrides, paddleboats, golf, and full- and half-day supervised Kids Adventure Kamp for children from "walking age" to 12.

For year-round fun, the indoor base facility has a game room, a bowling center, a pool, hot tubs, handball/racquetball courts, miniature golf, a fitness room, and a roller-skating center. There are several restaurants and a small shopping mall. During one winter visit, we encountered fresh powder for skiing, but then a nasty, rainy day that would've wrecked many other ski vacations. Here, we just played inside.

FAMILY-FRIENDLY RESTAURANTS

EAT'N PARK FAMILY RESTAURANTS

519 West Main Street, Uniontown; (724) 439-4579

Meals served: Breakfast, lunch, and dinner
Cuisine: American
Entree range: $5.95–15.95
Children's menu: Yes
Reservations: No
Payment: Major credit cards

A regional chain with locations in Pennsylvania, West Virginia, and Ohio, this place offers fast, straightforward eating with good service and no surprises. The baked goods are homemade, and kids get a smiley-face cookie with their meal. Seniors even have their own specials. Other locations in the region include Greensburg, North Huntingdon, Latrobe, and Somerset.

LIGONIER COUNTRY INN

Route 30 East, Laughlintown; (724) 238-3651

Meals served: Dinner and Sunday breakfast buffet and brunch
Cuisine: Continental
Entree range: $10.95−19.50
Children's menu: No, but will fulfill requests
Reservations: Yes
Payment: Major credit cards

Ligonier is a country inn with a charming dining room and also a pub. The inn prides itself on its "flowerpot bread," baked and served in a flowerpot, and its crab dip. Entrees range from pot pies to filet mignon.

Lake Erie Region

The northern tier stretches from mid-state to Lake Erie and the Ohio border. If that sounds like a lot of territory, it is. And much of it is untrammeled forest that will make you feel like you're miles from anywhere. You are.

The city of **Erie,** on the shores of Lake Erie, is the largest town in the region. A major shipping port in its own right, the city has a number of attractions to offer. The **Bicentennial Observation Tower** (call (814) 455-6055) stands 185 feet tall and yields impressive views. A new children's museum, **expERIEnce Children's Museum** (call (814) 453-3743), appeals very much to elementary-school-aged kids, and the **Erie Historical Museum and Planetarium** (call (814) 871-5790) offers worthwhile astronomy shows. The **Firefighters Historical Museum** (call (814) 456-5969) houses one of the finest displays of firefighting memorabilia you'll ever see. In **Sharon, Daffin's Candies** (call (412) 342-2892) is a small chocolate factory that gives tours and features a display of gigantic chocolate animals (like a 700-pound bunny). Choca-holics will want to then drive over to **Hermitage** to tour the **Philadelphia Candies Factory** (call (412) 981-6341) and then walk off all that candy with a stroll down the **Avenue of Flags,** claimed to be the world's largest flag display (444 of them). If you're in the **Oil City/Titusville** area between June and October, visit the **Otto Cupler Torpedo Company** (call (814) 827-2921), where you'll find out just how important nitroglycerin was to the area's oil industry in the nineteenth century, plus see a special nitro show. Canal buffs should visit the **Canal Museum** (call (412) 588-7540) in **Grenville,** while bird lovers should see the **Brucker Great Blue Heron Sanctuary** (on Route 18, south of town; (800) 248-4435), which houses a huge colony of these magnificent birds.

How to Get There

By Car. The far northwestern corner of the state is best reached by car. From the south, I-79 comes up from Pittsburgh, and I-90 serves the area coming from the north (Buffalo) or west (Ohio). U.S. 62 takes you to Oil City, while U.S. 6 runs east-west along the entire northern tier, producing one of the most scenic old-fashioned highways you'll ever drive.

How to Get Information before You Go

Erie Area Convention & Visitors Bureau, 10006 State Street, Erie, PA 16501; (814) 454-7191; www.eriepa.com.

Mercer Country Convention & Visitors Bureau, 835 Perry Highway, Mercer, PA 16137; (800) 637-2370 or (412) 748-5315; www.merlink.org.

The Best Parks and Beaches

Oil Creek State Park. Highlights here include a scenic excursion train ride and a paved 9.5-mile bike path through a picturesque gorge. You can also hike, fish, and canoe/kayak on easy runs. RR 1, Oil City; (814) 676-5915.

Presque Isle State Park. A curving sand spit jutting into Lake Erie, this is the state's only beach, located just four miles from downtown Erie. Activities include swimming, boating, water-skiing, scuba diving, fishing, hiking, bicycling, in-line skating, ice-fishing, ice-boating, and ice-skating. Erie; (814) 833-7424.

Pymatuning State Park. One of the state's largest park's, Pymatuning centers on a large reservoir and offers swimming, small-engine and paddle-powered boating, camping, fishing, ice-skating, cross-country skiing, ice-boating, and an island natural reserve. At the Visitor Center is the Waterfowl Museum. 2660 Williamsfield Road, Jamestown; (724) 932-3141.

Family Outdoor Adventures

Bicycling. Oil Creek State Park (see The Best Parks and Beaches, above) has a 9.5-mile paved bike trail that passes through Oil Creek Gorge. Rent bikes at the old Egbert Oil Office at Petroleum Centre. Ernst Bike Trail (French Creek Recreational Trails) has a five-mile bike path with a crushed-stone surface; Mercer Pike, Meadville; (814) 333-1235.

Camping. Pymatuning State Park (see The Best Parks and Beaches, above) has 657 campsites, some with electric hook-up, and 25 modern camping cabins.

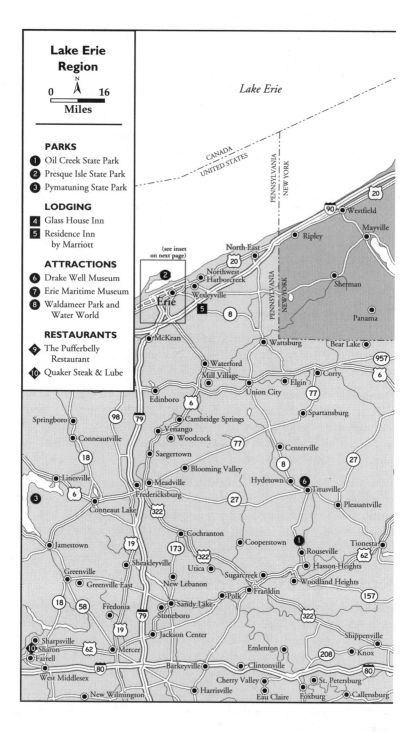

Lake Erie Region

N

0 — 16
Miles

PARKS
1. Oil Creek State Park
2. Presque Isle State Park
3. Pymatuning State Park

LODGING
4. Glass House Inn
5. Residence Inn by Marriott

ATTRACTIONS
6. Drake Well Museum
7. Erie Maritime Museum
8. Waldameer Park and Water World

RESTAURANTS
9. The Pufferbelly Restaurant
10. Quaker Steak & Lube

Lake Erie

CANADA
UNITED STATES

PENNSYLVANIA
NEW YORK

20

90 — Westfield

Ripley

Mayville

North-East

(see inset on next page)

20

Northwest Harborcreek

Sherman

Wesleyville

Erie

Panama

McKean

Wattsburg

Bear Lake

957

Waterford

Corry

6

Mill Village

Elgin

Union City

77

Edinboro

6

Spartansburg

Springboro

98

79

Cambridge Springs

Venango

Woodcock

77

Conneautville

Saegertown

Centerville

27

18

Blooming Valley

8

Linesville

Meadville

Hydetown

6

Titusville

3

6

Fredericksburg

27

Pleasantville

Conneaut Lake

322

Jamestown

19

173

Cochranton

Cooperstown

1

Rouseville

Tionesta

62

Sheakleyville

322

Hasson Heights

Greenville

Utica

Sugarcreek

Woodland Heights

Greenville East

New Lebanon

Franklin

157

18

58

Fredonia

Polk

Sandy Lake

322

Stoneboro

79

Sharpsville

19

Jackson Center

Shippenville

Sharon

62

Mercer

Emlenton

208

Knox

Farrell

Barkeyville

Clintonville

80

West Middlesex

Cherry Valley

St. Petersburg

New Wilmington

Harrisville

Eau Claire

Foxburg

Callensburg

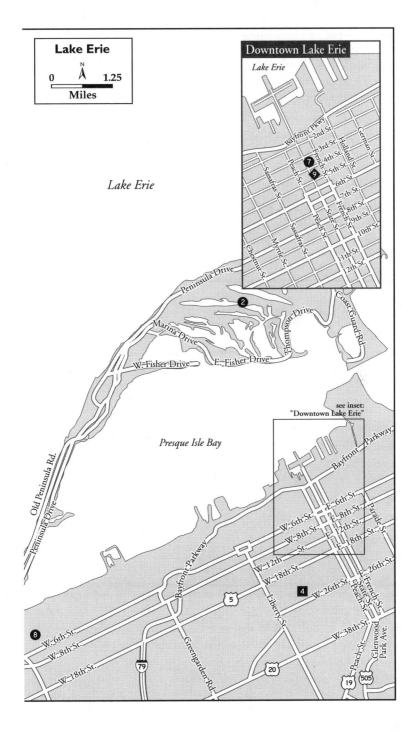

Lake Erie

0 ⫟ 1.25
Miles

Downtown Lake Erie

Lake Erie

Bayfront Pkwy.
2nd St.
3rd St.
French St.
Peach St.
4th St.
5th St.
6th St.
7th St.
8th St.
9th St.
10th St.
State St.
Peach St.
Sassafras St.
Myrtle St.
Chestnut St.
11th St.
12th St.
Holland St.
German St.
Coast Guard Rd.

7
9

Lake Erie

2

Peninsula Drive
Thompson Drive
Marina Drive
W. Fisher Drive
E. Fisher Drive

Old Peninsula Rd.
Peninsula Drive

Presque Isle Bay

see inset:
"Downtown Lake Erie"

Bayfront Parkway

W. 6th St.
W. 8th St.
E. 6th St.
E. 8th St.
E. 12th St.
E. 18th St.
Parade St.
St.

W. 12th St.
W. 18th St.

Bayfront Parkway

5

4
W. 26th St.
E. 26th St.
State St.
French St.
Peach St.

8
W. 6th St.
W. 8th St.
W. 18th St.

Greengarden Rd.
Liberty St.

W. 38th St.
Peach St.
Glenwood Park Ave.

79

20

19 **505**

Deep-Sea Fishing. A number of charter services operate out of Erie. For a list or general information, contact Pennsylvania/Lake Erie Charter Captains Association, P.O. Box 731, Fairview, PA 16415; (814) 474-2199.

Hiking. Oil Creek State Park (see The Best Parks and Beaches, above) has 52 miles of hiking trails, including one loop that circumnavigates the entire park, and a number of shorter inner loop trails. Erie National Wildlife Refuge offers a number of easy walking trails for spotting wildlife and birds; 11296 Wood Duck Lane, Guys Mills; (814) 789-3585.

Paddling. Pymatuning State Park (see The Best Parks and Beaches, above), has three marinas that rent float boats, motorboats, rowboats, canoes, and motors. French Creek Canoe & Kayak rents canoes and kayaks and offers a shuttle service as well as instruction and guided trips; P.O. Box 575, Edinboro, PA 16412; (814) 796-3366.

Family Lodging

Glass House Inn

In the heart of town, the family-owned and -operated Glass House Inn offers 30 rooms. It features an outdoor pool and free continental breakfast. Rates: $59–109. 3202 West 26th Street, Erie; (800) 956-7222 or (814) 833-7751; www.glasshouseinn.com.

Residence Inn by Marriott

Residence Inn is an all-suites hotel, and each suite has a kitchen. A breakfast buffet, an indoor pool, and other amenities are available. Rates: $99–239. 8061 Peach Street, Erie; (814) 864-2500.

Attractions

Drake Well Museum

RD 3, Titusville; (814) 827-2797; www.usachoice.net/drakewell

Hours: May–October, Monday–Saturday 9 a.m.–5 p.m. and Sunday 10 a.m.–5 p.m.; November–April, Tuesday–Saturday 9 a.m.–5 p.m. and Sunday noon–5 p.m.

Admission: $4 adults, $3.50 seniors 60 and older, $2 children ages 6–12, free for children 5 and under, $10 families

Appeal by Age Groups:

Pre-school	Grade School	Teens	Young Adults	Over 30	Seniors
★★	★★★★	★★★★	★★★★	★★★★★	★★★★★

Touring Time: Average 1½ hours, minimum 1 hour

Rainy-Day Touring: Yes

Services and Facilities:

Restaurants No	Lockers No
Alcoholic beverages No	Pet kennels No
Disabled access Yes	Rain check No
Wheelchair rental Yes; free	Private tours Yes; upon request
Baby stroller rental No	

Description and Comments   This is the site where Edwin L. Drake drilled the world's first oil well in 1859. You'll find a replica of his engine house, an oil derrick steam engine, and a wood-fired boiler. You can self-guide or join a guided tour (during summer), either way starting with the orientation video. Some 80 exhibits tell the early oil industry's story. The 219-acre grounds are a pleasant place to picnic or stroll. The Drake Well Museum also oversees the Pithole Visitor Center, located on the nearby site of a vanished 1865 oil boomtown.

Erie Maritime Museum

150 East Front Street, Erie; (814) 452-2744; www.brigniagara.org

Hours: Monday–Saturday 9 a.m.–5 p.m., Sunday noon–5 p.m.

Admission: $6 adults, $5 seniors, $3 children, $15 families; prices lower when the USS *Niagara* is not in port

Appeal by Age Groups:

Pre-school	Grade School	Teens	Young Adults	Over 30	Seniors
★★	★★★★	★★★★	★★★★	★★★★	★★★★★

Touring Time: Average 2 hours, minimum 1 hour

Rainy-Day Touring: Yes

Services and Facilities:

Restaurants Yes	Lockers No
Alcoholic beverages No	Pet kennels No
Disabled access Yes	Rain check No
Wheelchair rental Yes; free	Private tours No
Baby stroller rental No	

Description and Comments   The museum presents the story of the USS *Niagara*, a reconstructed flagship of Pennsylvania and the warship that won the Battle of Lake Erie in the War of 1812. The museum also features interactive exhibits on maritime life and the region's ecology. You can tour the *Niagara* when she's in port.

Waldameer Park and Water World

P.O. Box 8308, Route 832 North, Erie; (814) 838-3591;
www.waldameer.com

Hours: Hours vary from mid-May–Labor Day

Admission: Water World: $11.25 over 42 inches tall, $8.25 under 42
inches tall; Waldameer: $13 over 42 inches tall, $8.25 under 42 inches
tall; combination of both parks: $15.50 over 42 inches tall, $10.25
under 42 inches tall; individual ride tickets available

Appeal by Age Groups:

Pre-school	Grade School	Teens	Young Adults	Over 30	Seniors
★★★★★	★★★★★	★★★★★	★★★★★	★★★★★	★★★★★

Touring Time: Average 6 hours, minimum 4 hours

Rainy-Day Touring: No

Services and Facilities:

Restaurants Yes	Lockers Yes
Alcoholic beverages No	Pet kennels No
Disabled access Yes	Rain check No
Wheelchair rental Yes	Private tours No
Baby stroller rental Yes	

Description and Comments   This is a major water and amusement park
located just at the entrance to Presque Isle State Park. It has some 75 rides
and slides, live shows for kids and adults, and free fireworks displays Sunday and Monday of Memorial Day weekend, July Third and Fourth, and
the Sunday before Labor Day.

Family-Friendly Restaurants

THE PUFFERBELLY RESTAURANT

414 French Street, Erie; (814) 454-1557

Meals served: Lunch and dinner
Cuisine: American
Entree range: $5.95–15.95
Children's menu: Yes
Reservations: Yes
Payment: Major credit cards

A casual restaurant set in a firehouse, circa 1908. The name Pufferbelly
comes from the nickname given to the steam pumpers and engines of the

late 1800s, and the eatery is filled with antique firefighting artifacts. It's a good place to enjoy classic American fare after you've visited the Firefighters Historical Museum.

QUAKER STEAK & LUBE

101 Chestnut Street, Sharon; (724) 981-3123

Meals served: Lunch and dinner
Cuisine: American
Entree range: $5.99–14.99
Children's menu: No
Reservations: No
Payment: Major credit cards

Quaker Steak is a theme restaurant that appeals to folks who like mainstream food and fast cars. Burgers, hot wings, wraps, steaks, etc. round out the fare. Live nighttime entertainment.

Allegheny National Forest Region

North central Pennsylvania instills a sense of what this land was like when it was first settled by Europeans. Large, no, *huge* tracts of unsullied timberland stretch for miles in all directions, creating an environment that invites outdoor recreation and exploration. The towns are small, the trees are tall, and in the center of it all lies the so-called Grand Canyon of Pennsylvania—Pine Creek Gorge.

The region contains seemingly endless numbers of state parks, and each one has something worthwhile to offer. The towns include **Bradford**, where **Cook Farm** (call (814) 362-3906) re-creates an early nineteenth–century farmstead and the **Penn-Brad Oil Museum** (call (814) 362-5984) shows the 1890s oil industry. In **Wellsboro**, the **Tioga Central Railroad** (call (717) 724-0990) makes summer rides to the New York state line and back, while **Storms Horse Drawn Rides** (call (717) 376-3481) features 1.5-hour horse-drawn carriage rides and campfire meals. Another excellent train ride is the **Knox, Kane & Kinzua Railroad** (call (814) 927-8881), which runs out of **Marienville** for nearly 100 miles, crossing the famous 2,000-foot long, 300-foot high Kinsua Railroad Bridge in Kinzua State Park. Park visitors can walk across the bridge if they dare. The **Galeton** area is home to four state parks. **Cooksburg** is home to Cook Forest State Park, site of **Cook Forest Sawmill Center for the Arts** (call (814) 927- 6655), where several excellent festivals are staged through the year. At the Center for the Arts, kids can learn crafts-making skills and see art exhibits, performances, and demonstrations that run non-stop.

How to Get There

By Car. The main access is via I-80, which cuts east-west across the southern edge of the region. U.S. 6 runs parallel in the northern latitudes, and NY 17 does as well about ten miles north of the Pennsylvania/New York line. U.S. 219 runs north-south up the territory's middle, while U.S. 62 does the same along the western side.

How to Get Information before You Go

Allegheny National Forest Vacation Bureau, P.O. Drawer G, Junction 219 and 770, Custer City, PA 16725; (814) 368-9370; www.allegheny-vacation.com.

The Magic Forests Visitors Bureau, 175 Main Street, Brookville, PA 15825; (800) 348-9393 or (814) 849-5197; www.magicforests.org.

The Northern Alleghenies Vacation Region, 315 Second Avenue, Box 804, Warren PA 16365; (800) 624-7802 or (814) 726-1222.

Tioga County Visitors Bureau, 114 Main Street, Suite G, Wellsboro, PA 16901; (888) 846-4228 or (717) 724-0635; www.visittiogapa.com.

The Best Parks

Allegheny National Forest. Covering more than a half-million acres, the Allegheny Forest offers all kinds of recreational opportunities, from camping and hiking to boating and horseback riding and, in winter, cross-country skiing. (See Family Outdoor Adventures for some specific activities listings.) 222 Liberty Street, Warren; (814) 723-5150.

Cook Forest State Park. Covering 668 acres, the park is famous for its old-growth white pine and hemlock timber forest, which is classified as a National Natural Landmark and contains primeval white pine and hemlock trees ranging up to 350 years old and 200 feet tall. Recreation includes camping, log cabin camping, fishing, picnicking, swimming, canoeing, cross-country skiing, snowmobiling, sledding, and ice-skating. For an outstanding view, climb old fire tower 9. Cooksburg; (814) 744-84076.

Leonard Harrison State Park. This park is known for its spectacular vistas and views of Pine Creek Gorge, a.k.a. Pennsylvania's Grand Canyon. The hiking can be rugged, but the Pine Creek Trail, a converted railroad bed, runs through the bottom of the gorge and is great for walking and biking. RR 6, Wellsboro; (570) 724-3061.

Family Outdoor Adventures

Biking. Pine Creek Trail uses an abandoned railway along Pine Creek and features a groomed surface that's great for biking, hiking, and cross-country

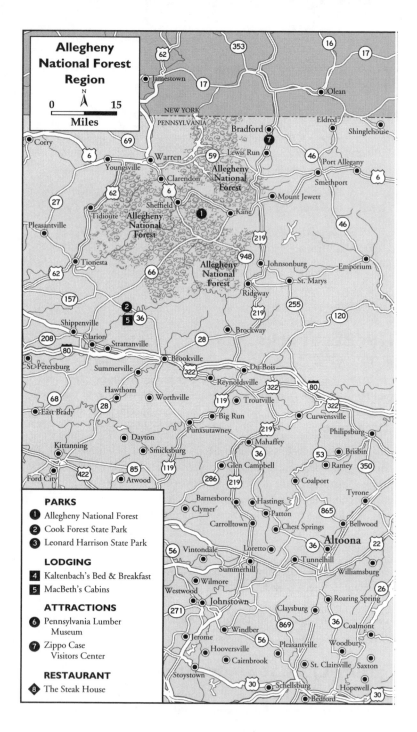

Allegheny National Forest Region

N

0 — 15
Miles

NEW YORK
PENNSYLVANIA

PARKS
1. Allegheny National Forest
2. Cook Forest State Park
3. Leonard Harrison State Park

LODGING
4. Kaltenbach's Bed & Breakfast
5. MacBeth's Cabins

ATTRACTIONS
6. Pennsylvania Lumber Museum
7. Zippo Case Visitors Center

RESTAURANT
8. The Steak House

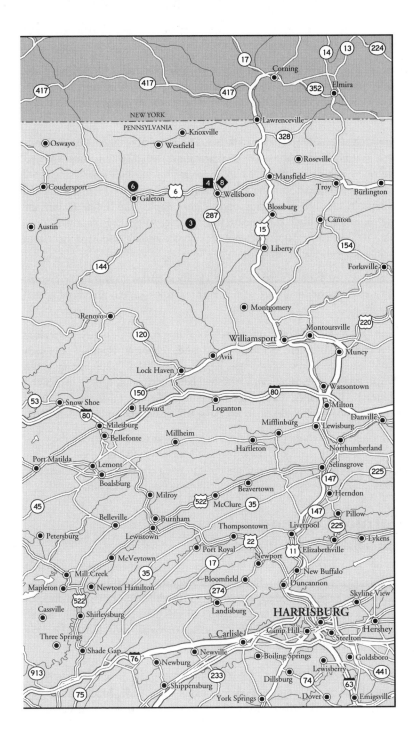

skiing. Pine Creek Outfitters Inc. rents bikes, including kid-sized bikes, trail-a-bikes, child seats, and kid-trailers. Pine Creek Outfitters runs shuttles to the Pine Creek Rail-Trail and shuttles for mountain bikers; RR 4, Wellsboro; (570) 724-3003; www.pinecrk.com.

Camping. Cook Forest State Park (see The Best Parks, above) has a family campground (Ridge Camp) open year-round with 226 tent sites. Twenty-five rustic cabins in two areas are available for families from early April through late December. The River Cabins are large, with four rooms and a fireplace, capable of sleeping up to eight people. The Indian Cabins are one-room and will accommodate four people. Allegheny National Forest (see The Best Parks, above) offers a variety of camping opportunities, from backpacking to trailer camping.

Hiking. Cook Forest State Park (see The Best Parks, above) has a 27-mile trail network, the longest of which is three miles; several are about a half-mile long.

Horseback Riding. This is great horseback riding country. Four outfitters lead rides through Allegheny National Forest lands: Flying W Ranch, (814) 463-7663; Hickory Creek Wilderness Ranch, (814) 484-7520; Spring Creek Ranch, (814) 489-5657; and Yellow Hammer Corral, (814) 463-3703. Mountain Trail Horse Center Inc. offers true Western outfitting with trips from a half-day or full day up to five days; RD 2, Wellsboro; (570) 376-5561.

Paddling. Pale Whale Canoe Livery is the largest canoe livery on the Clarion River in the heart of Cook Forest, Cooksburg; (814) 744-8300. Pine Creek Outfitters Inc. leads rafting and canoeing trips and rents canoes and kayaks; RR 4, Wellsboro; (570) 724-3003; www.pinecrk.com.

Family Lodging

Kaltenbach's Bed & Breakfast

Set on a 72-acre farm replete with sheep, pigs, and beef cattle, as well as wildlife, this ten-room inn features an all-you-can-eat country style breakfast that alone makes the trip out there worthwhile. Rooms feature king or queen beds (some have two beds), and all have private baths. Rates: $60–125 per night. Stony Fork Road, RD 6, Wellsboro; (800) 722-4954 or (570) 722-4954.

MacBeth's Cabins

Located just at the south entrance to Cook State Park, MacBeth's has 28 cabins in wooded settings. Most sleep up to eight people, one sleeps 12, and one is an apartment. A small playground and gas station/country store/gift shop are on-site. Rates $80–180 per night; weekly rates are available. Route 36, Cooksburg; (800) 331-6319 or (814) 744-8400.

Attractions

Pennsylvania Lumber Museum

5660 U.S. 6, Galeton; (814) 435-2652; www.lumbermuseum.org

Hours: April–November, daily 9 a.m.–5 p.m.; closed Columbus Day, Veterans Day, Thanksgiving Day, and the day after Thanksgiving; December–March, open by chance or by appointment

Admission: $3.50 adults, $3 seniors 60 and older, $1.50 children under age 12, $10 families

Appeal by Age Groups:

Pre-school	Grade School	Teens	Young Adults	Over 30	Seniors
★★★	★★★★★	★★★★	★★★★★	★★★★★	★★★★★

Touring Time: Average 1½ hours, minimum 1 hour

Rainy-Day Touring: Yes

Services and Facilities:

Restaurants No	Lockers No
Alcoholic beverages No	Pet kennels No
Disabled access Yes	Rain check No
Wheelchair rental Yes; free	Private tours No
Baby stroller rental No	

Description and Comments Lumber was as much a mainstay of the Pennsylvania economy as were coal and oil. This quaint museum takes you through the entire lumber-milling process. Start at the Visitor Center, where the short video serves as an intro, the Lumbermen Gallery depicts the industry's history, and another exhibit features the Civilian Conservation Corps' work in Pennsylvania. The bulk of the buildings depict a typical logging camp and a sawmill operation.

Zippo Case Visitors Center

1932 Zippo Drive, Bradford; (888) 442-1932; www.zippo.com/standard/about/zcvc

Hours: Monday–Saturday 9 a.m.–5 p.m.; closed major holidays

Admission: Free

Appeal by Age Groups:

Pre-school	Grade School	Teens	Young Adults	Over 30	Seniors
★★	★★★★	★★★★★	★★★★★	★★★★★	★★★★★

Touring Time: Average 1½ hours, minimum 1 hour

Rainy-Day Touring: Yes

Services and Facilities:

Restaurants No	Lockers No
Alcoholic beverages No	Pet kennels No
Disabled access Yes	Rain check No
Wheelchair rental No	Private tours No
Baby stroller rental No	

Description and Comments Zippo makes cigarette lighters. Case makes knives. Together this place makes one of the more unusual places you'll visit. In its 15,000 square-foot "museum," exhibits include rare Zippo lighters and Case knives. Interactive kiosks dazzle the eye with displays like a huge American flag made from nearly 3,500 red, white, and blue Zippo lighters, a "knife-in-motion" hologram, and a seven-foot audio/kinetic ball machine where the balls make their way up and down the gears and gizmos, as sounds and colors are produced. If you're lucky, the Zippo Car may be there. It's a 1947 Chrysler Saratoga–New Yorker topped by two gigantic lighters.

Family-Friendly Restaurant

THE STEAK HOUSE

29 Main Street, Wellsboro; (570) 724-9092

Meals served: Dinner
Cuisine: American
Entree range: $9.95–19.95
Children's menu: Yes
Reservations: No
Payment: Major credit cards

The Steak House is a small town restaurant in a small town. Pass up the chains and fast food places to come here and meet the locals and dine on seafood, steaks, and pasta.

Greater Pittsburgh

Located in the southwest corner of the state where the Monongahela and Allegheny rivers come together to form the Ohio River, Pittsburgh was once the steelmaking capital of the land. Back then, it was sooty, dirty, and dark. Today, it's clean, green, and one of the more family-friendly cities around. More than anything, it's a city of neighborhoods, starting with the **Downtown** area, an 11-square-block section at the point where the rivers converge. Downtown is where the major hotels, department stores, and **Point State Park,** home to **Fort Pitt Museum** (call (412) 281-9285) are located. **Oakland,** located three miles east of downtown, is home to many attractions, like the **Carnegie Museums of Art and Natural History,** but it's also the site of the **University of Pittsburgh** and **Carnegie Mellon University,** offering all the arts, culture, and good dining you'd expect to find where two major colleges are found. Be sure to take **The Nationality Rooms Tour** (call (412) 624-6000), where 24 classrooms depict the city's ethnic heritage in the University of Pittsburgh's **Cathedral of Learning** building.

The **Strip District** sounds raunchy, but it isn't—it's all about food and is one of our favorites places. You'll find an incredible wholesale and retail food market, with great restaurants and some interesting attractions, such as **The Senator John Heinz Pittsburgh Regional History Center** and, nearby, **The Society of Contemporary Crafts** (call (412) 261-7003), where everyone can create crafts or help work on an artist-designed project. Nearby, in **Shadyside,** you'll find **Sandcastle** (call (412) 465-6666), a very popular water park on the shore of the Monongahela River.

The **North Side** holds the **Andy Warhol Museum** (call (412) 237-8300) on Sandusky Street, as well as the **National Aviary,** the **Carnegie Science Center,** and **The Mattress Factory.** The **South Side,** across the Monogahela River, has **Station Square** (call (412) 471-5808), where you

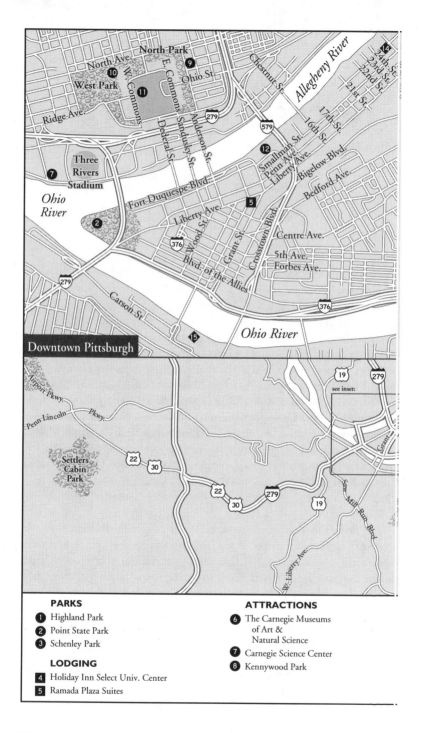

Downtown Pittsburgh

Allegheny River

Ohio River

Ohio River

North Park
West Park
Three Rivers Stadium

North Ave.
W. Commons
E. Commons
Ohio St.
Ridge Ave.
Anderson St.
Sandusky St.
Dedeal St.
Chestnut St.
17th St.
16th St.
21st St.
22nd St.
23rd St.
24th St.
Fort-Duquespe Blvd.
Smallman St.
Penn Ave.
Liberty Ave.
Bigelow Blvd.
Bedford Ave.
Liberty Ave.
Crosstown Blvd.
Grant St.
W. Pool St.
Centre Ave.
5th Ave.
Forbes Ave.
Blvd. of the Allies
Carson St.

279 · 579 · 376

Airport Pkwy.
Penn-Lincoln Pkwy.
Settlers Cabin Park
San Mill Run Blvd.
Grant
W. Liberty Ave.
see inset:

19 · 279 · 22 · 30

PARKS
1. Highland Park
2. Point State Park
3. Schenley Park

LODGING
4. Holiday Inn Select Univ. Center
5. Ramada Plaza Suites

ATTRACTIONS
6. The Carnegie Museums of Art & Natural Science
7. Carnegie Science Center
8. Kennywood Park

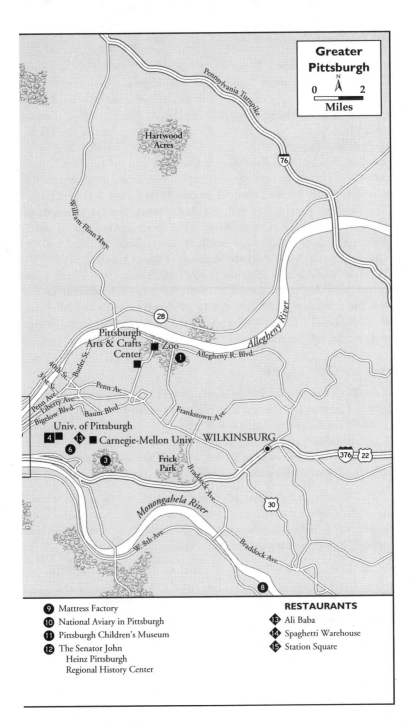

Greater Pittsburgh

0 ⋀ 2
N
Miles

Pennsylvania Turnpike

Hartwood Acres

76

William Flinn Hwy.

28

Pittsburgh Arts & Crafts Center ■ Zoo ❶

Allegheny River

Allegheny R. Blvd.

40th St.
31st St.
Butler St.

Penn Av.
Penn Ave.
Liberty Ave.
Bigelow Blvd.
Baum Blvd.

Frankstown Ave.

Univ. of Pittsburgh
❹ ■ ⓭ ■ Carnegie-Mellon Univ. WILKINSBURG
❻
❸
Frick Park
376 22

Monongahela River

Braddock Ave.

30

W. 8th Ave.
Braddock Ave.

❽

❾ Mattress Factory
❿ National Aviary in Pittsburgh
⓫ Pittsburgh Children's Museum
⓬ The Senator John
   Heinz Pittsburgh
   Regional History Center

RESTAURANTS
⓭ Ali Baba
⓮ Spaghetti Warehouse
⓯ Station Square

can board the **Gateway Clipper Fleet** (call (412) 355-7980) for a river tour. Above Station Square stands **Mt. Washington,** where the inclines offer a unique ride and great views and Grandview Avenue is lined with restaurants. The **Pittsburgh Zoo** (call (412) 665- 3640), with its Discovery Kingdom, is also on the south side of the Monogahela in the **Highland Park** section.

Beyond the city, **Tour-Ed Mine & Museum** (call (412) 224-4720) in **Tarentum** is a hard-hat, underground experience. In the northwest of the city in **New Castle** are the **Living Treasures Animal Park** (call (412) 924-9571), an exotic petting zoo, and the **Harlansburg Station Museum of Transportation** (call (724) 652-9002), which houses planes, trains, automobiles, and trucks of all kinds. **Avella,** about an hour southwest of the city, is home to the **Meadowcroft Museum of Rural Life** (call (412) 587-3412). The Meadowcroft Museum covers 16,000 years of life, as this site contains the oldest archeological evidence of human habitation in the region, but it focuses on life 150 years ago. **Pennsylvania Trolley Museum** (call (412) 228-9256) in **Washington** is yet another Pennsylvania site where you can ride wonderful old trolleys and see how they're restored.

HOW TO GET THERE

By Car. From the east, the Pennsylvania Turnpike (I-76) passes just east of the city. Leave it at I-376 to get into town. From the west, leave the Turnpike at I-79 South, and take that to I-279 South. From the north, take I-79 to I-279, as well. And, from the south, I-79 comes up from Morgantown, West Virginia. I-70 arrives from Wheeling, West Virginia, in the west, connecting to I-79 at Washington, Pennsylvania.

By Plane. Pittsburgh International Airport is among the most pleasant airports in the country, rather a cross between an airport and a major shopping mall. It's a hub for US Airways and is served by most major carriers; Route 60 North, Pittsburgh; (412) 472-5526.

By Train. Amtrak services Pittsburgh with three major trains daily through the downtown Union Station; (412) 471-6172 or (800) 872-7245.

THE INCLINES

What's an incline? It's a kind of cable railway (operated by attaching a rail car to a moving cable, just like the San Francisco cable cars) that's able to carry people up steep hillsides. Pittsburgh has two, each on the south side of the Monongahela, ascending Mount Washington. The **Duquesne Incline** is at 1220 Grandview Avenue, (412) 381-1665, while the **Monongahela Incline,** (412) 442-2000, leaves from Station Square. Both give a fun ride and great city views.

GETTING AROUND TOWN

Public transportation works pretty well in Pittsburgh. The "T," as the subway system is called, is a high-class operation, with art on display and classical music playing. Travel is free within the downtown area or $1 to cross the river to Station Square; the line also runs above ground to the southern suburbs. The bus system does a good job of connecting downtown to North Side and Oakland attractions; for information, contact Port Authority Transit Downtown Service Center, 534 Smithfield Street; (412) 442-2000. For those getting around by car, the city has instituted signage they call The Wayfinder System, which divides the city into five sections, each represented by signs of a different color; the Purple Belt creates a loop that leads the way to major attractions.

HOW TO GET INFORMATION BEFORE YOU GO

Greater Pittsburgh Convention & Visitors Bureau, Four Gateway Center, Pittsburgh, PA 15222; (800) 366-0093 or (412) 281-7711; www.pittsburgh-cvb.org.

The Best Parks

Highland Park. Highland is a 500-acre park that holds the Pittsburgh Zoo and a large reservoir with walkways and a bridge. Also in the park are a swimming pool with a wading pool, ten playgrounds, picnic areas, woodland trails, tennis courts, a softball field, sand volleyball courts, and a half-mile bike track/velodrome; Highland Avenue, Highland Park neighborhood.

Point State Park. Located at the Golden Triangle, where the rivers meet, this park has a paved, waterside promenade and is the site of the Fort Pitt Museum; in the Downtown neighborhood.

Schenley Park. Site of the Vintage Grand Prix and Smoky City Folk Festival, Schenley Park also hosts twice-weekly, summertime Cinema in the Parks free movies. There's an ice skating/in-line skating rink, cross-country skiing, and sled riding, as well as picnic areas, a swimming pool, six playgrounds, running and walking tracks and trails, tennis courts, and ballfields; Schenley Drive, Oakland neighborhood.

Family Lodging

Holiday Inn Select University Center

Recently renovated, this hotel is within walking distance of the University of Pittsburgh, many museums, and Schenley Park. A downtown bus stops at the door; leave the bus at the Smithfield Street Bridge, and from there you can walk across the bridge to Station Square. There's also a complimentary downtown shuttle. Rooms have coffee makers, irons and ironing boards, hair dryers, and cable TV. The hotel has a restaurant and indoor pool. Rates $109–155; children under age 18 stay free with parents; bed and breakfast packages are available. 100 Lytton Avenue, Pittsburgh; (412) 682-6200.

Ramada Plaza Suites and Conference Center

This Ramada is an all-suites hotel with junior or one- and two-bedroom suites. The hotel has an indoor pool and health club and an on-site restaurant. Suites have kitchenettes with coffee makers, microwaves, and refrigerators. Rates $99–300; ask about special "Getaway Packages." One Bigelow Square, Pittsburgh; (800) 225-5858 or (412) 281-5800.

Attractions

The Carnegie Museums of Art and Natural Science

4400 Forbes Avenue, Pittsburgh; (412) 622-3131; www.clph.org/moa

Hours: Tuesday–Saturday 10 a.m.–5 p.m. and Sunday 1–5 p.m.; closed Mondays and legal holidays

Admission: $6 adults, $5 seniors 62 and older, $4 children ages 3 and up and full-time students

Appeal by Age Groups:

Pre-school	Grade School	Teens	Young Adults	Over 30	Seniors
★★★	★★★★★	★★★★★	★★★★★	★★★★★	★★★★★

Touring Time: Average 3 hours, minimum 2 hours

Rainy-Day Touring: Yes

Services and Facilities:

Restaurants Yes	Baby stroller rental No
Alcoholic beverages Yes	Lockers Yes; coatroom
Disabled access Yes	Pet kennels No
Wheelchair rental Yes; free, call	Rain check No
(412) 622-3343	Private tours No

Description and Comments   The two museums are next door to each other, and one admission covers both. Natural History is a good fit for younger kids. The dinosaur collection is one of the best, and three's a Discovery Room for hands-on stuff. Bonehunters Quarry is an interactive fossil dig, and Earth Theater, a state-of-the-art digital theater with a wraparound screen, is definitely a kick. Computer kids go for Xtreme Earth, where 14 computer terminals relay earth, life, and environmental science news.

There's also geology, minerals, gems, fossils, and a cool interactive exhibit that explores the earth's interrelated natural and human resources. There's more, of course, including a whole section on insects and another on life at the north and south poles.

The art museum features a lot of Impressionist and modern works. The free Kids & Families ARTventures are of particular interest, as they involve hands-on art-making in the museum's galleries. Children can participate with or without parents for a few minutes or most of the day.

Carnegie Science Center

One Allegheny Avenue, Pittsburgh; (412) 237-3400;
www.CarnegieScienceCenter.org

Hours: Sunday–Friday 10 a.m.–6 p.m. and Saturday 10 a.m.–9 p.m.; closed Thanksgiving, Christmas, and New Year's days

Admission: Museum: $10 adults, $8 seniors 62 and older and children ages 3–18; Museum and Omnimax: $14 adults, $10 seniors 62 and older and children ages 3–18

Appeal by Age Groups:

Pre-school	Grade School	Teens	Young Adults	Over 30	Seniors
★★★★	★★★★★	★★★★★	★★★★★	★★★★★	★★★★★

Touring Time: Average 3 hours, minimum 2 hours

Rainy-Day Touring: Yes

Services and Facilities:

Restaurants Yes	Lockers Yes
Alcoholic beverages No	Pet kennels No
Disabled access Yes	Rain check No
Wheelchair rental Yes; free	Private tours No
Baby stroller rental Yes; free	

Description and Comments This is a terrific science museum with some 250 hands-on exhibits, an Omnimax Theater, a Digistar II Planetarium, and a World War II submarine to climb aboard. The problem, if there is one, is what to do first and how to schedule everything. We especially like the Weather Center, Vision Science, and the Sport Creative Technology Center. But we also like the SeaLife Aquarium and the live demonstrations at the ScienceStage and The Works Kitchen Theater, where cooking becomes a science.

Kennywood Park

4800 Kennywood Boulevard, West Mifflin; (412) 461-0500;
www.kennywood.com

Hours: Late April–mid-May, Saturday and Sunday 10:30 a.m.–10 p.m.; mid-May–Labor Day, daily 10:30 a.m.–10 p.m.

Admission: $22.95 Saturday and Sunday, $18.95 Monday–Friday, $7.50 guests over 21 or those subject to Kennywood's ride limitations due to height or physical restrictions; children under 3 enter free but pay for rides; general admission buyers can purchase individual ride tickets at 25 cents each or books of 20 tickets for $5 each; most adult rides require three to six tickets each; kiddieland requires one to two tickets per ride

Appeal by Age Groups:

Pre-school	Grade School	Teens	Young Adults	Over 30	Seniors
★★★★★	★★★★★	★★★★★	★★★★★	★★★★★	★★★★★

Touring Time: Average 6 hours, minimum 4 hours

Rainy-Day Touring: No

Services and Facilities:

Restaurants Yes	Lockers Yes
Alcoholic beverages No	Pet kennels No
Disabled access Yes	Rain check No
Wheelchair rental No	Private tours No
Baby stroller rental Yes	

Description and Comments An amusement park that's earned National and State Historic Landmark status, Kennywood features 31 major rides, including three wooden roller coasters, something called the Exterminator Roller Coaster, water rides, and a Kiddieland for the little ones. For an extra fee, you can play mini-golf, pilot paddleboats, and scare yourself to death on the Skycoaster. You'll also find games and arcades throughout the park. This one's a classic. *Note:* A $29.95 one-price pass good at Idlewild Park, Kennywood, the Pittsburgh Zoo, and Aquarium and Sandcastle Water Park can be bought on the Internet through a link at the Kennywood website, or by calling (800) 432-9386.

Mattress Factory

500 Samsonia Way, Pittsburgh; (412) 231-3169; www.mattress.org

Hours: Tuesday–Saturday 10 a.m.–5 p.m. and Sunday 1–5 p.m.; closed August

Admission: $6 adults, $4 seniors 55 and older and students, free for children ages 12 and under; free for everyone on Thursdays

Appeal by Age Groups:

Pre-school	Grade School	Teens	Young Adults	Over 30	Seniors
★★★★	★★★★★	★★★★★	★★★★★	★★★★★	★★★★★

Touring Time: Average 2 hours, minimum 1 hour

Rainy-Day Touring: Yes

Services and Facilities:

Restaurants No	Lockers No
Alcoholic beverages No	Pet kennels No
Disabled access Yes	Rain check No
Wheelchair rental Yes; free	Private tours Yes, with 3 weeks
Baby stroller rental No	notice; fee required

Description and Comments An old mattress factory has been converted into a unique museum specializing in site-specific art environments. They offer a printed student guide that makes it all a bit more comprehensible, but even without it, this is art-as-fun. You're going to want to try out the garden piece that encourages you to crawl through some tunnels and climb stairs to literally get inside the artwork. Another work features some neat lighting effects. This is near the Andy Warhol Museum, so you can make a whole day of kid-friendly art-going.

National Aviary in Pittsburgh

Allegheny Commons, West Pittsburgh; (412) 323-7235; www.aviary.org

Hours: Daily 9 a.m.–5 p.m.; closed Christmas Day

Admission: $5 adults, $4 seniors 60 and older, $3.50 children ages 2–12, free for children under age 2

Appeal by Age Groups:

Pre-school	Grade School	Teens	Young Adults	Over 30	Seniors
★★★★	★★★★★	★★★★★	★★★★★	★★★★★	★★★★★

Touring Time: Average 3 hours, minimum 2 hours

Rainy-Day Touring: Yes

Services and Facilities:

Restaurants No	Lockers Yes; coatroom
Alcoholic beverages No	Pet kennels No
Disabled access Yes	Rain check No
Wheelchair rental Yes; free	Private tours Yes
Baby stroller rental No	

Description and Comments The country's only independent avarian zoo, it holds more than 500 birds, representing over 200 different species. The free-flight atrium allows you to see the birds in action, and the staff always seems to have some hands-on demo going. For private tours, call (412) 323-7235 ext. 209 one week ahead of your visit.

Pittsburgh Children's Museum

10 Children's Way, Allegheny Center, Pittsburgh; (412) 322–5058;
www.pittsburghkids.org

Hours: During the school year, Tuesday, Thursday, and Saturday 10
a.m.–5 p.m., Friday 10 a.m.–8 p.m., and Sunday noon–5 p.m.;
mid-June–August, Monday–Saturday 10 a.m.–5 p.m. and Sunday
noon–5 p.m.

Admission: $5 adults, $4.50 seniors and children, free for children under
age 2; $3.50 for everyone on Thursdays; closed on major holidays

Appeal by Age Groups:

Pre-school	Grade School	Teens	Young Adults	Over 30	Seniors
★★★★★	★★★★★	★★	★★★	★★★★	★★★★

Touring Time: Average 4 hours, minimum 2 hours

Rainy-Day Touring: Yes

Services and Facilities:

Restaurants Yes	Lockers Yes; coatroom
Alcoholic beverages No	Pet kennels No
Disabled access Yes	Rain check No
Wheelchair rental No	Private tours No
Baby stroller rental No	

Description and Comments   Here's another of the excellent hands-on, participatory children's museums available to this younger generation. Set in the
classic Old Post Office Building, the museum makes much ado about Mr.
Rogers, whose TV show originated in Pittsburgh. They've also got a two-story
climbing environment, artworks to make, airplanes to make and fly, performances starring their own mascot, Stuffee, and a whole bunch of things to do
with puppets. Plus, there's a special new area for infants and toddlers.

The Senator John Heinz Pittsburgh Regional History Center

1212 Smallman Street, Pittsburgh; (412) 454-6000; www.pghhistory.org

Hours: Daily 10 a.m.–5 p.m.; closed Easter, Thanksgiving, Christmas
and New Years days

Admission: $6 adults, $4.50 seniors 62 and older and students, $3 chil-
dren ages 6–18

Appeal by Age Groups:

Pre-school	Grade School	Teens	Young Adults	Over 30	Seniors
★★★	★★★★★	★★★★★	★★★★★	★★★★★	★★★★★

Touring Time: Average 2 hours, minimum 1 hour

Rainy-Day Touring: Yes

Services and Facilities:

Restaurants Yes	Lockers Yes
Alcoholic beverages No	Pet kennels No
Disabled access Yes	Rain check No
Wheelchair rental Yes; free	Private tours Yes
Baby stroller rental Yes; free	

Description and Comments   One of Pittsburgh's newest museums, this one covers regional history from 1750 to today with lots of hands-on and interactive stuff. You're greeted by a robot, a trolley car, and a Conestoga wagon. You'll want to make a beeline for Discovery Place, where the hands-on experience is based on putting you into the lives of eight real-life kids, who did things like pack pickles and work in steel mills.

Family-Friendly Restaurants

ALI BABA

404 South Craig Street, Pittsburgh; (412) 682-2829

Meals served: Lunch and dinner
Cuisine: Middle Eastern
Entree range: $7.50–11.50 (dinner)
Children's menu: No
Reservations: No
Payment: Major credit cards

Only open Monday through Friday, this fine, easy-going place, serves Middle Eastern fare with enough plain stuff (like omelets and chicken in tomato sauce) to satisfy most picky kids. It's in the heart of university country, so it's usually lively and filled with international students.

SPAGHETTI WAREHOUSE

2601 Smallman Street, Pittsburgh; (412) 261-6511

Meals served: Lunch and dinner
Cuisine: Italian
Entree range: $6.95–19.95
Children's menu: Yes
Reservations: Yes
Payment: Major credit cards

A chain, it's true, but just the kind of thing that makes dining easy. It's not too exotic for conservative eaters. It's in the Strip District.

Station Square

Station Square is the hungry family's paradise, filled with an array of at least a dozen and a half riverside eateries, ranging from pizza and fast food to full gourmet, including some that are local and many chain names you'll recognize. It's a good bet if you're going on a Gateway Clipper cruise, up the Incline, or to a concert at I.C. Light Amphitheatre.

Part Three

Delaware

They call it "The First State." Why? Because its representatives were the first
to sign the Declaration of Independence. Delaware's also a pretty small
state. But it abounds in things to do, especially in its largest city, Wilmington, and along the shore. We start in northern Delaware, exploring **Wilmington, Newark,** and the countryside just south of Philadelphia. Then we
move south into central Delaware, site of **Dover,** the state capital, and
much history. We finish in southern Delaware, home to some of the East's
favorite shore towns, particularly **Rehoboth Beach.** Delaware may be
tightly packed between New Jersey, Pennsylvania, and Maryland, but don't
let that fool you. It's a pretty and fun place to visit. And remember, too, that
Delaware has no sales tax, so it can be a shopper's paradise.

Delaware's Not-to-Be-Missed Attractions	
Northern Delaware	Brandywine Creek State Park Fort Delaware State Park Hagley Museum Winterthur Museum
Central Delaware	Bombay Hook National Wildlife Refuge Air Mobility Command Museum Johnson Victrola Museum
Southern Delaware	Rehoboth Beach Cape Henlopen State Park

How to Get Information before You Go

Delaware Tourism Office, 99 Kings Highway, P.O. Box 1410, Dover, DE 19903; (800) 441-8846 or (302) 739-4271, fax (302) 739-4271; www.state.de.us.

Calendar of Festivals and Events

January

Northern Delaware: Hagley's Invention Convention. The Hagley Museum celebrates inventions of all kinds. Wilmington; (302) 658-2400.

February

Northern Delaware: Victorian Valentine Days. The Hagley Museum now celebrates an old-fashioned Valentine's Day. Wilmington; (302) 658-2400.

March

Northern Delaware: Spring Children's Festival. The Delaware Museum of Natural History becomes Kids Central. Wilmington; (302) 658-9111.

April

Northern Delaware: Brandywine Zoo's Earth Day Celebration. What better place to celebrate Earth Day than with the animals? Wilmington; (302) 571-7850 ext. 209.

Southern Delaware: Great Delaware Kite Festival. Cape Henlopen State Park is filled with kites and more kites. Lewes; (302) 645-8983.

May

Northern Delaware: St. Hedwig Polish Festival. Wilmington celebrates all things Polish. Polka, anyone? (302) 594-1402.

Northern Delaware: Eighth Annual Civil War Reenactment. The war comes to Brandywine Creek State Park. Montchanin; (302) 655-5740.

Central Delaware: Old Dover Days. A major festival in the state capital. Dover; (302) 734-1736.

June

Northern Delaware: Greek Festival. The city turns its attention to things Greek. Wilmington; (302) 654-4447.

Southern Delaware: Delmarva Chicken Festival. The chicken-raising capital of the world honors its favorite bird, including frying up hundreds of them in the world's largest frying pan.

Note: This festival moves around the Delmarva peninsula—one year in Delaware, the next in Maryland—so call for locale information; (302) 856-9037.

Southern Delaware: Delmarva Hot-Air Balloon and Craft Festival. A huge ballooning event. Milton; (302) 684-8404.

July

Central Delaware: Delaware State Fair. Delaware's big one. Harrington; (302) 398-3269.

Southern Delaware: Delaware Seashore Sandcastle Contest. How big can you build it? Dewey Beach; (302) 227-2800.

August

Northern Delaware: Garrison Weekend. Fort Delaware State Park arms for battle. Delaware City; (302) 834-7941.

Southern Delaware: Nanticoke River Festival. This little town comes alive with activities. Seaford; (302) 629-9690.

September

Northern Delaware: Craft Festival at Winterthur. Crafts and arts of all kinds at the museum. Wilmington; (302) 888-4600. Brandywine Arts Festival. Arts and crafts of all kinds in Brandywine Park. Wilmington; (302) 529-0761.

Southern Delaware: Nanticoke Indian Pow Wow. The state's major Native American festival. Millsboro; (302) 945-3400. Coastal Music and Arts Festival. Food, foot stompin', and other good stuff at the shore. Bethany Beach; (302) 537-2700.

October

Northern Delaware: Halloween Trail. Ghostly happenings at Cape Henlopen State Park. Lewes; (302) 645-6852.

Southern Delaware: Rehoboth Beach Jazz Festival. The entire shore from Rehoboth to Dewey Beach gets rhythm. (800) 296-8742.

November

Southern Delaware: World Championship Punkin Chunkin Competition. A local tradition—tossing chunks of pumpkin as far as you can—plus food, games, and other good stuff. Millsboro; (302) 856-1444.

December

Central Delaware: Farmer's Christmas. The Delaware Agricultural Museum and Village does Christmas the old-fashioned and rural way. Dover; (302) 734-1618.

Cool Web Sites for Delaware-Bound Kids

State of Delaware Kids Page: www.state.de.us/kidspage

General facts and information about Delaware:
www.50states.com/delaware.htm

The Groundhogs at HogHaven—groundhogs (or woodchucks) that live near Lums Pond State Park in Bear, Delaware:
www.hoghaven.com

Biographies of famous Delawareans:
www.state.de.us/facts/history/intrbio.htm

History of the early settlement of Delaware: www.geocities.com/siliconvalley/way/9301/historyday.html

---

Northern Delaware

Northern Delaware is pretty small, a piece of land wedged between New Jersey and Maryland. But it holds the state's largest city, Wilmington, and the University of Delaware in nearby Newark. Beyond the gleaming office towers of downtown Wilmington lies an antique neighborhood, **Quaker Hill Historic District** (call (302) 658-9295), which actually was the city's first residential neighborhood, settled in 1738. Three of the original homes survive, plus excellent examples of nineteenth-century architecture. Pick up a self-guided walking tour map at the visitors center. The **Old Town Hall Museum** (call (302) 655-7161) on Market Street, a building of Georgian-style architecture, houses Delaware history and arts exhibits. The **Kalmar Nyckel Shipyard** (call (302) 429-7447) holds a re-creation of the *Kalmar Nyckel,* a circa-1638 ship that brought Swedish settlers to the area; the replica functions as a living history museum. The shipyard itself delves into shipbuilding history. Just south in New Castle, the **Museum of the American Road** (call (302) 658-8800) is a motorcycle dealership/repair shop with a restaurant (see Family-Friendly Restaurants) and displays of motorcycle esoterica—like the only Harley-Davidson to have been ridden around the world. The **Delaware Museum of Natural History** (call (302) 658-9111), on Route 52 between Greenville and Centreville, offers a look at nature from prehistoric times forward. In Newark more Delaware birds, mammals, insects, reptiles, fossils, minerals, and prehistoric artifacts can be studied at the **Iron Hill Museum of Natural History** (call (302) 368-5703); the museum also maintains three nature trails. The **University of Delaware Mineralogical Museum** (call (302) 831-8242) shows off a lot of stones, rocks, and other such stuff that usually fascinates little boys.

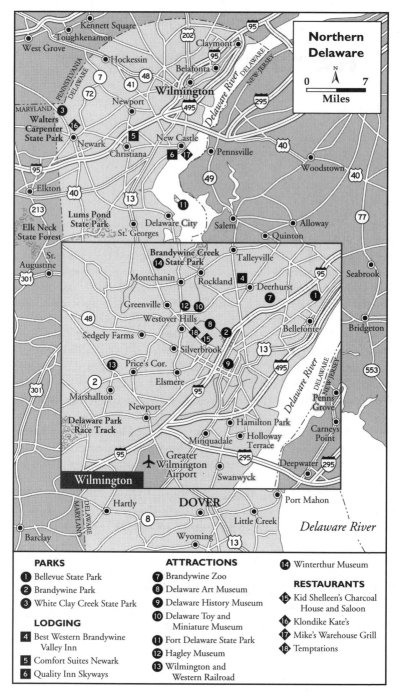

Northern Delaware

N

0 ⎯⎯⎯ 7

Miles

Wilmington

PARKS

1 Bellevue State Park
2 Brandywine Park
3 White Clay Creek State Park

LODGING

4 Best Western Brandywine Valley Inn
5 Comfort Suites Newark
6 Quality Inn Skyways

ATTRACTIONS

7 Brandywine Zoo
8 Delaware Art Museum
9 Delaware History Museum
10 Delaware Toy and Miniature Museum
11 Fort Delaware State Park
12 Hagley Museum
13 Wilmington and Western Railroad

14 Winterthur Museum

RESTAURANTS

15 Kid Shelleen's Charcoal House and Saloon
16 Klondike Kate's
17 Mike's Warehouse Grill
18 Temptations

How to Get There

By Car. I-95 (the Delaware Turnpike) is the main highway through the region; it travels through both Newark and Wilmington. U.S. 13 and State Route 1 parallel the coast north-south, while U.S. 301 parallels the Delaware/Maryland border south of Newark.

By Plane. Philadelphia International Airport is the closest to this region; Philadelphia, PA 19153; (215) 492-3181.

By Train. Amtrak provides regular service into Wilmington; (800) 872-7245. SEPTA provides commuter rail service between Philadelphia and Wilmington; (215) 580-7800.

How to Get Information before You Go

Greater Wilmington Convention and Visitors Bureau, 1300 Market Street, Suite 504, Wilmington, DE 19801; (800) 422-1181 or (302) 652-4088.

The Best Parks

Bellevue State Park. The park covers 328 acres and has hiking trails, a jogging track, a fishing pond, bicycling paths, tennis courts, game courts, picnic grounds, nature programs, and a regular schedule of summertime concerts. 800 Car Road, Wilmington, DE 19809; (302) 577-3390.

Brandywine Park. Set in the heart of Wilmington, this 1,000-acre park encompasses 14 miles of hiking trails and many open fields. You can fish (with the proper license) in Brandywine Creek and Wilsons Run, or canoe the Brandywine in a canoe rented from the park office. The Brandywine Creek Nature Center offers a variety of interpretive programs, as well as special programs in storytelling and folk music. They offer a nifty introduction-to-backpacking program—all gear supplied—on certain weekends. P.O. Box 3782, Wilmington, DE 19807; (302) 577-3534.

White Clay Creek State Park. A 2,500-acre oasis in the midst of suburbia, the park offers 20 miles of hiking trails, a fitness trail, a large picnic area, fishing, equestrian trails, a refreshment stand, and a series of nature programs and summer concerts; 425 Wedgewood Road, Newark, DE 19711; (302) 369-6900.

Family Outdoor Adventures

Hiking. White Clay Creek State Park and Brandywine Park (see The Best Parks, above).

Horseback Riding. Carousel Farm Riding Stable offers trail rides, hayrides, lessons, and pony rides; 3700 Limestone Road, Wilmington, DE 19808; (302) 999-1922.

Paddling. Brandywine Park (see The Best Parks, above). Wilderness Canoe Trips organizes two- and four-hour canoe and tubing trips on the Brandywine River that are excellent for beginners; 2111 Concord Pike, Wilmington, DE 19803; (302) 654-2227.

Family Lodging

Best Western Brandywine Valley Inn

A full-service facility with 98 rooms, pool, wading pool, a dozen efficiency units, and special packages that include admission to various area attractions.

1807 Concord Pike, Wilmington, DE 19803; (302) 656-9436. Rates $79–132.

Comfort Suites Newark

A 65-room all-suites property with an indoor pool, exercise area, free continental breakfast, in-room movies and coffee, and two TVs in each suite.

56 Old Baltimore Pike, Newark, DE 19701; (800) 322-5999 or (302) 266-6600. Rates $79–119.

Quality Inn Skyways

A 100-room property in a central location to many attractions, with a pool, wading pool, horseshoe and volleyball courts, in-room coffee, and an on-site restaurant.

147 North Dupont Highway, New Castle, DE 19720; (800) 775-7352 or (302) 328-6666. Rates $69–109.

Attractions

Brandywine Zoo

Brandywine Park, 1001 North Park Drive, Wilmington, DE 19802; (302) 571-7850; www.k12.de.us/warner/zoointro.htm

Hours: Daily 10 a.m.–4 p.m.

Admission: $3 adults, $1.50 seniors 62+ and children ages 3–11; free November–March

Appeal by Age Groups:

Pre-school	Grade School	Teens	Young Adults	Over 30	Seniors
★★★★★	★★★★★	★★★	★★★★	★★★★	★★★★

Touring Time: Average 3 hours, minimum 1½ hours

Rainy-Day Touring: Yes

Services and Facilities:

Restaurants Yes; snack bar	Lockers No
Alcoholic beverages No	Pet kennels No
Disabled access Yes	Rain check No
Wheelchair rental No	Private tours No
Baby stroller rental No	

Description and Comments A small but delightful zoo that offers some great programs for kids from 18 months to 6 years old, who must be accompanied by an adult. Program activities include meeting the animals up close and personal, storytelling, crafts, and other events. There's a program fee of $7 per child; call or visit the Web site for dates. Another program, "Animal Tales," is designed for all ages.

Delaware Art Museum

2301 Kentmere Parkway, Wilmington, DE 19806; (302) 571-9590; www.delart.org

Hours: Tuesday and Thursday–Saturday 9 a.m.–4 p.m., Wednesday 9 a.m.–9 p.m., Sunday 10 a.m.–4 p.m.

Admission: $7 adults, $5 seniors, $2.50 students, free for children 6 and under; free on Wednesday evenings

Appeal by Age Groups:

Pre-school	Grade School	Teens	Young Adults	Over 30	Seniors
★★★	★★★★	★★★★	★★★★★	★★★★★	★★★★★

Touring Time: Average 2 hours, minimum 1 hour

Rainy-Day Touring: Yes

Services and Facilities:

Restaurants Yes	Lockers Yes; coatroom
Alcoholic beverages No	Pet kennels No
Disabled access Yes	Rain check No
Wheelchair rental Yes	Private tours Yes, for a $25 fee;
Baby stroller rental No	call ahead

Description and Comments The museum holds a significant collection of nineteenth- and twentieth-century American art, from Winslow Homer and Thomas Eakins to Edward Hopper and Andrew Wyeth. But, for younger kids, the big attraction here is the participatory gallery, where they can use a variety of media and tools to create their own artworks.

Delaware History Museum

505 Market Street, Wilmington, DE 19801; (302) 655-7161;
www.hsd.org

Hours: Monday–Friday noon– 4 p.m., Saturday 10 a.m.– 4 p.m.

Admission: $4 adults, $3 seniors 65+ and students, $2 children 18 and
under, free for children under 2

Appeal by Age Groups:

Pre-school	Grade School	Teens	Young Adults	Over 30	Seniors
★★★★	★★★★★	★★★★	★★★★	★★★★★	★★★★★

Touring Time: Average 2 hours, minimum 1 hour

Rainy-Day Touring: Yes

Services and Facilities:

Restaurants No	Lockers Yes
Alcoholic beverages No	Pet kennels Yes
Disabled access Yes	Rain check No
Wheelchair rental No	Private tours No
Baby stroller rental No	

Description and Comments   Here's Delaware history, dating from the earliest European settlements of the 1600s, brought to life in a 1940s Woolworth store, using high-tech, interactive exhibitions. Most noteworthy: the Grandma's Attic Discovery Center, where kids 12 and under can put their hands on history: there are vintage clothes to wear, old-fashioned toys to play with, history games to try, old books and magazines to browse through, and a 1940s market/corner store to shop at—after which they can sort, store, and play with their purchases in the 1940s kitchen. The museum's other galleries offer changing exhibits for all ages.

Delaware Toy and Miniature Museum

P.O. Box 4053, Route 141, Wilmington, DE 19807; (302) 427-8697;
www.thomes.net/toys

Hours: Tuesday–Saturday 10 a.m.– 4 p.m., Sunday noon– 4 p.m.

Admission: $5 adults, $4 seniors 62+, $3 children 12 and under, free for
children 2 and under

Appeal by Age Groups:

Pre-school	Grade School	Teens	Young Adults	Over 30	Seniors
★★	★★★★	★★★★	★★★★	★★★★★	★★★★★

Touring Time: Average 2 hours, minimum 1 hour

Rainy-Day Touring: Yes

Services and Facilities:

Restaurants No	Lockers No
Alcoholic beverages No	Pet kennels No
Disabled access Yes	Rain check No
Wheelchair rental No	Private tours Yes
Baby stroller rental No	

Description and Comments   One of only three museums of its kind in the country, this unique site displays dollhouses, dolls, and toys dating from 1770 and miniature vases dating back to 600 B.C. It's a fascinating look at antique (and some contemporary) dollhouses, miniature furniture, dolls, toys, trains, boats, and planes from Europe and America. There are more than 100 dollhouses in all, and then there are those teeny vases—some 700 of them, from a dozen and a half countries, ranging in size from half an inch to five inches tall.

Fort Delaware State Park

P.O. Box 170, Delaware City, DE 19706; (302) 834-7941

Hours: Mid-June–Labor Day, Wednesday–Sunday and holidays 10 a.m.–6 p.m.; Labor Day–end of September and late-April–mid-June, Saturday–Sunday and holidays 10 a.m.–6 p.m.

Admission: Ferry: $6 adults, $4 children ages 2–12

Appeal by Age Groups:

Pre-school	Grade School	Teens	Young Adults	Over 30	Seniors
★★★	★★★★	★★★★	★★★★★	★★★★★	★★★★★

Touring Time: Average 3 hours, minimum 1½ hours

Rainy-Day Touring: Yes

Services and Facilities:

Restaurants Yes; concession stand	Lockers No
Alcoholic beverages No	Pet kennels No
Disabled access Yes	Rain check No
Wheelchair rental Yes	Private tours Yes, free; reserve
Baby stroller rental Yes	ahead

Description and Comments   Fort Delaware was built as a Union fortress in 1859 and was used during the Civil War as a prison for captured Confederate soldiers. You reach the fort via a half-mile ferry ride to Pea Patch Island, followed by a short jitney ride. From that point on it's 1863, and you're guided through the fort by interpreters in historic dress. There's lots of hands-on stuff to do—help the blacksmith, do the laundry, prepare food, or see the soldiers load up and fire the eight-inch cannon—plus a variety of exhibits about the island's past.

Hagley Museum

Route 141, P.O. Box 3630, Wilmington, DE 19807; (302)-658-2400;
www.hagley.org

Hours: March 15–December 30, daily 9:30 a.m.–4:30 p.m.; January 1–
March 14, Saturday–Sunday 9:30 a.m.–4:30 p.m.; closed Thanksgiving
Day, Christmas Day, and December 31

Admission: $9.75 adults, $7.50 students and seniors, $3.50 children ages
6–14, $26.50 family, free for children under 6

Appeal by Age Groups:

Pre-school	Grade School	Teens	Young Adults	Over 30	Seniors
★	★★★	★★★★	★★★★	★★★★★	★★★★★

Touring Time: Average 3 hours, minimum 1½ hours

Rainy-Day Touring: Yes

Services and Facilities:

Restaurants Yes	Lockers Yes; coatroom
Alcoholic beverages No	Pet kennels No
Disabled access Yes	Rain check No
Wheelchair rental Yes; free	Private tours No
Baby stroller rental No	

Description and Comments   The museum traces American manufacturing
and economic history through interpretive displays and living history reenactments depicting nineteenth-century life. The grounds cover some 235
acres along the Brandywine River on the site of the original Du Pont mills,
estate, and gardens. Kids tend to like the working mill, antique automobiles, and working machine shop, as well as the powdermen and machinists
who demonstrate the water turbine, steam engine, gunpowder tester, and
other machines. The Blacksmith Hill section focuses on the social and family history of the workers who operated the powder mills. A number of kid-
friendly special events are staged during the course of the year, such as the
annual Storybook Garden Party in late April.

Wilmington and Western Railroad

Greenbank Station, Route 41, P.O. Box 5787, Wilmington, DE 19808;
(302) 998-1930; www.wwrr.com

Hours: Vary according to season

Admission: $8–12 adults, $5–7 children, $7 seniors 60+, free for children
under 2; prices vary according to specific train ride and special events

Appeal by Age Groups:

Pre-school	Grade School	Teens	Young Adults	Over 30	Seniors
★★★	★★★★★	★★★★	★★★★	★★★★★	★★★★★

Touring Time: Varies according to train ride

Rainy-Day Touring: Varies according to train ride

Services and Facilities:

Restaurants Yes; snack bar	Lockers No
Alcoholic beverages No	Pet kennels No
Disabled access No	Rain check No
Wheelchair rental No	Private tours No
Baby stroller rental No	

Description and Comments The main attraction here is the turn-of-the-century steam engine. The trip travels through the Red Clay Valley, revealing nice scenery and some interesting history. Some trains utilize an antique diesel engine, so ask before you commit yourself, especially if the steam engine is what you prefer. The railroad operates many special events— special kids' days, dinner trains, murder mystery tours, a Civil War skirmish ride, trips with the Easter Bunny and Santa Claus, and the Trick or Treat Halloween Express.

Winterthur Museum

Route 52, Winterthur, DE 19735; (800) 448-3883 or (302) 888-4600; www.winterthur.org

Hours: Monday–Saturday 9 a.m.–5 p.m., Sunday noon–5 p.m.; closed Thanksgiving, Christmas, and New Year's days

Admission: $8 adults, $6 seniors 62+ and students, $4 children ages 5–11, free for children under 5

Appeal by Age Groups:

Pre-school	Grade School	Teens	Young Adults	Over 30	Seniors
★	★★★	★★★★	★★★★★	★★★★★	★★★★★

Touring Time: Average 3½ hours, minimum 2 hours

Rainy-Day Touring: Yes

Services and Facilities:

Restaurants Yes	Lockers No
Alcoholic beverages Yes	Pet kennels No
Disabled access Yes	Rain check No

Wheelchair rental Yes   Private tours No
Baby stroller rental Yes

Description and Comments   The museum displays Henry Francis du Pont's collection of decorative arts made or used in America between 1640 and 1860, the largest collection of its kind. The galleries present an introductory exhibition, "Perspectives on the Decorative Arts in Early America," while the period rooms can be explored through 45-minute guided tours. Kids will best like the Touch-It Room, where they can dress up in vintage clothes and play old-time games. The Dominy Clock Shop and Woodworking Shop will also hold their interest. These are reconstructions of the shops used by four generations of artisans who made clocks, chairs, case pieces, looking glasses, and tables from the mid-1700s to the mid-1800s, complete with photographs, templates, machinery, and tools.

The gardens here cover 1,000 acres. A good way to explore them is on the garden tram. It follows a regular schedule, weather permitting, and stops at designated locations throughout the garden, allowing you to get on and off and mix your walking with some riding

Family-Friendly Restaurants

KID SHELLEEN'S CHARCOAL HOUSE AND SALOON

14th and Scott Streets, Wilmington; (302) 658-4600

Meals served: Lunch and dinner
Cuisine: American
Entree range: $5.95–16.95 (lunch and dinner)
Children's menu: Yes
Reservations: Yes
Payment: Major credit cards

Steaks, ribs, enchiladas, pizza, seafood—this hip spot has a bit of everything, and it's a good value. You can eat on the patio or inside, and even though there can be a busy bar scene, kids are more than welcome.

KLONDIKE KATE'S

158 East Main Street, Newark; (302) 737-6100

Meals served: Lunch and dinner
Cuisine: American, with fajitas and some Italian dishes
Entree range: $8.95–17.95
Children's menu: Yes

Reservations: Yes
Payment: Major credit cards

This is a major hangout for University of Delaware undergrads and thus can get raucous in the evenings. But it's set in a building that's been functioning as some kind of a restaurant or tavern since at least 1757, with the exception of 1905–15, when it functioned as a courtroom and jail. (The jail cells are still there, in the basement.) The food is straight-ahead, middle-of-the-road stuff that won't surprise anyone but won't draw complaints either. In summer, you can dine outside.

MIKE'S WAREHOUSE GRILL

2164 New Castle Avenue, New Castle; (302) 658-5900

Meals served: Breakfast, lunch, and dinner
Cuisine: American
Entree range: $2.95–6.95 (breakfast, lunch, and dinner)
Children's menu: Yes
Reservations: Yes
Payment: Major credit cards

A theme restaurant attached to a motorcycle museum and Harley Davidson dealership/repair shop. The ambience is converted warehouse, with huge windows through which motorcycles can often be seen coming and going. A steel racking grid serves as a dining counter. Or you can choose the Boiler Room, a faux boiler large enough to seat six. Flashing lights simulate welding arcs, while rusty chains, gears and cogs comprise the wall art, and diners can watch motorcycle mechanics work on bikes through a special window adjacent to the restaurant. The food, by the way, runs to burgers and such, but that doesn't really matter much.

TEMPTATIONS

11 Trolley Square #A, Wilmington; (302) 429-9162

A local favorite for ice cream or sandwiches, in the heart of things.

Central Delaware

Dover, the state capital, is this region's major city. You can visit **Legislative Hall** (call (302) 739-5807 or (302) 739-4114), meeting site for the state's General Assembly, on weekdays, and take a guided tour of the **State House** (call (302) 739-4266), the state's symbolic capitol—a building dating from 1792 that contains period and reproduction furnishings and an eighteenth-century courtroom and legislative chamber. It's located on **The Green,** a square laid out in 1717 in accordance with the orders of William Penn, and the site where the Declaration of Independence was read to the public and where Delaware voted to ratify the U.S. Constitution (it was the first state to do so). Nearby, the **Delaware Archaeology Museum** (call (302) 739-4266) occupies a 1790 church on Meeting House Square. It houses exhibits illustrating Delaware's archaeology, history, and culture. The **John Dickinson Plantation** (call (302) 739-3277), located south of town on Route 113, is a Revolutionary War–era farm with outbuildings and a log cabin typifying eighteenth-century life in Kent County.

In the region's southern section, the town of **Harrington** is home to the **Harrington Museum** (call (302) 398-3698), which houses displays of local historical artifacts, including household items, a miniature re-creation of Harrington circa 1910, and an old-fashioned soda fountain and kitchen. The **Harrington Railroad Museum** (call (302) 398-3698) has a preserved signal tower, a restored 1926 caboose, and a crossing guard watchman's house. The **Messick Agricultural Museum** (call (800) 237-1272 or (302) 398-3729) looks at past life on the farm through old tractors, implements, tools, smokehouse equipment, and the first tractor John Deere ever made.

HOW TO GET THERE

By Car. The main north-south access is via U.S 13, which runs from Wilmington to Dover and on south to Harrington. State Route 1 and U.S. 113 parallel it more to the east.

By Plane. Philadelphia International Airport is the closest to this region; Philadelphia, PA 19153; (215) 492-3181.

By Train. Amtrak provides daily service into Wilmington and Philadelphia; (800) 872-7245.

HOW TO GET INFORMATION BEFORE YOU GO

Central Delaware Chamber of Commerce, 9 East Lockerman Street, Dover, DE 19904; (302) 678-0892.

The Best Parks

Bombay Hook National Wildlife Refuge. Located east of Smyrna in the region's center, just off Route 9, the refuge covers 15,978 acres and has been created as a haven for waterfowl and other migratory birds. One interesting option is to obtain an interpretive audiocassette tape at the visitors center and then follow the 12-mile auto tour route, which includes a few observation towers. The refuge also has several nature trails, ranging from one-quarter mile to one mile long, three of which lead to 30-foot observation towers. The refuge is open daily from sunrise to sunset; the visitors center is open Monday–Friday 8 a.m.– 4 p.m. 2591 Whitehall Neck Road, Smyrna, DE 19977; (302) 653-6872; www2.newszap.com/community/bombayhook.

Killens Pond State Park. Located a mile east of U.S. 13, south of Felton, the park offers camping, camping cabins, and the state's only water park. The 66-acre lake is the park's centerpiece. It can be explored by canoe, kayak, or rowboat, all of which can be rented during the summer months, and also offers good fishing. Paddleboats and surf bikes can also be rented. Paddlers can take on the Murderkill River Canoe Trail. Other recreational options include extensive hiking trails, a disc golf course, a bike path, and ball courts. But certainly the park's biggest attraction is its water park. It features water slides, bubblers, a tot pool with little slides, lap swimming lanes, and a full bathhouse and concession area. 5025 Killens Pond Road, Felton, DE 19943; (302) 284-4526; www.destateparks.com/kpsp/kpsp.htm.

Silver Lake Park. A city park featuring play areas, swimming, fishing, a fitness trail, and a launching ramp for small boats. Entrances from Washington Street, Dover, DE 19901; (302) 736-7050.

Family Outdoor Adventures

Camping. Killens Pond State Park (see The Best Parks, above) has 59 full-service sites with electric and water hookups, accommodating tents and/or RVs, plus tent-only, primitive camping at 17 secluded sites. Ten camping cabins and one lake-view cottage are also available. The cabins sleep four and are outfitted with an efficiency kitchen, eating area, bedroom, bath

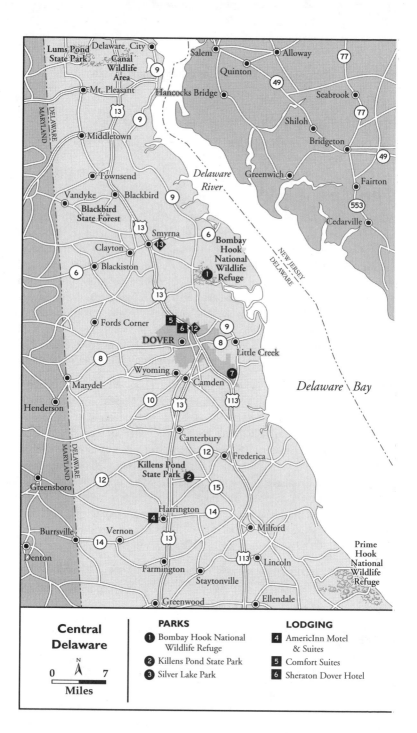

Central Delaware

N

0 —— 7

Miles

PARKS

1 Bombay Hook National
Wildlife Refuge

2 Killens Pond State Park

3 Silver Lake Park

LODGING

4 AmericInn Motel
& Suites

5 Comfort Suites

6 Sheraton Dover Hotel

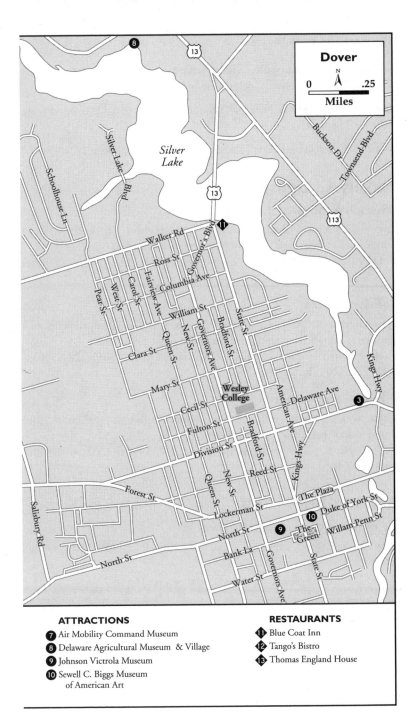

Dover

0 .25
Miles

Silver Lake

Silver Lake Blvd

Schoolhouse Ln

Buckson Dr

Townsend Blvd

Walker Rd

Governor's Blvd

Ross St

Columbia Ave

Fairview Ave

Carol St

West St

Pear St

William St

New St

Queen St

Governors Ave

Bradford St

State St

Clara St

Mary St

Cecil St

Wesley College

American Ave

Delaware Ave

Fulton St

Kings Hwy

Division St

Bradford St

Reed St

New St

Queen St

Forest St

Salisbury Rd

Lockerman St

The Plaza

Duke of York St

Willam Penn St

North St

The Green

North St

Bank La

Governors Ave

State St

Water St

Kings Hwy

ATTRACTIONS
⑦ Air Mobility Command Museum
⑧ Delaware Agricultural Museum & Village
⑨ Johnson Victrola Museum
⑩ Sewell C. Biggs Museum
   of American Art

RESTAURANTS
⑪ Blue Coat Inn
⑫ Tango's Bistro
⑬ Thomas England House

with shower, air-conditioning, heat, picnic table, grill, and porch. Subject to availability, cabin rentals include the use of a canoe and rowboats.

Hiking. Bombay Hook National Wildlife Refuge and Killens Pond State Park (see The Best Parks, above).

Paddling. Killens Pond State Park (see The Best Parks, above).

Family Lodging

AmericInn Motel and Suites

Forty-eight rooms and suites, located 18 miles south of Dover, with an indoor pool and hot tub and complimentary continental breakfast.

1259 Corn Crib Road, Harrington, DE 19952; (302) 398-3900. Rates $77–97.

Comfort Suites

A 64-room motel with an outdoor pool and suites equipped with coffeemakers, mini-refrigerators, and microwaves.

1654 North DuPont Highway, Dover, DE 19901; (800) 228-5150 or (302) 736-1204. Rates $84–200.

Sheraton Dover Hotel

A hotel with 153 large, well-appointed rooms, a fully equipped health club, heated indoor pool, and on-site dining.

1570 North DuPont Highway, Dover, DE 19901; (302) 678-8500. Rates $95–105.

Attractions

Air Mobility Command Museum

1301 Heritage Road, Dover Air Force Base, DE 19902; (302) 677-5938; www.amcmuseum.org

Hours: Daily 9 a.m.–4 p.m.; closed on federal holidays

Admission: Free

Appeal by Age Groups:

Pre-school	Grade School	Teens	Young Adults	Over 30	Seniors
★★	★★★★	★★★★★	★★★★★	★★★★★	★★★★★

Touring Time: Average 2 hours, minimum 1 hour

Rainy-Day Touring: Yes

Services and Facilities:

Restaurants No	Lockers No
Alcoholic beverages No	Pet kennels No
Disabled access Yes	Rain check No
Wheelchair rental Yes	Private tours Yes; call ahead
Baby stroller rental No	

Description and Comments Located on Dover Air Force Base, the museum displays vintage aircraft and artifacts showing military airplane and Dover Air Force Base history. During World War II, Hangar 1301 was the site of a secret rocket development program. Among the planes on view there today are a C-47 used on D-Day, a C-141 four-engine jet transport, a B-17G Flying Fortress, and a P-51 Mustang.

Delaware Agricultural Museum and Village

866 North DuPont Highway, Dover, DE 19901; (302) 734-1618; www.agriculturalmuseum.org

Hours: April–December, Tuesday–Saturday 10 a.m.–4 p.m. and Sunday 1 p.m.–4 p.m.; January–March, Monday–Friday 10 a.m.–4 p.m.

Admission: $3 adults, $2 seniors 59+ and children ages 6–17, free for children 5 and under

Appeal by Age Groups:

Pre-school	Grade School	Teens	Young Adults	Over 30	Seniors
★★	★★★★	★★★★	★★★★★	★★★★★	★★★★★

Touring Time: Average 2½ hours, minimum 1½ hours

Rainy-Day Touring: Yes

Services and Facilities:

Restaurants No	Lockers No
Alcoholic beverages No	Pet kennels No
Disabled access Yes; partially	Rain check No
Wheelchair rental Yes	Private tours Yes; call ahead
Baby stroller rental Yes	

Description and Comments The museum shows village life and farm life in central Delaware in the 1890s. Antique tractors, farming implements, and other artifacts dating from 1670 through 1950 are on display. Buildings on the site include an old-time sawmill, a barbershop, a one-room schoolhouse, a farmhouse, and blacksmith and wheelwright shops. Living history programs and nineteenth-century arts and crafts workshops are offered seasonally; call or visit their Web site to obtain the schedule.

Johnson Victrola Museum

Bank Lane and New Street, Dover DE 19901; (302) 739-4266;
www.destatemuseums.org

Hours: Tuesday–Saturday 10 a.m.–3:30 p.m.; closed Sundays, Mondays,
and state holidays

Admission: Free

Appeal by Age Groups:

Pre-school	Grade School	Teens	Young Adults	Over 30	Seniors
★★	★★★★	★★★★★	★★★★★	★★★★★	★★★★★

Touring Time: Average 1½ hours, minimum 1 hour

Rainy-Day Touring: Yes

Services and Facilities:

Restaurants No	Lockers No
Alcoholic beverages No	Pet kennels No
Disabled access Yes	Rain check No
Wheelchair rental No	Private tours Yes
Baby stroller rental No	

Description and Comments   This nifty museum is a tribute to Eldridge Reeves Johnson, inventor of the Victrola and founder of the Victor Talking Machine Company. The theme is a 1920s Victrola retail store, which is filled with an extensive collection of talking machines, Victrolas, early recordings, and memorabilia. A wonderful chance to take the kids back to their grandparent's heyday—so maybe you should bring the grandparents along.

Sewell C. Biggs Museum of American Art

406 Federal Street, Dover, DE 19901; (302) 674-2111;
www.biggsmuseum.org

Hours: Wednesday–Saturday 10 a.m.–4 p.m., Sunday 1:30–4:30 p.m.;
closed Monday, Tuesday, and state holidays

Admission: Free

Appeal by Age Groups:

Pre-school	Grade School	Teens	Young Adults	Over 30	Seniors
★	★★	★★★★	★★★★★	★★★★★	★★★★★

Touring Time: Average 2 hours, minimum 1 hour

Rainy-Day Touring: Yes

Services and Facilities:

Restaurants No	Lockers Yes; coatroom
Alcoholic beverages No	Pet kennels No
Disabled access Yes	Rain check No
Wheelchair rental No	Private tours Yes
Baby stroller rental No	

Description and Comments This is a rather serious art museum with an impressive collection of fine and decorative arts, covering 200 years of American cultural history, and including some emphasis on works from and about Delaware. There are 14 galleries in all. It's a place best suited to older and more mature children.

Family-Friendly Restaurants

BLUE COAT INN

800 North State Street, Dover; (302) 674-1776

Meals served: Lunch and dinner
Cuisine: American/seafood
Entree range: $4.25–24.95 (lunch and dinner)
Children's menu: Yes
Reservations: Yes
Payment: AE, DC, MC, V

The lakeside setting is pleasant, and the seafood is excellent, as are the steak and poultry dishes. The Blue Coat is well regarded and a longtime local favorite.

TANGO'S BISTRO

Sheraton Dover Hotel, 1570 North DuPont Highway, Dover; (302) 678-8500

Meals served: Lunch and dinner
Cuisine: American
Entree range: $4.95–24.95 (lunch and dinner)
Children's menu: Yes
Reservations: Yes
Payment: Major credit cards

A touch of California in Delaware, and certainly very convenient if you're staying at the Sheraton. The food's excellent, and the atmosphere is upscale and contemporary.

THOMAS ENGLAND HOUSE

1165 South DuPont Boulevard, Smyrna; (302) 653-1420

Meals served: Lunch and dinner
Cuisine: Continental
Entree range: $4.95–28.95 (lunch and dinner)
Children's menu: Yes
Reservations: Yes
Payment: AE, DC, MC, V

This is a converted Greek Colonial–style mansion dating from 1711 that has five dining rooms, fine food, and a very attentive staff. Seafood is the specialty; there's excellent prime rib as well, plus poultry and beef.

Southern Delaware

Southern Delaware is prime beach country. The ocean and Delaware Bay playgrounds draw visitors from all over the East and the Midwest. But it's not all water play down here. In the inland town of Bridgeville, the **Firehouse Museum** (call (302) 739-5318) shows off antique firefighting equipment. Millsboro, in south-central Delaware, holds the **Nanticoke Indian Museum** (call (302) 945-7022) of the Nanticoke tribe, who stage an impressive pow-wow over Labor Day weekend. South of Bridgeville, in Seaford, the **UNOI Grain Mill** (call (302) 629-4083) is Delaware's last operating flour mill; it's been producing and selling corn meal, Dove brand flour, and buckwheat pancake mixes since 1885. Just west of town, the **Woodland Ferry** (call (302) 629-9690), a cable-operated vessel, still crosses the Nanticoke River, as it has done since 1793. East of Seaford, the **Seacoast Speedway** (call (302) 629-5720) stages stock and vintage car racing in Georgetown. In the region's far southern reaches, NHRA drag racing takes place at the U.S. 13 Dragway (call (302) 846-3968) in Delmar. Between Bridgeville and the coast, Milton is home to the **Lydia Ann B. Cannon Museum** (call (302) 684-3256), where early shipbuilding tools and artifacts are displayed.

Along the shore, in Lewes (pronounced "Lewis"), the **Cannonball House Marine Museum** (call (302) 645-7670 or (302) 645-8073) is housed in a building that was struck by a cannonball during the War of 1812. From **Fisherman's Wharf** (call (302) 645-8862) board fishing or dolphin- and whale-watching cruises are available. **Queen Anne's Railroad** (call (302) 644-1720) runs one-hour scenic trips from July to Labor Day, plus dinner and murder mystery trains. Between Bethany Beach and Dewey Beach, the **Indian River Lifesaving Station** (call (302) 227-0478) was built in 1876 and now displays the history and artifacts of the "surfmen" who rescued sailors and ship passengers in the nearby sea. In North Ocean City, the **Fenwick Island Lighthouse** (call (302) 539-2100)—opened in 1859—can be toured on select summer days.

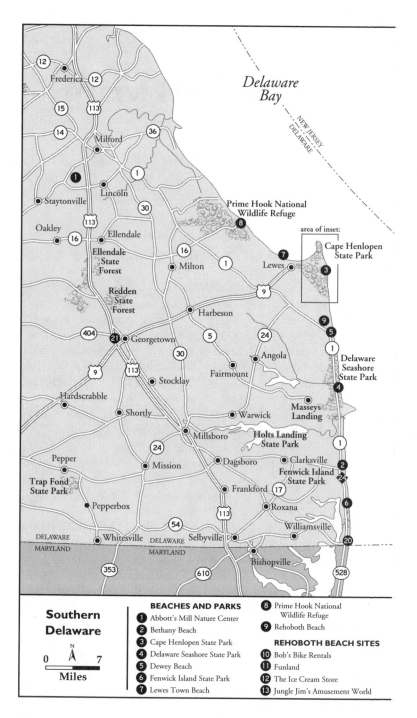

Delaware
Bay

NEW JERSEY
DELAWARE

area of inset:
Cape Henlopen
State Park

Prime Hook National
Wildlife Refuge

Frederica

Milford

Lincoln

Staytonville

Oakley

Ellendale

Ellendale
State
Forest

Milton

Redden
State
Forest

Harbeson

Lewes

Georgetown

Angola

Fairmount

Stocklay

Hardscrabble

Shortly

Warwick

Masseys
Landing

Delaware
Seashore
State Park

Millsboro

Holts Landing
State Park

Pepper

Mission

Dagsboro

Clarksville

Fenwick Island
State Park

Trap Fond
State Park

Frankford

Roxana

Pepperbox

Williamsville

DELAWARE
MARYLAND

Whitesville

DELAWARE
MARYLAND

Selbyville

Bishopville

Southern Delaware

N

0 ——— 7
Miles

BEACHES AND PARKS

1. Abbott's Mill Nature Center
2. Bethany Beach
3. Cape Henlopen State Park
4. Delaware Seashore State Park
5. Dewey Beach
6. Fenwick Island State Park
7. Lewes Town Beach
8. Prime Hook National
   Wildlife Refuge
9. Rehoboth Beach

REHOBOTH BEACH SITES

10. Bob's Bike Rentals
11. Funland
12. The Ice Cream Store
13. Jungle Jim's Amusement World

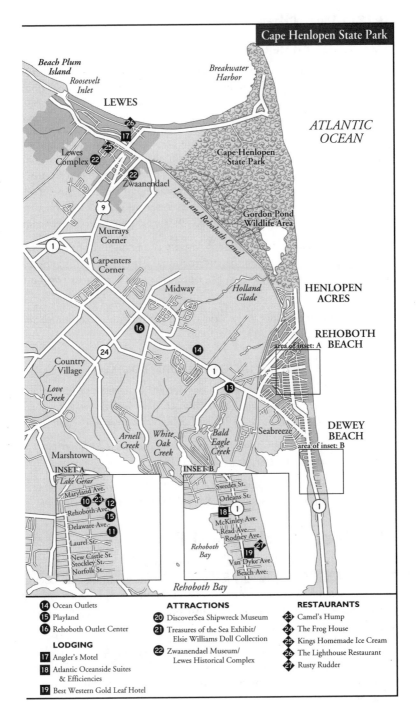

Beach Plum
Island
Roosevelt
Inlet

Breakwater
Harbor

LEWES

Lewes
Complex

Zwaanendael

Cape Henlopen
State Park

ATLANTIC
OCEAN

Gordon Pond
Wildlife Area

Murrays
Corner

Carpenters
Corner

Midway

Holland
Glade

HENLOPEN
ACRES

Country
Village

Love
Creek

Arnell
Creek

White
Oak
Creek

Bald
Eagle
Creek

Seabreeze

REHOBOTH
BEACH

area of inset: A

DEWEY
BEACH

area of inset: B

Marshtown

INSET A

Lake Gerar

Maryland Ave.

Rehoboth Ave.

Delaware Ave.

Laurel St.

New Castle St.
Stockley St.
Norfolk St.

INSET B

Swedes St.

Orleans St.

McKinley Ave.
Read Ave.
Rodney Ave.

Rehoboth
Bay

Van Dyke Ave.
Beach Ave.

Rehoboth Bay

14 Ocean Outlets
15 Playland
16 Rehoboth Outlet Center

LODGING

17 Angler's Motel
18 Atlantic Oceanside Suites
& Efficiencies
19 Best Western Gold Leaf Hotel

ATTRACTIONS

20 DiscoverSea Shipwreck Museum
21 Treasures of the Sea Exhibit/
Elsie Williams Doll Collection
22 Zwaanendael Museum/
Lewes Historical Complex

RESTAURANTS

23 Camel's Hump
24 The Frog House
25 Kings Homemade Ice Cream
26 The Lighthouse Restaurant
27 Rusty Rudder

How to Get There

By Car. Coming from Wilmington and the north, follow State Route 9 to State Route 1; from Dover, follow U.S. 113 to State Route 1. Coming from the south, U.S. 13 is the main thoroughfare; take it to U.S. 9 eastbound. From Baltimore and the west, follow U.S. 50 to State Route 404.

By Ferry. The Cape May–Lewes Ferry runs between Cape May, New Jersey, and Lewes, Delaware. It's a 70-minute trip that's very pleasant in good weather and open to folks with cars, on foot, or with bikes. There's a snack bar on board, and occasionally there's entertainment. Shuttle bus service into Lewis and Rehoboth Beach is available. Reservations are recommended during summer weekends. (800) 643-3779; www.capemay-lewesferry.com.

By Plane. Philadelphia International Airport is one airport option; (215) 492-3181. Baltimore/Washington International Airport (BWI) is another; (800) 435-9294 or (410) 859-7111. Both are about a one- to two-hour drive from the region.

By Train. Amtrak provides daily service into Wilmington, Baltimore, and Philadelphia. (800) 872-7245.

How to Get Information before You Go

Rehoboth Beach–Dewey Beach Chamber of Commerce and Visitor Center, 501 Rehoboth Avenue, P.O. Box 216, Rehoboth Beach, DE 19971; (800) 441-1329 or (302) 227-2233; www.beach-fun.com.

Lewes Chamber of Commerce and Visitors Bureau, 120 Kings Highway, Lewes, DE 19958; (302) 645-8073.

Southern Delaware Tourism, P.O. Box 240, Georgetown, DE 19947; (800) 357-1818 or (302) 856-1818; www.visitdelaware.com.

The Best Beaches and Parks

Abbott's Mill Nature Center. Located southwest of Milford, this is a Delaware Nature Society Facility featuring a historic gristmill, a number of hiking trails, and canoeing at Abbott's Pond. Nature programs are offered year-round for all ages and families. Just off U.S. 113; (302) 422-0847; www.delawarenaturesociety.org.

Bethany Beach. A small, quiet place with an easygoing feel, a boardwalk lined with low-rise condominiums, and a small downtown area. The town beach is pleasant, and changing rooms are available. Nearby is Fenwick Island State Park.

Cape Henlopen State Park. Cape Henlopen has the best beaches in the area—two of them. The northern swimming area has a modern bathhouse with showers, changing rooms, and a food concession. Umbrella rentals are available at both. In addition, the park has a fishing pier, surf fishing, a campground, nature trails, some neat World War II defense bunkers to clamber around in, and two observation towers that afford great views of the park and the bay. The Cape Henlopen Seaside Nature Center, (302) 645-6852, has aquariums and a touch tank and presents a range of programs, from beach hikes and dolphin watching to canoe trips and crabbing lessons. The park also has hiking trails and a nature trail. 42 Cape Henlopen Drive, Lewes; (302) 645-8983, campground (302) 645-2103; www.dnrec. state.de.us/parks/dsp1st.htm.

Delaware Seashore State Park. The park is tucked between the ocean, Rehoboth Bay, and Indian River Bay and has some excellent beaches, two lifeguarded ocean swimming areas, and bathhouses with snack bars and umbrellas/chair/raft rentals. There's a short nature trail that yields salt-marsh views, and a large campground. Inlet 850, Rehoboth Beach; (302) 227-2800; www.destateparks.com/dssp/dssp.htm.

Dewey Beach. The beach in Dewey Beach is relatively undeveloped and far less crowded than that in Rehoboth Beach, but it has no changing facilities, so it's a good option only if you're lodging here. The excellent beaches of Delaware Seashore State Park are just a few minutes away. Route 1, Dewey Beach; (302) 227-2233.

Fenwick Island State Park. Covering three miles of barrier island between Bethany Beach and Fenwick Island, the park encompasses 344 acres and is another excellent spot for noncommercial beachgoing. There's a bathhouse with a gift shop and snack bar, and you can rent not only umbrellas, chairs, and rafts but also sailboards, Jet-Skis, and catamarans. Naturalist-led beach walks are offered each Wednesday afternoon in summer. C/o Holts Landing State Park, P.O. Box 76, Routes 1 and 54, Millville; (302) 539-9060; www.destateparks.com/fenwick/fisp.htm.

Lewes Town Beach. The beach here stretches for about a mile on the Delaware Bay and is a particularly good place for families with smaller children due to its lack of crowds and large waves and the adjacent parking lot, bathhouse, concession stand, and boogie board and raft rentals; (302) 645-8073.

Prime Hook National Wildlife Refuge. This pristine refuge has two major hiking trails (one of which is a boardwalk trail through the marshlands), boat ramps, and seven miles of canoe trails. County Road 236, Milton; (302) 684-8419.

Rehoboth Beach

Delaware's major beach town, Rehoboth Beach, lies within easy driving distance of Ocean City, Maryland, and Assateague National Seashore. The boardwalk is lively, with all the requisite shops. The small downtown area offers a range of shopping and eating. Free concerts are staged at the boardwalk band shell at the end of Rehoboth Avenue. And out on busy Route 1, the main road leading into town, the outlet malls are sprouting up like weeds, letting folks take advantage of the absence of sales tax. The town beach can get crowded, and it offers no bathhouse/changing facilities, although rest rooms can be found at Maryland and Delaware Avenues. The south end of the beach has become something of a gay haven—a fact to be aware of in case it bothers or attracts you.

Parking can be a pain. The main areas are metered—and closely monitored. Residential streets require a parking permit. There are metered lots as well.

Transportation The Jolly Trolley runs between Rehoboth Beach and Dewey Beach; (302) 227-1197. A park-and-ride bus runs during summer months on Route 1 between Rehoboth Beach and Dewey Beach, with service to the outlet malls and the town center; (800) 553-3278. From mid-June through Labor Day, daily shuttle bus service is offered from the Cape May–Lewes Ferry terminal to Rehoboth Beach and the outlet mall; weekend service is available in the spring and autumn; (302) 644-6030.

Reheboth Beach Amusements

Beach Food. The Ice Cream Store serves up homemade ice cream, Rehoboth Avenue at Boardwalk; (302) 227-4609. Grotto Pizza, a regional chain, has seven full-service locations in the area, plus seasonal spots on the Rehoboth Beach and Dewey Beach boardwalks.

Bike Rentals. Bob's Bike Rentals offers bicycles and bike/surreys for kids and adults; First and Maryland Avenues; (302) 227-7996.

Funland. You'll find rides, games, and an arcade at Boardwalk and Delaware Avenue; (302) 227-1921.

Jungle Jim's Amusement World. Just off Route 1, it has three go-cart tracks, a water slide, baseball batting cages, bumper boats, and other attractions; 273 Country Club Road, Rehoboth, DE 19971; (302) 227-8444.

Miniature Golf. Coastal Golf, Highway 1; (302) 227-4653. Shell We Golf and Sea Shell Shop, 4405 Highway 1; (302) 227-4323. Bayside Adventures, Highway 1 at Collins Street; (302) 226-2012.

Playland. This arcade is located at Boardwalk and Wilmington Avenue; (302) 226-1415.

Shopping. Stop at the visitors center and pick up a copy of Beach and Bay Outlet Shopper, or visit www.outletsonline.com to get the overview of all the options. The two major outlet shopping malls are: Rehoboth Outlet Center, with some 50 stores; Route 1 at Midway, Rehoboth Beach, DE 19971; (302) 644-2000; and Ocean Outlets, located on Route 1 between Routes 9 and 1-A, a two-part complex with 100 stores; 1600 Ocean Outlets, Rehoboth Beach, DE 19971; (302) 226-9223.

Family Outdoor Adventures

Camping. Cape Henlopen State Park (see The Best Beaches and Parks, above) offers camping at 159 sites, some with hook-ups. Delaware Seashore State Park (see Best Parks and Beaches above) has a large campground— 145 sites with water, electric, and sewer, and 133 sites without hookups.

Paddling. Beaston's Marina rents canoes and small boats; 19 Hassell Avenue, Bethany Beach, DE 19930; (302) 539-3452. Broadkill River Canoe Trail, operated by the Delaware Nature Society and the Town of Milton, runs along the McCabe Preserve on the Broadkill River; rental canoes can be obtained from Wilson's Marine; 309 Front Street, Milton, DE 19968; (302) 684-3425 or (302) 539-3452.

Family Lodging

Rehoboth Beach and Dewey Beach offer the full range of lodging, from rental houses and apartments to simple motels; contact the area chamber of commerce for full listings: (800) 441-1329 or (302) 227-2233; www.beach-fun.com.

Angler's Motel

This simple, 25-room motel in Lewes has a pool, is clean and reasonably priced, overlooks the canal, and is near town. A few efficiency units are available.

100 Anglers Road, Lewes, DE 19958; (302) 645-2831. Rates $60–100.

Atlantic Oceanside Suites and Efficiencies

A variety of suites ranging in size to hold up to eight people; pool, free movies, barbecue grills; two blocks from the beach and near the boardwalk.

2800 Highway One, Rehoboth Beach, DE 19971; (800) 442-0481 or (302) 227-3430. Rates $89–299.

Best Western Gold Leaf Hotel

Set half a block from the ocean and near the bay, the property offers a rooftop swimming pool, a sun deck, fishing and watersports equipment, laundry facilities, free continental breakfast, in-room refrigerators and microwaves, and private balconies.

1400 Highway One, Dewey Beach, DE 19971; (800) 422-8566 or (302) 226-1100. Rates $99–199.

Attractions

DiscoverSea Shipwreck Museum

708 Ocean Highway, Fenwick Island, DE 19944; (888) 743-5524 or (302) 539-9366; www.discoversea.com

Hours: Memorial Day–Labor Day, daily 10 a.m.–9 p.m.; September– October, daily 11 a.m.–4 p.m.; November–March, Saturday–Sunday 11 a.m.–4 p.m.; April–Memorial Day, daily 10 a.m.–4 p.m.

Admission: Donation

Appeal by Age Groups:

Pre-school	Grade School	Teens	Young Adults	Over 30	Seniors
★★	★★★	★★★	★★★★	★★★★	★★★★

Touring Time: Average 1½ hours, minimum 1 hour

Rainy-Day Touring: Yes

Services and Facilities:

Restaurants No	Lockers No
Alcoholic beverages No	Pet kennels No
Disabled access No	Rain check No
Wheelchair rental No	Private tours No
Baby stroller rental No	

Description and Comments   A small museum in a strip-mall-like setting (on the second floor of the Sea Shell City store) that holds a fascinating store of artifacts recovered from shipwrecks off the Delaware coast, plus things like a huge shell collection and lighthouse paraphernalia. Some hands-on learning goes on, maritime films are screened in the theater, and beach exploration walks are sometimes offered.

Treasures of the Sea Exhibit/Elsie Williams Doll Collection

Route 18, Delaware Technical and Community College, Georgetown, DE 19947; (302)-856-5700; www.treasuresofthesea.org

Hours: Sea exhibit: Monday–Tuesday 10 a.m.–4 p.m., Friday noon– 4 p.m., Saturday 9 a.m.–1 p.m.; Doll collection: Monday–Thursday 8 a.m.–10:30 p.m., Friday 8 a.m.–4:30 p.m., Saturday 8:30 a.m.– 1 p.m.; both are closed major holidays and school vacations

Admission: Sea exhibit: $2 adults, $1 seniors 64+, children 4 and over, and students; free for children under age 4; doll collection: free

Appeal by Age Groups:

Pre-school	Grade School	Teens	Young Adults	Over 30	Seniors
★★	★★★★	★★★★	★★★★	★★★★	★★★★

Touring Time: Average 1½ hours, minimum 1 hour

Rainy-Day Touring: Yes

Services and Facilities:

Restaurants No	Lockers No
Alcoholic beverages No	Pet kennels No
Disabled access Yes	Rain check No
Wheelchair rental No	Private tours No
Baby stroller rental No	

Description and Comments The "Treasures of the Sea" exhibit displays gold ingots, silver coins, and jewels salvaged from the Spanish galleon *Atocha,* shipwrecked in 1622 while carrying an estimated $4 million in treasure. Start by watching the half-hour video on the discovery of the ship.

The Elsie Williams Doll Collection, set in the school library, includes hundreds of collectible dolls by famous makers. In addition, while you're on campus, you might want to stop in at the art gallery in the West Building and visit the "Trees of the States" arboretum for a self-guided walking tour of nearly all the state trees.

Zwaanendael Museum/Lewes Historical Complex

102 Kings Highway, Lewes, DE 19958; (302) 645-1148;
www.destatemuseums.org/zwa

Hours: Tuesday–Saturday 10 a.m.–4:30 p.m., Sunday 1:30–4:30 p.m.

Admission: Free

Appeal by Age Groups:

Pre-school	Grade School	Teens	Young Adults	Over 30	Seniors
★★	★★★	★★★	★★★★	★★★★	★★★★

Touring Time: Average 1 hour (museum), minimum 30 minutes

Rainy-Day Touring: Yes

Services and Facilities:

Restaurants No	Baby stroller rental No
Alcoholic beverages No	Lockers No
Disabled access Yes; first floor only	Pet kennels No
	Rain check No
Wheelchair rental No	Private tours No

Description and Comments The museum building is modeled after the City Hall in Hoorn, the Netherlands. It houses exhibits on local history and the HMB *DeBraak,* a British brig that sank near Lewes in 1798. Artifacts from the War of 1812 and items dating as far back as 1631 are also on display.

The historical complex comprises various restored buildings and a country store that have been moved to Lewes. Walking tours are offered from mid-June until Labor Day, beginning at the Thompson Store at 110 Shipcarpenter Street. Tour information: (302) 645-7670 or (302) 645-8073.

Family-Friendly Restaurants

CAMEL'S HUMP

21 Baltimore Avenue, Rehoboth Beach; (302) 227-0947

Meals served: Lunch and dinner
Cuisine: Middle Eastern
Entree range: $5.95−24.95 (lunch and dinner)
Children's menu: Yes
Reservations: Yes
Payment: MC, V

Now, here's something different right in the heart of town. The waiters dress up in puffy pants out of the *Arabian Nights,* and the decor is from the lands of sands—but desert sands, not the beach. The food's authentic, and they'll help you out with picky kids.

CHEZ LA MER

210 Sedon Street, Rehoboth Beach; (302) 227-6494

Meals served: Dinner
Cuisine: Seafood
Entree range: $15.95−19.95
Children's menu: Yes
Reservations: Yes
Payment: Major credit cards

An excellent restaurant in a renovated house that serves seafood with a continental flair, plus some meat and vegetarian dishes. You can dine on the deck, the sunporch, or indoors.

THE FROG HOUSE

116 Garfield Parkway, Bethany Beach; (302) 539-4500

Meals served: Breakfast, lunch, and dinner
Cuisine: American—steaks, seafood, pasta, and poultry
Entree range: $7.25–14.65
Children's menu: Yes
Reservations: Yes
Payment: Major credit cards

A great family-oriented atmosphere with a wide range of mainstream foods, and items on the children's menu that are real food (i.e., Maryland crab cakes) in small portions, or kiddie classics like PB&J and chocolate milk.

KINGS HOMEMADE ICE CREAM

201 Second Street, Lewes; (302) 645-9425

Real homemade ice cream and something very special they call a "brownie ice cream sandwich." Open mid-March through September.

THE LIGHTHOUSE RESTAURANT

Angler's Road, Lewes; (302) 645-6271

Meals served: Lunch and dinner
Cuisine: Seafood
Entree range: $4.95–29.95 (lunch and dinner)
Children's menu: Yes
Reservations: Yes
Payment: MC, V

A longtime Lewes family dining fixture set right waterside in the harbor with a view of the drawbridge. (If you're lucky, the bridge will open while you dine—always a hit with the kids.) The lighthouse/nautical theme is cute, the food is good, and you can dine on the big deck on nice summer days.

RUSTY RUDDER

113 Dickson Street, Dewey Beach; (302) 227-3888

Meals served: Lunch and dinner
Cuisine: Seafood and ribs
Entree range: $5.95–25.95 (lunch and dinner)
Children's menu: Yes
Reservations: Yes
Payment: Major credit cards

Its nautical theme, very casual atmosphere, near-the-beach location, and locally renowned all-you-can-eat buffet combine to make this a good spot for families.

Part Four

Maryland

Maryland's a small state, but it offers big-state diversity and resources. Travelers can choose their destinations from among beach, farmland, major metropolises, mountains, and any combination of those elements. History abounds. Major battles from the Civil War and the War of 1812 were fought here, the "Star-Spangled Banner" was composed here, and the canal era of the Industrial Revolution almost blossomed here. The state loosely divides into topographic and population zones: **Western Maryland** is mountainous country; the **Capital Region** borders Washington, D.C., on three sides; **Central Maryland** holds Baltimore—as kid-friendly a city as you'll find anywhere—as well as history-rich Annapolis; **Southern Maryland** holds on to its rural, farming roots while reaching back to some of the country's first settlements; and the **Eastern Shore** has long reigned as one of the East's best beach getaways. During the Civil War, Maryland remained in the Union despite its strong southern culture. Clearly, this state is one where all passions can find their place.

Maryland's Not-to-Be-Missed Attractions	
Western Maryland	Swallow Falls State Park
	Deep Creek Lake State Park
	Antietam National Battlefield
Baltimore	National Aquarium in Baltimore
	Port Discovery
	Baltimore Museum of Industry
	B&O Railroad Museum
	Grab a Bite at Lexington Market

Maryland's Not-to-Be-Missed Attractions (continued)	
Annapolis	Naval Academy Guide Service
Capital Region	Cunningham Falls State Park/ Cacotin Mountain National Park
	National Colonial Farm
	College Park Aviation Museum
	Canal Clipper at the C&O Canal National Historical Park
Eastern Shore	Ocean City
	Assateague Island National Seashore
	Ocean City Life-Saving Station Museum
Southern Maryland	Calvert Marine Museum
	Historic St. Mary's City

How to Get Information before You Go

Maryland Office of Tourism Development, 217 E. Redwood Street, Baltimore, MD 21202; (877) 333-4455 or (410) 767-3400; www.mdisfun.org.

Calendar of Festivals and Events

January

Baltimore: Baltimore on Ice Winter Fest. Learn to ski or skate, rock at the "sock hop on ice," and watch an ice-carving competition and sled dog competitions, in the heart of the city. (800) 282-6632 or (410) 837-4636.

February

Western Maryland: Cabin Fever Weekend. Spruce Forest Artisan Village features storytellers and entertainment. Grantsville; (301) 895-3332.

March

Southern Maryland: Maryland Days. Maryland's first capital celebrates the state's founding, in 1634. St. Mary's City; (800) 762-1634 or (301) 862-0990.

April

Eastern Shore: Maryland International Kite Festival. World-class kite flying in an Olympic format. Ocean City; (800) 626-2326 or (410) 289-2800; www.oceancity.org.

May

Eastern Shore: Mid-Atlantic Maritime Festival. The Chesapeake Bay Maritime Museum fetes the nautical life. St. Michael's; (410) 820-8606 or (410) 745-2916; www.cbmm.org.

Annapolis: Chesapeake Bay Bridge Walk. Walk the magnificent 4.3-mile span, return by bus. In Stevensville, the "Bridge Walk Rendezvous" fair is held. (410) 228-8405; rendezvous information, (410) 643-8530.

Western Maryland: C&O Canal Fest. Celebrating the C&O Canal at its western terminus. Cumberland; (301) 724-3655.

June

Capital Region: Capital Jazz Fest. They call it "the world's largest showcase of contemporary jazz music" or "the Super Bowl of Contemporary Jazz." Columbia; (301) 218-0404; www.capitaljazz.com.

Baltimore: CitySand. Harborplace hosts professional architects and designers to help kids create sand sculptures and castles while teaching about manmade environments. (800) 427-2671; www.harborplace.com.

July

Baltimore: Ice Cream Festival. Lexington Market goes ice cream mad. Delicious. (410) 685-6169.

Eastern Shore: Kent County Fair. Tolchester; (410) 778-0767.

August

Annapolis: Kunta Kinte Heritage Festival. St. Johns College celebrates the African American, African, and African Caribbean cultures in memory of Kunte Kinte, a slave who arrived in Annapolis in 1767 and was Alex Haley's ancestor. (410) 349-0338.

Baltimore: Maryland State Fair. Timonium (in Baltimore County); (410) 252-0200.

September

Southern Maryland: Working Hands. Spend Labor Day weekend as a seventeenth-century laborer. St. Mary's City; (800) 762-1634 or (301) 862-0990.

Southern Maryland: Calvert County Fair. Prince Frederick; (410) 535-0026.

Capital Region: Great Frederick Fair. Frederick; (301) 663-5895; www.great frederickfair.com.

October

Capital Region: Catoctin Colorfest. Autumn's onset lures 150,000 people for arts and crafts, food, and entertainment. Thurmont; (301) 271-4432.

November

Eastern Shore: Winterfest of Lights. Huge animated characters, oversized ornaments, and 800,000 lights at the beach. Ocean City; (800)-626-2326 or (410) 289-2800; www.oceancity.org.

December

Baltimore: Christmas at Harborplace. Harborplace as holiday wonderland. (800) 427-2671; www.harborplace.com.

Cool Web Sites for Maryland-Bound Kids
Maryland's Kids' Page: www.sos.state.md.us/sos/kids/html/ kidhome.html
Fort McHenry: www.bcpl.lib.md.us/~etowner/patriots.html
Student Chesapeake Bay Savers: www.savethebay.cbf.org/sbs
Stately Knowledge: www.ipl.org/youth/stateknow

Western Maryland

Mountains and Maryland are probably not synonymous for most people. But here, the Cumberland Gap is where westward-bound settlers overcame their first major obstacles—the Allegheny Mountains. Most of America's early wars included action in the area—from the French and Indian War through the Civil War. Indeed, in Boonsboro, you can visit the War Correspondents Arch, erected to honor Civil War correspondent George Alfred Townsend, and the world's only monument to a war journalist. Cumberland, the town at the Cumberland Gap, displays architecture from the full span of the nation's early history in its Washington Street Historic District. Its **C&O Canal Boat Replica** (call (301) 729-3136) illustrates life on the canal, while the **C&O Canal Paw Paw Tunnel** (call (301) 722-8226) was one of the canal's major engineering feats. The towpath runs right through its 3,118-foot length, and so can you.

The **Deep Creek Lake** area ranks as the region's major attraction/destination. With 65 miles of shoreline, a number of state parks, skiing, and most other forms of recreation, it lures people of every stripe. A visit to **Swallow Falls State Park** (call (301) 334-9180) is a must with kids. You can easily hike to three spectacular waterfalls. Younger children will enjoy the **School House Earth Petting Zoo and Craft Shop** (call (301) 746-8603), which features a farm animal petting zoo. At **Valley View Country Store and Farm** (call (301) 334-4381), you'll see animals like ostrich, emu, rhea, llama, and miniature donkeys.

In **Friendsville,** the **Frostburg Museum** (call (301) 689-6853), set in an 1890s schoolhouse, depicts local history, the National Road, and mining. The **Thrasher Carriage Museum** (call (301) 689-3380) is considered to hold one of the country's best collections of horse-drawn vehicles. Another worthwhile stop along the **National Road** (the first federally funded highway) can be found at **Casselman River Bridge State Park**

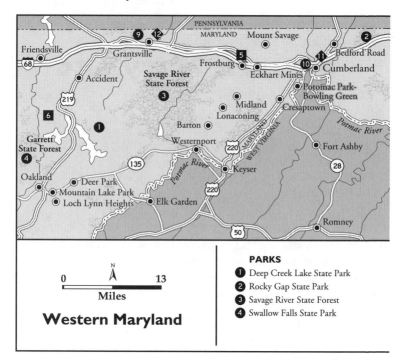

PENNSYLVANIA
MARYLAND   Mount Savage

Friendsville
68
Grantsville
Frostburg
Eckhart Mines
Bedford Road
Cumberland
2
11
10
5
9 12

Accident
Savage River
State Forest
Potomac Park-
Bowling Green
219
3
Midland
Lonaconing
Cresaptown
6
1
Barton

Garrett
State Forest
4
Westernport
220
Fort Ashby
Potomac River

Oakland
135
Keyser
28

Deer Park
Mountain Lake Park
Loch Lynn Heights
Elk Garden
220

Romney
50

N
0   13
Miles

Western Maryland

PARKS
1 Deep Creek Lake State Park
2 Rocky Gap State Park
3 Savage River State Forest
4 Swallow Falls State Park

(call (301) 895-5453), site of the nation's largest stone bridge, which was built in 1813. The **Sideling Hill Exhibit Center** (call (301) 842-2155) on I-68, just west of **Hancock,** reveals a 350-million-year-old rock formation in geological cross section.

Hagerstown is the cultural center of the region. The **Maryland Theatre** (call (301) 790-3500) presents a variety of performing arts events, including the **Maryland Symphony Orchestra** (call (301) 797-4000). At the **Hagerstown Roundhouse Museum** (call (301) 739-4665), you'll find the history of six railroads. Prefer fast cars? The **Hagerstown Speedway** (call (301) 582-0640) stages dirt-track auto racing. A more peaceful pastime can be found at the **Albert Powell Trout Hatchery** (call (301) 791-4736), where some 200,000 fish are raised annually.

HOW TO GET THERE

By Car. Western Maryland is best reached by using I-68. Traveling from the west, I-68 intersects I-79 at Morgantown, West Virginia. Traveling from the east, I-68 intersects I-70 at Hancock, Maryland, about 20 minutes west of Hagerstown.

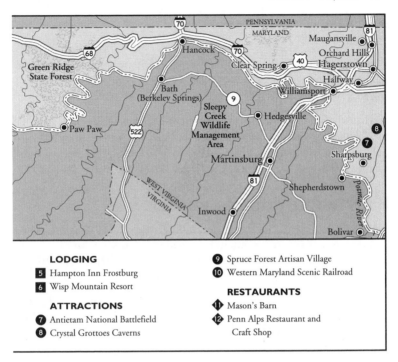

LODGING

5 Hampton Inn Frostburg

6 Wisp Mountain Resort

ATTRACTIONS

7 Antietam National Battlefield

8 Crystal Grottoes Caverns

9 Spruce Forest Artisan Village

10 Western Maryland Scenic Railroad

RESTAURANTS

11 Mason's Barn

12 Penn Alps Restaurant and
Craft Shop

How to Get Information before You Go

Hagerstown/Washington County Convention and Visitors Bureau, Elizabeth Hager Center, Hagerstown, MD 21740; (888) 257-2600 or (301) 791-3246; www.hagerstowncvb.org.

Allegany County Convention and Visitors Bureau, P.O. Box 1445, Cumberland, MD 21502; (800) 508-4748; www.mdmountainside.com.

Garrett County Chamber of Commerce, 15 Visitors Center Drive, McHenry, MD 21541; (301) 387-4386; www.garrettchamber.com.

The Best Parks

Deep Creek Lake State Park. Set on the lake's shoreline, this is a great place to swim, boat, try other water activities, have a picnic, or visit the Discovery Center. 898 State Park Road, Swanton, MD 21561; (301) 387-4111.

Rocky Gap State Park. The main attraction at this park (nestled between two mountains) is the 243-acre lake, but there's excellent hiking and even an 18-hole golf course. 12500 Pleasant Valley Road, Flintstone, MD 21530; (301) 777-2139.

Savage River State Forest. At 53,000 acres, this is the state's largest. It features year-round activities. 349 Headquarters Lane, Grantsville, MD 21536; (301) 895-5453.

Swallow Falls State Park. Nine miles west of Oakland/Deep Creek Lake, the park holds a wonderful, easy hiking trail that kids love because it leads to three waterfalls, including 54-foot Muddy Creek Falls; some great fishing is found here, too. 222 Herrington Lane, Oakland, MD 21550; (301) 334-9180.

Family Outdoor Adventures

Allegany Expeditions. Guided rock climbing, rappeling, kayaking, canoeing, caving, cross-country skiing, bass fishing, fly fishing, and backpacking. 10310 Columbus Avenue, Cumberland, MD 21502; (800) 819-5170 or (301) 722-5170.

Camping. Herrington Manor State Park. The park, located five miles from Oakland/Deep Creek Lake, has 20 log cabins for cabin-camping, plus a 53-acre lake. (301) 334-9180.

Cross-Country Skiing. Savage River State Forest holds ten miles of cross-country ski trails. Trails are also maintained at Herrington Manor State Park and New Germany State Park.

Guiding Services. Adventure Guides and Travel, 113 East Main Street, Frostburg, MD 21532; (301) 689-0345: instruction, guiding, and equipment rental for rock and ice climbing, caving, rappeling, scuba/snorkeling, kayaking, canoeing, fishing, and cycling.

Hiking. Savage River and Rocky Gap State Parks (see The Best Parks, above). South Mountain State Park, 21843 National Pike, Boonsboro, MD 21713; (301) 791-4767; contains 40 miles of the Appalachian Trail.

Horseback Riding. Western Trails in Oakland, mounts by the hour, half-day or full-day for all abilities; (301) 387-6155 or (301) 387-6890.

Small Oaks Riding Stables, in Oakland, offers trail rides by the hour, as well as pony rides, buggy rides, hayrides, and sleigh rides in winter; (301) 334-5733 or (301) 334-4991.

Mountain Biking. Savage River State Forest allows mountain bikes on most of its trail system. Trail access also available at Green Ridge State Park, Flintstone, MD 21530; (301) 478-3124.

Waterskiing. High Mountain Sport's Water Ski School in McHenry gives instruction to children and adults by reservation; (301) 387-4199.

Family Lodging

Hampton Inn Frostburg

Hotel features a large continental breakfast bar, an indoor heated pool, and a fitness center. All rooms have iron, ironing board, coffeemaker, hairdryer, and microfridge.

11200 New George's Creek Road, Frostburg; (301) 689-1998 or (800) HAMPTON; www.hampton-inn.com/hi/frostburg. Rates $79–95.

Wisp Mountain Resort

A 169-room hotel at the base of the ski area and golf course, it holds 102 suites and 66 efficiencies and/or deluxe rooms. Indoor pool, in-room coffee, activity discount coupons, and several on-site dining options.

290 Marsh Hill Drive, McHenry, MD 21541; (800) 462-9477 or (301) 5581. Rates $129–169 for suites; multiday and week-long packages available with breakfast.

DEEP CREEK LAKE: TRY A CONDO, COTTAGE, OR HOUSE

Deep Creek Lake is the kind of place that lends itself to renting a unit with all the comforts of home. Here are some options.

Railey Mountain Lake Vacations

Houses by the week or more, from two-bedroom/one-bath to eight bed-rooms/6½ baths, starting at $695 per week. Multiple day rates also available. 22491 Garrett Highway, McHenry; (800) 846-7368 or (301) 387-2124.

Will o' the Wisp

Within walking distance of a marina, restaurant, movie house, and mini-golf. Efficiencies, up to three-bedroom/two-bath condo units, range from $96 to $282; one- and two-bedroom rustic cottages (no air-conditioning) from $80 to $162. 20160 Garrett Highway, Oakland; information (301) 387-5503, reservations (301) 387-6990.

Attractions

Antietam National Battlefield

P.O. Box 158, Sharpsburg, MD 21782; (301) 432-5124;
www.nps.gov/anti

Hours: Summer, daily 8:30 a.m.–6 p.m.; winter, daily 8:30 a.m.–5 p.m.; closed Thanksgiving, Christmas, and New Year's days

Admission: $2 adults, $4 per family; free for children age 16 and under

Appeal by Age Groups:

Pre-school	Grade School	Teens	Young Adults	Over 30	Seniors
★★	★★★★	★★★★	★★★★	★★★★★	★★★★★

Touring Time: Average 2 hours, minimum 1 hour

Rainy-Day Touring: Yes

Services and Facilities:

Restaurants No	Lockers No
Alcoholic beverages No	Pet kennels No
Disabled access No	Rain check No
Wheelchair rental No	Private tours No
Baby stroller rental No	

Description and Comments   Site of one of the bloodiest battles of the Civil War, in September 1862. More than 23,000 men were killed, wounded, or missing here after one single day, and the battle prompted President Lincoln to issue the Emancipation Proclamation. Start at the visitors center by viewing the 26-minute film *Antietam Visit* (screened on the hour), which re-creates the battle and President Lincoln's subsequent visit. Park personnel recommend taking a self-guided driving tour. The tour road is 8.5 miles long and contains 11 stops. You can walk or bike the route. Audiotape narrations—which are well worth it—can be purchased or rented at the bookstore.

Crystal Grottoes Caverns

198 Shepherdstown Pike, Boonsboro, MD 21713; (301) 432-6336

Hours: April 1–October 31, daily 10 a.m.–5 p.m.; November–March, weekends 11 a.m.–4 p.m.

Admission: $8.50 adults, $4.50 children under 12

Appeal by Age Groups:

Pre-school	Grade School	Teens	Young Adults	Over 30	Seniors
★★★	★★★★	★★★★	★★★★	★★★★	★★★★

Touring Time: 30-minute tour runs every 15 minutes

Rainy-Day Touring: Yes

Services and Facilities:

Restaurants No	Lockers No
Alcoholic beverages No	Pet kennels No
Disabled access No	Rain check No
Wheelchair rental No	Private tours No
Baby stroller rental No	

Description and Comments These 250-million-year-old caverns were "discovered" in 1920, when the State Roads Commission was quarrying to build a highway. The cave, 86 feet underground, opened as a public attraction in 1922. Compared to some commercial caves, it's a small, stark place, but the natural wonders get center stage. You see formations resembling chandeliers, bacon, an Egyptian mummy, the U.S. Capitol building, and a reflecting pool. Easy walking.

Spruce Forest Artisan Village

177 Casselman Road, Grantsville, MD 21536; (301) 895-3332; www.spruceforest.org

Hours: Monday–Saturday 10 a.m.–5 p.m.

Admission: Free; nominal fee for some special events

Appeal by Age Groups:

Pre-school	Grade School	Teens	Young Adults	Over 30	Seniors
★★★	★★★★	★★★★	★★★★	★★★★★	★★★★★

Touring Time: Average 2 hours, minimum 1 hour

Rainy-Day Touring: Yes

Services and Facilities:

Restaurants No	Lockers No
Alcoholic beverages No	Pet kennels No
Disabled access Yes	Rain check No
Wheelchair rental No	Private tours No
Baby stroller rental No	

Description and Comments This collection of genuine log cabins houses many working artisans, such as blacksmiths, spinners, weavers, potters, and sculptors, and visitors can meet and talk with them. Other high-quality crafts produced here include baskets, stained glass, and teddy bears.

Western Maryland Scenic Railroad

13 Canal Street, Cumberland, MD 21502; (800) 872-4650 or (301) 759-4400; www.wmsr.com

Hours: 11:30 a.m. for regular trip departures; call for special-event train schedule and to determine exactly when the steam trains and diesel trains operate

Admission: Steam train: May–mid-September, $17.50 adults, $16 seniors 60+, $11 children ages 2–12; children under 2 ride free when not occupying a seat; mid-September–December, $19.50 adults, $19 seniors, $12 children. Diesel train: May–mid-September, $15.50

adults, $14 seniors, $9 children; mid-September–December, $17.50
adults, $17 seniors, $10 children

Appeal by Age Groups:

Pre-school	Grade School	Teens	Young Adults	Over 30	Seniors
★★	★★★★	★★★	★★★	★★★★	★★★★★

Touring Time: 3 hours

Rainy-Day Touring: Yes

Services and Facilities:

Restaurants Yes; in Old Frostburg	Baby stroller rental No
Station at end of ride	Lockers No
Alcoholic beverages No	Pet kennels No
Disabled access Yes	Rain check No
Wheelchair rental No	Private tours No

Description and Comments   The scenery is beautiful no matter which train you take—the track winds through the Alleghenies, crosses an iron truss bridge, goes around Helmstetter's Horseshoe Curve, and travels through the Brush Tunnel under Piney Mountain—but the steam train bespeaks that illustrious bygone era. The 16-mile run takes three hours round-trip, stopping in Frostburg, site of the Frostburg Depot Restaurant and the Thrasher Carriage Museum.

Wisp Ski and Golf Resort

296 Marsh Hill Road, McHenry, MD 21541; (301) 387-4911;
www.gcnet.net/wisp

Hours: Skiing early November–mid-December, Tuesday–Saturday 8:30
a.m.–9 p.m.; mid-December–mid-March, Tuesday–Saturday 8:30
a.m.–10 p.m.; all season, Sunday–Monday 8:30 a.m.–4:30 p.m.

Lift tickets: $35 adult all day, $25 child all day, $21 adult afternoon or night, $16 child afternoon or night; multiday ticket available. Weekends and holidays: $42 adult all day, $29 children all day

Appeal by Age Groups:

Pre-school	Grade School	Teens	Young Adults	Over 30	Seniors
★★★	★★★★	★★★★★	★★★★	★★★	★★

Services and Facilities:

Restaurants Yes	Lockers Yes
Alcoholic beverages No	Pet kennels No
Disabled access Yes	Rain check No
Wheelchair rental Yes	Private tours No
Baby stroller rental No	

Description and Comments Wisp is Maryland's only ski resort. It holds 23 trails on 80 acres of skiable terrain, with a 610-foot vertical drop and 14 miles of trails. The longest trail runs about 1.5 miles. Snowboarders like the state's only halfpipe. Beginner trails comprise 20 percent of the skiing, intermediate 50 percent, and expert 30 percent. Ninety percent of the mountain is lit for night skiing. Uphill transportation: two triple chairlifts, three double chairlifts, one rope tow, and one handle tow. On-site golf in summer.

Family-Friendly Restaurants

MASON'S BARN

Ali Ghan Road, I-68 Exit 46, Cumberland; (301) 722-6155

Meals served: Breakfast, lunch, and dinner
Cuisine: American
Entree range: $6.95–17.95
Children's menu: Yes
Reservations: Yes
Payment: Major credit cards

A local institution in family dining since 1954. The decor is punctuated with primitive antiques, but the food is a basic, simple homemade-type affair.

PENN ALPS RESTAURANT AND CRAFT SHOP

125 Casselman Road, Grantsville; (301) 895-5985

Meals served: Breakfast, lunch, and dinner
Cuisine: American
Entree range: $2.95 (breakfast)–15.95 (dinner)
Children's menu: Yes; $2.75–7.95
Reservations: Yes
Payment: Major credit cards

Adjacent to Spruce Grove Artisan Village, this is plain, good old-fashioned American food at reasonable prices. They serve a buffet Friday and Saturday nights, and a Sunday brunch, where kids under five eat free. It's the kind of place that has PB&J with fries on the children's menu. Mmmmm.

WISP/THE PLACE

290 Marsh Hill Road, McHenry; (301) 387-4911, ext. 2159

Meals served: Breakfast, lunch, and dinner
Cuisine: Pasta, seafood, and steaks

Entree range: $6.95–16.95 (dinner)
Children's menu: Yes
Reservations: Yes
Payment: Major credit cards

Located in the Wisp Resort Hotel at the base of the ski area, this restaurant describes itself as "informal, irreverent, yet sophisticated." It offers good food, like large sandwiches convenient during a day of skiing.

Baltimore

My goodness, **Baltimore** has come a long way. Twenty years ago, it was a city struggling against decline. Today it's a visitor's treasure trove. We've brought our kids to Baltimore many times, and it never loses its appeal. Among our favorite stops is **Lexington Market** (call (410) 685-6169), an old-fashioned, indoor, fresh-food market that's been in operation since 1782. If your timing's right, indulge in their chocolate or ice cream festivals. Baltimore overflows with museums, and to see them all requires several days. In addition to the attractions we've listed, kids will also like the **Babe Ruth Birthplace Museum** (call (410) 727-1539); the **American Visionary Art Museum** (call (410) 244-1900), the country's official national museum dedicated to inventive art by self-taught artists; the **Baltimore Public Works Museum** (call (410) 396-5565), where the inner workings of tunnels, bridges, and water systems are revealed; the **Baltimore Zoo** (call (410) 396-6620); the **Maryland Science Center** (call (410) 685-2370), which combines hands-on science with a planetarium and an IMAX theater; **Fort McHenry National Monument** (call (410) 962-4290), where Francis Scott Key was inspired to write the national anthem; the navy's last all-sail battleship, the USS *Constellation* (call (410) 539-1797), along with the Coast Guard cutter *Taney,* the World War II submarine *Torsk,* and the lightship *Chesapeake* (call (410) 396-3453), all of which can be boarded and toured; and **Oriole Park at Camden Yards** (call (410) 547-6234), which offers an excellent behind-the-scenes tour and also happens to be a great place to watch a baseball game.

Teens like visiting **Fells Point,** a neighborhood that dates to 1730 and thrives with shops, street performers, and nightlife, but we'd admonish parents that the scene may not be appropriate on weekend evenings. The **Power Plant** features a *Hard Rock Cafe* and the first *ESPN The Zone.* And, some excellent dining choices can be found in **Little Italy.** Winter visitors

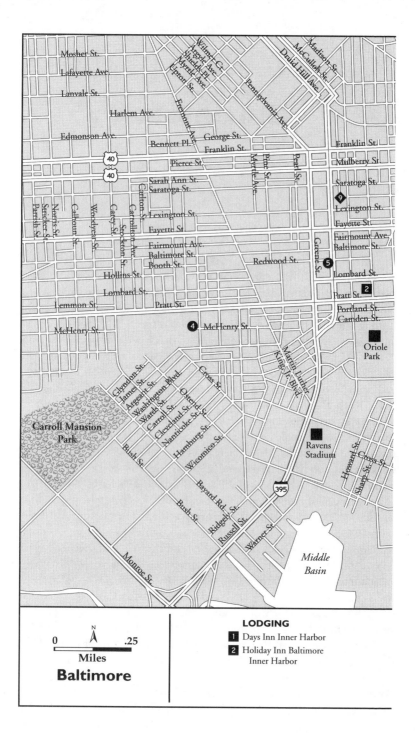

LODGING

1 Days Inn Inner Harbor
2 Holiday Inn Baltimore
Inner Harbor

0   N   .25

Miles

Baltimore

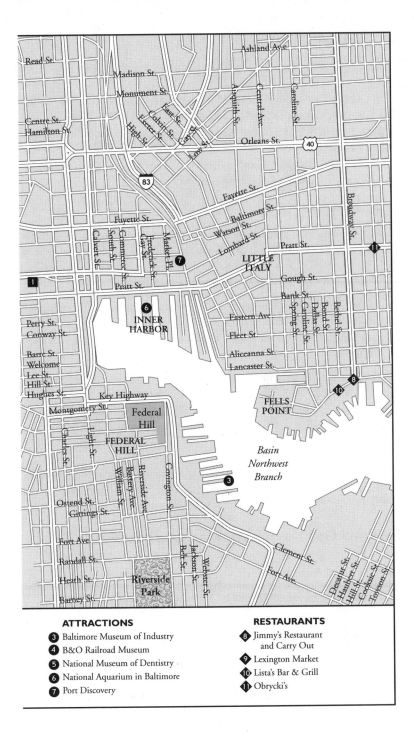

ATTRACTIONS

3 Baltimore Museum of Industry
4 B&O Railroad Museum
5 National Museum of Dentistry
6 National Aquarium in Baltimore
7 Port Discovery

RESTAURANTS

8 Jimmy's Restaurant
  and Carry Out
9 Lexington Market
10 Lista's Bar & Grill
11 Obrycki's

can ice-skate at **Baltimore on Ice** (call (410) 752-8632) right at the Inner Harbor.

Your best bet for getting around the Inner Harbor area is to buy an all-day ticket on either the **Harbor Shuttle** ($4 adults, $2 children ten and under; (410) 675-2900) or the **Water Taxi** ($5 adults, $2 children ten and under; (410) 563-3901).

The **Ladew Topiary Gardens** in nearby Monkton (call (410) 557-9570) offers 15 thematic topiary and flower gardens.

HOW TO GET THERE

By Car. Baltimore is easily accessible by car from the north by I-83, from the south by I-97, from both north and south by I-95, and from the west by I-70. The I-695 Beltway circles the metro area and can cause confusion, so be alert and read the signs.

By Plane. Baltimore/Washington International Airport (BWI) is located just south of the city and is served by most major airlines. The airport's observation gallery offers a variety of diversions for kids. (800) 435-9294 or (410) 859-7111.

By Train. Amtrak's northeast corridor service runs right through Baltimore; (800) 872-7245. The Light Rail system will take you from Amtrak's Penn Station to downtown and the Inner Harbor. MARC commuter trains run on weekdays to and from Washington, D.C.; (800) 325-7245.

Public Transportation

The MTA sells an all-day pass for $3 that allows unlimited rides on buses, the Light Rail, and the Metro subway; ask for their *Visitors Ride Guide.* (800) 543-9809 or (410) 539-5000; www.mtamaryland.com.

HOW TO GET INFORMATION BEFORE YOU GO

Baltimore Area Convention and Visitors Association; 100 Light Street, 12th Floor; (800) 343-3468; www.baltconvstr.com.

Howard County; (800) 288-8747; www.howardcountymdtour.com.

Family Lodging

Days Inn, Inner Harbor

A 250-room, high-rise hotel located three blocks from the Inner Harbor. It offers large guest rooms and suites and has an outdoor pool and a full-service restaurant.

100 Hopkins Place, Baltimore, MD 21201; (410) 576-1000 or (800) 544-8313. Rates $99–199.

Holiday Inn Baltimore Inner Harbor

Newly renovated, this Holiday Inn is three blocks from the Inner Harbor and offers a restaurant and pool.

301 West Lombard Street, Baltimore, MD 21201; (410) 685-3500. Rates $89–199, children 12 and under stay free in parents' room, packages available that include breakfast. On-site parking, $8/day.

Attractions

Baltimore Museum of Industry

1415 Key Highway, Baltimore, MD 21230; (410) 727-4808

Hours: Memorial Day–Labor Day, Tuesday–Saturday 10 a.m.–5 p.m.; Labor Day–Memorial Day, Thursday–Saturday 10 a.m.–5 p.m.; open Mondays celebrated as federal holidays; closed Thanksgiving Day, Christmas Eve, and Christmas Day

Admission: $6 adults, $4.50 seniors and students; free for children under 6; $20 per family

Appeal by Age Groups:

Pre-school	Grade School	Teens	Young Adults	Over 30	Seniors
★★★	★★★★★	★★★★	★★★★	★★★★★	★★★★★

Touring Time: Average 2 hours, minimum 1 hour

Rainy-Day Touring: Yes

Services and Facilities:

Restaurants No	Lockers No; coat check
Alcoholic beverages No	Pet kennels No
Disabled access Yes	Rain check No
Wheelchair rental No	Private tours No; docents avail-
Baby stroller rental No	able to guide

Description and Comments What a delightful jumble of gizmos and machines this is! Set, appropriately, next door to the Domino Sugar processing plant in an old (circa 1865) oyster-canning house, the museum covers the gamut of nineteenth- and twentieth-century industry—from food processing, to a 1930s grocery store, to modern sheet-metal making—focusing on companies from and items made in Maryland. Did you know that the first metal skis were made in Baltimore? We didn't. There's an incredible machine shop section where, when all the machines are grinding away, the noise reaches, well, industrial levels. Kids can experience how oyster-canning factories worked, how precomputer printing was done, and how umbrellas—a major Baltimore product—were made. The entrance yard features a huge crane and lots of other heavy-duty industrial machines that immediately set the mood. Weekends are the best time to visit because there are always plenty of participatory activities happening. Note for those arriving by water: The Harbor Shuttle docks right at the museum, while the Water Taxi does not.

B&O Railroad Museum

901 Pratt Street, Baltimore, MD 21223; (410) 752-2490;
www.borail.org

Hours: Daily 10 a.m.–5 p.m.; closed Easter, Thanksgiving, Christmas, and New Year's days

Admission: $7 adults, $6 seniors 60+, $5 ages 3–12; free for children 2 and under

Appeal by Age Groups:

Pre-school	Grade School	Teens	Young Adults	Over 30	Seniors
★★★★	★★★★★	★★★★	★★★★	★★★★★	★★★★★

Touring Time: Average 2½ hours, minimum 1½ hours

Rainy-Day Touring: Yes

Services and Facilities:

Restaurants Yes	available for loan
Alcoholic beverages No	Lockers No
Disabled access Yes	Pet kennels No
Wheelchair rental Yes; one avail-able for loan	Rain check No
Baby stroller rental Yes; one	Private tours No; but volunteers available to guide

Description and Comments   There are railroad museums and then there are *railroad* museums. Two things make this one special: (1) the huge rolling stock collection, and (2) the roundhouse. The roundhouse is an incredible building—ornate yet industrial, and filled with unique railroad cars and engines, including the Tom Thumb, the original steam engine that raced the horse-drawn train, and the horse-drawn train, too. Outside, there's an immense 2-6-6-4 Allegheny locomotive (the largest ever built). You can climb aboard and play engineer on it. Upstairs, there's a huge HO-scale layout that some kids (big and small) might just eyeball for hours.

Dr. Samuel D. Harris National Museum of Dentistry

31 South Greene Street, Baltimore, MD 21201; (410) 706-0600;
www.dentalmuseum.org

Hours: Wednesday–Saturday 10 a.m.–4 p.m., Sunday 1–4 p.m.

Admission: $4.50 adults, $2.50 seniors 60+, $2.50 ages 7–18, free for
children 6 and under

Appeal by Age Groups:

Pre-school	Grade School	Teens	Young Adults	Over 30	Seniors
★★	★★★★	★★★★	★★★★	★★★★★	★★★★★

Touring Time: Average 1½ hours, minimum 1 hour

Rainy-Day Touring: Yes

Services and Facilities:

Restaurants No	Lockers No
Alcoholic beverages No	Pet kennels No
Disabled access Yes	Rain check No
Wheelchair rental No	Private tours No; but special
Baby stroller rental No	arrangements can be made

Description and Comments Few folks know about this place, but it's
unique and worth a visit. You'll find all kinds of dental artifacts. We liked
the interactive touch-screens that show film clips with a dentistry theme.
Among them: old toothpaste television ads ("You'll wonder where the yellow went," etc.), and clips from old-time movies, like Little Rascals or
Charlie Chaplin movies, involving dentists. They even have George Washington's famous dentures on display, as well as a two-story "Tower of
Chairs" sculpture.

National Aquarium in Baltimore

Pier 3, 501 East Pratt Street, Baltimore, MD 21202; (410) 576-3800;
www.aqua.org

Hours: July and August, daily 9 a.m.–8 p.m.; November–February,
Saturday–Thursday 10 a.m.–5 p.m., Friday 10 a.m.–8 p.m.;
March–June, September and October, Saturday–Thursday 9 a.m.–
5 p.m., Friday 9 a.m.–8 p.m. *Note:* The above "closing" times are the
latest you can enter the building; the aquarium actually closes two
hours after the "last entry" time

Admission: $14 adults, $10.50 seniors 60+, $7.50 children ages 3–11, free
for children under 3; $5 admission for everyone on Fridays after 5 p.m.,

mid-September through mid-March. *Note:* Tickets can be purchased in advance by calling TicketMaster at (800) 551-7328 or (410) 481-7328

Appeal by Age Groups:

Pre-school	Grade School	Teens	Young Adults	Over 30	Seniors
★★★★★	★★★★★	★★★★★	★★★★★	★★★★★	★★★★★

Touring Time: Average 2½ hours, minimum 1½ hours

Rainy-Day Touring: Yes

Services and Facilities:

Restaurants Yes	backs provided
Alcoholic beverages Yes; beer	Lockers No; coat and stroller
Disabled access Yes	check
Wheelchair rental Yes; free	Pet kennels No
Baby stroller rental No; strollers	Rain check No
not permitted; kid-carrying	Private tours Yes

Description and Comments   We love this place—and everybody else does, too! It gets crowded. Arrive before 11 a.m. or after 3 p.m. if possible, and buy tickets in advance (up to 30 days ahead) from either the ticket office or TicketMaster.

Start outside and see the harbor and gray seals. Once inside, just follow the lines on the floor. "Wings in the Water"—stingrays and small sharks—comes first and is most popular at feeding time, when divers enter the tank. Level 2 covers Maryland habitats; level 3 is devoted to animal adaptations and includes creatures such as octopi, moray and electric eels, and seahorses; level 4 features the aquarium's newest exhibit, "The Amazon Rain Forest," a fascinating portrayal of an Amazon tributary river at flood time and after flooding has receded (can you find the anaconda? He's huge, but hard to locate). Level 5 puts you inside a tropical rain forest, after which wind down a ramp among tropical fish and then big sharks. The Marine Mammal Pavilion holds a 1,300-seat amphitheater, where dolphins perform several times each day, and also houses the Exploration Station, a high-tech center of participatory exhibits.

Special tours are offered several times a year. Adult behind-the-scenes tours (ages 12 and up) cost $18 per person; parent-and-child behind-the-scenes tours (for children ages 8–11) cost $20 per parent/child team. Early-opening educational tours for ages 3–5 focus on specific topics, like "Frogs," and cost $15 per parent/child team, plus $6 for an extra child.

Port Discovery

35 Market Place, Baltimore, MD 21202; (410) 864-2680;
   www.portdiscovery.org

Hours: Memorial Day–Labor Day, daily 10 a.m.–5:30 p.m.; Labor

Day–Memorial Day, Tuesday–Sunday 10 a.m.–5:30 p.m.; closed
Thanksgiving and Christmas days

Admission: $10 adults, $7.50 children ages 3–12, free for children under 3

Appeal by Age Groups:

Pre-school	Grade School	Teens	Young Adults	Over 30	Seniors
★★★★	★★★★★	★★★	★★★★	★★★★	★★★

Touring Time: Average 3 hours, minimum 2 hours

Rainy-Day Touring: Yes

Services and Facilities:

Restaurants Yes; McDonald's on site, many more nearby	**Baby stroller rental** No
	Lockers Yes
Alcoholic beverages No	**Pet kennels** No
Disabled access Yes	**Rain check** No
Wheelchair rental Yes; free	**Private tours** No

Description and Comments The concept here is to let kids develop personal skills—goal setting, problem solving, critical thinking, risk taking, creativity, and interpersonal skills—unconsciously in a fun environment. The museum centers on a three-story climbing environment called Kid-Works made from ropes, ladders, and netting, and topped with a rope bridge. Other environments include "Miss Perception's Mystery House" and "Adventure Expeditions," where you find clues and solve problems to find a missing person or venture back into ancient Egypt. In other rooms, kids can build things using real tools under supervision or create their own TV show. There's even a branch of the public library on site that augments their experiences with learning resources. The environments, created by Disney Imagineering, are well thought out, and everyone has a wonderful time. Grandparents, however, might find the noise level a bit much.

Family-Friendly Restaurants

The Inner Harbor holds two mall-like centers, **Light Street Pavilion** and **The Gallery,** each of which offers a food court with a variety of choices. All the chains—from Hard Rock Cafe to Johnny Rockets—can be found there as well.

JIMMY'S RESTAURANT AND CARRY OUT

801 South Broadway, Baltimore; (410) 327-3273

Meals served: Breakfast, lunch, and dinner
Cuisine: American diner

Entree range: $5.50–7.95
Children's menu: No
Reservations: No
Payment: Major credit cards

A Baltimore landmark. Indeed, when we asked the Harbor Shuttle captain where he'd recommend taking the kids, he said "Jimmy's!" without hesitation. Breakfast is served all day and is a major attraction. You'll get lots of local flavor with your food here.

LEXINGTON MARKET

Lexington and Eutlaw Streets, Baltimore; (410) 685-6169

Meals served: Breakfast, lunch, and early dinner
Cuisine: Eclectic
Entree range: $2.95 and up
Children's menu: No
Reservations: No
Payment: Major credit cards at most sites; cash only at some

Lexington Market is the city's oldest indoor market, and you can find just about anything here, from stalls selling fresh seafood or meats to seafood eateries, delis, ice cream shops, sub shops—you name it. One of the best markets in the Mid-Atlantic.

LISTA'S BAR AND GRILL

1637 Thames Street, Baltimore; (410) 327-0046

Meals served: Lunch and dinner
Cuisine: Mexican
Entree range: $6–15
Children's menu: No
Reservations: Yes
Payment: Major credit cards

A friendly restaurant in the heart of Fell's Point, and just across the street from a terrific CD shop. If your kids don't like spicy stuff, they can get a burger or chicken fingers.

OBRYCKI'S CRAB HOUSE AND SEAFOOD RESTAURANT

1727 East Pratt Street, Baltimore; (410) 732-6399

Meals served: Lunch and dinner
Cuisine: Seafood
Entree range: $6.50–28.95
Children's menu: No
Reservations: Yes, but only during limited hours
Payment: Major credit cards

At some point while in Maryland, you *must* eat Maryland crab. This is a good spot to do it not only because it's been a Baltimore landmark for more than 50 years but also because they provide you with how-to instructions for eating hard-shell crabs. Obrycki's is set in an old warehouse with antique/old-time Baltimore decor (an oak board bar top and door, and window casings from a monastery dating to 1927; artifacts from the original 1865 building locale; and artwork depicting Baltimore history) that's fun and funky. In addition to crab, they make great crab cakes, fried shrimp, fancy seafood dishes, and, if you must, they'll serve up a hamburger.

Annapolis

Although it's the state capitol, Annapolis is dominated by the U.S. Naval Academy's presence. "Middies," as the midshipmen are called, are everywhere. It's a history-rich town that, because of its setting along Chesapeake Bay, also presents abundant water-oriented activities. A number of companies, like **Harbor Cruises** (call (800) 695-5239) or the **Harbor Queen** (call (410) 260-7600), offer narrated cruises. Fishermen can choose from a number of charters and outfitters. Or you can rent a boat from **The Waterfront** (call (410) 263-7873). On land, the **Chesapeake Children's Museum** (call (410) 266-0677) is chock-full of hands-on and interactive exhibits. Mega–amusement park **Six Flags America** (call (301) 249-1500) is in Largo, about 20 minutes away. And if your timing's right, **The Talent Machine** (call (410) 956-0512), a Broadway musical–performing group featuring 5- to 19-year-olds, may be performing while you're in town. **City Dock** is the hub of things. You'll find lots of shopping and dining there and along adjacent **Main Street**.

HOW TO GET THERE

By Car. Access is from State Route 50; connect to it from I-97 or I-495 (the Washington Beltway). Parking on the city's old streets is difficult at best, but two public garages and the Navy–Marine Corps Memorial Stadium parking lot provide excellent alternatives. Metered parking maxes out at two hours, a time limit that's diligently enforced. Parking info can be found at 1620 AM on your car radio. The city is very walking-friendly; the Jiffy Water Taxi (410-263-0033) can get you from City Dock to any point along the waterfront.

By Plane. Baltimore/Washington International Airport (BWI) is the closest. See the Baltimore section for specifics.

How to Get Information before You Go

Annapolis and Anne Arundel County Conference and Visitors Bureau, 26 West Street, Annapolis, MD 21401; (410) 280-0445, fax (410) 263-9591; www.visit-annapolis.org.

The Best Parks

Sandy Point State Park. A swimming beach, picnic grounds, playground, hiking trails, and boat rentals. Watch the freighters on Chesapeake Bay. 1100 East College Parkway, Annapolis; (410) 974-2149.

Truxton Park. Seventy acres with all kinds of fields and courts, plus a public outdoor swimming pool and playground. Hilltop Lane, Annapolis; (410) 263-7958. Fee for swimming.

Family Outdoor Adventures

Boating. Many companies offer charter services. Contact the Annapolis and Anne Arundel County Conference and Visitors Bureau at (410) 280-0445 for a list. American Powerboat Schools and Charters presents daily tours, rents boats, and offers boating instruction; 222 Severn Avenue, Pier 3, Skip 18, Annapolis, MD 21401; (410) 721-7517. *Beginagain* sails three times daily, and no sailing experience is required; City Dock, Annapolis, MD 21401; (410) 626-1422.

Hiking/Biking. The Baltimore and Annapolis Trail runs 13 miles along an abandoned rail bed from Glen Burnie to Annapolis, passing through forest, farmland, and urban settings. Park Headquarters, Earleigh Heights Road, Severna Park, MD 21146; (410) 222-6244.

Sea Kayaking. You can kayak right from City Dock in Annapolis. Amphibious Horizons offers tours, overnights, instruction, and rentals. 600 Quiet Waters Park Road, Annapolis, MD 21403; (888) 458-8786 or (410) 267-8742.

Family Lodging

Annapolis Marriott Waterfront Hotel

This 150-room luxury hotel can be pricey, but it's right in the heart of things in the City Dock area. Many rooms feature private balconies overlooking the Chesapeake Bay, while others offer Annapolis Harbor and City

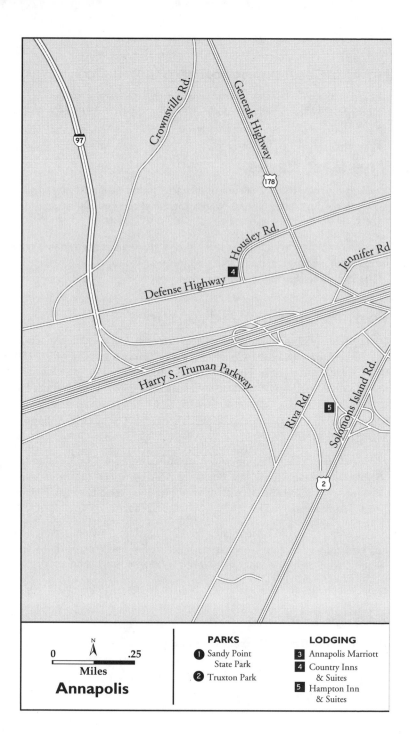

PARKS

1 Sandy Point
  State Park
2 Truxton Park

LODGING

3 Annapolis Marriott
4 Country Inns
  & Suites
5 Hampton Inn
  & Suites

Miles

Annapolis

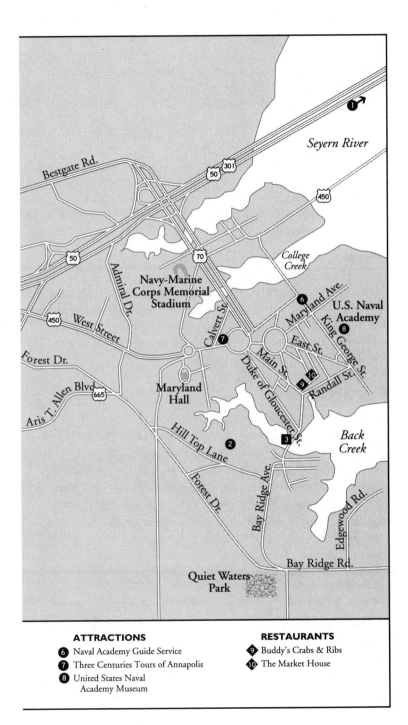

Seyern River

Bestgate Rd.

50 301

50

450

Admiral Dr.

70

College Creek

Navy-Marine Corps Memorial Stadium

Calvert St.

450 West Street

6

Maryland Ave.

U.S. Naval Academy

King George St.

8

7

East St.

Forest Dr.

Main St.

Aris T. Allen Blvd.

665

Maryland Hall

Duke of Gloucester St.

9 10

Randall St.

Hill Top Lane

2

Back Creek

3

Forest Dr.

Bay Ridge Ave.

Edgewood Rd.

Bay Ridge Rd.

Quiet Waters Park

ATTRACTIONS

6 Naval Academy Guide Service
7 Three Centuries Tours of Annapolis
8 United States Naval
   Academy Museum

RESTAURANTS

9 Buddy's Crabs & Ribs
10 The Market House

Dock views. In-room movies and an on-site restaurant and health club round out the amenities.

80 Compromise Street, Annapolis, MD 21401; (410) 268-7555. Rates $134–389.

Country Inns and Suites

A newly built, 100-room all-suite property with indoor pool and plentiful continental breakfast included. A bit of a drive from the city proper, but very close to the area's only shopping mall.

2600 Housely Road, Annapolis, MD 21401; (800) 456-4000 or (410) 571-6700; www.countryinns.com.

Hampton Inn and Suites Annapolis

We like Hampton Inns—they always have a pool, and the free continental breakfast is reasonably diverse and good. This one also offers connecting rooms. It's located near the Galleria Shopping Mall about three miles from the historic district and U.S. Naval Academy.

124 Womack Drive, Annapolis, MD 21401; (800) 426-7866 or (410) 571-0200. Rates $91–149.

Attractions

Naval Academy Guide Service

52 King George Street, Annapolis, MD 21402; (410) 263-6933

Hours: June–Labor Day, every half-hour Monday–Saturday 9:30 a.m.–3:30 p.m. and Sunday 12:15 p.m.–3:30 p.m.; September–November and March–Memorial Day, hourly Monday–Friday 10 a.m.–3 p.m., Saturday 10 a.m.–3:30 p.m., and Sunday 12:30 p.m.–3:30 p.m.

Admission: $6 adults, $5 seniors 62+, $4 students grades 1–12; free for preschoolers

Appeal by Age Groups:

Pre-school	Grade School	Teens	Young Adults	Over 30	Seniors
★★	★★★★	★★★★	★★★★	★★★★	★★★★

Touring Time: 1 hour

Rainy-Day Touring: Yes

Services and Facilities:

Restaurants Yes	Lockers No
Alcoholic beverages No	Pet kennels No
Disabled access Yes	Rain check No

Wheelchair rental No   Private tours No
Baby stroller rental No

Description and Comments   Naval Academy tours are shorter and probably better suited for younger children than the longer city tours. Start at
the Armel-Leftwich Visitor Center, where the film *To Lead and to Serve*
presents a general background and where you'll find exhibits on midshipmen's life and the *Freedom 7* space capsule, as well as a café. Kids of all ages
get a kick out of visiting Bancroft Hall, the dorm in which all 4,000 midshipmen live. Yes, it's huge.

Three Centuries Tours of Annapolis

48 Maryland Avenue, P.O. Box 29, Annapolis, MD 21404; (410) 263-
5401; www.annapolis-tours.com

Hours: April 1–October 31, daily 10:30 a.m. and 1:30 p.m.; November
1–March 31, daily 2:30 p.m.

Admission: $9 adults, $3 students

Appeal by Age Groups:

Pre-school	Grade School	Teens	Young Adults	Over 30	Seniors
★	★★★	★★★★	★★★★	★★★★★	★★★★★

Touring Time: 2 hours

Rainy-Day Touring: No

Services and Facilities:

Restaurants No   Lockers No
Alcoholic beverages No   Pet kennels No
Disabled access No   Rain check No
Wheelchair rental No   Private tours No
Baby stroller rental No

Description and Comments   Costumed interpreters lead these tours. They're
entertaining and extremely informative, not only about Annapolis but also,
more generally, about life in colonial America. The tours cover the historic
district, St. Mary's College, and highlights of the Naval Academy. Children
are welcome, but please judge whether or not they can hold up for a two-
hour walking tour. If they can't, consider limiting yourselves to a tour of the
Naval Academy, which is generally of most interest to kids (see below).

United States Naval Academy Museum

118 Maryland Avenue, Preble Hall, U.S. Naval Academy Annapolis, MD
21402; (410) 293-2108

Hours: Monday–Saturday 9 a.m.–5 p.m., Sunday 11 a.m.–5 p.m.; closed Thanksgiving, Christmas, and New Year's days

Admission: Free

Appeal by Age Groups:

Pre-school	Grade School	Teens	Young Adults	Over 30	Seniors
★★	★★★★	★★★★	★★★★	★★★★	★★★★★

Touring Time: Average 1 hour, minimum 45 minutes

Rainy-Day Touring: Yes

Services and Facilities:

Restaurants No	Lockers No
Alcoholic beverages No	Pet kennels No
Disabled access Yes	Rain check No
Wheelchair rental No	Private tours No
Baby stroller rental No	

Description and Comments   Home of the Rogers Ship Models Collection, 108 ship and boat models dating from 1650 to 1850. The models were built for the British Admiralty and are displayed in seventeenth-century cabinets.

Family-Friendly Restaurants

BUDDY'S CRABS AND RIBS

110 Main Street, Annapolis; (410) 626-1100; www.buddysonline.com

Meals served: Lunch and dinner; Sunday breakfast buffet
Cuisine: Seafood, ribs, and steaks
Entree range: $6.95–29.95 (lunch and dinner); buffets $7.95–10.95
Children's menu: Yes
Reservations: Yes
Payment: Major credit cards

Buddy's is busy. Lots of noise, lots of character, lots of food. Kids are handed a coloring pad and a balloon when they walk in. Kids ten and under eat free from the kids' menu, or one child eats free with each full-price adult entree. Everything's good, from the raw bar to the super crab cakes or the baby-back ribs. Portions are generous, and the buffets are enormous.

THE MARKET HOUSE

City Dock, Annapolis; (410) 269-0941

Meals served: Breakfast, lunch, and dinner
Cuisine: Seafood, deli, pizza, bakery, and more
Entree range: $2.50 and up
Children's menu: No
Reservations: No
Payment: Major credit cards; cash at some stands

Market House is the old-time market center and a great place to pick up "fast food." A fish market and raw bar, pizza place, Baskin Robbins, and a deli. Eat at tables outside, or on the run.

Capital Region

It's easy to think of Maryland's Beltway area as nothing but a series of face-less suburbs. But it's rich in semihidden treasures and surprises that can not only be reached within reasonable driving times from D.C. and environs but often can be reached on the District's easy-to-use Metro system. Young kids and granddads will love the **National Capital Trolley Museum** (call (301) 384-6088) in **Silver Spring,** where you can take a 20-minute ride on a vintage Washington, D.C., trolley car. Horse lovers enjoy learning about thoroughbreds at the **Belair Stable Museum** (call (301) 809-3088) in **Bowie.** In **Greenbelt,** the **NASA/Goddard Space Flight Center/Museum** (call (301) 286-8981) uses interactive activities to convey ideas about space and space travel. **Oxon Hill Farm** in **Oxon Hill** (call (301) 839-1177) brings old-time farming to life. South on the Beltway, **Six Flags America** (call (301) 249-1500) is a major theme and water park located in Largo.

　Frederick is a history-rich little town that sits about 45 minutes north of the D.C. Beltway and calls itself "The Crossroads of American History." The local historical society offers an excellent walking tour, but it's proba-bly too long for kids. Stop in at the **Visitors Center** (call (800) 999-3613) and pick up a self-guiding tour brochure to catch the highlights. From April through December, families with older children can join a guide-led walk-ing tour (call (301) 775-8687) or hop aboard a horse-drawn carriage for a tour (call (301) 775-2670). The historic district holds plenty of shops and restaurants, so there are plenty of modern diversions. Check out **I Made This** (call (301) 624-4030), a pottery store where you can make your own. The town holds some 30 antique dealers, for those who like that sort of thing, and regularly hosts a farmer's market in **Everedy Square. Baker Park** contains playgrounds, ball fields, and lots of room to run.

　In nearby **Brunswick,** southwest of Frederick, railroad buffs will like the **Brunswick Railroad Museum** (call (301) 834- 7100), set in an 1891

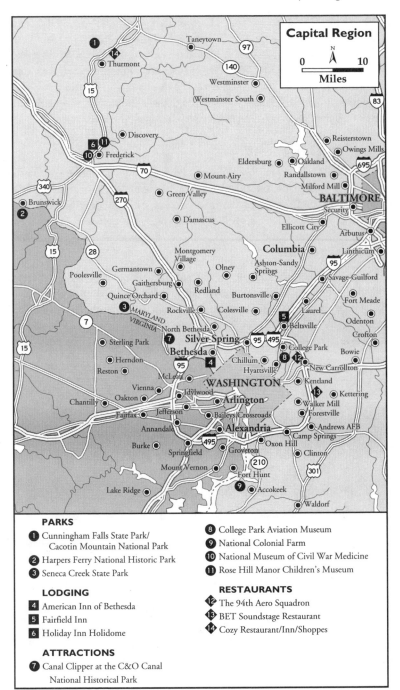

Capital Region

N

0   10
Miles

Taneytown

Thurmont

Westminster

Westminster South

Discovery

Frederick

Brunswick

Reisterstown

Owings Mills

Eldersburg   Oakland

Randallstown

Milford Mill

BALTIMORE

Security

Mount Airy

Green Valley

Damascus

Ellicott City

Arbutus

Montgomery
Village

Olney

Ashton-Sandy
Springs

Columbia

Linthicum

Poolesville

Germantown

Gaithersburg

Quince Orchard

Redland

Burtonsville

Savage-Guilford

Fort Meade

MARYLAND
VIRGINIA

Rockville

Colesville

Laurel

Odenton

North Bethesda

Sterling Park

Silver Spring

Bethesda

Beltsville

College Park

Crofton

Bowie

Herndon

Reston

McLean

Chillum

Hyattsville

WASHINGTON

New Carrollton

Kendall

Vienna

Idylwood

Arlington

Walker Mill

Kettering

Chantilly

Oakton

Forestville

Fairfax

Jefferson

Baileys Crossroads

Annandale

Alexandria

Andrews AFB

Burke

Springfield

Groveton

Oxon Hill

Camp Springs

Clinton

Mount Vernon

Fort Hunt

Lake Ridge

Accokeek

Waldorf

PARKS

❶ Cunningham Falls State Park/
Cacotin Mountain National Park

❷ Harpers Ferry National Historic Park

❸ Seneca Creek State Park

LODGING

4 American Inn of Bethesda

5 Fairfield Inn

6 Holiday Inn Holidome

ATTRACTIONS

❼ Canal Clipper at the C&O Canal
National Historical Park

❽ College Park Aviation Museum

❾ National Colonial Farm

❿ National Museum of Civil War Medicine

⓫ Rose Hill Manor Children's Museum

RESTAURANTS

⓬ The 94th Aero Squadron

⓭ BET Soundstage Restaurant

⓮ Cozy Restaurant/Inn/Shoppes

train station. The **C&O Canal Historic Park** (call (301) 739-4200) runs through here for an easy hike or bike ride. In **Thurmont,** not far from Cunningham Falls Park and Cacotin Mountain Park, the **Cacotin Wildlife Preserve and Zoo** (call (301) 271- 3180) is set on 26 natural acres. **Antietam National Battlefield** (call (301) 432-5124), site of one of the Civil War's bloodiest one-day battles and considered the war's best-preserved battlefield, can be reached in a half-hour's drive west along Route 40A.

HOW TO GET THERE

By Car. I-95 is the main north-south thoroughfare whether you're coming from New York or Richmond. I-495, the infamous "Beltway," circles Washington, D.C., and from it you'll find access to most attractions in the region's southern section. I-270 runs northwest-southeast between Rockville (a Washington suburb) and Frederick, while I-70 runs east-west between Baltimore and Frederick.

By Plane. Baltimore/Washington International Airport (BWI) best serves the region's more northerly areas; (800) 435-9294; www.bwairport.com. Washington's two Virginia-based airports are best for southerly destinations in the region: Ronald Regan Washington National Airport, or Washington Dulles International Airport; (703) 419-8000; www.metwashairports.com.

By Train. Amtrak serves both Washington, D.C., and Baltimore, as well as several points between; (800) 872-7245; www.amtrak.com.

HOW TO GET INFORMATION BEFORE YOU GO

Conference and Visitors Bureau of Montgomery County, 12900 Middlebrook Road, Suite 1400, Germantown, MD 20874; (800) 925-0880; www.cvbmontco.com.

Prince George's County; (888) 925-8300.

Tourism Council of Frederick County, 19 East Church Street, Frederick, MD 21701; (800) 800-9699; (301) 663-8687; www.visitfrederick.org.

The Best Parks

Cunningham Falls State Park/Cacotin Mountain National Park. Within an hour's drive of metro Washington, these paired parks offer the perfect introduction to the lush Maryland mountains. The hike to Cunningham Falls is an easy, annotated half-mile, and the nearby lake offers swimming and picnicking. At the south end, which has a separate entrance, the Cacotin Iron Furnace Historical Site reveals the area's past iron mining and processing industries, and the Manor Area holds a recycled tire playground. Cacotin Mountain Park, home to the presidential retreat Camp David, offers a variety of trails ranging from one-third mile to nine miles long. Camping is available in both parks. Cunningham Falls Park and Cacotin Park information: 14039 Cacotin Hollow Road, Thurmont, MD 21788; (301) 271-7574, TDD (410) 260-8835.

Harpers Ferry National Historical Park. See page 410 in the West Virginia chapter. P.O. Box 65, Harpers Ferry, WV 25425; (304) 535-6298; www.nps.gov/hafe.

Seneca Creek State Park. Day visitors to this park, which encompasses more than 6,000 acres, can play disc golf, rent a boat or canoe, fish, hike, or horseback ride. 11950 Clopper Road, Gaithersburg, MD 20828; (301) 924-2127.

Family Outdoor Adventures

Biking and Canoeing. The tow path that winds throughout the C&O Canal National Historic Park offers terrific, relatively flat and easy cycling and paddling; (202) 653-5844 or (301) 299-3613.

Hiking and Camping. See Cunningham Falls State Park and Cacotin Mountain National Park under The Best Parks.

Family Lodging

American Inn of Bethesda

A comfortable, moderately priced hotel in the heart of Bethesda—two miles south of I-270 and I-495 (the Capital Beltway) and within walking distance of the Washington Metro—that could be used as an alternative to more expensive in-town D.C. hotels. This 76-room property has an outdoor pool, free e-mail and Internet access, and a complimentary continental breakfast. As for restaurants, downtown Bethesda has some 170 of them.

8130 Wisconsin Avenue, Bethesda, MD 20814; (800) 323-7081; www.american-inn.com. Rates $84–150; children under age 18 stay free in same room with parents.

Fairfield Inn Capital Beltway

Fairfield Inn is a reliable chain, and this one is located near College Park and within easy driving distance of everything from Baltimore to Washington, D.C. It has 169 rooms, an on-site restaurant (with several others nearby), a pool, and complimentary continental breakfast.

4050 Powder Mill Road, Beltsville, MD 20705; (301) 572-7100. Rates $79–139.

Holiday Inn Holidome and Conference Center

We like these Holidomes—their interior atriums are very kid friendly. This one features a heated indoor pool, sauna, Jacuzzi, miniature golf, volleyball, horseshoes, and on-site restaurant. It's within walking distance of the local shopping mall (more than 75 stores) and restaurants and a mile from the historic district.

5400 Holiday Drive, Frederick, MD 21703; (800) 868-0094 or (301) 694-7500. Rates $79–109; special breakfast-included rates available; children age 19 and under stay free in same room with parents.

Attractions

Canal Clipper at the C&O Canal National Historical Park

Great Falls Visitor Center, 11710 MacArthur Boulevard, Potomac, MD 20854; Georgetown Visitor Center, 1057 Thomas Jefferson Street NW, Washington, D.C. 20007; Great Falls, (301) 299-3163; Georgetown, (202) 653-5844; www.nps.gov/choh

Hours: Boat tours vary by season: April–early June and mid-September–early November, departing Thursday–Sunday at 11 a.m. and 3 p.m., with a 1:30 p.m. excursion on weekends; mid-June–mid-September cruises add Wednesdays, as well as a 1:30 p.m. departure Wednesday–Friday and 1:30 p.m. and 4:30 p.m. trips on weekends; schedules change, so call ahead to verify

Admission: $7.50 adults, $6 seniors 62+, $4 children ages 4–14, free for children 3 and under

Appeal by Age Groups:

Pre-school	Grade School	Teens	Young Adults	Over 30	Seniors
★★★	★★★★	★★★★	★★★★	★★★★★	★★★★★

Touring Time: 1 hour

Rainy-Day Touring: Yes

Services and Facilities:

Restaurants No	Baby stroller rental No
Alcoholic beverages No	Lockers No
Disabled access Yes; at Georgetown	Pet kennels No
	Rain check No
Wheelchair rental No	Private tours No

Description and Comments   The C&O Canal runs 130-plus miles from Washington, D.C., to Cumberland, Maryland, passing through 74 lift locks. These two sites offer rides aboard the mule-drawn canal boats that hauled iron, grain, and other products in the mid-nineteenth century. Narration is provided by a park ranger. When we rode the boat, the guide was engaging and funny and had all the children well involved in her stories. The mules were downright adorable. And feeling the boat rise and fall as the lock filled and emptied was deemed cool by all aboard. Visitors to the Great Falls center can also take a short walk to observe the falls. Canoes, rowboats, and bikes can be rented near the Great Falls center at Swain's Lock (call (301) 299-9006) and at Thompson Boat Center in Georgetown (call (202) 333-4861). Just south of Great Falls, Cabin John Park in Bethesda holds an excellent playground.

College Park Aviation Museum

1985 Corporal Frank Scott Drive, College Park, MD 20740;
  (301) 864-6029

Hours: Daily 10 a.m.–5 p.m.; closed major holidays

Admission: $4 adults, $3 seniors 60+, $3 children ages 2–13, free for children 2 and under

Appeal by Age Groups:

Pre-school	Grade School	Teens	Young Adults	Over 30	Seniors
★★★	★★★★★	★★★	★★★★	★★★★★	★★★★★

Touring Time: Average 1½ hours, minimum 45 minutes

Rainy-Day Touring: Yes

Services and Facilities:

Restaurants No; one located in a 5-minute walk	**Lockers** No
	Pet kennels No
Alcoholic beverages No	**Rain check** No
Disabled access Yes	**Private tours** Yes; by appointment
Wheelchair rental Yes; for loan	
Baby stroller rental No	

Description and Comments College Park, home to the University of Maryland, was where the Wright brothers developed their flying machine into a profitable business. Indeed, the museum is on the grounds of the world's oldest continually operated airport. It's a small, user-friendly museum that makes an excellent, calmer alternative to the usually bustling and crowded Air and Space Museum in D.C.. You're greeted by an animatronic Wilbur Wright, who welcomes you to the airfield and his workshop, and from there you head into the main exhibit area, where a handful of vintage planes are displayed, including a replica 1911 Wright Brothers Model B. Take a close look at the 1924 Berliner helicopter, the first vertical flight machine; it looks far too complicated to actually fly. Plenty of hands-on activities are featured, including flight simulators; preschoolers love the pedal-powered mini-biplanes they can drive on the outdoor patio. Special programs are scheduled regularly for all ages from preschool through high school. Get there via the D.C. Metro, which stops three blocks away.

National Colonial Farm

3400 Bryan Point Road, Accokeek, MD 20607; (301) 283-2113; www.accokeek.org

Hours: Mid-march–mid-December, Tuesday–Sunday 10 a.m.–5 p.m.; Piscataway Park itself is open daily from sunrise to sunset

Admission: $2 adults, $.50 children ages 3–12, free for children under 3; Mt. Vernon Connector Ferry runs mid-May–mid-September: $7 adults, $5 children; Mt. Vernon package, including admission at both attractions and two-way ferry ride: $15 adults, $9 children

Appeal by Age Groups:

Pre-school	Grade School	Teens	Young Adults	Over 30	Seniors
★★	★★★★	★★★	★★★★	★★★★★	★★★★★

Touring Time: Average 2½ hours, minimum 1½ hours

Rainy-Day Touring: Yes

Services and Facilities:

Restaurants No; snacks in gift shop	Baby stroller rental No
Alcoholic beverages No	Lockers No
Disabled access Yes, to the grounds; no, to the buildings	Pet kennels No
	Rain check No
Wheelchair rental Yes; free	Private tours No

Description and Comments Unlike many historical re-creations and preservation sites that focus on the famous or well-to-do, the National Farm centers around the life of a typical middle-class farm family circa 1775. Set on beautiful lowlands bordering the Potomac River in the midst of the Piscataway Park natural preserve, the farm features a farmhouse, out-kitchen, tobacco barn, smokehouse, crop fields, and demonstration gardens. In addition, the adjoining Ecosystem Farm offers a look at a fully functioning co-operative community farm that produces its own energy and is devoted to sustaining the land. An interpreter in period costume will accompany you, focusing particularly on the theme of the month, which has included such topics as herbs, colonial lighting, or the eco-farm. You can tour on your own if you prefer. Visit in the spring, when the heirloom livestock—such as the Hog Island sheep—are expanding their families. The farm offers a low-key look into a combination of history and environmentalism in a beautiful setting. Bring a picnic lunch; walk one of the six interpretive hiking trails (ranging from a half mile to a mile and a half long).

The Farm offers combination tickets for entrance to Mt. Vernon (see page 327 in the Virginia chapter) that, in summertime, includes a ferry trip across the Potomac in a period dory riverboat.

National Museum of Civil War Medicine

48 East Patrick Street, Frederick, MD 21701; (301) 695-1864; www.civilwarmed.org

Hours: Mid-March–mid-November, Monday–Saturday 10 a.m.–5 p.m., Sunday 11 a.m.–5 p.m. Mid-November–mid-March, Monday–Saturday 10 a.m.–4 p.m., Sunday 11 a.m.–4 p.m.

Admission: $6.50 adults, $6 seniors 60+, $4.50 children ages 6–10, free for children 9 and under. *Note:* Admission charges were scheduled to be increased; call for exact fee

Appeal by Age Groups:

Pre-school	Grade School	Teens	Young Adults	Over 30	Seniors
★	★★★	★★★★	★★★★	★★★★★	★★★★★

Touring Time: Average 2 hours, minimum 1 hour

Rainy-Day Touring: Yes

Services and Facilities:

Restaurants No; several nearby	Lockers No
Alcoholic beverages No	Pet kennels No
Disabled access Yes	Rain check No
Wheelchair rental Yes, free	Private tours No
Baby stroller rental No	

Description and Comments Billed as the only museum devoted exclusively to the medical aspect of the Civil War, this small but eye-opening place is best visited during a special event. Living history events take place throughout the summer months, usually on weekends and holidays, and can include vivid and lively demonstrations of nursing and the duties of the wartime medical steward (or doctor's assistant), embalming (which was not a common practice until that war), and the life of the drummer boy. Where else can a kid try his or her hand at producing medicinal pills with 1860s technology and techniques? Beyond the living history, younger kids might find the exhibits a trifle boring or difficult to comprehend, but the facts one learns are quite surprising. Hospitals, for example, employed full-time bands, staged theatrical productions, and did many other things to amuse their long-suffering, bedridden patients. And did you know that the war was so bloody and devastating that it necessitated the development of many new medical techniques and spawned a variety of treatment breakthroughs? There's also a tribute to the African American doctors, nurses, and soldiers who suffered through this calamitous period in U.S. history.

Rose Hill Manor Children's Museum

1611 North Market Street, Frederick, MD 21701; (301) 694-1648; www.co.frederick.md.us/govt/parks/rosehill.htm

Hours: April–October, Monday–Saturday 10 a.m.– 4 p.m., Sunday 1 p.m.– 4 p.m.

Admission: $3 adults, $2 seniors 55+, $2 children ages 3–17

Appeal by Age Groups:

Pre-school	Grade School	Teens	Young Adults	Over 30	Seniors
★★	★★★★★	★★★	★★★	★★★★	★★★★★

Touring Time: Average 2½ hours, minimum 1 hour

Rainy-Day Touring: Yes

Services and Facilities:

Restaurants No	Baby stroller rental No
Alcoholic beverages No	Lockers No
Disabled access Yes; with some limitations	Pet kennels No
	Rain check No
Wheelchair rental No	Private tours No

Description and Comments   A history museum aimed specifically at elementary school kids, Rose Hill Manor focuses on life in the early nineteenth century through guided and self- guided tours. The self-guided tour of the Farm Museum features exhibits on late-nineteenth-century and early-twentieth-century agricultural practices and farm family life. Manor House tours are guided by costumed interpreters. A visit includes hands-on activities, such as weaving, carding wool, playing with replica period toys, and doing chores. The carriage museum will be of interest to those who like wheeled vehicles. For adults, the museum offers architectural and historic interpretation.

Family-Friendly Restaurants

THE 94TH AERO SQUADRON

5240 Pain Beach Parkway, College Park; (301) 633-9400

Meals served: Lunch and dinner
Cuisine: Eclectic mix of American, Italian, and seafood

Entree range: $8.95 – 24.95
Children's menu: Yes
Reservations: Yes
Payment: Major credit cards

Part of a small chain with installations in the Midwest and Northeast, the theme here is World War II aviation. The food is good—but the real attraction is the theme. A cadre of real WWII war planes guards the entrance to a building designed to invoke a French countryside farmhouse—right down to a bombed-out section of the leftmost wing. Take a table by the window so you can watch the modern-day private planes come and go from the College Park Airport.

BET SOUNDSTAGE RESTAURANT

9640 Lottsford Court, Largo; (301) 883-9500

Meals served: Lunch, dinner, and Sunday brunch
Cuisine: Southern and Caribbean-style, plus steaks
Entree range: $7.50 – 15.95 (lunch and dinner)
Children's menu: Yes
Reservations: Yes
Payment: Major credit cards

If you're traveling with a teen who's into rap, R&B, soul, Motown, or hip-hop, this is a very cool place to be. It's the first of a planned series of eateries that takes its theme from the Black Entertainment Television network, often featuring live celebrity entertainment and always showing the latest black artists on dozens of large and small TV screens. Soundstage is oddly located—in a remote area amid office suburban complexes and just a couple of miles from the new Redskins football stadium—but the food is excellent, kids of all ages will love the active, nonstop music environment, and it's near Six Flags America.

COZY RESTAURANT COUNTRY INN AND VILLAGE OF SHOPPES

Route 806, Thurmont; (301) 271-4301

Meals served: Breakfast, lunch, and dinner
Cuisine: American
Entree range: $2.09 – 14.49 (breakfast, lunch, and dinner)
Children's menu: Yes
Reservations: Yes
Payment: Major credit cards

Set 15 miles north of Frederick and 5 miles from Camp David, Cunningham State Park, and Cacotin Mountain Park (see The Best Parks above), the Cozy is a local legend. In business on this site since the 1920s, it started as a tourist court with gas station and restaurant. Today, the busy decor features mementos of all the sports and political celebrities who have dined and lodged here. They specialize in buffets for all three meals, and brunch on Sundays, but you can also order from the menu. After you dine, trek across the street to the shops, where gifts and crafts are sold.

Eastern Shore

"Maryland's Eastern Shore." The phrase holds magic for Baltimore and D.C. dwellers, who flock to sites along the ocean and the bay seeking water-based relief from the summer heat. This is quintessential "low" country, where the grasses grow tall, farming is still a way of life, and the sea is a place both to play and to make a living. It's also a place where small-town living holds the day. **St. Michael's,** home to cute shops and some surprisingly good restaurants, personifies that lifestyle. If you want to sample the oysterman's life, **Chesapeake Skipjack Sailing Tours** (call (410) 745-6080) will show you how it's done. European settlement on **Tilghman Island** goes back to 1650, and life there today can seem much the same. If you're looking for something laid-back and uncrowded, this island, just three miles long, is it.

Ocean City, of course, is the region's main attraction. It's situated on a long, narrow peninsula; the ocean lies on the east side, and Sinepuxtent and Assawoman Bays on the west. The streets are laid out in a grid, and those running east-west are numbered: First Street is the southernmost, and 146th Street actually falls at the Maryland/Delaware state line. Ocean City's beach is wide and meticulously manicured and features some nifty little-kid play structures—a pirate ship, a huge truck, etc.—fitted with climbing elements and slides, plus, for older kids, a series of beach volleyball courts, at least one of which is lit for night play. The boardwalk, three miles long, offers all the usual ticky-tacky attractions and shops that shore boardwalks do, but it's well kept, clean, and approachable. The **Kite Loft** (call (410) 289-7855) can be found at three locations; it's an Ocean City tradition for anything that flies, flaps, or flutters in the wind. **Wheels of Yesterday** (call (410) 213-7329) is an antique and classic car museum in West Ocean City. The **Model Train Garden,** located at 94th Street and open Thursday–Sunday during summer (and weekends otherwise), features 1,600 square

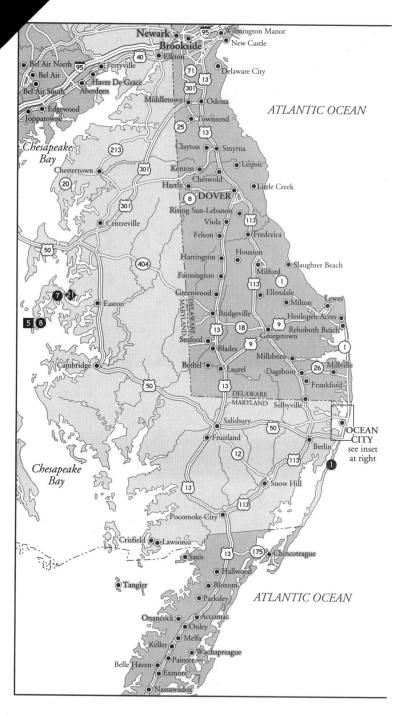

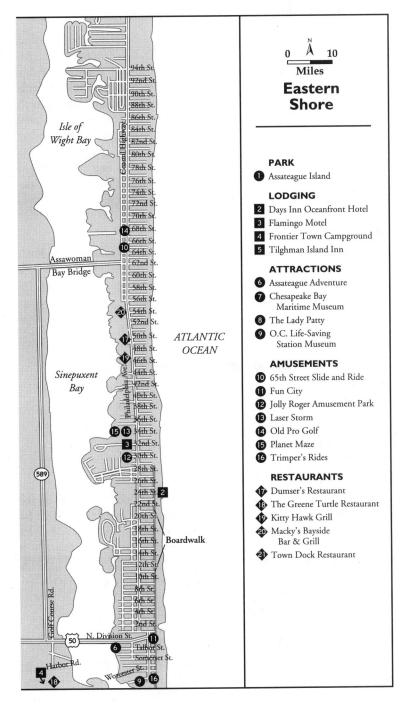

94th St.
92nd St.
90th St.
88th St.
86th St.
84th St.
82nd St.
80th St.
78th St.
76th St.
74th St.
72nd St.
70th St.
68th St.
66th St.
64th St.
62nd St.
60th St.
58th St.
56th St.
54th St.
52nd St.
50th St.
48th St.
46th St.
44th St.
42nd St.
40th St.
38th St.
36th St.
34th St.
32nd St.
30th St.
28th St.
26th St.
24th St.
22nd St.
20th St.
18th St.
16th St.
14th St.
12th St.
10th St.
8th St.
6th St.
4th St.
2nd St.

Isle of Wight Bay

Coastal Highway

Assawoman
Bay Bridge

Sinepuxent Bay

Philadelphia Ave.

589

ATLANTIC OCEAN

Boardwalk

Golf Course Rd.

50 N. Division St.
Talbot St.
Somerset St.
Harbor Rd.
Worcester St.

0   N   10
Miles

Eastern Shore

PARK
1. Assateague Island

LODGING
2. Days Inn Oceanfront Hotel
3. Flamingo Motel
4. Frontier Town Campground
5. Tilghman Island Inn

ATTRACTIONS
6. Assateague Adventure
7. Chesapeake Bay Maritime Museum
8. The Lady Patty
9. O.C. Life-Saving Station Museum

AMUSEMENTS
10. 65th Street Slide and Ride
11. Fun City
12. Jolly Roger Amusement Park
13. Laser Storm
14. Old Pro Golf
15. Planet Maze
16. Trimper's Rides

RESTAURANTS
17. Dumser's Restaurant
18. The Greene Turtle Restaurant
19. Kitty Hawk Grill
20. Macky's Bayside Bar & Grill
21. Town Dock Restaurant

feet of Lionel O-gauge trains and no admission fee. **Nite Lite** (call (410) 289-6313), an under-21 dance club at Boardwalk and Worcester Street, fills the need for teens craving nightlife. The town maintains a variety of public parks. The **Northside Park** at 127th Street covers 58 acres, with ball fields, tot-lots, a fishing lagoon, and a marvelous jogging/in-line skating path. **Ocean City Skate Park** at Third Street holds an excellent reputation among East Coast trick in-line skaters and skateboarders; the park also has basketball and tennis courts.

If you need an inland day trip, visit the **Salisbury Zoo and Park** (call (410) 548-3188), located about 20 minutes west of Ocean City in Salisbury. It's one of the country's better small zoos—and it's free.

HOW TO GET THERE

Most folks arrive in the Eastern Shore from the west, traveling from D.C., Baltimore, or Annapolis. Most folks also arrive by car. Heading to most major southern points, including Ocean City, from the west, follow U.S. Route 50 across the Chesapeake Bay. If you want to head north from there, follow U.S. 301. Coming *from* the north, exit I-95 at Elkton and follow State Route 213 south to Route 301.

HOW TO GET INFORMATION BEFORE YOU GO

Queen Anne's County Office of Tourism, 425 Piney Narrows Road, Suite 3, Chester, MD 21619; (888) 400-7787; www.qac.org.

Ocean City Office of Tourism, 4001 Coastal Highway, Ocean City, MD 21842; (800) 626-2326; www.ocean-city.com.

GETTING AROUND OCEAN CITY

You'll most likely arrive by car, but there's no need to drive everywhere you go. Local buses run the length of town, stopping at every other block for a fare of $1 per day; a trolley runs the same route, and rides on it are included in the bus fare. The Boardwalk Train, a tourist-style conveyance pulled by a slow-moving Jeep, runs the three-mile length of the boardwalk. You can get on or off anywhere along the route. The ride makes a nice diversion for tired kids, but at $2.25 per person one-way, you'll want to reserve it for special occasions.

OCEAN BEACH DISABLED BEACH ACCESS

The City of Ocean Beach has created beach access for the disabled at 20 locations. Seventeen of those offer special beach chairs on a first-come, first-served basis: Inlet Beach, 12th Street, 25th Street, 35th Street, 37th Street in the Sand Hotel, 40th Street, 48th Street, 59th Street, 70th Street, 81st Street, 89th Street, 94th Street, 107th Street, 120th Street, 130th Street, 139th Street, and 145th Street. The Ocean City Visitors Center has one beach chair available for multiday use by advanced reservation; call (410) 289-2800.

Family Outdoor Adventures

Biking. For cycling in the St. Michael's/Tilghman's Island area, rent a bike at Wheel Doctor Cycle and Sport, (410) 745-6676; www.wheeldrbicycle.com.

Bicycling the boardwalk is a tradition, and Ocean City holds a number of places to rent bikes. Generally the price runs from $4 to $20, depending on what you rent, which can be anything from an old-fashioned two-wheeler to a bike with attached stroller or a low-rider. Boardwalk cycling hours are 6–10 a.m. Cyclists are also welcome in Assateague National Seashore.

Boating. Explore the Chesapeake by rowboat, sailboat, or motorboat. In the St. Michael's/Tilghman Island area, Deep Reef rents small craft of all kinds, (410) 886-2545.

Deep-Sea Fishing. The *Nancy Ellen* can be chartered out of Knapps Narrows Marine at Tilghman Island, (410) 745-6022. A number of operators provide service out of Ocean City; call (800) 622-2326 or (410) 289-2800, or visit www.ocean-city.com for a list.

Sea Kayaking and Canoeing. Island Kayak, (410) 886-2083, explores the Tilghman Island area with paddle; you can either join guided tours or go on your own. The cypress swamps and waterways of the southeastern Eastern Shore can be explored with guided trips from Poconoke River Canoe, 312 North Washington Street, Snow Hill, MD 21863; (800) 258-0905; or Tangier Sound Outfitters, 27582 Farm Market Road, Marion, MD 21838; (410) 968-1803.

Surfing. K-Coast Surf Shop at 78th Street and Coastal Highway, (410) 723-3330, stages surf camps from 8 a.m. to 10 a.m. on Tuesday, Wednesday, and Thursday in July and August. Camps include use of surfboards, wetsuits, bodyboards, personalized lessons, and water safety instruction.

Family Lodging

Days Inn Oceanfront Hotel

On the boardwalk, but out of earshot of the noisiest sections, the property features two outdoor pools and a kiddie pool. Rooms have microwaves, refrigerators, and coffeemakers. Efficiencies and suites available with the same, plus cooktop, stove, cookware, and utensils. Complimentary cribs.

Assateague Island

Just ten miles or so south of Ocean City lies **Assateague Island,** famous for its free-running wild ponies. Both a national and a state park are located there, each offering ocean and bay swimming, as well as camping. If you're going to camp, one local describes the difference between the two parks this way: the state park has new, modern bathhouses with hot showers, whereas the national park does not. The national park, however, has campsites that are more isolated. Both are plagued by mosquitoes that are almost as famous as the ponies. For day beachgoing, best to pick a day with an easterly, offshore wind, which tends to blow the bugs inland and off the beach. Bathing with small children is best on the bay side, where the water remains shallow for a great distance.

Assateague Island National Seashore offers many kid-friendly and family-oriented programs and facilities. Their Junior Ranger program is aimed at 6- to 14-year-olds and includes a booklet filled with learning activities to follow. Throughout the summer, the park offers a series of programs such as marsh walks, aquarium and campfire talks, and canoe trips. In addition, the visitors center shows videos about the park, including one about the ponies, and has an aquarium with local fish and a "please touch" room. Pick up the park newspaper upon arrival for current activities and programs.

Information: Assateague Island National Seashore, 7206 National Seashore Lane, Berlin, MD 21811; (800) 365-2267 or (410) 641-1441; www.nps.gov/asis; visitors center open daily 9 a.m.–5 p.m. Assateague State Park, 7303 Stephen Decatur Highway, Berlin, MD 21811; (888) 432-2267 or (410) 641-2120; www.dnr.state.md.us.

2210 Baltimore Avenue, Ocean City, MD 21842; (800) 926-1122. Rates $39–259; children 18 and under stay free in room with parents.

Flamingo Motel

A moderately priced, well-kept, multi-building motel three blocks north of the boardwalk. It has regular rooms, kitchenette units and suites (no ovens, just microwaves), and a nice indoor pool.

3100 Baltimore Avenue, Ocean City, MD 21842; (800) 394-7465 or (410) 289-6464. Rates $29–139; children 16 and under stay free with paying adult.

Frontier Town Campground

A commercial campground with 500 sites for RVs and tents. The park also offers cabin camping sites and rental vacation trailer sites. Swimming pool and water park, plus mini-golf, fishing and crabbing pier, nature trails, and other activities (see Frontier Town in the Attractions section).

Route 611, P.O. Box 691, Ocean City, MD 21843; (800) 228-5590 or (410) 641-0880. Rates for site, $20–33.50; for cabins, $41–61; for vacation trailers, $58.50–$99.

Tilghman Island Inn

A comfortable, 20-room inn set right on the water, with small boats for rent, a swimming pool, and an on-site restaurant. Adjacent to the *Lady Patty* sailing cruises and ten miles from St. Michael's.

21384 Cooper Road, Tilghman, MD 21671; (800) 866-2141 or (410) 886-2141; www.tilghmanislandinn.com. Rates $75–160; multiday packages including dinner and breakfast are available.

Attractions

Assateague Adventure

Talbot Street on the Bay, Ocean City, MD; (410) 289-3500; www.ocean-city.com/boatrides/assateague.htm

Hours: Mid-May–mid-June, daily 9:30 a.m., 12:30 p.m., and 3:30 p.m.; mid-June–August, Monday–Friday 8:30 a.m., 10:30 a.m., 12:30 p.m., 2:30 p.m., 4:30 p.m., 6:30 p.m., Saturday–Sunday 10:30 a.m., 12:30 p.m., 2:30 p.m., and 4:30 p.m.; September–mid-October, daily 9:30 a.m., 12:30 p.m., and 3:30 p.m.

Admission: $14.50 adults, $12 seniors, $8 children ages 7–12, free for children under 7

Appeal by Age Groups:

Pre-school	Grade School	Teens	Young Adults	Over 30	Seniors
★★	★★★★	★★★★	★★★★★	★★★★★	★★★★

Touring Time: 1½ hours

Rainy-Day Touring: Yes

Services and Facilities:

Restaurants No	Lockers No
Alcoholic beverages No	Pet kennels No
Disabled access Partial	Rain check No
Wheelchair rental No	Private tours No
Baby stroller rental No	

Description and Comments   A 90-minute cruise to Assateague Island, including a landing on the island to explore the ecosystem and look for birds and the famous wild ponies. Clam dredging and hands-on crabbing and crab-pot demonstrations, too. This is a fun, alternative way to visit Assateague with a knowledgeable guide.

Chesapeake Bay Maritime Museum

Mill Street, P.O. Box 636, St. Michael's, MD 21663; (410) 745-2916; www.cbmm.org

Hours: June–September, daily 9 a.m.–6 p.m.; March–May, September–November, daily 9 a.m.–5 p.m.; December–February, daily 9 a.m.–4 p.m.; closed Thanksgiving, Christmas, and New Year's days

Admission: $7.50 adults, $6.50 seniors 65+, $3 children ages 6–17, free for children under 6

Appeal by Age Groups:

Pre-school	Grade School	Teens	Young Adults	Over 30	Seniors
★★★	★★★★★	★★★	★★★★	★★★★★	★★★★★

Touring Time: Average 1½ hours, minimum 45 minutes

Rainy-Day Touring: Yes

Services and Facilities:

Restaurants No; several nearby	Baby stroller rental No
Alcoholic beverages No	Lockers No
Disabled access Yes; but not to lighthouse	Pet kennels No
	Rain check No
Wheelchair rental Yes; two available for free	Private tours Yes; call ahead

Description and Comments   A small museum, with nine exhibit buildings, devoted to the history and culture of the Chesapeake Bay. The 1879 "screwpile" lighthouse is the highlight exhibit, but kids will like the chance to try their hand at oystering and setting a trotline for crabbing. There are also a variety of boats to climb on and explore. In high season, Wednesday morning special programs are offered for kids grouped by ages. Special events take place throughout the spring, summer, and fall. The museum expects to greatly increase the number of interactive exhibits during 2001 and 2002. The grounds are pretty and make a good picnic place.

Frontier Town

Route 611, P.O. Box 691, Ocean City, MD 21843; (800) 228-5590 or (410) 289-7877; www.frontiertown.com

Hours: Memorial Day–Labor Day, daily 10 a.m.–6 p.m.; gates close at 4:30 p.m., rides close at 5:30 p.m.

Admission: $10 adults and teens 14 and up, $8 children ages 4–13, free for children 3 and under; on-site campers: $8 adults and teens 14 and up, $6.50 children ages 4–13; includes all shows and rides; unlimited, all-day mini-golf and water park for everyone: $6

Appeal by Age Groups:

Pre-school	Grade School	Teens	Young Adults	Over 30	Seniors
★★★★	★★★★★	★★★★	★★★	★★★	★★

Touring Time: Average 4 hours, minimum 3 hours

Rainy-Day Touring: No

Services and Facilities:

Restaurants Yes	Lockers Yes
Alcoholic beverages Yes	Pet kennels No
Disabled access Yes	Rain check No
Wheelchair rental No	Private tours No
Baby stroller rental No	

Description and Comments   This is a campground/water park/Wild West show with miniature golf. The Wild West show runs daily to a specific schedule, including rodeo, gunfights, and Indian dancing. Kids can also try the rides—stagecoach, steam train, trail, pony, train, and paddleboats. The water park is for kids standing at least 42 inches tall, but there is a wading pool for the little ones.

The Lady Patty

5907 Tilghman Island Road, P.O. Box 248, Tilghman Island, MD 21671; (800) 690-5080 or (410) 886-2215; www.sailladypatty.com

Hours: Vary

Admission: $30–45 per person

Appeal by Age Groups:

Pre-school	Grade School	Teens	Young Adults	Over 30	Seniors
★★★	★★★★★	★★★★	★★★★★	★★★★★	★★★★★

Touring Time: 2 or 4 hours depending on the cruise

Rainy-Day Touring: No

Services and Facilities:

Restaurants No	Lockers No
Alcoholic beverages No	Pet kennels No
Disabled access Yes	Rain check No
Wheelchair rental No	Private tours Yes
Baby stroller rental No	

Description and Comments   Captain Mike Richards, an ex-navy man, guides you on the Chesapeake in his classic 45-foot teak and bronze Bay Ketch, built in 1935. A personable guide, Richards operates two-hour, four-hour, and sunset sail-powered cruises to Sharps Island and other spots near Tilghman Island. Kids get to steer the 16-passenger ship while Captain Mike regales everyone with sea stories, tall and otherwise.

Ocean City Life-Saving Station Museum

P.O. Box 603, Ocean City, MD 21843; (410) 289-4991;
www.ocmuseum.org

Hours: June–September, daily 11 a.m.–10 p.m.; October and May, daily 11 a.m.–4 p.m.; November–April, Saturdays and Sundays 11 a.m.–4 p.m.

Admission: $2 adults, $1 children 12 and under

Appeal by Age Groups:

Pre-school	Grade School	Teens	Young Adults	Over 30	Seniors
★★★	★★★★★	★★★★	★★★★★	★★★★★	★★★★★

Touring Time: Average 1½ hours, minimum 45 minutes

Rainy-Day Touring: Yes

Services and Facilities:

Restaurants No; many nearby	Lockers No
Alcoholic beverages No	Pet kennels No
Disabled access Yes	Rain check No
Wheelchair rental No	Private tours No
Baby stroller rental No	

Description and Comments At the south end of the boardwalk sits this unobtrusive historic building that houses Ocean City and U.S. Life-Saving Service history—and more. Exhibits cover such unusual esoterica as replicas of hotels that once stood along the boardwalk, shipwreck artifacts, a mermaid collection, bathing suits from the past, and a "Sand from around the World" exhibit. A variety of small aquariums and a dollhouse are in here, too. At 10 a.m. on weekdays, in fair weather, special programs take place: fish feeding, Ocean City history, knot tying, and sharks.

OCEAN CITY AMUSEMENTS

Anytime you go to a bustling Atlantic Ocean resort, amusement centers will be part of the deal. Set two budgets with your kids: one for the number of amusement center visits you'll make during your stay; the second for the amount of money they can spend on rides and souvenirs. Then stick to your guns. They'll shed fewer tears, and everyone will have more fun. The best Ocean City amusements are:

65th Street Slide and Ride. A water park on the bay side of town that also has bumper cars, kiddie cars, and batting cages; (410) 524-5270.

Fun City. Located at the Boardwalk at Caroline Street, this is strictly arcade gaming, with electronic and video games and the always elusive chance to win prizes; (410) 289-9742.

Jolly Roger Amusement Park. At 30th Street and Coastal Highway, this place has a bit of everything, from rides to a water park to mini-golf; (410) 289-9742.

Laser Storm. Next door to Planet Maze at 33rd and Coastal, Laser Storm offers laser tag; (410) 524-4386.

Old Pro Golf. It has four locations between 23rd Street and 136th Street where elaborate, themed mini-golf courses make Putt-Putt more fun. The 68th Street entry features indoor mini-golf; (410) 524-2645.

Planet Maze. At 33rd Street. Planet Maze has indoor and outdoor amusements and an arcade; (410) 524-4348.

Trimper's Rides. At South First Street at the southern end of the boardwalk, it holds more than 100 rides, including a vintage 1902 Herschel-Spellman carousel and plenty of small-child-friendly amusements; (410) 524-5270.

Family-Friendly Restaurants

GREENE TURTLE RESTAURANT AND SPORTS BAR

116th Street, bay side, Ocean City; (410) 723-2120
Route 611, West Ocean City; (410) 213-1500

Meals served: Lunch and dinner
Cuisine: Seafood and American
Entree range: $4.95–19.95
Children's menu: Yes
Reservations: Yes
Payment: Major credit cards

Two locations, and a good choice for families with teenagers. They've got video games and pool tables (available to teens until 10 p.m.), ball games playing on dozens of televisions, and, at times, live entertainment. And the food is surprisingly good. Little kids will do fine here, too.

TOWN DOCK RESTAURANT

125 Mulberry Street, St. Michael's; (800) 884-0103 or
(410) 745-5577

Meals served: Lunch and dinner
Cuisine: Seafood; also poultry, beef, and pasta dishes
Entree range: $6.95–20.95 (lunch and dinner)
Children's menu: Yes; $5.95 entrees
Reservations: Yes
Payment: Major credit cards

Eat indoors or out on the deck overlooking the marina. There's even an outdoor side deck with a bar and a raw bar. Very pleasant. You can dine on plain stuff, like grilled pork loin, or unusual, like sashimi tuna. The kids' menu features "dirt and worms," a dessert made from chocolate pudding, Oreo crumbs, and gummy worms.

OTHER OCEAN CITY RESTAURANT SUGGESTIONS

There's a restaurant or food stand every 15 feet. How to choose? Some quick thoughts:

Dough Rollers. A breakfast/sandwich place that also offers Italian dinners. Four locations, and it's a good bet for pancakes. Kids get color-on menus with crayons and can pick a toy prize from the toy chest.

Dumser's Restaurant. A local ice cream parlor institution at two locations—49th Street, and 123rd Street at Coastal Highway; kids get draw-on placemats with crayons; sandwiches and desserts.

Kitty Hawk Grill. Seafood and California cuisine at 46th Street, bay side; kids receive a coloring book and crayons.

Macky's Bay Side Bar and Grill. American cuisine right on the bay, with its own private beach and outdoor dining, so kids can play in the sand while they wait for their food.

Some Boardwalk Munchie Musts. Thrasher's fries, Fisher's popcorn, and Dolle's caramel corn and saltwater taffy.

Southern Maryland

The southern section of Maryland—Calvert, St. Mary's, and Charles Counties—is too often overlooked, yet it's just a 90-minute drive from Washington and only slightly more from Baltimore. With the Chesapeake Bay on one side and the Potomac River on the other, it holds some magnificent low-country scenery and no small amount of American history. True, you're not going to find a plethora of amusement parks and glitter, but you'll find Mother Nature hard at work and plenty of maritime wonders.

Beachgoers can find a quiet, controlled environment at **Chesapeake Beach** and **North Beach.** Chesapeake Beach features the **Chesapeake Beach Water Park** (call (410) 257-1404 or (301) 855-3803), which may be a bit tame compared to bigger parks but still has plenty of slides and a kiddie pool and slow river for those who like to take things easy. The **Chesapeake Railway Museum** (call (410) 257-3892) is set in a circa-1900 station. The **Rod 'n Reel Restaurant** (call (410) 257-2735 or (301) 855-8351) has been a local favorite since 1946. North Beach holds a small boardwalk, a fishing/crabbing pier, and a bike trail.

In **Prince Frederick,** you should follow the boardwalk trail through **Battle Creek Cypress Swamp Sanctuary** (call (410) 535-5327), home to the northernmost stand of bald cypress trees in the United States; the site's nature center contains interesting exhibits and also offers kids' programs. As unlikely as it might sound to some of us, the **Calvert Cliffs Nuclear Power Plant Visitors Center** (call (410) 495-4673), set in a nineteenth-century tobacco barn in the town of **Lusby,** is a worthwhile stop. Entertaining, hands-on exhibits demonstrate energy generation, and agricultural and archeological displays reveal much of the local history and lifestyle. At **Flag Ponds Nature Park** (call (410) 586-1477), pick up a "Beachcombers Checklist" before heading down to the bayside beach, where you're guaranteed to find some kind of fossil, particularly fossilized sharks' teeth. The swimming's good down there

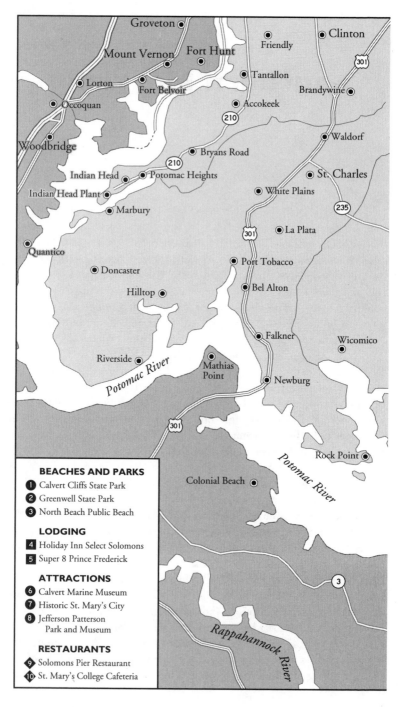

BEACHES AND PARKS
1 Calvert Cliffs State Park
2 Greenwell State Park
3 North Beach Public Beach

LODGING
4 Holiday Inn Select Solomons
5 Super 8 Prince Frederick

ATTRACTIONS
6 Calvert Marine Museum
7 Historic St. Mary's City
8 Jefferson Patterson
   Park and Museum

RESTAURANTS
9 Solomons Pier Restaurant
10 St. Mary's College Cafeteria

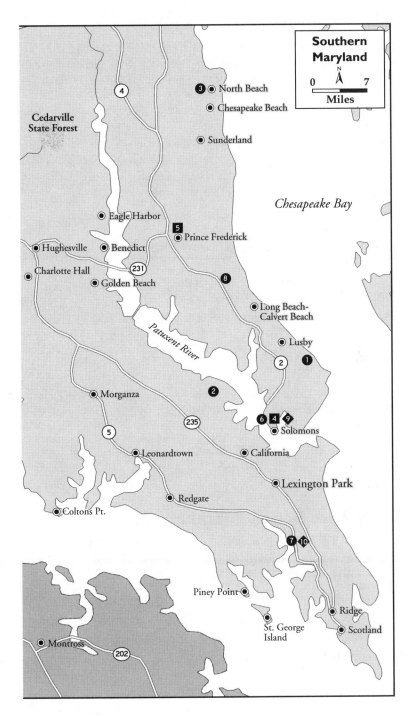

Southern Maryland

0 ⟨N⟩ 7
Miles

Cedarville
State Forest

④

❸ ⊙ North Beach
⊙ Chesapeake Beach

⊙ Sunderland

Chesapeake Bay

⊙ Eagle Harbor

❺ Prince Frederick

⊙ Hughesville ⊙ Benedict
⟨231⟩
⊙ Charlotte Hall
⊙ Golden Beach

❽

Patuxent River

⊙ Long Beach-
Calvert Beach

⊙ Lusby
⟨2⟩ ❶

❷

⊙ Morganza

⟨235⟩

❻ ❹ ❾
⊙ Solomons

⟨5⟩

⊙ Leonardtown ⊙ California

⊙ Lexington Park

⊙ Redgate

⊙ Coltons Pt.

❼ ❿

Piney Point ⊙

⊙ Ridge
St. George ⊙ Scotland
Island

⊙ Montross
⟨202⟩

(although there are no lifeguards), as are the fishing and hiking. The **Annmarie Garden on St. John** (call (410) 326-4640) in **Solomons** will give the kids a different perspective on art—major outdoor artworks are seeded throughout a woodland along the St. John River.

Coltons Point, in St. Mary's County, features the **Potomac River Museum** (call (301) 769-2222) and weekend boat tours to historic **St. Clement's Island.** Lighthouse buffs will want to visit the **Piney Point Lighthouse** (call (301) 769-2222), an 1836 building. Charles County's **La Plata** is home to the **African-American Heritage Museum** (call (301) 843-0371), which can be toured by appointment.

HOW TO GET THERE

By Car. The region is most easily accessed via Routes 2 and 4 from Washington, D.C., and Baltimore.

By Plane. Fly into BWI or one of the D.C. airports, then rent a car.

HOW TO GET INFORMATION BEFORE YOU GO

Calvert County Department of Economic Development, 175 Mains Street, Prince Frederick, MD 20678; (800) 331-9771 or (410) 535-4583; www.co.cal.us/cced.

St. Mary's County Division of Tourism, P.O. Box 653, Washington Street, Leonardstown, MD 20650; (800) 327-9023 or (301) 475-4626; www.saintmayscountymd.com/decd.

Charles County Tourism Division, 8190 Port Tobacco Road, Port Tobacco, MD 20677; (800) 766-3386, ext. 146 or (301) 934-9305 ext. 195.

The Best Beaches and Parks

Calvert Cliffs State Park. Nearly 1,500 acres of woodlands and Chesapeake Bay shoreline offers the hearty-on-foot a chance to hike, fish, and hunt for fossils; (301) 872-5688.

Greenwell State Park. Hiking and fishing along the Patuxent River; (301) 872-5389.

North Beach Public Beach. The town of North Beach offers free beach access on the Chesapeake; (410) 257-9618.

Family Outdoor Adventures

Biking. The region offers plenty of road biking opportunities. Obtain a

"Southern Maryland Bicycle Map," which details the best routes and pinpoints bike shop locations, from (800) 331-9771.

Camping. A commercial site, Breezy Point Beach and Campground in Chesapeake Beach, holds 80 sites for tents, trailers, and RVs, (410) 535-0259. State-run facilities can be found at Cedarville State Forest (301-326-3241) and, where the Chesapeake and Potomac River come together, Point Lookout State Park (301-872-5688).

Deep-Sea Fishing/Boat Rentals. In Solomons, Bunky's Charter Boats rents 16-foot skiffs for fishing and crabbing on the Patuxent River, (410) 326-3241; Solomons Boat Rental hires out 15- to 20-foot power boats by the hour, half-day and full-day, (410) 326-4060.

Hiking. Calvert Cliffs State Park (see The Best Beaches and Parks above) and Cedarville State Forest (see Mountain Biking below) offer the most extensive trail networks in the region.

Kayaking and Canoeing. Island Creek Outfitters on Broomes Island offers kayaking instruction, rentals, and trips, (410) 286-0950.

Mountain Biking. Cedarville State Forest holds a mountain bike trail network. (301) 888-1410.

Family Lodging

Holiday Inn Select Solomons

A new, 326-room, full-service hotel with outdoor pool, restaurant, fitness center, tennis and volleyball courts, and marina. Regular rooms and suites available.

155 Holiday Drive, P.O. Box 1099, Solomons, MD 20688; (800) 356-2009 or (410) 326-6311. Rates $99–189.

Super 8 Prince Frederick

Centrally located in the region, this motel offers standard rooms, executive doubles with refrigerator and sitting area, and suites. Complimentary continental breakfast is included, and there's an on-site fitness center with a hot tub.

40 Commerce Lane, Prince Frederick, MD 20678; (800) 800-8000 or (410) 535-8668. Rates $55–130.

Attractions

Calvert Marine Museum

State Route 2, P.O. Box 2042, Solomons, MD 20688; (410) 326-2042; www.calvertmarinemuseum.com

Hours: Daily 10 a.m.–5 p.m.; closed Thanksgiving, Christmas, and New Year's days

Admission: $5 adults, $4 seniors 55+, $2 children ages 5–12, free for children under 5

Appeal by Age Groups:

Pre-school	Grade School	Teens	Young Adults	Over 30	Seniors
★★★★	★★★★★	★★★★	★★★★★	★★★★★	★★★★★

Touring Time: Average 2 hours, minimum 1 hour

Rainy-Day Touring: Yes

Services and Facilities:

Restaurants No	Baby stroller rental Yes; free
Alcoholic beverages No	Lockers No
Disabled access Yes; except lighthouse	Pet kennels No
	Rain check No
Wheelchair rental Yes; free	Private tours No

Description and Comments   What a pleasant surprise this is! Dedicated to three themes—local maritime history, the paleontology of the nearby Calvert Cliffs, and the estuarine life of the tidal Patuxent River and Chesapeake Bay—this museum is small but sophisticated and beautifully presented. You can actually visit the hands-on Discovery Room, watch the introductory films, and see the sturgeon exhibit without paying the entrance fee. But you're going to want to enter. The museum's aquaria, including one magnificent one that beautifully displays incandescent jellyfish, are few enough in number to allows close scrutiny. And the resident river otters will hold everyone's attention for a long time. Other exhibits include a boat building shop, where the carpenters are often in action; a screwpile lighthouse (sign up for tours); many small craft; and the area's industrial and boats history. Solomons was the site of military training for the World War II D-Day landing, and each August the town stages a unique reenactment. Half a mile south of the main museum, the J.C. Lore Oyster House reveals the story of the region's seafood industries.

Historic St. Mary's City

Rosecroft Road, P.O. Box 39, St. Mary's City, MD 20686; (800) 762-1634 or (301) 862-0990; www.webgraphic.com/hsmic

Hours: Mid-March–November, Wednesday–Sunday 10 a.m.–5 p.m.

Admission: $7.50 adults, $6 seniors 60+, $6 students 12+, $3.50 children ages 6–12, free for children 5 and under

Appeal by Age Groups:

Pre-school	Grade School	Teens	Young Adults	Over 30	Seniors
★★★	★★★★	★★★	★★★★	★★★★	★★★★★

Touring Time: Average 3 hours, minimum 2 hours

Rainy-Day Touring: Yes

Services and Facilities:

Restaurants No	Baby stroller rental Yes; free
Alcoholic beverages No	Radio Flyer wagons
Disabled access Yes; but not to	Lockers No
the boat, *Maryland Dove*	Pet kennels No
Wheelchair rental Yes; free	Rain check No
	Private tours No

Description and Comments An 850-acre living history museum on the site of the fourth permanent European settlement in British North America and the first capital of Maryland Province. St. Mary's City was settled in 1634, and it thrived until 1695. This re-creation depicts St. Mary's City at its peak, during the 1660s and 1670s, and includes an inn, the State House, a chapel, a tobacco farm, an Indian hamlet, and the Maryland Dove, a working replica of the square-riggers that once plied these waters. Each restored building is hosted by costumed interpreters, who are very adept at drawing visitors of all ages into the stories of their lives and work. The visitors center's exhibit gives basic background information, augmented by a short film narrated by Walter Cronkite.

Jefferson Patterson Park and Museum

10514 Mackall Road, St. Leonard, MD 20685; (410) 586-8500; www.dhcd.state.md.us

Hours: April 15–October 15, Wednesday–Sunday 10 a.m.–5 p.m.

Admission: Free

Appeal by Age Groups:

Pre-school	Grade School	Teens	Young Adults	Over 30	Seniors
★★	★★★★	★★★	★★★★	★★★★	★★★★

Touring Time: Average 1½ hours, minimum 45 minutes

Rainy-Day Touring: Yes

Services and Facilities:

Restaurants No	Lockers No
Alcoholic beverages No	Pet kennels No

Disabled access Yes	Rain check No
Wheelchair rental No	Private tours No
Baby stroller rental No	

Description and Comments This is another of those little-known gems. No bells and whistles, but a beautiful setting and some fascinating history and activities. The single largest battle of the War of 1812 took place on and near the 512-acre site. In addition, archeological surveys have revealed evidence of some 70 significant sites ranging back 9,000 years, including Native American, colonial, and postcolonial artifacts. Visitors can participate in an active archeology dig from mid-May through June, open to ages 15 and up, and to younger kids with parental accompaniment. A series of special events, including tours by kayak, spinning and weaving demonstrations, a Celtic Festival and an African American Family Community Day, highlight the season. Elementary-school-age kids especially will like the visitors center's "please touch" room, where they can work with colonial tools and discover fossils. The Farm Exhibit Building holds a potpourri of old-time machines and implements. Finally, the property contains two one-hour trails that, when followed with the trail guide, take you through the site's history and ecology.

Family-Friendly Restaurants

SOLOMONS PIER RESTAURANT

14575 Solomons Island Road, Solomons; (410) 326-2424

Meals served: Lunch and dinner
Cuisine: Seafood and American
Entree range: $9.95–20.50 (dinner)
Children's menu: Yes; $3.50–6.95
Reservations: Yes
Payment: Major credit cards

A pleasant place with outdoor waterfront dining that offers great views; kids will like watching traffic pass over the modern arched Routes 2/4 bridge. The food's good, and though the kid's menu only offers a half-dozen items, it comes with paper-and-pencil puzzles and games.

ST. MARY'S COLLEGE OF MARYLAND CAFETERIA

18952 East Fisher Road, St. Mary's City; (301) 862-0200

Meals served: Breakfast, lunch, and dinner
Cuisine: Varied
Entree range: $4.50
Children's menu: No
Reservations: No
Payment: Cash or major credit cards

Okay, so you're thinking, "College cafeteria: joke, right?" Nope. You dine in the "Great Room," under a vaulted ceiling, on cherry-wood tables and chairs set on a slate floor. There's a full selection, ranging from burgers and Mexican to a huge salad bar, dessert bar, and hot entrees. Eat as much as you want, and all for four and a half bucks. Plus, it's a spankin' new building, really very pleasant, and kids will love hanging out with the collegiate types. The full cafeteria is closed during the latter part of May, but the snack cafeteria still does pretty well.

Part Five

Washington, D.C.

The nation's capital is one place every family should visit at least once. There's so much to do and see, however, that several visits are probably required. It's a large, world-class city and, of course, the seat of our national government. That factor alone can make it intimidating. Toss in all the sites to see, all the museums to visit, and all the buildings, restaurants, and shops to explore, and you could easily wonder how to stay sane. Two pieces of advice: plan and don't overdo it. If you do a bit of planning, you can explore the city without getting exhausted. And, as with any major city, remember that you can't see and do everything all at once. So prioritize (for which we've given you a bit of help by marking the most kid-luring attractions with an asterisk), and resist the temptation to try to do everything right now. Better to, as they used to say in vaudeville, leave 'em wanting more.

How to Get Information before You Go

Washington, D.C., Convention and Visitors Bureau, 1212 New York Avenue NW, Washington, D.C. 20005; (202) 789-7000; www.washington.org.

Visitor Information Center, 1300 Pennsylvania Avenue NW, Washington, D.C. 20005; (202) 328-4748; www.dcvisit.com.

D.C. Committee to Promote Washington, 1212 New York Avenue NW, Washington, D.C. 20005; (202) 724-5644.

Smithsonian Information Center, Smithsonian Institution, Washington, D.C. 20560; (202) 357-2700; www.si.edu.

Washington, D.C.'s Not-to-Be-Missed Attractions	

Around Washington	Rock Creek Park
	Explorers Hall, National Geographic
	  Society
	Lincoln Memorial
	Thomas Jefferson Memorial
	U.S. Capitol
	Washington Monument
	Smithsonian Institution: Arts and
	  Industries Building
	Smithsonian Institution: National
	  Air and Space Museum
	Smithsonian Institution: National
	  Museum of American History
	Smithsonian Institution: National
	  Zoo

Calendar of Festivals and Events

February

Lincoln's Birthday Observance. Concerts by military bands, and a dramatic reading of the Gettysburg Address. Lincoln Memorial; (703) 619-7222.

March

National Cherry Blossom Festival. Two weeks of events of all kinds all over the city during late March and early April; (202) 547-1500.

April

White House Easter Egg Roll. For ages three to six accompanied by an adult; eggs and entertainment provided. White House; (202) 456-2200.

May

Memorial Day Concert with the National Symphony. At the U.S. Capitol; (202) 619-7222.

June

Military Band Concerts. Free concerts every night of the week from Memorial Day through Labor Day at various locations; Army Band (703) 696-3399; Marine Band (202) 433-4011; Navy Band (202) 433-2525; and Air Force Band (202) 767-5658.

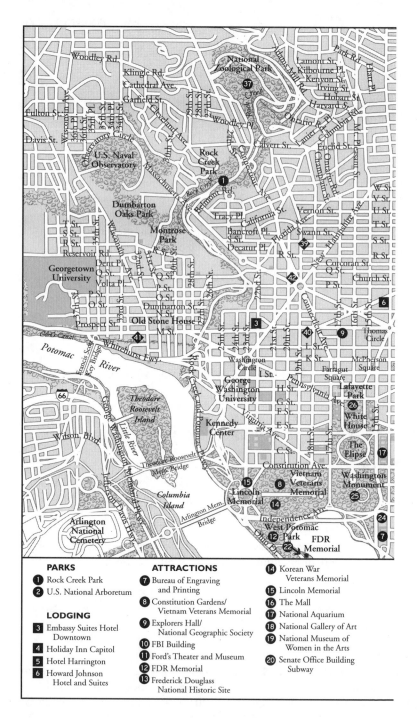

PARKS

1 Rock Creek Park
2 U.S. National Arboretum

LODGING

3 Embassy Suites Hotel
Downtown
4 Holiday Inn Capitol
5 Hotel Harrington
6 Howard Johnson
Hotel and Suites

ATTRACTIONS

7 Bureau of Engraving
and Printing
8 Constitution Gardens/
Vietnam Veterans Memorial
9 Explorers Hall/
National Geographic Society
10 FBI Building
11 Ford's Theater and Museum
12 FDR Memorial
13 Frederick Douglass
National Historic Site

14 Korean War
Veterans Memorial
15 Lincoln Memorial
16 The Mall
17 National Aquarium
18 National Gallery of Art
19 National Museum of
Women in the Arts
20 Senate Office Building
Subway

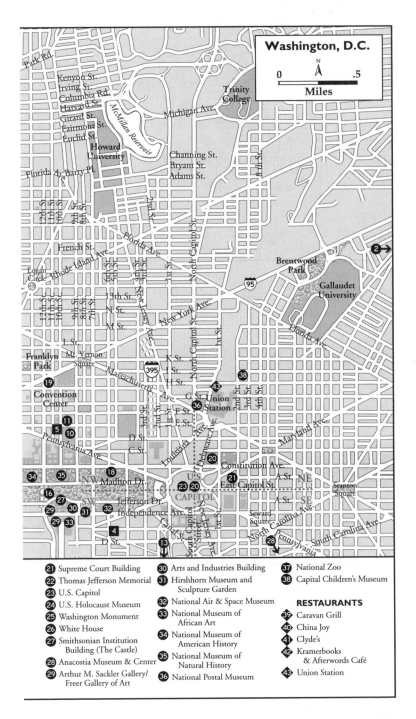

Washington, D.C.

N

0 .5

Miles

Park Rd.

Kenyon St.
Irving St.
Columbia Rd.
Harvard St.
Girard St.
Fairmont St.
Euclid St.

McMillan Reservoir

Michigan Ave.

Trinity College

Howard University

Channing St.
Bryant St.
Adams St.

Florida A. Barry Pl.

French St.

Brentwood Park

Gallaudet University

Logan Circle

Rhode Island Ave.

Florida Ave.

13th St.

New Jersey Ave.

New York Ave.

Florida Ave.

N St.

M St.

L St.

Mt. Vernon Square

Franklin Park

Massachusetts Ave.

K St.
I St.
H St.

Union Station

G St.
F St.
E St.

Convention Center

Pennsylvania Ave.

D St.

C St.

Louisiana Ave.

Delaware Ave.

Constitution Ave.

Maryland Ave.

Madison Dr.

U.S. CAPITOL

East Capitol St.

A St.

NE

Stanton Square

NW
SW
SE

Jefferson Dr.

Independence Ave.

Seward Square

North Carolina Ave.

Pennsylvania Ave.

South Carolina Ave.

D St.

Maine Ave.

21 Supreme Court Building
22 Thomas Jefferson Memorial
23 U.S. Capitol
24 U.S. Holocaust Museum
25 Washington Monument
26 White House
27 Smithsonian Institution Building (The Castle)
28 Anacostia Museum & Center
29 Arthur M. Sackler Gallery/ Freer Gallery of Art

30 Arts and Industries Building
31 Hirshhorn Museum and Sculpture Garden
32 National Air & Space Museum
33 National Museum of African Art
34 National Museum of American History
35 National Museum of Natural History
36 National Postal Museum

37 National Zoo
38 Capital Children's Museum

RESTAURANTS

39 Caravan Grill
40 China Joy
41 Clyde's
42 Kramerbooks & Afterwords Café
43 Union Station

July

Festival of American Folklife. A huge festival sponsored by the Smithsonian Institution with exhibits, foods, music, and arts from a range of American and international cultures. Smithsonian; (202) 357-2700.

National Independence Day Celebration. An all-day affair on the Fourth of July, starting with a parade down Constitution Avenue, entertainment at the Sylvan Theatre on the Washington Monument grounds, a National Symphony Orchestra concert, and a spectacular fireworks display over the Washington Monument. (202) 619-7222.

August

National Frisbee Festival. World Frisbee champions and disc-catching dogs take over the grounds of the Washington Monument. (301) 645-5043.

September

Black Family Reunion. A cultural celebration of the African American family, with performances, food, and themed pavilions. National Mall; (202) 659-0006.

December

Pageant of Peace: National Christmas Tree Lighting. The president lights the National Christmas Tree, followed by a choral performance and a spectacular display of lighted Christmas trees representing each U.S. state and territory; The Ellipse; (202) 619-7222.

Holidays around the World. The Capital Children's Museum marks holiday traditions of children from around the world; (202) 675-4120.

Cool Web Sites for D.C.-Bound Kids

Visitor Information Center Kids' Page: www.dcvisit.com/kids

National Zoo (cool videos, games, and the Orangutan Language Project): natzoo.si.edu

The White House for Kids:
www.whitehouse.gov/wh/kids/html/home.html

HOW TO GET THERE

By Car. The Capital Beltway (I-495) encircles the city. It can be used, therefore, to access any area in the city. From the north on the eastern side, I-95 comes down from Baltimore, as does the Baltimore-Washington Parkway. I-95 is also the main thoroughfare from Richmond and the south. I-270 comes in from the northwest and Frederick, Maryland, while I-66 arrives from the west and Fairfax, Virginia. Once you're in the District, park your car and leave it; use the Metro or bus system instead. Trying to drive and park here isn't worth the trial.

By Plane. Ronald Reagan Washington National Airport is located in Arlington just across the river from Washington; (703) 417-8000. Washington Dulles International Airport is located due west of downtown D.C.; (703) 572-2700. Washington Flyer provides bus service from the airports to major downtown hotels for round-trip fares of $14 from National and $26 from Dulles; (703) 685-1400. The Metro stops at National, as do Metro system buses. Cab fare from National to downtown is about $12; from Dulles, about $45.

By Train. Amtrak service arrives at revitalized Union Station, First Street and Massachusetts Avenue NE; (800) 872-7245 or (202) 906-3000.

GETTING AROUND

The Layout. Although it's sometimes hard to believe, the city was carefully laid out into four quadrants of a grid; that's why all the addresses have NW, SW, NE, and SE attached to them. Most of the major tourist attractions are found in the northwest quarter. Numbered streets run north-south; lettered streets run east-west; major avenues with states' names run diagonally. Where major avenues meet, traffic circles are formed. However, sometimes anomalies occur, such as when Pennsylvania Avenue is interrupted by the White House and the Ellipse. Keep a map handy.

By Metro. The Washington Metro serves most areas of the District, plus northern Virginia and nearby Maryland cities. It's clean, pleasant, efficient, and, for kids especially, fun. All four lines—Red, Yellow, Orange, and Blue—cut through the heart of town and interconnect with each other. Fares are based on how far and what time of day you travel. Buy a Farecard from a machine at any station (have small bills ready). You can buy single or round-trip fares or a $20 debit card, which saves 10%. A full-day pass costs $5 and is good from 9:30 a.m. to closing (usually midnight). Other multiuse passes are also available. Up to two children under age five ride for free with each paying customer. Information: (202) 637-7000.

By Bus. Metro system buses can get you to nearly any spot in the city. Fare is $1.10, exact fare required. Extra zone fares are charged on buses that cross into Maryland and Virginia. Information: (202) 637-7000.

TOUR OPTIONS

Tour companies and options abound. We like these:

Tourmobile Sightseeing. This service makes 25 stops on a narrated tour from which you can get on and off at will; buy tickets from TicketMaster (800) 551-7328, at Arlington Cemetery, or at the Capitol Mall; two-day tickets available; call for prices; (202) 554-5100.

Li'l Red Trolley All Day Tour. Part of Gray Line, this tour offers two-hour or all-day passes for a route that hits all the major attractions and monuments; $19 adults, $9 children ages 3–11; 50 Massachusetts Avenue NW; (202) 289-1995.

D.C. Ducks Land and Sea Tours. Offers 90-minute narrated tours on the Potomac River in reconditioned World War II amphibious vehicles from April through October; call for prices; tickets at 50 Massachusetts Avenue; mailing address 1323 Pennsylvania Avenue NW, Washington, D.C. 20004; (202) 966-3825.

MAJOR LEAGUE PROFESSIONAL SPORTS

The NFL's Redskins play at FedEx Field in Landover, MD; general information (301) 276-6000, ticket office (301) 276-6050. The NHL Capitals and NBA Wizards play hockey and basketball at the MCI Center, 601 F Street NW; ticket information (202) 432-7328.

The Best Parks

Chesapeake and Ohio Canal National Historical Park. The in-town base for this park is in Georgetown. From here you can participate in ranger-led walks and talks, take a mule-drawn canal boat ride (see Maryland, Capitol District), bike, and canoe or kayak from Georgetown to Violettes Lock; 1057 Thomas Jefferson Street NW; (202) 653-5190; www.nps.gov/choh.

Rock Creek Park. This ranks among the largest forested urban parks in the United States, covering some 1,754 acres. Activities include biking, fishing, hiking, horseback riding, nature walks, a nature center with exhibits and a discovery room for younger children, and a planetarium. 3545 Williamburg Lane NW; (202) 426-6828 or (202) 282-1063; www.nps.gov/rocr.

U.S. National Arboretum. A 446-acre park with a huge variety of plants, some native to this country, some imported, including dwarf conifers (which kids will get a kick out of) and lots of flowering plants; a series of trails allows for fun exploration. New York Avenue and R Street SE; (202) 245-2726.

Family Outdoor Adventures

Hiking. Chesapeake and Ohio Canal National Historical Park and Rock Creek Park (see The Best Parks above).

Horseback Riding. Rock Creek Park Horse Center offers hour-long trail rides through Rock Creek Park; 5100 Glover Road NW; (202) 262-0118; www.nps.gov/rocr/visitorcenter/horsecenter.htm.

Paddling and Bicycling. Thompson Boat Center rents canoes, kayaks and bicycles for use in Rock Creek Park or C&O Canal Park; 2900 Virginia Avenue, Georgetown; (202) 333-9543.

Family Lodging

Note: For a visit to Washington, lodging in Arlington or Alexandria can be much more economical, while providing excellent access to both the city and the surrounding countryside. Both these cities offer a full range of lodging from the well-known chains. See the Northern Virginia section on page 321.

HotelsDC is a hotel booking service that represents more than 80 capital-area lodging facilities and can act as a reasonable central booking and information service; (800) 323-2149; www.hotelsdc.com.

Embassy Suites Hotel, Downtown

Another full-service hotel in an excellent location, this one all suites, with an indoor pool, on-site restaurant, in-room coffee, and complimentary full breakfast.

1250 22nd Street NW, Washington, D.C. 20037; (202) 857-3388. Rates $129–$249.

Holiday Inn Capitol

Its location just eight blocks from the Smithsonian and one block from the Metro, plus the on-site sight-seeing tour pickups, make this Holiday Inn a good choice. There's also a summertime swimming pool, on-site restaurant and Pizza Hut, and in-room coffee, and suites with fridge and microwave are available.

550 C Street SW, Washington, D.C. 20024; (888) 874-7232 or (202) 479-4000. Rates $114–$199; children age 19 and under stay free; children age 12 and under stay and eat free.

Hotel Harrington

A low-priced, family-owned hotel that wins applause for affordability combined with good location and friendliness. In addition to standard rooms, the hotel offers some family rooms that will sleep up to eight, and some two-room/two-bath family suites.

11th and E Streets NW, Washington, D.C. 20004; (800) 424-8532 or (202) 628-8140. Rates $75–$89; children under age 16 stay free.

Howard Johnson Hotel and Suites

A 184-room hotel with some junior and one-bedroom suites, and a few standard hotel rooms with kitchenettes. The rooftop pool is a welcome amenity, as is the on-site restaurant; the hotel also has a video game room.

1430 Rhode Island Avenue NW, Washington, D.C. 20005; (800) 368-5690 or (202) 462-7777. Rates $89–$169; children under age 18 stay free.

Attractions

Washington contains a plethora of free sites to visit, from monuments to museums. We summarize these, then cover the various installations of the Smithsonian Institution. Again, attractions with an asterisk (*) are the ones that are generally most popular with school-age children.

U.S. Senate and House of Representatives Gallery Tickets

If you want to watch the Senate or House in action, you'll need to obtain tickets from your senator or district representative. Tickets are limited, so it's suggested that you reserve them three months ahead; five tickets is the limit for each person reserving them. To contact your legislator, call and ask to be connected to his or her office. Capitol Hill; (202) 224-3121.

Bureau of Engraving and Printing

14th and C Streets; (202) 874-3019

Hours: April–September, Monday–Friday 9 a.m.–1:40 p.m.; June–August, Monday–Friday 9 a.m.–1:40 p.m., 5–6:40 p.m.; October–March, 9 a.m.–2 p.m.

Touring Time: 1 hour

Appeal by Age Groups:

Pre-school	Grade School	Teens	Young Adults	Over 30	Seniors
★	★★★★	★★★★★	★★★★★	★★★★★	★★★★★

Comments   See paper money and postage stamps printed.

*Constitution Gardens/Vietnam Veterans Memorial

Constitution Avenue, 17th–23rd Streets; (202) 426-6841

Hours: Daily 24 hours

Touring Time: 1 hour

Appeal by Age Groups:

Pre-school	Grade School	Teens	Young Adults	Over 30	Seniors
★★	★★★	★★★★	★★★★★	★★★★★	★★★★★

Comments   The renowned and moving "wall" is set in a 52-acre park with a 6-acre lake near the Lincoln Memorial.

*Explorers Hall, National Geographic Society

17th and M Streets NW; (202) 857-7588

Hours: Monday–Saturday 9 a.m.–5 p.m.; Sunday 10 a.m.–5 p.m.

Touring Time: 1½ hours

Appeal by Age Groups:

Pre-school	Grade School	Teens	Young Adults	Over 30	Seniors
★★★	★★★★★	★★★★★	★★★★★	★★★★★	★★★★★

Comments   An interactive geography and science center with focus on sea exploration, weather, early humans, insects, and animals.

FBI Building

Ninth and Tenth Streets NW; (202) 324-3447

Hours: Monday–Friday 8:45 a.m.–4:15 p.m.

Touring Time: 1 hour

Appeal by Age Groups:

Pre-school	Grade School	Teens	Young Adults	Over 30	Seniors
★★	★★★	★★★★★	★★★★★	★★★★★	★★★★★

Comments   One-hour tours include firearms demonstrations and a review of FBI history.

Ford's Theater and Museum

511 10th Street NW; (202) 426-6924

Hours: Daily 9 a.m.–5 p.m.; no tours during performances—call

Touring Time: 1 hour

Appeal by Age Groups:

Pre-school	Grade School	Teens	Young Adults	Over 30	Seniors
★	★★★	★★★★	★★★★★	★★★★★	★★★★★

Comments   Site of Lincoln's assassination, the theater is used for stage productions but can also be toured. The museum depicts the assassination. Across the street, at 516 Tenth Street, is the Peterson House, where Lincoln died.

FDR Memorial

West Potomac Park; (202) 619-7222

Hours: Daily 24 hours

Touring Time: 1 hour

Appeal by Age Groups:

Pre-school	Grade School	Teens	Young Adults	Over 30	Seniors
★★	★★★	★★★★	★★★★★	★★★★★	★★★★★

Comments   The new memorial to Franklin Roosevelt contains a dozen sculptures, carved quotations, and World War II and Great Depression exhibitions. Youngest kids will like the statue of FDR and his dog.

Frederick Douglass National Historic Site

1411 W Street SE; (202) 426-5961

Hours: Daily 9 a.m.–5 p.m.

Time to Allow: 1 hour

Appeal by Age Groups:

Pre-school	Grade School	Teens	Young Adults	Over 30	Seniors
★★	★★★★	★★★★	★★★★★	★★★★★	★★★★★

Comments   Last home of the slave-turned-statesman and civil rights activist. Exhibits and an introductory film interpret his life. Tours available for a fee.

Korean War Veterans Memorial

The Mall; (202) 619-7222

Hours: Daily 24 hours

Touring Time: ½ hour

Appeal by Age Groups:

Pre-school	Grade School	Teens	Young Adults	Over 30	Seniors
★★	★★★	★★★★	★★★★★	★★★★★	★★★★★

Comments Dedicated to the 1.5 million Americans who served in Korea, the memorial is dominated by a sculpture of 19 soldiers and a 164-foot wall that magically changes from images of hilly terrain (when seen from a distance) to military photographs (when seen close up).

*Lincoln Memorial

The Mall; (202) 426-6895

Hours: Daily 24 hours

Touring Time: ½ hour

Appeal by Age Groups:

Pre-school	Grade School	Teens	Young Adults	Over 30	Seniors
★★★	★★★★★	★★★★★	★★★★★	★★★★★	★★★★★

Comments It's among the city's must-see spots, with its famous, huge statue of Lincoln sitting and its 36 columns. The lower lobby contains a student exhibition, "Lincoln's Legacy," and allegorical murals. Guided tours available.

*The Mall

Runs from the Capitol to the Lincoln Memorial

Hours: Daily 24 hours

Touring Time: Varies

Appeal by Age Groups:

Pre-school	Grade School	Teens	Young Adults	Over 30	Seniors
★★★★★	★★★★★	★★★★★	★★★★★	★★★★★	★★★★★

Comments The Mall encompasses the Washington Monument, the Smithsonian Institution, and Grant Memorial. A major gathering place filled with people and vendors.

National Aquarium

Department of Commerce Building, 13th Street and Constitution
Avenue NW; (202) 482-2825

Admission: $2, 75¢ ages 2–10

Hours: Daily 9 a.m.–5 p.m.

Touring Time: 1 hour

Appeal by Age Groups:

Pre-school	Grade School	Teens	Young Adults	Over 30	Seniors
★★★	★★★★★	★★★★	★★★★★	★★★★★	★★★★★

Comments Oldest public aquarium in the country, it holds some 250 species, a touch tank, sharks, and piranhas (call for feeding times).

National Gallery of Art

Constitution Avenue at Third and Seventh Streets NW; (202) 737-4215

Hours: Monday–Saturday 10 a.m.–5 p.m.; Sunday 11 a.m.–6 p.m.

Touring Time: 2–3 hours

Appeal by Age Groups:

Pre-school	Grade School	Teens	Young Adults	Over 30	Seniors
★★	★★★	★★★★	★★★★★	★★★★★	★★★★★

Comments Two huge buildings filled with paintings and sculpture, an interactive, multimedia computer room, a 6-acre sculpture garden, and a café. Tours available.

National Museum of Women in the Arts

New York Avenue and 13th Street NW; (202) 783-5000

Hours: Monday–Saturday 10 a.m.–5 p.m.; Sunday 12–5 p.m.

Touring Time: 1 hour

Appeal by Age Groups:

Pre-school	Grade School	Teens	Young Adults	Over 30	Seniors
★★	★★★	★★★★	★★★★★	★★★★★	★★★★★

Comments A permanent collection of 1,500 works by women artists.

Senate Office Building Subway

Capitol Plaza; (202) 224-3121

Hours: Monday–Friday 8 a.m.–6 p.m.; Saturday 9 a.m.–1 p.m.

Touring Time: ½ hour

Appeal by Age Groups:

Pre-school	Grade School	Teens	Young Adults	Over 30	Seniors
★★★★	★★★★★	★★★★★	★★★★	★★★	★★★

Comments Have a meal in the House Office Building cafeteria, then take the short mini-subway ride to the Capitol, just like the senators do. Just a fun thing to do.

Supreme Court Building

Maryland Avenue and East Capitol Street NE; (202) 479-3000

Hours: Monday–Friday 9 a.m.–4:30 p.m.; call for court session hours

Touring Time: 1–2 hours

Appeal by Age Groups:

Pre-school	Grade School	Teens	Young Adults	Over 30	Seniors
★	★	★★★★	★★★★★	★★★★★	★★★★★

Comments The court is in session two weeks a month and is open to the public on a first-come, first-served basis. The ground floor offers exhibits and a film about the Court and how it works.

*Thomas Jefferson Memorial

Tidal Basin; (202) 426-6821

Hours: Daily 24 hours

Touring Time: ½ hour

Appeal by Age Groups:

Pre-school	Grade School	Teens	Young Adults	Over 30	Seniors
★★	★★★	★★★★★	★★★★★	★★★★★	★★★★★

Comments A circular dome structure in which the huge statue of Jefferson is surrounded by inscriptions from his writings.

*U.S. Capitol

Capitol Plaza; (202) 225-6827

Hours: March–August, daily 9 a.m.–8 p.m.; September–February, daily 9 a.m.–4:30 p.m. Tours offered Monday–Saturday.

Touring Time: 1 hour

Appeal by Age Groups:

Pre-school	Grade School	Teens	Young Adults	Over 30	Seniors
★★	★★★	★★★★★	★★★★★	★★★★★	★★★★★

Comments Home to the Senate and House of Representatives, highlighted by the center dome.

U.S. Holocaust Museum

100 Raoul Wallenberg Place SW; (202) 488-0400

Hours: Daily 10 a.m.–5:30 p.m.

Touring Time: 3 hours

Appeal by Age Groups:

Pre-school	Grade School	Teens	Young Adults	Over 30	Seniors
★	★★	★★★★★	★★★★★	★★★★★	★★★★★

Comments The history of the World War II Holocaust extermination of Jews, gypsies, and others killed by German Nazis. Remarkable, but heavy going. Entrance to the permanent exhibition requires timed passes; call (800) 400-9373 for information on advance-issue passes.

*Washington Monument

The Mall; (202) 426-6841

Hours: April–Labor Day, daily 8 a.m.–11:45 p.m.; Labor Day–March, daily 9 a.m.–5 p.m.

Touring Time: 1 hour

Appeal by Age Groups:

Pre-school	Grade School	Teens	Young Adults	Over 30	Seniors
★★★★	★★★★★	★★★★★	★★★★★	★★★★★	★★★★★

Comments One of D.C.'s most recognizable attractions, it stands 555 feet tall. You can no longer walk up, but you can ride the elevator to the 500-foot level. Timed tickets are required and can be obtained at the 15th Street kiosk at the monument.

White House

1600 Pennsylvania Avenue; (202) 456-7041

Hours: Tour ticket distribution starts at 7:30 a.m. Tuesday–Saturday.

Touring Time: 1 hour from tour start

Appeal by Age Groups:

Pre-school	Grade School	Teens	Young Adults	Over 30	Seniors
★	★★★	★★★★	★★★★★	★★★★★	★★★★★

Comments Where the president lives. Self-guided tours are available of areas open to the public. Timed tickets are required; get them at the White House Visitor Center at E and 15th Streets. If you want to tour, get there early.

THE SMITHSONIAN INSTITUTION

Smithsonian Information, SI Building, Room 153, Washington, D.C. 20560; (202) 357-2700; www.si.edu

Hours: In general, the museums are open daily 10 a.m.–5:30 p.m.

Admission: Free

Rainy-Day Touring: Yes

Services and Facilities:

Restaurants Yes
Alcoholic beverages Yes
Disabled access Yes
Wheelchair rental Yes; free
Baby stroller rental Yes; zoo only

Lockers Yes; at some facilities
Pet kennels No
Rain check No
Private tours No

Comments The Smithsonian comprises 16 museums, 14 of which are in Washington, D.C.; of these 14, most are found on the Mall. Most museums offer free highlights tours daily on a walk-in basis. If you or your older kid(s) have a keen interest in airplane restoration, you can tour the Air and Space Museum's off-site Paul E. Garber Preservation, Restoration, and Storage Facility; reservations are necessary, three weeks in advance; call (202) 357-1400.

The following section reviews the Smithsonian's various installations.

Note: We have not profiled the Smithsonian American Art Museum and the National Portrait Gallery here, as both are closed for renovation until 2003.

Smithsonian Institution Building (The Castle)

1000 Jefferson Drive SW; (202) 357-2700

Appeal by Age Groups:

Pre-school	Grade School	Teens	Young Adults	Over 30	Seniors
★★	★★★	★★★	★★★	★★★	★★★

Touring Time: 30 minutes

Restaurants: No

Description and Comments All first-time Smithsonian visitors should start here to gather general and current event information. You can collect maps and guides to the Smithsonian, as well as general materials on Washington, and pick up a current Smithsonian event calendar. Stop in at one of the orientation theaters to view the half-hour introductory video; it plays continuously. The scale models of Washington and electronic wall maps and touch-screens highlighting D.C. attractions will keep the kids entertained while you figure out where to go next.

Anacostia Museum and Center for African American History and Culture

1901 Fort Place SE; (202) 287-3369

Appeal by Age Groups:

Pre-school	Grade School	Teens	Young Adults	Over 30	Seniors
★★	★★★	★★★★	★★★★★	★★★★★	★★★★★

Touring Time: Average 2 hours, minimum 1 hour
Restaurants: No

Description and Comments The Anacostia is dedicated to increasing awareness of the black experience in America and preserving African American history, specifically from the Upper South region. Best for older kids, the exhibits here yield an insight into black southern life that's revealing, incisive, and more far-ranging than usual.

Note: The museum is closed for major renovation through the summer of 2001.

Arthur M. Sackler Gallery and Freer Gallery of Art

Sackler Gallery: 1050 Independence Avenue SW; (202) 357-3200
Freer Gallery: Jefferson Drive at 12th Street SW; (202) 357-4880

Appeal by Age Groups:

Pre-school	Grade School	Teens	Young Adults	Over 30	Seniors
★★★	★★★★	★★★★	★★★★	★★★★★	★★★★★

Touring Time: Average 2 hours, minimum 1 hour
Restaurants: No

Description and Comments The two national museums of Asian art are connected by an under-street tunnel. The Sackler features Chinese paintings and lacquerware, ancient Near Eastern ceramics and metalware, and sculpture from South and Southeast Asia. The Freer collection comes from China, Japan, Korea, South and Southeast Asia, and the Near East. It also holds a collection of nineteenth-century and early-twentieth-century American art. Walk-in tours are offered daily, except Wednesdays, at 11 a.m.

Arts and Industries Building

900 Jefferson Drive SW; (202) 357-1500

Appeal by Age Groups:

Pre-school	Grade School	Teens	Young Adults	Over 30	Seniors
★★★★★	★★★★★	★★★★	★★★★★	★★★★★	★★★★★

Note: The ratings and average tour time are based on a visit that includes seeing a performance at the Discovery Theater.

Touring Time: Average 3 hours, minimum 2 hours
Restaurants: No

Description and Comments This was the original building in which the Smithsonian was housed. Today it contains exhibits in various art media covering a wide range of subjects. We love the Discovery Theater, where child-oriented live theater performances are staged in puppetry, theater, dance, storytelling, and musicals, much of it interactive. Performances are aimed at specific age groups, ranging from pre-K through senior high school. A Saturday Special series is also offered.

Hirshhorn Museum and Sculpture Garden

Independence Avenue at Seventh Street SW; (202) 357-1618 or (202) 357-3091

Appeal by Age Groups:

Pre-school	Grade School	Teens	Young Adults	Over 30	Seniors
★★★	★★★★	★★★★	★★★★★	★★★★★	★★★★★

Touring Time: Average 3 hours, minimum 1½ hours

Restaurants: Yes

Description and Comments A building of thoroughly modern design that caused some controversy when it first opened, it showcases art from the late nineteenth century to today. Our kids always enjoyed the sunken sculpture garden, where large works in various styles and materials seem larger than life. Walk-in tours are offered weekdays at noon, Saturdays and Sundays at noon and 2 p.m.

Two programs will interest families with elementary-school-age children: "Young at Art," for ages six to nine (accompanied by adults), meets Saturdays 10 a.m.–noon in a program that combines looking at art with creating your own; preregistration is required; "Improv Art," a drop-in program, meets Saturdays 10:30 a.m.–1 p.m. for ages 5 to 11 (accompanied by an adult); it combines activity-sheet gallery tours with creating original artworks to take home.

*National Air and Space Museum

Seventh Street and Independence Avenue SW; tour information (202) 357-1400, theater and planetarium recorded information (202) 357-1686, general information (202) 357-2700

Admission: Planetarium shows: $3.75 per person; IMAX only: $5.50 adults, $4.25 seniors 55+ and children ages 2–17; IMAX/Planetarium combination: $8 adults, $7 seniors and children

Appeal by Age Groups:

Pre-school	Grade School	Teens	Young Adults	Over 30	Seniors
★★★★	★★★★★	★★★★★	★★★★★	★★★★★	★★★★★

Touring Time: Average 3 hours, minimum 2 hours

Restaurants: Yes

Description and Comments   Air and Space is a hit with almost all kids—and adults, too, for that matter. In 23 main exhibition galleries, the museum displays major artifacts covering the history of manned flight—from the Wright brothers to space travel. Before you embark on a visit here, get a museum map and make a plan. There's a lot to see and do, it's usually crowded, and the going can be hectic. In addition to exhibits, shows are put on daily in the Albert Einstein Planetarium, and the Samuel P. Langley Theater has a five-story IMAX screen that's seven stories wide. Free docent-led tours are given daily; audio tours are available for a per-headset fee of $5 adults and $4.50 students and seniors.

Note: The museum is undergoing a renovation scheduled for completion in July 2001, but it will remain open during the project.

National Museum of African Art

950 Independence Avenue SW; (202) 357-4600

Appeal by Age Groups:

Pre-school	Grade School	Teens	Young Adults	Over 30	Seniors
★★	★★★★	★★★★★	★★★★★	★★★★★	★★★★★

Touring Time: Average 2 hours, minimum 1 hour
Restaurants: No

Description and Comments   An in-depth look at the incredibly wide range and diversity of African cultures is what you find here. Some of the visual arts exhibited are remarkably colorful and striking, and other exhibits, like the temporary Audible Art installation, take you to Africa by way of your other senses. All African areas are represented, in both ancient and contemporary works. Among the permanent exhibits that might best appeal to kids is "Art of the Personal Object." The museum also sponsors ongoing arts workshops for children, and family programs, such as storytelling sessions.

*National Museum of American History

14th Street and Constitution Avenue NW; (202) 357-2700

Appeal by Age Groups:

Pre-school	Grade School	Teens	Young Adults	Over 30	Seniors
★★	★★★★	★★★★★	★★★★★	★★★★★	★★★★★

Touring Time: Average 3 hours, minimum 1½ hours
Restaurants: Yes

Description and Comments   You must stop in here, if for no other reason, to see the American flag that inspired the writing of the National Anthem and one of the original Edison lightbulbs. Beyond that, the museum does a terrific job of bringing history to life, covering topics ranging from "After the Revolution: Everyday Life in America, 1780–1800" to "The Information Age: People, Information, and Technology." Better still are the Hands-On History Room and the Hands-On Science Center. In the Hands-On History Room (children ages 5 to 12 must be accompanied by an adult), nearly three dozen activities help kids (and parents) experience and feel life in past times. Three of our favorites are "Sorting the Mail by Rail," in which you try to sort the mail with the same quickness and dexterity that were needed to do the job in the old-time railcars; "Travel with the Peddler," which puts you out on the street with a push-cart peddler; and "More Work for Mother," where you try out inventions from the late 1800s designed to make housekeeping easier. The Hands-On Science Center serves a similar function, allowing kids to try lasers, understand DNA, find food dyes in different beverages, test water for pollutants the way scientists did in the 1890s, and so on. The Hands-On rooms are open 12 noon to 3 p.m., Tuesday through Sunday; tickets (no charge) are required during weekends and busy times.

*National Museum of Natural History

Tenth Street and Constitution Avenue NW; (202) 357-2700

IMAX Admission: 2-D films: $5.50 adults, $4.50 seniors 55+ and children ages 2–17; 3-D films: $6.50 adults, $5.50 seniors 55+ and children ages 2–17

Appeal by Age Groups:

Pre-school	Grade School	Teens	Young Adults	Over 30	Seniors
★★★	★★★★★	★★★★★	★★★★★	★★★★★	★★★★★

Touring Time: Average 2 hours, minimum 1 hour

Restaurants: Yes

Description and Comments Butterflies, dinosaurs, and rocks highlight this museum. The new butterfly garden encompasses four habitats—wetland, meadow, wood's edge, and urban gardens—and is just fascinating. Dinosaur Hall is, of course, a long-standing favorite. Somehow these giant creatures never cease to stimulate our imaginations. If you've got a nine-year-old who's collecting rocks (like some of us did), the Hall of Geology is a must-see. For hands-on doings, the museum has a Discovery Room. We like the Insect Zoo, by the way, especially when the tarantulas are feeding! There's a lot more, of course: sea ecology, the African bush elephant, African cultures, and lots of life-sized models of huge animals, current and prehistoric. Free weekday highlights tours are available Monday through Thursday at 10:30 and 1:30, Friday at 10:30.

National Postal Museum

2 Massachusetts Avenue NE; (202) 633-9360

Appeal by Age Groups:

Pre-school	Grade School	Teens	Young Adults	Over 30	Seniors
★★	★★★	★★★★	★★★★	★★★★	★★★★★

Touring Time: Average 2 hours, minimum 1 hour

Restaurants: No

Description and Comments   The United States Postal Service delivers over 600 million pieces of mail every day. No wonder letters get lost! This hall contains six major exhibit galleries covering the history, whys, and wherefores of the U.S. Postal Service, with installations like "Binding the Nation," which tells how the post helped bring the country together, and "Moving the Mail," describing just how it all works. The museum does have a Discovery Center where kids can pick up activity kits, play games focused on museum topics, do self-directed crafts, or design their own commemorative stamp. But the center's only open on the third Saturday of each month from 1 p.m. to 3 p.m.

*National Zoo

3001 Connecticut Avenue NW; general information (202) 673-4717; guided tours (202) 673-4955

Appeal by Age Groups:

Pre-school	Grade School	Teens	Young Adults	Over 30	Seniors
★★★★★	★★★★★	★★★★★	★★★★★	★★★★★	★★★★★

Touring Time: Average 5 hours, minimum 3 hours

Restaurants: Yes

Description and Comments   What a wonderful zoo this is—even if the famous Chinese pandas are no longer there (which for a long time was the main reason our kids wanted to visit). As with most modern zoos, the orientation here is preservation and species ecology, not amusing display, and the whole experience is much more educational—and fun. Check out the Pollinarium, where you can explore how animals help plants cross-pollinate and just what's in it for the animals; the Think Tank, a place to learn how animals think; the orangutans, who are becoming computer literate; and the Komodo dragons and Golden Lion Tamarins. Also of special interest are Amazonia, a re-creation of a tropical river and forest; the Reptile Discovery Center, where you can see reptiles and amphibians up close and personal; and the Invertebrate Exhibit, which covers everything from ants to octopuses.

Capital Children's Museum

800 Third Street NE; Washington, D.C.; (202) 675-4120; www.ccm.org

Hours: Easter–Labor Day, daily 10 a.m.–6 p.m.; Labor Day–Easter, 10 a.m.–5 p.m.

Admission: $6 per person, $4 seniors 55+; free for children age 2 and under; half-price on Sunday before noon

Appeal by Age Groups:

Pre-school	Grade School	Teens	Young Adults	Over 30	Seniors
★★★★	★★★★★	★★	★★	★★	★★

Touring Time: Average 2 hours, minimum 1 hour

Rainy-Day Touring: Yes

Services and Facilities:

Restaurants No	Lockers No
Alcoholic beverages No	Pet kennels No
Disabled access Yes	Rain check No
Wheelchair rental No	Private tours No
Baby stroller rental No	

Description and Comments   This hands-on museum shows a lot of emphasis on cultures—Japan, Mexico, etc. It has five permanent exhibits and always offers a traveling exhibit as well. Among the permanent exhibit topics: Mexico; Chemical Science; Chuck Jones, covering the art, history, and science of animation; Cityscapes; and the Peace Sculpture, an interesting house-shaped construction stuffed with violent toys that, over time, is to be transformed into a peace sculpture by being covered over with kids' messages promoting peace. Like many of the growing number of fine children's museums, this is an excellent place to spend a few hours learning while you play.

Family-Friendly Restaurants

CARAVAN GRILL

1825 18th Street NW; (202) 518-0444

Meals served: Lunch and dinner
Cuisine: Persian/Middle Eastern
Entree range: $12.95–17.95 (dinner); buffet $7.95–10.95
Children's menu: No, but kids' buffet is half-price
Reservations: Yes
Payment: AE, MC, DC, V

About half of the dishes offered here are from northern Iran, which is quite unusual. Best bet with kids is to come for lunch and go for the buffet.

CHINA JOY

1827 M Street NW; (202) 296-6082

Meals served: Lunch and dinner
Cuisine: Chinese
Entree range: $5.95–19.95 (lunch and dinner)
Children's menu: No
Reservations: Yes
Payment: Major credit cards

This small place serves up excellent Chinese cuisine and offers a wide choice of noodle dishes to satisfy the little ones who aren't too adventurous.

CLYDES

3236 M Street NW; (202) 333-9180

Meals served: Lunch and dinner
Cuisine: Seafood and ribs
Entree range: $6.95–14.95 (lunch and dinner)
Children's menu: Yes
Reservations: Yes
Payment: Major credit cards

This restaurant is a comfortable place to bring the children, but it still manages to offer food worthy of its Georgetown surroundings. You can dine in the atrium if you want a more spacious feeling.

KRAMERBOOKS AND AFTERWORDS CAFÉ

1517 Connecticut Avenue NW; (202) 387-1462

Meals served: Breakfast, lunch, and dinner
Cuisine: Eclectic
Entree range: $3.95–13.75
Children's menu: No
Reservations: No
Payment: MC, V, AE, DC

The tables are packed tight at this combination bookstore and restaurant, but the menu is huge and has something for every taste: vegetarian chili, pasta in huge bowls, enormous sandwiches, and even fancy trendy entrees. Fun and busy.

Union Station
The classic railroad terminal has been renovated and is filled with shops, a food court, and a variety of restaurants. A good place to take a break. First Street and Massachusetts Avenue; (202) 371-9441.

Part Six

Virginia

Few states can match Virginia's diversity. From major urban areas and seats of government to the ocean to the mountains and across the farmlands and horse country in between, the state can supply just about any kind of vacation your family craves. We start our tour in **Northern Virginia,** looking at the cities and countryside near Washington, D.C. We then creep down the state's coast, covering the **Chesapeake Bay and Eastern Shore,** where maritime and beach vacations predominate. From there, it's farther south along the ocean to **Tidewater and Hampton Roads,** home to much of the country's illustrious colonial, maritime, and military history. We move on to the large, triangle-shaped midlands of **Central Virginia,** including the state capital of Richmond and some water-related vacation spots at the state's southern border. And, finally, we look at the western edge along the **Shenandoah Valley and Southwest Blue Ridge** regions, where the mountains provide an outdoor wonderland.

How to Get Information before You Go

Virginia Tourism Corporation, 901 E. Byrd Street, Richmond, VA 23219; (800) 742-3935 or (804) 371-8169; www.virginia.org.

Virginia Bicycling Guide, (800) 825-1203.

Virginia's Not-to-Be-Missed Attractions
Northern Virginia Newseum
Arlington National Cemetery
Mt. Vernon Estate and Gardens

Virginia's Not-to-Be-Missed Attractions (continued)

Chesapeake Bay and Eastern Shore

Chincoteague National Wildlife
Refuge
Chesapeake Bay Bridge and Tunnel
NASA WFF Visitor Center

Tidewater and Hampton Roads

Virginia Beach
First Landing/Seashore State Park
Virginia Air and Space Center
Hampton Roads History Center
Jamestown Settlement
Yorktown Victory Center
Natuticus, The National Maritime
Center
Colonial Williamsburg
Busch Gardens Williamsburg/
Water Country USA

Central Virginia Maymont
Appomattox Court House National
Historical Park
Monticello
Virginia Museum of Fine Arts
Wintergreen Resort

Shenandoah Valley and Southwest Blue Ridge

George Washington and Jefferson
National Forests
Shenandoah National Park
The Homestead
Center in the Square

Calendar of Festivals and Events

March

Shenandoah Valley and Southwest Blue Ridge: Highland Maple Festival, Monterey. Celebrate the coming of maple syrup; (540) 468-2550.

April

Statewide: Historic Garden Week in Virginia. More than 250 landmark homes and gardens offer open houses; (804) 644-1776.

Tidewater and Hampton Roads: Easter Eggstravaganza, Virginia Beach. The boardwalk goes wild with an Easter celebration; (800) 822-3224.

May

Northern Virginia: Alexandria Family History Festival, Alexandria. A day of history-oriented events around town; (703) 838-4242.

Tidewater and Hampton Roads: Children's Festival of Friends, Newport News. Newport News Park celebrates diversity and friendship for all kids; (757) 926-8451.

Chesapeake Bay and Eastern Shore: Spring on the Plantation. George Washington Birthplace National Monument; planting and life on the Colonial farm are celebrated; (804) 224-8687.

Central Virginia: Family Day at Jefferson's Retreat, Forest. Thomas Jefferson's Poplar Forest comes alive with Colonial family fun. Forest; (804) 525-1806.

June

Northern Virginia: Fairfax Fair, Fairfax County Government Center, Fairfax. An old-time fair with all the fixings; (703) 324-3247.

Tidewater and Hampton Roads: Seawall Festival, Portsmouth. Olde Towne comes alive with things maritime, old and new. (800) 296-9933 or (757) 393-9933.

Chesapeake Bay and Eastern Shore: Annual Potomac River Festival, Colonial Beach. Music, food, water events, games, and lots of fun; (804) 224-0732.

Central Virginia: James River Bateau Festival, Lynchburg and Appomattox. Boats from long ago float the river while everyone eats and makes merry; (804) 845-5966.

July

Northern Virginia: Civil War Weekend, Manassas. A major fair, encampment, etc.; (800) 432-1792.

Tidewater and Hampton Roads: Children's Colonial Weekend, Jamestown and Yorktown. Jamestown Settlement and Yorktown Victory Center take kids back to life in the old, old days; (888) 593-4682 or (757) 253-4838.

Chesapeake Bay and Eastern Shore: Annual Pony Swim and Auction, Chincoteague Island. The wild pony herds are rounded up to check their health and get a head count. Some are offered for sale to control their numbers; (757) 336-6161.

Shenandoah Valley and Southwest Blue Ridge: Virginia Highlands Arts & Crafts Festival, Abingdon. Lots of arts and crafts, plus hot air ballooning, music, and, of course, food; (800) 435-3440.

August

Northern Virginia: Somerset Steam & Gas Pasture Party, Somerset. Old-time farming gizmos are celebrated; (540) 672-2495.

Shenandoah Valley and Southwest Blue Ridge: Virginia Mountain Peak Festival, Roanoke. The downtown and market areas come alive with all kinds of good stuff; (540) 342-2028.

September

Northern Virginia: Warrenton Horse Show, Warrenton Horse Show Grounds. An equestrian fiesta on Labor Day; (540) 347-9442 or (540) 347-4414.

Tidewater and Hampton Roads: Isle of Wight County Fair, Isle of Wight. A good old county fair on a special island; (757) 357-2291.

Central Virginia: State Fair of Virginia, Strawberry Hill Fairgrounds, Richmond. The big one; (800) 588-3247 or (804) 228-3200.

October

Shenandoah Valley and Southwest Blue Ridge: Fall Foliage Festival, Clifton Forge. A wide variety of events, food, entertainment, and sights to see; (540) 862-4463.

November

Northern Virginia: Trains at Christmas Model Train Show, Fredericksburg. Toy trains fill the Fredericksburg National Guard Armory; (800) 768-4748.

Shenandoah Valley and Southwest Blue Ridge: Fantasyland, Center in the Square, Roanoke. Celebrating the holiday season with events, performances, food—the whole nine yards; (540) 342-5770.

VIRGINIA CIVIL WAR SITES

The Virginia Civil War Trails program interprets 250 Civil War sites and provides up-to-date Civil War event information. Contact them at P.O. Box 4232, Richmond, VA 23220.

Northern Virginia

Fredericksburg & Spotsylvania Military Park. The park contains portions of several major battlefields— Fredericksburg, Chancellorsville, the Wilderness,

Spotsylvania Court House—and several other smaller historic sites, plus picnic areas and trails. 120 Chatham Lane, Fredericksburg; (540) 371-0802.

Manassas Museum. This state-of-the-art museum displays an extensive exhibit on the Civil War era. 9101 Prince William Street, Manassas; (703) 368-1873.

Manassas National Battlefield Park. Site of the war's first major battle and of the Second Battle of Manassas. The Visitor Center presents electronic maps and displays of equipment and memorabilia, and the staff regularly stages interpretative presentations. Walking and driving tours can be undertaken. 6511 Sudley Road, (Route 234), Manassas; (703) 361-1339.

Sailor's Creek Battlefield. The site of Virginia's last major battle, where Lee lost more than half his army, forcing him to surrender at Appomattox three days later. Re-enactment and interpretive programs are offered in summer. Twin Lakes State Park, Route 2, Green Bay; (804) 392-3435.

Virginia Civil War Trails—Caroline County. Drive to five sites in Caroline County: the Town of Bowling Green, Bethel Church, Carmel Church, Guinea Station, and the Star Hotel, all associated with the North Anna Campaign, where Lee and Grant first met in battle. 104 South Main Street, Bowling Green; (804) 633-7826.

Chesapeake Bay and Eastern Shore

Stratford Hall Plantation. (See Attractions, page 339.) Ancestral home of the Lee family. Stratford; (804) 493-8038 or (804) 493-8371.

Central Virginia

Appomattox Court House National Historical Park. (See Attractions, page 369.) Site of the war's end. Route 24, Appomattox; (804) 352-8987.

Blandford Church and Cemetery. An eighteenth-century parish church with 15 Tiffany stained-glass windows memorializing the 30,000 Confederate soldiers buried in the cemetery. Cemetery tours offered at special times, and a night tour is staged during Halloween. 111 Rochelle Lane, Petersburg; (800) 368-3595 or (804) 733-2396.

Living History at the Museum of the Confederacy. Costumed interpreters tell about life during the Civil War for a broad spectrum of the population, black and white, Federal and Confederate. 1201 East Clay Street, Richmond; (804) 649-1861.

Pamplin Historical Park & The National Museum of the Civil War Soldier. A 422-acre park containing museums, an antebellum plantation home, and a battlefield where, in 1865, Union forces broke through and captured

Richmond; less than a week later, Lee surrendered. Living history demonstrations staged regularly. 6125 Boydton Plank Road, Petersburg; (877) 726-7546 or (804) 861-2408.

Petersburg National Battlefield. Site of several battles in 1864 and 1865 and a nine-month siege, the longest ever in American warfare. 1539 Hickory Hill Road, Petersburg; (804) 732-3531.

Siege Museum. Tells the story of how the people of Petersburg lived before, during, and immediately after the Civil War, including a 20-minute film. 15 West Bank Street, Petersburg; (800) 368-3595 or (804) 733-2404.

Richmond National Battlefield Park. Commemorates 11 different sites associated with Union attempts to capture Richmond. The park covers 763 acres. The Visitor Center exhibits artifacts and a scale model hospital and shows a 22-minute film. 3215 East Broad Street, Richmond; (804) 771-2808.

Staunton River Battlefield State Park. Site of the Battle of the Old Men and Young Boys, so called because an unlikely group of Confederate old men and boys held a bridge of strategic importance. The park features a visitor center, battlefield exhibits, earthworks, nature walking trails, wildlife observation towers, and prehistoric Native American artifacts. 1021 Fort Hill Drive, Randolph; (804) 454-4312.

Shenandoah Valley and Southwest Blue Ridge

Kernstown Battlefield. This small town, site of two major battles, has changed little since the Civil War. Opequon Church Lane, Route 11, Winchester; (540) 722-3647.

Stonewall Country—Theater at Lime Kiln. A live performance focused on Stonewall Jackson, both fact and legend, plus a realistic portrayal of the Civil War's effect on the people of its era. Bordan Road, Lexington; (540) 463-3074.

Shenandoah Valley Heritage Museum. Depicts local history, including an electronic map of Stonewall Jackson's Valley campaign. 382 High Street, Dayton; (540) 879-2616.

Virginia Military Institute Museum. A mural of the famous VMI cadet charge during the Battle of New Market, plus Stonewall Jackson's war horse and other Civil War exhibits. Jackson Memorial Hall, Lexington, VA 24450; (703) 464-7232.

VIRGINIA BIKING

Virginia presents a huge array of bicycling opportunities, from short seaside rides to multiday mountain adventures. The state government publishes

The Virginia Bicycling Guide, which provides an excellent overview of the rides found here. State Bicycle Coordinator, Virginia Department of Transportation, 1401 East Broad Street, Richmond, VA 23219; (800) 835-1203 or (804) 371-4869. You might also want to check out *Mountain Bike! Virginia,* published by Menasha Ridge Press; to order, call (800) 243-0495.

Cool Web Sites for Virginia-Bound Kids

Alexandria Archaeology Kid's Page: ci.alexandria.va.us/oha/archaeology/ar-kids.html

Mount Vernon Pioneer Farmer: learn what it was like to work on a farm in George Washington's day: www.mountvernon.org/pioneer

Northern Virginia

Northern Virginia can provide an alternative access to Washington, D.C., offer a number of its own urban attractions, or readily take you out into the countryside. **Alexandria** is a vibrant metropolis in its own right. Worthwhile sites include **The Lyceum** (call (703) 838-4997), which covers the city's history; the **Alexandria African-American Heritage Park** (call (703) 838-4356), where a historic graveyard, natural wetlands, and a sculpture garden create a unique destination; and the **Alexandria Black History Resource Center** (call (703) 838-4356), which interprets African Americans' contributions to local history. The **Fort Ward Museum and Historic Site** (call (703) 838-4848) is a restored Union fort. The **Torpedo Factory Art Center** (call (703) 838-4565) displays the work of some 85 artists in all media. **Mt. Vernon Cruise** (call (703) 548- 9000) offers a boat trip to **Mt. Vernon** and a tour of the grounds. Also in Mt. Vernon is **Frank Lloyd Wright's Pope-Leighey House** (call (703) 780-4000). Just east, **Fairfax** is home to the **Fairfax Museum and Visitors Center** (call (800) 545-7950), which is devoted to local history; the **George Mason University Center for the Arts** (call (703) 993-8888), where world-class entertainment is presented; and the **Sully Historic Site** (call (703) 437-1794), a Federal period home with a museum, outbuildings, gardens, and living history tours.

Northeast lies **McLean,** where the **Claude Moore Colonial Farm** (call (703) 442-7557) reproduces an eighteenth-century tenant tobacco farm. Near Dulles Airport, **Herndon** has the 1930s **Kidwell Farm at Frying Pan Park** (call (703) 437-9101), and **Leesburg** is home to **Morven Park** (call (703) 777-2414), which features a mansion tour, carriage collection, and a fox-hunting museum. **Oatlands Plantation** (call (703) 777-3174), also in Leesburg, is another historic mansion with magnificent formal gardens.

Moving south, **Manassas** has the **Manassas National Battlefield Park** (call (703) 361-1339), site of the Battles of Bull Run, and **Splashdown**

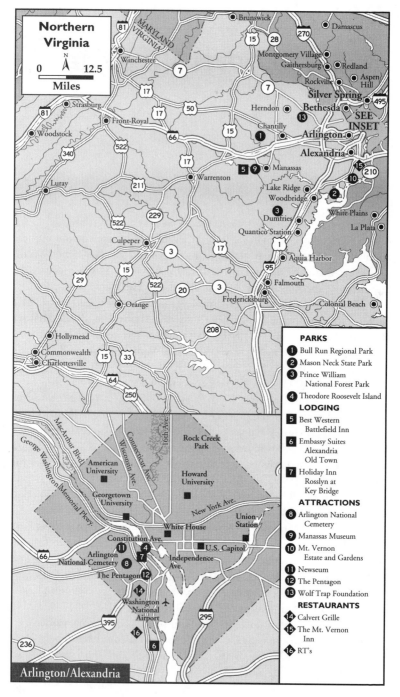

Northern Virginia

N

0 ⤒ 12.5

Miles

Brunswick

Damascus

Montgomery Village
Gaithersburg ● Redland

Rockville ● Aspen Hill

Winchester

Silver Spring

Herndon ● **Bethesda** **SEE INSET**

Strasburg

Woodstock

Front-Royal

Chantilly

Arlington

Alexandria

Luray

Warrenton

Manassas

Lake Ridge
Woodbridge

White Plains

Culpeper

Dumfries

La Plata

Quantico Station

Aquia Harbor

Falmouth

Orange

Fredericksburg

Colonial Beach

Hollymead

Commonwealth
Charlottesville

PARKS

❶ Bull Run Regional Park

❷ Mason Neck State Park

❸ Prince William
   National Forest Park

❹ Theodore Roosevelt Island

LODGING

❺ Best Western
   Battlefield Inn

❻ Embassy Suites
   Alexandria
   Old Town

❼ Holiday Inn
   Rosslyn at
   Key Bridge

ATTRACTIONS

❽ Arlington National
   Cemetery

❾ Manassas Museum

❿ Mt. Vernon
   Estate and Gardens

⓫ Newseum

⓬ The Pentagon

⓭ Wolf Trap Foundation

RESTAURANTS

⓮ Calvert Grille

⓯ The Mt. Vernon
   Inn

⓰ RT's

Rock Creek
Park

American
University

Howard
University

Georgetown
University

New York Ave.

Union
Station

White House

Constitution Ave.

U.S. Capitol

Arlington
National Cemetery

Independence
Ave.

The Pentagon

Washington
National
Airport

Arlington/Alexandria

Water Park (call (703) 361-4451), a good place to obtain relief from the summer heat. **Warrenton** has the **Old Jail Museum** (call (540) 347-5525). **Fredericksburg,** a major Civil War site, is home to the **Fredericksburg Area Museum and Cultural Center** (call (540) 371-3037), which covers the area from pre-history to modern times; **George Washington's Ferry Farm** (call (540) 371-6066), the president's boyhood home; and **Wilderness Battlefield** (call (540) 371- 0802), site of Lee and Grant's first encounter.

How to Get There

By Car. The area near Washington, D.C., including Alexandria, Arlington, and Mt. Vernon, is accessed from I-495, the Beltway, which encircles the greater D.C. area. State Route 267 runs west to Vienna, while I-66 travels southwest through Falls Church to Manassas. I-95 provides the primary access for those arriving from Richmond and the south.

By Plane. Ronald Reagan Washington National Airport (call (703) 417-8000) is located right in Arlington just across the river from Washington, D.C., and is served by the Metro subway system. Washington Dulles International Airport (call (703) 572-2700) is located due west of downtown D.C. For more information, contact the Metropolitan Washington Airports Authority, 1 Aviation Circle, Washington, DC 20001; (703) 417-8600.

By Train. Amtrak offers frequent service into Washington; (800) 872-7245.

By Subway. The Washington Metro serves many of Northern Virginia's cities. The Metro is clean, pleasant, efficient, and, for kids especially, fun. The Blue Line runs through Arlington into Alexandria, past Arlington Cemetery, the Pentagon, and National Airport, finally traveling just across the Fairfax County line. The Yellow Line reaches similar destinations more directly from central D.C., but does not stop at the cemetery. The Orange Line runs out to Falls Church, accessing Wolf Trap via connecting bus shuttle. Fares are based on how far you travel and time of day. Buy a Farecard from a machine at any station (have small bills ready). You can buy fares for round-trip or get a $20 debit card, which saves ten percent. A full-day pass costs $5, good from 9:30 a.m. to closing (usually midnight). Other multiuse passes are also available. Up to two children under age five ride free with each paying customer. For information, call (202) 637-7000.

How to Get Information before You Go

Alexandria Visitors Center, 221 King Street, Alexandria, VA 22314; (703) 838-4200; www.funside.com.

Fairfax County Visitors Center, 8180-A Silverbrook Road, Lorton, VA 22079; (703) 550-2450; www.cvb.co.fairfax.va.us.

Fredericksburg Visitors Center, 7806 Caroline Street, Fredericksburg, VA 22401; (800) 678-4748; www.fredericksburgva.com.

Historic Manassas Visitors Center, 9431 West Street, Manassas, VA 20110; (703) 361-6599.

Prince William County Visitors Center, 200 Mill Street, P.O. Box 123, Occoquan, VA 22125; (703) 491-4045; www.visitpwc.com.

The Best Parks

Bull Run Regional Park. The park has a campground, hiking trails, and a pool, along with an indoor archery range, minigolf and a Frisbee golf course; 7700 Bull Run Drive, Centreville; (703) 631-0550.

Mason Neck State Park. Just north of the Chesapeake Bay–Potomac River confluence, the park has hiking, fishing, picnicking, and biking. It's also adjacent to the Mason Neck Wildlife Refuge; 7301 High Point Road, Lorton; (703) 550-0960.

Prince William National Forest Park. Covers 17,000 acres and features streams, waterfalls, ponds, 35 miles of hiking trails, and all kinds of camping, including cabin camping; State Route 619 West, Triangle; (703) 221-7181.

Theodore Roosevelt Island. An 88-acre island in the Potomac River, this park has walking trails and a Teddy Roosevelt Memorial and is great for birding; (703) 289-2530.

Family Outdoor Adventures

Biking. W&OD Railroad Regional Park offers rails-to-trail biking and walking; 21293 Smiths Switch Road, Ashburn; (703) 729-0596. The Mt. Vernon Trail runs 18 miles between Theodore Roosevelt Island and Mt. Vernon; (800) 835-1203. Manassas National Battlefield Park allows cycling on its battlefield-touring road; 12521 Lee Highway, Manassas; (703) 754-1861.

Camping. Prince William National Forest Park (see The Best Parks, above).

Hiking. Prince William National Forest Park (see The Best Parks, above).

Family Lodging

Note: Lodging in Arlington or Alexandria can be an economical choice for a Washington, D.C., visit. Both cities provide convenient access to D.C.

and the surrounding countryside. Both cities offer a full range of lodging from the well-known chains.

Best Western Battlefield Inn

A 121-room, two-story motel, the Best Western Battlefield Inn has a pool, an on-site restaurant, free continental breakfast, and rooms available with microwaves and refrigerators. Cribs are available at no charge. Pets are welcome. Rates: $65–75; children under age 18 stay free with parents. 10820 Balls Ford Road, Manassas; (703) 361-8000.

Embassy Suites Alexandria Old Town

This is a 268-room, all-suites hotel in historic Old Town and within a block of the Metro. It offers an indoor pool and complimentary breakfast. Rates: $120–210; special package plans are available. 1900 Diagonal Road, Alexandria; (703) 884-5900.

Holiday Inn Rosslyn at Key Bridge

A 306-room hotel within one block of the Metro, Holiday Inn Rosslyn has an on-site restaurant that features panoramic views of the Capitol. It has a health/fitness center with an indoor pool. Cribs are available at no charge. Rates: $103–160 with breakfast on weekender rate; children under age 18 stay free with parents. 1900 North Fort Myer Drive, Arlington; (800) 368-3408 or (703) 807-2000.

Attractions

(See also Virginia Civil War Sites, pages 317–319.)

Arlington National Cemetery

Arlington; (703) 607-8052; www.arlingtoncemetery.com

Hours: Cemetery: April–September, daily 8 a.m.–7 p.m.; October–March, daily 8 a.m.–5 p.m. Tourmobile Guided Tour: April–September, daily 8:30 a.m.–6:30 p.m.; October–March, daily 9:30 a.m.–4:30 p.m.

Admission: Cemetery: free; Tourmobile: $4.75 adult, $2.25 children ages 3–11

Appeal by Age Groups:

Pre-school	Grade School	Teens	Young Adults	Over 30	Seniors
★★★★	★★★★★	★★★★★	★★★★★	★★★★★	★★★★★

Touring Time: Average 2 hours (Tourmobile), minimum 1 hour
Rainy-Day Touring: Yes

Services and Facilities:

Restaurants No	Lockers No
Alcoholic beverages No	Pet kennels No
Disabled access Yes	Rain check No
Wheelchair rental No	Private tours No
Baby stroller rental No	

Description and Comments   Arlington National Cemetery is a must-see for any Washington, D.C., or Northern Virginia visit. If nothing else, visit the Tomb of the Unknown Soldier and the Netherlands Carillon, the latter of which yields terrific views. The Visitor Center is just across Memorial Bridge from D.C. It houses historical displays and a small gift shop and distributes free maps and information. Changing of the guard ceremonies are conducted at the Tomb of the Unknowns every 30 minutes from April 1 through September 30 and every hour on the hour from October 1 through March 31.

Manassas Museum

9101 Prince William Street, Manassas; (703) 368-1873;
  www.manassasmuseum.org

Hours: Tuesday–Sunday 10 a.m.–5 p.m.; closed Mondays (except for Federal Holidays) and Thanksgiving, Christmas Eve, Christmas, and New Year's days

Admission: $3 adults, $2 children age 12 and under

Appeal by Age Groups:

Pre-school	Grade School	Teens	Young Adults	Over 30	Seniors
★★★	★★★★	★★★★	★★★★★	★★★★★	★★★★★

Touring Time: Average 2 hours, minimum 1 hour

Rainy-Day Touring: Yes

Services and Facilities:

Restaurants No	Lockers No
Alcoholic beverages No	Pet kennels No
Disabled access Yes	Rain check No
Wheelchair rental No	Private tours No
Baby stroller rental No	

Description and Comments   The museum interprets Manassas and Northern Virginia history and culture, ranging from prehistoric times, through the Civil War, and into the twentieth century. Start with the video programs, "A Place of Passages" and "A Community at War." They describe the region's early settlers and the Civil War's legacy. In summer, evening concerts are offered on the museum lawn.

Mt. Vernon Estate and Gardens

George Washington Parkway, Mount Vernon; (703) 780-2000;
www.mountvernon.org

Hours: April–August, daily 8 a.m.–5 p.m.; March and September–
October, daily 9 a.m.–5 p.m.; November–February, daily 9 a.m.–4 p.m.

Admission: $9 adults, $8.50 seniors 62 and older, $4.50 children ages
6–11, free for children age 5 and under; audio tour rental, $3

Appeal by Age Groups:

Pre-school	Grade School	Teens	Young Adults	Over 30	Seniors
★	★★★★	★★★★	★★★★★	★★★★★	★★★★★

Touring Time: Average 2 hours, minimum 1 hour

Rainy-Day Touring: Yes

Services and Facilities:

Restaurants Yes	Lockers No
Alcoholic beverages Yes	Pet kennels No
Disabled access Yes	Rain check No
Wheelchair rental Yes; free	Private tours No
Baby stroller rental No	

Description and Comments   This was George Washington's home for some
45 years. It's the second-most visited home in America, behind only the
White House. Maybe the most interesting thing about it is this: it looks to
be made of stone, but it's not; it's actually constructed of pine that has
been "rusticated" to look like rock. Washington designed the two-story
piazza that overlooks the Potomac River himself. The grounds, which he
also designed, cover some 500 acres. Costumed docents offer insights
throughout the estate. Kids probably best like touring the grounds, which,
in addition to the gardens and park-like setting, include a stable, mule
shed, paddock, coach house, spinning room, and salt house. The on-
property grist mill will open to the public in 2001. You can get here by
boat from Arlington or, with a combined admission, from the National
Farm in Accokeek, Maryland (see Maryland, Capital Region, page 258).

Newseum

1101 Wilson Boulevard, Arlington; (888) 639-7386 or (703) 284-3544;
www.newseum.org

Hours: Tuesday–Sunday 10 a.m.–5 p.m.; closed Thanksgiving, Christmas, and New Year's days

Admission: Free

Appeal by Age Groups:

Pre-school	Grade School	Teens	Young Adults	Over 30	Seniors
★★★	★★★★★	★★★★★	★★★★★	★★★★★	★★★★★

Touring Time: Average 3 hours, minimum 1½ hours

Rainy-Day Touring: Yes

Services and Facilities:

Restaurants Yes	Lockers Yes; coatroom
Alcoholic beverages No	Pet kennels No
Disabled access Yes	Rain check No
Wheelchair rental Yes; free	Private tours No
Baby stroller rental Yes; free	

Description and Comments Kids love this place, and adults do, too. It's the only interactive museum of news anywhere, disclosing a behind-the-scenes experience of how and why news is reported. You can be a reporter or a television newscaster. You can see current news happening on the block-long video news wall. We like being able to re-experience the great news stories of different eras. And there are lots of interactive exhibits to dabble in and films to watch. Don't miss the journalism game series, which takes place on 32 interactive stations. Among the roles everybody can play are a photo journalist, an investigative reporter, or a managing editor. The Domed Theater shows "great moments in the news" on a huge, high-definition video screen. Real radio and TV news programs are produced in the Broadcast Studio, where you can talk with the journalists and newsmakers.

Outside, Freedom Park is all about, well, freedom. Among the international symbols of "the fight to be free" are original Berlin Wall pieces and the Freedom Forum Journalists Memorial, honoring journalists who died while reporting the news. Reach the museum by taking the Metro to the Rosslyn Station.

The Pentagon

Arlington; (703) 695-1776; www.defenselink.mil/pubs/pentagon

Hours: Monday–Friday 9 a.m.–3 p.m.

Admission: Free

Appeal by Age Groups:

Pre-school	Grade School	Teens	Young Adults	Over 30	Seniors
★	★★★	★★★★	★★★★★	★★★★★	★★★★★

Touring Time: 1½ hours

Rainy-Day Touring: Yes

Services and Facilities:

Restaurants Yes	Lockers No
Alcoholic beverages No	Pet kennels No
Disabled access Yes	Rain check No
Wheelchair rental No	Private tours No
Baby stroller rental No	

Description and Comments   There's something forbiddingly fascinating about the Pentagon. It implies top secret activities and super spy stuff. This tour involves a 1.5-mile walk through one of the world's largest buildings, featuring 20 displays in many areas of interest. Each military branch is covered. *Note:* A photo ID is required for anyone age 16 and older. Get there by taking the Metro to the Pentagon stop.

Wolf Trap Foundation for the Performing Arts

1624 Wolf Trap Road, Vienna; (703) 255-1916; ticket information,
(703) 255-1860; www.wolf-trap.org

Hours: Vary by performance schedule

Admission: Varies by performance

Appeal by Age Groups:

Pre-school	Grade School	Teens	Young Adults	Over 30	Seniors
★★★★	★★★★★	★★★★★	★★★★★	★★★★★	★★★★★

Touring Time: Varies by performance

Rainy-Day Touring: Yes

Services and Facilities:

Restaurants Yes	Lockers No
Alcoholic beverages Yes	Pet kennels No
Disabled access Yes	Rain check No
Wheelchair rental No	Private tours No
Baby stroller rental No	

Description and Comments   This is the country's "national performing arts center," placed in a bucolic, wooded setting not far from Dulles Airport. It offers three performance venues: the Filene Center, the main theater; the Barns of Wolf Trap, a smaller facility; and Theatre-in-the-Woods, an amphitheater set in a thick grove of trees. Performances run the musical gamut from folk, pop, and rock to the National Symphony and opera. You can sit on the sloped lawn for concerts at the Filene Center (where slightly more than half the seating is under cover in the open-sided hall), and you can picnic before and during the performance. It's awfully pleasant, but be aware that if it rains, you'll get wet sitting out there. A series of children's performances are staged each summer at the Theatre-in-the-Woods, including music, dance, mime, storytelling, comic basketball, puppetry, and clowning. All in all, it's a wonderful place to be entertained.

Family-Friendly Restaurants

CALVERT GRILLE

3106 Mt. Vernon Avenue, Arlington; (703) 836-8425

Meals served: Breakfast, lunch, and dinner
Cuisine: American
Entree range: $3.95–11.95 (lunch and dinner)
Children's menu: Yes
Reservations: Yes
Payment: Major credit cards

Calvert Grille is a very family-friendly place, complete with a kids' playroom and a wall to draw on. Food runs to crab cakes, baby-back ribs, and local specialties.

THE MT. VERNON INN

George Washington Memorial Parkway, Mt. Vernon; (703) 780-0011

Meals served: Lunch and dinner
Cuisine: American
Entree range: $4.95–24.95 (lunch and dinner)
Children's menu: Yes
Reservations: Yes
Payment: Major credit cards

You have to dress up a bit here (semiformal, they say), but the experience is worth the bother. The decor and costumed servers take you back to George Washington's day, and specialties on the menu emphasize that time in this region (peanut-chestnut soup, for example).

RT'S

3804 Mt. Vernon Avenue, Alexandria; (703) 684-6010

Meals served: Lunch and dinner
Cuisine: Seafood

Entree range: $12.95–17.95 (dinner)
Children's menu: Yes
Reservations: Yes
Payment: Major credit cards

RT's is an award-winning, neighborhood seafood restaurant in the heart of Alexandria's Old Town. The she-crab soup is a specialty, as is the Jack Daniels shrimp. If seafood is not your thing, the menu also includes meats and pasta.

Chesapeake Bay and Eastern Shore

What's in a name? Sometimes everything. They call this area along the Chesapeake Bay the Northern Neck, and while the name has a kind of grisly air, it is descriptive of the "neck" of land on which it sits. This is really lowland country, some of it heavily forested, much of it cut or bordered by large rivers. It's also farm country, and the **Westmoreland Berry Farm and Orchard** (call (800) 997-2377) in **Oak Grove** is a fun place to pick your own fruit, have a picnic, and taste the agricultural life. In **Reedville,** all the way out where the land meets the bay, the **Reedville Fishermen's Museum** (call (804) 453-6529) displays the fishing and crabbing life. In **King William,** the **Mattaponi Indian Museum Minnie Ha Ha Educational Trading Post** (call (804) 769-2194) is home to many artifacts, including a necklace once belonging to Pocahontas, and a nature trail. Our first president was born in this neck of the woods, in **Westmoreland,** where the **George Washington Birthplace National Monument** (call (804) 224-1732) is a Colonial living history farmstead.

The Eastern Shore is a small spit of land extending south from Ocean City, Maryland, almost to Virginia Beach. Almost, but not quite, which created an excuse to build the Chesapeake Bay Bridge-Tunnel, one of the more fun roads on which to ride. The area highlights are Chincoteague Island and Chincoteague Village adjacent to Assateague National Seashore. You'll also enjoy the **Eastern Shore Railway Museum** (call (757) 665-4618) in **Parksley,** and the **Hopkins and Bros. Store & Eastern Shore Steamboat Co.** (call (757) 787-3100), one of the oldest general stores on the East Coast, in **Onancock.**

HOW TO GET THERE

By Car. From Fredericksburg, U.S. 17 travels north-south down the mainland side of the area, west of the Rappahannock River. Between the river and the bay, State Route 3 provides the primary access. You must arrive at the Eastern Shore either from Maryland to the north or, from the mainland, via the Chesapeake Bay Bridge-Tunnel, which is U.S. 13 from Virginia Beach.

How to Get Information before You Go

Chesapeake Bay/Northern Neck Visitor Center, 3450 James Madison Parkway, King George, VA 22485; (540) 663-3205; www.northernneck.org.

Eastern Shore Visitor Center & Tourism Commission, P.O. Box 460, U.S. Route 13 South, Melfa, VA 23410; (757) 787-2460; www.esva.net/~esvatourism.

Chincoteague Chamber of Commerce, P.O. Box 258, Chincoteague, VA 23336; (757) 336-6161; www.chincoteaguechamber.com.

The Best Beaches and Parks

Assateague National Seashore (see Maryland, Eastern Shore, page 274).

Chincoteague National Wildlife Refuge. A birdwatcher's and photographer's paradise, this is home to more than 100 bird species birds at any time. More famous, however, are the wild ponies. Take the Chincoteague Wildlife Loop to see the ponies and other wildlife; it's reserved for hikers and bicyclists until 3 p.m., after which it's open to cars. Maddox Boulevard Extension, Chincoteague; (804) 336-6122.

Colonial Beach. Just a stone's throw west of Fredericksburg, this is a laid-back town along the Potomac River with a wide, sandy beach, a boardwalk, and not too much commercial development; (804) 244-8145 or (804) 224-1781.

Eastern Shore Wildlife Refuge. Located near the entrance to the Chesapeake Bay Bridge-Tunnel, the refuge has exhibits and nature trails. 5003 Hallot Circle, Cape Charles; (757) 331-2760.

Hughlett's Point Natural Area. A preserve with a long sandy beach and Chesapeake Bay views. There are no facilities here, but it's a terrific beach if you go for natural surroundings; Route 605 in Northumberland County.

Westmoreland State Park. Just south of Colonial Beach and adjacent to the birthplaces of George Washington and Robert E. Lee, the park fronts the Potomac for about 1.5 miles. Its most famous aspect is Horsehead Cliffs,

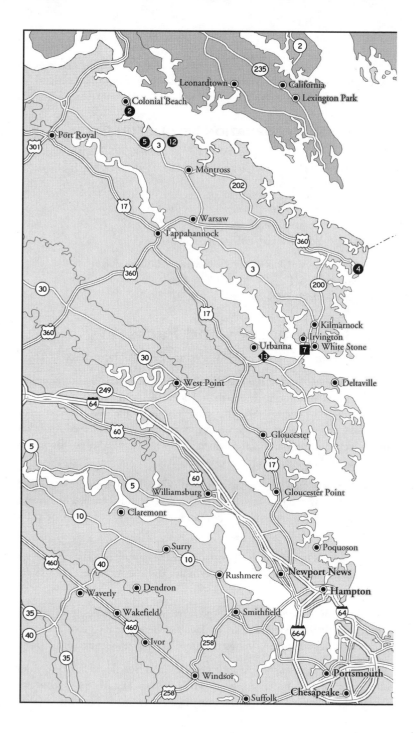

Chesapeake Bay and Eastern Shore

N

0   12.5

Miles

CHESAPEAKE BAY

CHESAPEAKE BAY

ATLANTIC OCEAN

MARYLAND
VIRGINIA

Hebron

Salisbury

Fruitland

12

Princess Anne

13

Snow Hill

113

Pocomoke City

Crisfield

Lawsonia

Saxis

13

Hallwood

Tangier

Bloxom

Parksley

Accomac

Onancock

Onley

Melfa

Keller

Wachapreague

Painter

Belle Haven

Exmore

Nassawadox

13

Eastville

Cheriton

Cape Charles

13

60

Virginia Beach

175

Chincoteague

BEACHES AND PARKS

1. Chincoteague National Wildlife Refuge
2. Colonial Beach
3. Eastern Shore Wildlife Refuge
4. Hughlett's Point Natural Area
5. Westmoreland State Park

LODGING

6. The Sunrise Motor Inn
7. The Tides

ATTRACTIONS

8. Chesapeake Bay Bridge and Tunnel
9. Island Aquarium
10. NASA WFF Visitor Center
11. Oyster and Maritime Museum
12. Stratford Hall Plantation

RESTAURANTS

13. Marshall's Drugstore
14. Muller's Old Fashioned Ice Cream Parlour
15. Steamers Seafood Restaurant

which offers spectacular river views. You can hike, camp, cabin camp, fish, boat, and swim; 1650 State Park Road, Montross; (804) 493-8821.

Family Outdoor Adventures

Biking. There's a lot of good cycling on the Eastern Shore peninsula. Bikes can be rented from the following: The Bike Depot, 7058 Maddox Boulevard, Chincoteague, (757) 336-5511; Just Bikes, 6527 Maddox Boulevard, Chincoteague, (757) 336-6700; Piney Island Country Store, 7805 Maddox Boulevard, Chincoteague, (757) 336-6212.

Fishing. More than a dozen charter boat services operate out of the area. Contact one of the Visitor Centers for a list (see How to Get Information before You Go).

Hiking. Caledon Natural Area, the summer home for one of the largest concentrations of bald eagles on the East Coast, has five hiking trails that wander through marshlands and woodlands, plus a visitor center with bald eagle exhibits; 11617 Caledon Road, King George, (540) 663-3861. Bushmill Stream Natural Area has a streamside trail that's fun to hike; Route 642, Heathsville, (804) 462-5030. Corotoman River Nature Trail, runs along the river through forest and marshlands; Route 3, Lancaster, (804) 843-5402.

Horseback Riding. Breezewood Farms has guided trail rides and western riding lessons; Irvington Road, Irvington; (804) 438-5141.

Paddling. Belle Isle State Park features guided canoe tours of Mulberry Creek and the Rappahannock River for minimal fees, (804) 462-5030. Westmoreland State Park (see The Best Beaches and Parks, above) has kayaking below the Horsehead Cliffs that's appropriate for beginners and includes basic instruction, a guided tour of the shoreline, and a fossil search. Mattaponi Canoe & Kayak in Aylett offers canoe and kayak rentals, natural history paddle tours, and water-based environmental education throughout Virginia's Middle Peninsula, (800) 769-3545, www.mattaponi.com. Intracoastal Kayak Company offers a wide range of guided trips; 6250 Maddox Boulevard, Chincoteague, (757) 336-0070.

Family Lodging

The Sunrise Motor Inn

There's nothing fancy about this place, but it's a good, solid motel with a pool and a restaurant nearby. It's within walking distance to shops, bike rentals, and miniature golf, and it's less than a mile from the entrance to the Chincoteague National Wildlife Refuge and the Assateague National Seashore. Rates: $41–45 per night; one- and two-bedroom efficiencies are

$325–585 per week; children under age 12 stay free. Maddox Boulevard, Chincoteague; (800) 673-5211 or (757) 336-6671; www.chincoteague. com/sunrise.

The Tides

The Tides is an upscale, family-run, self-contained resort that offers all the sports and pastimes you'd expect, plus a supervised kids' program—Crab Net Kids—with both daytime and evening hours. The play pavilion is always open, with a pool table, Ping-Pong, a video arcade, and other indoor games. Shuffleboard, croquet, horseshoes, basketball, and a playground are on-site. Bicycles can be borrowed. The inn has Family Rooms designed to accommodate families with two or three small children; the Lodge and Cove Cottage offer more accommodations. Inn rates: $162–217, Modified American Plan; children under age 10 stay free in room with parents; children ages 10–15 are charged $65 day, MAP. Lodge rates: $119–179, room only. Children's program: $20 per day and $10 per evening. 480 King Carter Drive, Irvington; (800) 843-3746 or (804) 438-5000; www.the tides.com.

Attractions

Chesapeake Bay Bridge and Tunnel

U.S. 13, Cape Charles; (757) 331-2960; www.cbbt.com

Hours: Restaurant hours: October–March, daily 7 a.m.–6 p.m.;
April–September, daily 6 a.m.–10 p.m.

Admission: $10 per car, one-way toll

Description and Comments Okay, it may seem a bit odd to include a bridge as a tourist attraction, but if you're anywhere near this place, it's worth driving over (or over and back) just to experience it. Even the most jaded teens respond to the size and scope of this engineering project—a 20-mile, four-lane roadway over low-level trestles, with two mile-long tunnels and two high-level bridges. Four man-made ten-acre islands are located at each end of the tunnels. The southernmost, Sea Gull Island, affords an opportunity to stop, eat, fish, birdwatch, or gape at the view. There's an interpretive display about the Bridge-Tunnel's construction, and a Shipwatcher's Guide that describes the U.S. Navy ships you see sailing out of Hampton Roads. A scenic overlook is located on the west side of the roadway at the southern tip of Virginia's Eastern Shore, offering great photo opportunities.

Island Aquarium

8162 Landmark Plaza, Chincoteague; (757) 336-2212;
www.assateague.com/aquarium.htm

Hours: Daily 10 a.m.–5 p.m.

Admission: $3 for adults, $2 for children

Appeal by Age Groups:

Pre-school	Grade School	Teens	Young Adults	Over 30	Seniors
★★★★	★★★★★	★★★	★★★	★★★★	★★★★

Touring Time: 1 hour

Rainy-Day Touring: Yes

Services and Facilities:

Restaurants No	Lockers No
Alcoholic beverages No	Pet kennels No
Disabled access Yes	Rain check No
Wheelchair rental No	Private tours No
Baby stroller rental No	

Description and Comments   A very small but fun aquarium focused on local marine life. The touch tank features horseshoe crabs, spider crabs, starfish, whelks, and others. The water for the aquarium comes in directly from the Chincoteague Channel, and the animals are released back into local waters regularly, meaning that the fish you see will vary seasonally. There's also a marsh exhibit, explaining local habitat.

NASA WFF Visitor Center

Building J-17, Route 175, Wallops Island; (757) 824-1344 or (757) 824-2298; www.wff.nasa.gov/pages/visitor.htm

Hours: July and August, daily 10 a.m.–4 p.m.; March–June and September–November, Thursday–Monday 10 a.m.–4 p.m.

Admission: Free

Appeal by Age Groups:

Pre-school	Grade School	Teens	Young Adults	Over 30	Seniors
★★★★★	★★★★★	★★★★	★★★★	★★★★★	★★★★★

Touring Time: Average 3 hours, minimum 2 hours

Rainy-Day Touring: Yes

Services and Facilities:

Restaurants No	Lockers No
Alcoholic beverages No	Pet kennels No
Disabled access Yes	Rain check No
Wheelchair rental No	Private tours No
Baby stroller rental No	

Description and Comments   Some of us were previously unaware that space stuff went on here, but it does, and the Visitor Center is a must-see for flight and space-flight fans. There are displays on current and future NASA projects, with full-scale aircraft and rockets, and scale models of space probes and satellites. There's even a moon rock. Some of the hands-on activities include building and launching a bottle rocket and an exploration of satellite data transmission. Kids ages five to ten can earn their Space Ace Certificate by completing an activity sheet. On weekends, a ten-minute Puppets in Space program is presented at 11 a.m. Aimed at all ages, it uses puppet astronauts and Sam the monkey to explain space flight and how astronauts' space suits work. An eight-minute film follows. On Sundays, the 30-minute *Humans in Space* is presented at 1 p.m. Also aimed at all ages, it shows what it's like to live and work in space, after which kids can build their own space helmet.

Oyster and Maritime Museum

7125 Maddox Boulevard, Chincoteague Island; (757) 336-6117;
www.chincoteaguechamber.com/oyster/omm.htm

Hours: Monday–Friday 9 a.m.–5 p.m., Saturday 10 a.m.–5 p.m.,
Sunday noon–4 p.m.

Admission: $3 adults, $1.50 seniors 65 and older, $1 children ages 12
and under

Appeal by Age Groups:

Pre-school	Grade School	Teens	Young Adults	Over 30	Seniors
★★	★★★★	★★★	★★★★	★★★★	★★★★★

Touring Time: 1 hour

Rainy-Day Touring: Yes

Services and Facilities:

Restaurants No	Lockers No
Alcoholic beverages No	Pet kennels No
Disabled access Yes	Rain check No
Wheelchair rental No	Private tours No
Baby stroller rental No	

Description and Comments   Another small museum, this one is solely devoted to oysters and the lifestyle of those who fish them. Displays cover the oyster industry, oyster by-products, a shell collection, fossils, and oyster oddities.

Stratford Hall Plantation

Stratford; (804) 493-8038 or (804) 493-8371; www.stratfordhall.org

Hours: Daily 9 a.m.–4:30 p.m.; closed Thanksgiving, Christmas, and New Year's days

Admission: $7 adults, $6 seniors and military, $3 children ages 6–17, free for children 5 and under

Appeal by Age Groups:

Pre-school	Grade School	Teens	Young Adults	Over 30	Seniors
★★	★★★★	★★★★	★★★★★	★★★★★	★★★★★

Touring Time: Average 2 hours, minimum 1 hour

Rainy-Day Touring: Yes

Services and Facilities:

Restaurants Yes	Lockers No
Alcoholic beverages Yes	Pet kennels No
Disabled access Yes	Rain check No
Wheelchair rental Yes; free	Private tours Yes; of special
Baby stroller rental No	focus: garden, decos, etc.

Description and Comments This is Robert E. Lee's birthplace, beautifully set above the Potomac River and known for its unique architectural style. The Plantation is still managed as a farm, and younger kids will enjoy seeing the animals and farm workings. The main building, Stratford Hall, was built in the late 1730s and is furnished with eighteenth-century American and English decorative arts. The nursery will also appeal to kids, with its period toys and smaller furnishings. There are three gardens to explore—East, West, and Slave—and a nature trail, lined with wildflowers, which provides an enjoyable walk through fields and woods.

Family-Friendly Restaurants

MARSHALL'S DRUGSTORE

50 Cross Street, Urbanna; (804) 758-5344

Meals served: Breakfast, lunch, and early dinner
Cuisine: Short order and soda fountain
Entree range: $3.95–8.95
Children's menu: No
Reservations: No
Payment: Cash only

An authentic, old-fashioned drugstore fountain, Marshall's has been here since 1930. They serves things like milk shakes made with real ice cream, fresh-squeezed limeade and lemonade, and homemade sandwiches and burgers. It's hard to find a seat on weekdays before 9 a.m.—too many locals are catching up on the latest gossip.

MULLER'S OLD FASHIONED ICE CREAM PARLOUR

4034 Main Street, Chincoteague Island; (757) 336-5894

Meals served: Dessert
Cuisine: Sweets
Entree range: $1.95–6.95
Children's menu: No
Reservations: No
Payment: Cash only

In an 1875 home, Muller's serves up good, old-fashioned sweet stuff— fresh fruit sundaes, splits, malts, ice cream sodas, fountain drinks, and frozen yogurt. Oh, and for those who must: Belgian waffles served with ice cream, fresh fruit, and homemade whipped cream. They have superb root beer on draft, too.

STEAMERS SEAFOOD RESTAURANT

6251 Maddox Boulevard, Chincoteague Island; (757) 336-5478

Meals served: Dinner
Cuisine: Seafood
Entree range: $9.95–16.95
Children's menu: Yes
Reservations: No
Payment: V, MC, D

Steamed seafood dishes are the speciality here—spicy shrimp and local crabs—but you can get good fried chicken, too.

Tidewater and Hampton Roads

Visitors to this area may encounter a problem: too much to do. So rich is the region in activities, history, museums, science, maritime attractions, and other goodies that it's important to leave yourself sufficient time to explore. In **Hampton,** for example, a ride around town on the **Hampton Trolley** (call (757) 826-6351) is a must, but to get an even wider view, **Miss Hampton II Harbor Cruises** (call (800) 800-2202) offers three-hour rides that show off huge commercial cargo ships, Norfolk Naval Base, Blackbeard's Point, Old Point Comfort, and a stop at Fort Wool, an island fortress. **Air Power Park** (call (757) 727-1163) has a fine outdoor exhibit of rockets and military aircraft. **Hampton Carousel,** in **Carousel Park** (call (757) 727-1102) is a restored 1920 go-round that operates in the warm months. For something countrified, try **Bluebird Gap Farm** (call (757) 727-6739), where you can pick your own of whatever's in season and visit the small zoo and playground.

Newport News offers a bevy of sites. **Battle Dam No. 1** (call (757) 886-7912) is an extensive Civil War earthworks, where you'll find interpretive trails. For international flair, **Japanese Tea House in Virginia** (call (757) 594-7331) purports to be the only authentic Japanese tea house in the east. The **Newsome House Museum and Cultural Center** (call (757) 928-6754) houses a superb black history collection, while **Peninsula Fine Arts Center** (call (757) 596-8175) has a neat hands-on kids gallery. The **U.S. Army Transportation Museum** (call (757) 878-1115) displays all kinds of military "vehicles," even a flying saucer, and the **Virginia War Museum** (call (757) 247-8523) displays one of the country's largest military collections, dating from 1775.

Norfolk offers another kind of cruise: two- or three-hour sailing jaunts from **American Rover Tall Ship Cruises** (call (757) 627- 7245). The **Chrysler Museum of Art** (call (757) 664-6201) ranks among the country's finest art museums. More militaria can be seen at the **Hampton**

Roads Naval Museum (call (757) 444-8971), the state's official naval museum, and in a narrated tour of **Norfolk Naval Base** (call (757) 445-0348), the world's largest. **Norfolk Botanical Gardens** (call (757) 441-5830) has more than 20 theme gardens. The **Tugboat Museum** (call (757) 627-4884) features exhibits aboard an actual tugboat.

Next door, **Portsmouth** features a National Historic Landmark lightship at the **Lightship Portsmouth Museum** (call (757) 393-8741). **The Museum of Military History** (call (757) 393-2773) includes every war we've ever fought in. The **Naval Shipyard Museum** (call (757) 393-8591) covers local naval history. The **Pokey Smokey Steam Locomotive** (call (757) 465-2937) is a working scale model kids can ride. We like places like the **Virginia Sports Hall of Fame & Museum** (call (757) 393- 8031) because it's fun seeing which athletes we remember.

In addition to beaches and myriad amusements, **Virginia Beach** has the **Atlantic Wildfowl Heritage Museum** (call (757) 437-8432), a venue for the work of wildfowl artists. The **Chesapeake Bay Bridge and Tunnel** (see Eastern Shore section, page 337) leaves the mainland from the area and is a fun drive. The **Oceana Naval Air Station Tour** (call (757) 640-0300) displays more than 200 aircraft. **Old Cape Henry Lighthouse in Fort Story** (call (757) 422-9421) was built in 1791, while **The Old Coast Guard Station** (call (757) 422-1587) showcases local maritime history, including wrecks and rescues.

Williamsburg has **Colonial Williamsburg** (see Attractions, page 351). It also has **America's Railroads on Parade** (call (757) 220-8725), a model train wonderland; **Berkeley Plantation** (call (804) 829-6018), a magnificent mansion beside the James River; and **Sherwood Forest Plantation** (call (804) 829-5377), the home to president John Tyler. Tyler's home is still occupied by his family, who allow tours.

HOW TO GET THERE

By Car. Primary access to the main attraction locations is via I-64, which runs east-west out of Richmond. Approaching along I-95 from the south, you can take U.S. 58 east from Emporia, which will take you to the I-64/I-664 loop at Portsmouth/Norfolk; it continues on to Virginia Beach.

By Plane. Newport News-Williamsburg International Airport, is served by AirTran Airlines, US Airways/US Airways Express and United/United Express; 900 Bland Boulevard, Newport News; (757) 877-0221. Norfolk International Airport is served by a half-dozen major carriers; 2200 Norview Avenue, Norfolk; (757) 857-3351.

Richmond International Airport is served by 18 airlines and is about 50 miles from Williamsburg and 80 miles from Virginia Beach; 1 Richard E. Byrd Terminal Drive, Richmond International Airport; (804) 226-3000.

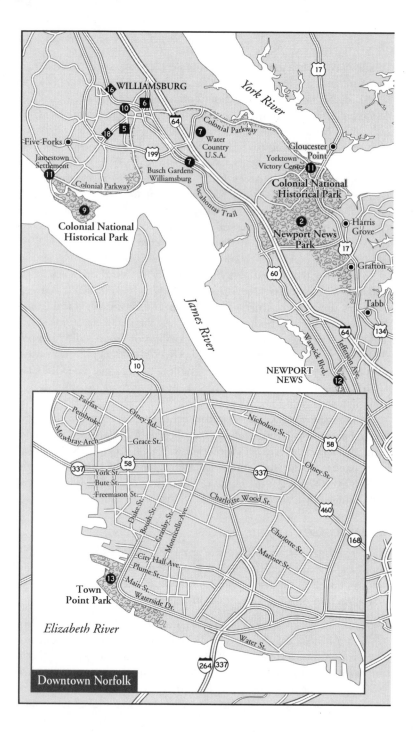

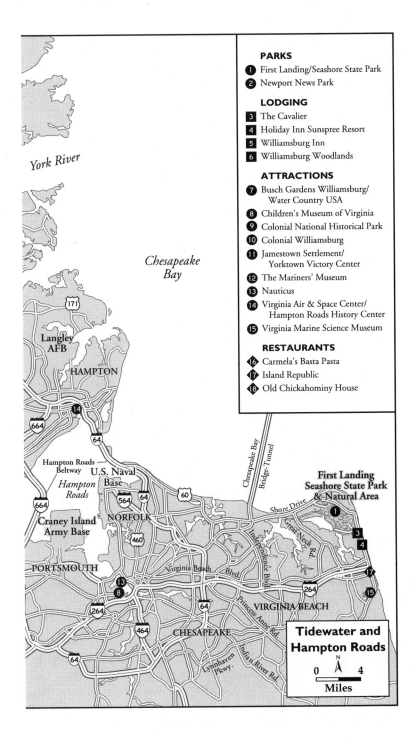

PARKS
1. First Landing/Seashore State Park
2. Newport News Park

LODGING
3. The Cavalier
4. Holiday Inn Sunspree Resort
5. Williamsburg Inn
6. Williamsburg Woodlands

ATTRACTIONS
7. Busch Gardens Williamsburg/ Water Country USA
8. Children's Museum of Virginia
9. Colonial National Historical Park
10. Colonial Williamsburg
11. Jamestown Settlement/ Yorktown Victory Center
12. The Mariners' Museum
13. Nauticus
14. Virginia Air & Space Center/ Hampton Roads History Center
15. Virginia Marine Science Museum

RESTAURANTS
16. Carmela's Basta Pasta
17. Island Republic
18. Old Chickahominy House

York River

Chesapeake Bay

171

Langley AFB

HAMPTON

14

664

64

Hampton Roads Beltway

U.S. Naval Base

Hampton Roads

664

Craney Island Army Base

564

64

60

NORFOLK

460

PORTSMOUTH

13

8

264

464

CHESAPEAKE

64

Virginia Beach Blvd

Princess Anne Rd.

64

Lynnhaven Pkwy.

Indian River Rd

Chesapeake Bay Bridge-Tunnel

First Landing Seashore State Park & Natural Area

Shore Drive

1

Great Neck Rd.

Independence Blvd

3

4

17

264

15

VIRGINIA BEACH

Tidewater and Hampton Roads

N

0   4

Miles

By Train. Amtrak serves the area through Washington, D.C., and Richmond; (800) 872-7245.

HOW TO GET INFORMATION BEFORE YOU GO

Virginia Beach Visitors Center, 2100 Parks Avenue, Virginia Beach, VA 23451; (800) 446-8038; www.city.virginia-beach.va.us or www.vabeach.com.

Williamsburg Area Convention & Visitors Bureau, 201 Penniman Road, Williamsburg, VA 23187; (800) 368-6511; www.visitwilliamsburg.com.

Norfolk Visitors Information Center, Fourth View Street, Norfolk, VA 23503; (800) 368-3097; www.norfolk.va.us.

Portsmouth Visitors Center, 6 Crawford Parkway, Portsmouth, VA 23704; (800) 767-8782; www.ci.portsmouth.va.us.

Newport News Tourist Information Center, 13560 Jefferson Avenue, Newport news, VA 23603; (888) 493-7386; www.visit.newportnews.org.

Hampton Visitors Center, 710 Settlers Landing Road, Hampton, VA 23669; (800) 800-2202; www.hampton.va.us/tourism.

Hampton Roads regional "Family Fun" vacation packages are available at www.coastalvirginia.com or (800) 976-1618.

Williamsburg's Revolutionary Fun Package (call (800) 211-7169) offers families package rates on multi-day visits, with admission to Colonial Williamsburg, Jamestown Settlement, Yorktown Victory Center, Busch Gardens, and Water Country USA.

The Best Beaches and Parks

First Landing/Seashore State Park. Virginia's most popular state park, it has 2,700 acres with camping, displays, three indoor aquariums, rest rooms, and showers. It offers hiking, water sports and equipment rentals, bicycle trails and bike rentals; 2500 Shore Drive, Virginia Beach; (757) 412-2300.

Newport News Park. An 8,000-acre municipal park with two freshwater reservoirs, an "aeromodel" flying field, an archery range, bicycle rentals, disc golf, freshwater fishing, a boat ramp, boat rentals, a 180-site campground, a Civil War battle site, a golf course, a horse show arena, interpretive programs, a wildlife rehabilitation center, picnic shelters, a playground, rest rooms, a stage, a Tourist Information Center, 30 miles of hiking trails, a five-mile mountain bike trail, and a 5.3-mile bikeway; 13564 Jefferson Avenue, Newport News; (757) 886-7912.

Virginia Beach. (See pages 357–360.)

Family Outdoor Adventures

Biking. Great Dismal Swamp National Wildlife Refuge (see Hiking) has many unpaved roads, of which the Washington Ditch Road is best for bikes. York River State Park (see Hiking) has 25 miles of hiking/biking trails, including two exclusively for mountain bikes.

Camping. First Landing State Park (see The Best Beaches and Parks, above) has no hook-ups, but it does have tent-camping sites with bathhouses and 20 camping cabins. Newport News Park (see The Best Beaches and Parks, above) holds an 180-site campground located in a wooded setting adjacent to the Lee Hall Reservoir, with heated rest rooms, hot showers, flush toilets, a laundry room, hook-ups at most sites, a camp store, and a playground; (800) 203-8322 or (757) 888-3333.

Hiking. First Landing State Park (see The Best Beaches and Parks, above) has an extensive hiking network, including a self-guided nature trail. Grandview Nature Preserve offers trails along the Chesapeake Bay and a 2.5-mile natural beachfront; Beach Road, Hampton; (757) 727-6347. Great Dismal Swamp National Wildlife Refuge covers almost 107,000 acres of forested wetlands and has hiking and self-guiding interpretive trails, including the Boardwalk Trail, which runs for about a mile; Route 32, Suffolk; (804) 986-3705. York River State Park has 25 miles of hiking/biking trails; 5526 Riverview Road, Williamsburg; (757) 566-3036.

Paddling. Wild River Outfitters leads sea kayak tours and also runs a large retail store; 3636 Virginia Beach Boulevard, Suite 108, Virginia Beach; (877) 431-8566 or (757) 431-8566; www.wildriveroutfitters.com.

Family Lodging

As would be expected, lodging choices run the full gamut in these major vacation destinations. Many offer special packages with breakfast and attractions admission included in the room rate. In Williamsburg, however, we recommend staying in one of the Colonial Williamsburg properties if possible. When you integrate the historical town into your stay, parking, getting around, and attending evening events becomes much easier. Virginia Beach offers every chain, plus innumerable beachfront properties.

The Cavalier

A world-class resort, the Cavalier includes five restaurants, indoor and outdoor Olympic-size swimming pools, a health club, and the only private beach in Virginia. Camp Cavalier for children ages 4–12, a free, supervised program with morning and afternoon sessions, is available during summer months. There's also Kids Café, a free dining room for kids only. Rates: $180–280, suites to $795. Oceanfront at 42nd Street, Virginia Beach; (800) 446-8199 or (757) 425-8555.

Holiday Inn Sunspree Resort

A 266-room property with 55 efficiency suites, all with ocean views, refrigerators, coffee makers, irons, ironing boards, in-room movies, and Nintendo. Efficiency suites also have microwaves. Indoor and outdoor pools will make the kids happy. The Kidzone activity program offers supervised activities for children ages 4–11. Rates: $162–250. 39th Street and Oceanfront, Virginia Beach; (800) 942-3224 or (757) 428-1711.

Williamsburg Inn

A luxury property with 91 rooms, a fitness center, an indoor pool, outdoor tennis courts, croquet, lawn bowling greens, outdoor swimming pools, ponds, and nature walks. Afternoon tea is served daily. Children are welcome at the Young Colonials' Club. The Historic Area is just a few steps away. Rates: $245–345; various package and multi-day plans available. Francis Street, Williamsburg; (800) 447-8079.

Williamsburg Woodlands

In a true park-like setting, these low-rise rooms are accessed by walking paths that wind through trees past a miniature golf course, tennis courts, a table tennis area, a horseshoe pit, badminton and shuffleboard courts, and a fitness course. Two pools and a wading pool are on-site. Children ages 5–12 can, for a fee, participate in the Young Colonials' Club, both daytime (lunch and kids-only visits to the Historic Area) and evening (dinner and entertainment, music, magic, and games), during summer months. Rates: $95–125; various package and multi-day plans available. Visitor Center Drive, Williamsburg; (757) 229-1000.

Attractions

Busch Gardens Williamsburg/Water Country USA

1 Busch Gardens Boulevard, Williamsburg; (757) 253-3350; www.buschgardens.com

Hours: Busch Gardens: March–October, variable hours; Water Country USA: early May–mid-September, variable hours

Admission: Busch Gardens only: $37 adults one day, $30 children ages
3–6 one day; Water Country USA: $28 adults one day, $20.50 children
one day; variety of multiple-day and multiple-attractions tickets available, including combination admission with Colonial Williamsburg

Appeal by Age Groups:

Pre-school	Grade School	Teens	Young Adults	Over 30	Seniors
★★★★★	★★★★★	★★★★★	★★★★★	★★★★★	★★★★★

Touring Time: Average 6 hours each attraction; minimum 4 hours Busch
Gardens, 3 hours Water Country

Rainy-Day Touring: Yes, Busch; No, Water Country

Services and Facilities:

Restaurants Yes	Lockers Yes
Alcoholic beverages Yes	Pet kennels No
Disabled access Yes	Rain check No
Wheelchair rental Yes	Private tours No
Baby stroller rental Yes	

Description and Comments   Even those of us who don't much like theme
parks have to admit that Busch Gardens is a happy place. Set up around
five theme villages—Germany, Italy, France, England, and Scotland—the
park covers more than 100 acres. (An Irish village debuts in summer
2001.) All the expected offerings are here—thrill rides, a kiddie park, a
petting zoo, live performances, and tons of places to eat and shop. It is, by
the way, a roller coaster aficionado's paradise. One thing that sets Busch
Gardens apart from the others is its beauty. Super landscaping is combined
with beautiful gardens and a nature preserve-like setting to create a less fre-
netic feeling than you get at most theme parks. An example: In summer
2000, the park introduced an attraction devoted to the gray wolf, offering
an up-close, interactive encounter with this animal and an educational
look at why the species needs protection. A new, interactive aviary was also
introduced, where guests become human perches upon which brilliantly
colorful Australian lorikeets can alight.

Water Country USA is one of the larger water parks in the Mid-
Atlantic. It, too, has all the expected features—from a wave pool and super
slides to a wading pool and kiddie slides. Live entertainment is also offered,
as well as shops and restaurants. One nice resource: plastic swim diapers for
little ones, required throughout the park, can be bought on-site. Everyone
enjoys the Caban-a-rama Theater, where a gymnastic and dive show is presented daily, and the young ones love the Minnow Matinee Theater's
"Jump, Jive and Duck!" musical review.

Busch Gardens and Water Country USA provide the perfect balance to
Colonial Williamsburg. Mix them—a day of history, a day of theme

park, a half-day of history with a half-day of water, etc.—and you'll keep everybody active and happy. And remember that Williamsburg's Revolutionary Fun Package (call (800) 211-7169) provides package deals with entry to all.

Children's Museum of Virginia

221 High Street, Portsmouth; (757) 393-5258

Hours: Tuesday–Saturday 10 a.m.–5 p.m., Sunday 1–5p.m.; closed Monday

Admission: $4 per person, free for children under age 2

Appeal by Age Groups:

Pre-school	Grade School	Teens	Young Adults	Over 30	Seniors
★★★★★	★★★★★	★★★	★★★★	★★★★	★★★★

Touring Time: Average 2½ hours, minimum 1½ hours

Rainy-Day Touring: Yes

Services and Facilities:

Restaurants No	back packs
Alcoholic beverages No	Lockers Yes
Disabled access Yes	Pet kennels No
Wheelchair rental Yes; free	Rain check No
Baby stroller rental Yes; front and	Private tours No

Description and Comments   The Children's Museum of Virginia is another in the growing line-up of super kids' museums. Among the cooler exhibits: feel yourself shrinking as you climb into a giant chair; become a maestro conductor by using light beams; climb inside a giant bubble; climb a rock wall. There's a lot more, of course, including one of the largest antique toy train collections in the east. We commend the Quiet Room for toddlers, as well. Note: A $5 "Museum Key Pass" permits entry to the Children's Museum plus the Lightship Museum, the Portsmouth Naval Shipyard Museum, and the Arts Center of the Portsmouth Museums. But all museums must be visited on the same day.

Colonial National Historical Park

Colonial Parkway, Yorktown; (757) 898-2410;
www.nps.gov/colo/home.htm

Hours: Jamestown Visitor Center: daily 9 a.m.–5 p.m. Yorktown Visitor Center: April–mid-June and mid-August–late October, daily 8:30 a.m.–5 p.m.; mid-June–mid-August, daily 8:30 a.m.–5:30 p.m.; late-October–early April, daily 9 a.m.–5 p.m.; closed Christmas Day

Admission: Yorktown: $4 adults, free for children ages 16 and under; Jamestown: $5 adults; Jamestown-Yorktown Passport: $7 adults; admission good for seven days

Appeal by Age Groups:

Pre-school	Grade School	Teens	Young Adults	Over 30	Seniors
★★	★★★★	★★★★★	★★★★★	★★★★★	★★★★★

Touring Time: Average 2 hours each attraction, minimum 1 hour each attraction

Rainy-Day Touring: Yes

Services and Facilities:

Restaurants No	Lockers No
Alcoholic beverages No	Pet kennels No
Disabled access Yes; partial	Rain check No
Wheelchair rental Yes; free	Private tours No
Baby stroller rental No	

Description and Comments These are the actual sites of Jamestown and Yorktown, and they lack the "tourist appeal" of the re-creations at Jamestown Settlement and the Yorktown Victory Center. They are, however, suitable for pre-teens and teens. At Yorktown, you'll find an introductory film, a museum, the original reconstructed eighteenth- and nineteenth-century earthworks, the Surrender Field, several original eighteenth-century buildings, a Victory Monument, a French Memorial, and the Civil War–era Yorktown National Cemetery. Rent an audio cassette guide and drive the seven-mile battlefield and nine-mile allied encampment auto tours.

Jamestown Island is a 1,500-acre site where you'll find a museum, another introductory film, a museum/bookstore, and the reconstructed foundations of archeological remains. Guided tours are sometimes offered. Costumed craftsmen demonstrate seventeenth-century glassblowing, and there is an active archeological dig and an archeological lab on-site. Self-guiding tours include walking through the New Towne and Old Town sites, and three- and five-mile auto loops around the island. Here, too, it's worth renting the audio tape available for the Old Town site and drive tours.

Colonial Williamsburg

134 North Henry Street, Williamsburg; (800) 447-8079 or (757) 229-1000; www.colonialwilliamsburg.org

Hours: Daily 9:30 a.m.–5 p.m., plus a variety of evening programs and events

Admission: $30 adults one day, $18 children ages 6–17 five days; various other passes good for multiple days or one year from $35–65 adults and $22.50 children

Appeal by Age Groups:

Pre-school	Grade School	Teens	Young Adults	Over 30	Seniors
★★★★★	★★★★★	★★★★★	★★★★★	★★★★★	★★★★★

Touring Time: Average 2–3 days, minimum 1 day

Rainy-Day Touring: Yes

Services and Facilities:

Restaurants Yes	Lockers No
Alcoholic beverages Yes	Pet kennels No
Disabled access Yes; mostly	Rain check No
Wheelchair rental Yes	Private tours No
Baby stroller rental No	

Description and Comments   Colonial Williamsburg is one of the finest living history attractions in the country. Period. If there's a problem it's that it can be overwhelming, as it covers 170-plus acres and has more than 500 buildings. Colonial Williamsburg accurately and effectively depicts life here in the eighteenth century, when folks like George Washington and Thomas Jefferson were residents serving in the legislature. There's no problem keeping a multiple-generation family happy, especially if you mix in trips to Busch Gardens and Water Country USA. The key to a successful stay is simple: plan ahead.

Start at the Visitors Center by picking up a copy of *Visitor's Companion,* a weekly newspaper that lists the hours for each building and the schedule of events. After you've watched the introductory film *Williamsburg: The Story of a Patriot,* study the newspaper and map, and plot a course. We heartily recommend one of the introductory tours. The costumed interpreters for those—and for all other sites and events—are magnificently trained, never breaking character and always supplying information thoroughly. Take in as many events or special tours as you can, like the Witch Trial, and one of the nighttime Lantern Tours.

Some of the on-site accommodations offer special kids' programs at extra cost. Free shuttle buses circulate around the historic area regularly, making it easy to get from any point to any other. But, we emphasize, this place requires planning.

Jamestown Settlement/Yorktown Victory Center

Route 31 and Colonial Parkway, Williamsburg; (888) 593-4682 or (757) 253-4838; www.historyisfun.org

Hours: August 16–June 14, daily 9 a.m.–5 p.m.; June 15–August 15, daily 9 a.m.–7 p.m.

Admission: Jamestown Settlement: $10.25 adults, $5 children ages 6–12; Yorktown Victory Center: $7.75 adults, $3.75 children; combination ticket: $15.25 adults, $7.25 children

Appeal by Age Groups:

Pre-school	Grade School	Teens	Young Adults	Over 30	Seniors
★★	★★★★★	★★★★	★★★★★	★★★★★	★★★★★

Touring Time: Average 3 hours each attraction, minimum 2 hours each attraction

Rainy-Day Touring: Yes

Services and Facilities:

Restaurants	Yes	Lockers	No
Alcoholic beverages	No	Pet kennels	No
Disabled access	Yes	Rain check	No
Wheelchair rental	Yes; free	Private tours	No
Baby stroller rental	Yes; free		

Description and Comments   Founded in 1607 as America's first permanent English colony, Jamestown was Virginia's capital until 1699, when it was moved to Williamsburg. While this is not the settlement's actual site, it's a faithful re-creation of the Colonial fort and a Powhatan Indian village. It also includes re-creations of the three ships that brought the settlers to Virginia. Start with the introductory film, *Jamestown: The Beginning,* which gives a good overview, then let the kids go out and grind corn, weave marsh grasses into rope, and build a dugout canoe. On the ships, they can set the sails, lower cargo into the hold, and poke around in the sailor's "see" chest.

Yorktown Victory Center depicts life in the Revolutionary army and celebrates the final victory over the British. Here, too, start with the film, *A Time of Revolution,* after which you can explore the re-created Continental Army encampment as well as a re-created eighteenth-century farm. Among the military experiences: eighteenth-century medical techniques, camp cooking, musket drills, and wartime punishments. On the farm you can process tobacco, bundle flax, garden, explore the farmhouse, and watch the cooking. (Both sites use well-trained and effective costumed interpreters.) The Discovery Room is particularly interesting for younger children; they can try on period clothing, copy from a "hornbook," make crayon rubbings of woodcuts, play the African game *mancala,* and investigate the identity of artifacts.

The Mariners' Museum

100 Museum Drive, Newport News; (800) 581-7245 or (757) 596-2222; www.mariner.org

Hours: Daily 10 a.m.–5 p.m.; closed Thanksgiving and Christmas days

Admission: $5 adults, $3 students of any age, $13 family of four, free for children ages 5 and under

Appeal by Age Groups:

Pre-school	Grade School	Teens	Young Adults	Over 30	Seniors
★★	★★★★	★★★★	★★★★★	★★★★★	★★★★★

Touring Time: Average 3 hours, minimum 2 hours

Rainy-Day Touring: Yes

Services and Facilities:

Restaurants Yes	Lockers No; coatroom
Alcoholic beverages No	Pet kennels No
Disabled access Yes	Rain check No
Wheelchair rental Yes; free	Private tours Yes; call one week
Baby stroller rental Yes; free	in advance

Description and Comments   If it's maritime, it's here. Best to start with the introductory film, *Mariner,* which gives an overview of mariners and their changing roles through history. Younger kids will probably most like the extensive collection of ship models and miniature ships, as well as the costumed interpreters—a model ship builder, an eighteenth-century sea captain, and a nineteenth-century whaler. Extensive collections of maritime paintings, decorative arts, carved figureheads, working steam engines, maps, and rare books are also on display. In the "Age of Exploration" exhibit, there's good use of short videos to bring the era to life. The Small Craft Collection shows more than 50 vessels from five continents, including an Italian gondola, African canoes, and sampans from China and Burma.

Nauticus, The National Maritime Center

1 Waterside Drive, Norfolk; (800) 664-1080 or (757) 664-1000; www.nauticus.org

Hours: Memorial Day–Labor Day, daily 10 a.m.–6 p.m.; Labor Day–Memorial Day, Tuesday–Saturday 10 a.m.–5 p.m., Sunday noon–5 p.m.; closed Thanksgiving Day, Christmas Eve, and Christmas Day

Admission: $7.50 adults, $6.50 seniors, $5 children ages 4–12, free for children ages 3 and under

Appeal by Age Groups:

Pre-school	Grade School	Teens	Young Adults	Over 30	Seniors
★★★★★	★★★★★	★★★★★	★★★★★	★★★★★	★★★★★

Touring Time: Average 3½ hours, minimum 2 hours

Rainy-Day Touring: Yes

Services and Facilities:

Restaurants Yes	Lockers Yes
Alcoholic beverages No	Pet kennels Yes
Disabled access Yes	Rain check Yes
Wheelchair rental Yes; free	Private tours No
Baby stroller rental Yes	

Description and Comments   Yet another of this region's monuments to the maritime life, Nauticus offers a lot of computer and video interactive exhibits. Subject areas include Maritime Commerce, The Modern Navy (where you can experience nifty flight simulations), Aegis Command Center, Aquaria, and The Environment. Some kids will love the Aegis Command Center, where they can command an Aegis-class destroyer through a simulated battle. Aquaria has touch pools (including a shark touch-tank) and various cool, exotic creatures. The Environment section focuses on weather, and you can tape your own weather forecast in a TV studio. (See if you can be just as wrong as the professionals!)

Virginia Air and Space Center/ Hampton Roads History Center

600 Settlers Landing Road, Hampton; (800) 296-0800 or (757) 727-0900; www.vasc.org

Hours: Memorial Day–Labor Day, Monday–Wednesday 10 a.m.–5 p.m and Thursday–Sunday 10 a.m.–7 p.m.; Labor Day–Memorial Day, Monday–Sunday 10 a.m.–5 p.m.; open evenings for special programs and IMAX films; closed Thanksgiving and Christmas days

Admission: Exhibits only: $6.50 adults, $5.50 seniors 65 and older and military/NASA members, $4.50 children ages 3–11; exhibits and IMAX: $9.50 adults, $8.50 seniors, $7.50 children; exhibits and 2 IMAX shows: $12 adults, $11 seniors, $10 children

Appeal by Age Groups:

Pre-school	Grade School	Teens	Young Adults	Over 30	Seniors
★★★★	★★★★★	★★★★★	★★★★★	★★★★★	★★★★★

Touring Time: Average 4 hours, minimum 2½ hours

Rainy-Day Touring: Yes

Services and Facilities:

Restaurants Yes	Lockers No
Alcoholic beverages No	Pet kennels No
Disabled access Yes	Rain check No
Wheelchair rental Yes; free	Private tours No
Baby stroller rental No	

Description and Comments   One of a pair of fine aerospace museums in the region, this one houses more than 100 interactive exhibits focused on NASA. Everyone will want to take an up-close look at the moon rock from Apollo 17 (1969)—no doubt you'll tell the kids where *you* were when they landed! But, the kids will probably like the hands-on stuff better—driving a space shuttle landing simulator or working as part of the launch team at Mission Control. "Up, Up and Away! Those Magnificent Flying Machines" teaches flying's four basic principles—lift, drag, gravity, and thrust—and how to keep them in balance by putting you in control in a wind chamber.

Some fascinating links to the past, near and distant, are covered, too: Mars memorabilia from the 1950s and 1960s, ham radio then and now, a Tuskegee Airmen exhibit, showcasing the first black aviators of World War II.

At the Hampton Roads History Center, explore the region's past, dating back 400 years to the first European explorers' arrival, plus replicas of the USS *Yorktown,* and an eighteenth-century custom house and tavern.

Note: You can visit the Virginia Air and Space Center in Hampton and Nauticus in Norfolk using the Harborlink Ferry for transportation; cost is $20 and includes exhibit admission and one IMAX film at the Air and Space Center, plus exhibit admission at Nauticus.

NASA Langley Motor Tours   Narrated tours via a mini-bus leave from the Virginia Air and Space Center during the summer months at 11 a.m. and 2 p.m. Langley is a key site in the U.S. aerospace industry, and its role is explored. You see NASA's wind tunnels, research labs, and Langley Air Force Base's Flight Line. Admission is $7 per person or $5 per person with the purchase of any Air and Space Center admission. It's best for kids age seven and up.

Virginia Marine Science Museum

717 General Booth Boulevard, Virginia Beach; (757) 425-3474;
   www.vmsm.com

Hours: Mid-June–Labor Day, daily 9 a.m.–9 p.m.; Labor Day–early
   June, daily 9 a.m.–5 p.m.; closed Thanksgiving and Christmas days

Admission: Museum: $8.95 adults, $7.95 seniors, $5.95 children. Museum and IMAX: $12.95 adults, $11.95 seniors, $9.95 children. Museum, IMAX, and Creek Cruise: $15.45 adults, $14.45 seniors, $12.45 children

Appeal by Age Groups:

Pre-school	Grade School	Teens	Young Adults	Over 30	Seniors
★★★★★	★★★★★	★★★★★	★★★★★	★★★★★	★★★★★

Touring Time: Average 5 hours, minimum 3 hours

Rainy-Day Touring: Yes

Services and Facilities:

Restaurants Yes	Lockers No
Alcoholic beverages No	Pet kennels No
Disabled access Yes	Rain check No
Wheelchair rental Yes; free	Private tours Yes
Baby stroller rental No	

Description and Comments This fine aquarium has recently undergone a major expansion. It occupies two buildings—the Atlantic Ocean Pavilion, site of the main exhibits, and the Owls Creek Marsh Pavilion, which focuses on life in Owls Creek salt marsh, the waterway on which the museum is located. A short Nature Trail connects them. Kids, of course, will love the exhibits that feature sharks, stingrays, whales, and the harbor seals. There's a lot of coverage of the local sea and lowland environment that's well presented and fun to see. Favorites in the Pavilion are the river otters, sea horses, and the macro-marsh, a place where teeny animals and plants are magnified to ten times their normal size. A ten-minute film, *The Secret Life of Owls Creek,* which reveals the many unseen goings-on among the plants and wildlife, is quite worthwhile. For an extra fee, the museum offers half-hour salt marsh tours in a 50-passenger pontoon boat.

VIRGINIA BEACH: A BASIC GUIDE

Virginia Beach stretches from the Chesapeake Bay to the North Carolina border, encompassing 28 miles of oceanfront and bay beaches, thus laying claim to being the largest resort city in the world. No matter what shore activity you and your family enjoy, you'll find it here—swimming, surfing, in-line skating, biking, tennis, golf, deep-sea fishing, sailing, water-skiing, scuba diving, and more amusements than you could ever hope to patronize. When you're tired of all the hubbub, head to Seashore State Park with its woodlands and 27 miles of nature trails.

The Layout. Beach life centers on a three-mile boardwalk. The commercial strip begins at First Street and runs north. The beach is lined with large hotels for about 40 blocks. The main streets running north-south, paralleling the ocean, are Atlantic, Pacific, Arctic, Baltic, and Mediterranean avenues. 17th Street becomes Virginia Beach Boulevard and is a main east-west thoroughfare, as is Laskin Road (also U.S. 58), which is the extension of 31st Street. State Route 44 (The Expressway) provides the main east-west access, becoming 21st and 22nd streets once in town. The Virginia Beach Visitor Information Center is worth a stop. You'll find it at 2100 Parks Avenue, on the left at the first traffic light off Route 44, as you enter the resort area. Off of the oceanfront, Virginia Beach is a sprawling city with a very suburban feel.

The Boardwalk. It's a paved walk, not literally a wooden "board" walk. A bike path parallels the walk, which means that here, unlike most beach towns, you can cycle or in-line skate during peak hours. Even skateboarders are welcome—a true rarity. The walk is grass-lined and calm—not filled with kitschy amusements and shops—and each block is well marked. Large resort hotels and motor inns line the landward side, as do many restaurants. The 7th, 17th, and 24th Street Stages present performances nightly throughout the summer; look for the schedule on bulletin boards mounted along the boardwalk.

The Beach. The main beach, along hotel row and the boardwalk, is wide, clean, and well-kept, but it can get crowded. You'll find changing facilities at First Street and Atlantic Avenue, plus several public rest rooms. Parking can be a problem; look for public lots at 4th and Atlantic or 19th and Pacific, plus the occasional private lot. Metered street parking is hard to find. Seashore State Park has a small beachfront, its own parking, and few folks. Locals like Little Island Park, a city park that partially borders a wildlife refuge; it has plenty of fee-parking, rest rooms, a snack bar, and a fishing pier.

Getting Around. Trolleys run from 2nd to 42nd Streets on Atlantic Avenue; from 19th Street and Pacific Avenue south on General Booth Boulevard; and to Lynnhaven Mall via the Route 44 Expressway. The Entertainment Express runs a circuit of all the major nightspots and hotels until 2:30 a.m. The North Seashore Park Trolley operates from 19th and Pacific Avenue to 68th Street.

Amusements. Ocean Breeze Fun Park, 848 General Booth Boulevard, (757) 422-4444, has a water park, 36-hole mini-golf course, batting cages, and go-kart track with one-third-scale Indy cars. Fun Spot Action Park, Virginia Beach Boulevard and 17th Street, (757) 422-1401, has go-kart tracks, a Ferris wheel, bumper boats, and kiddie rides.

Oceanfront Carousel, by the 15th Street Fishing Pier, has a carousel, carnival games, and kids' rides; (757) 428-2333. Around the World Mini-Golf,

16th Street and Pacific Avenue, (757) 428-3658, has 36 holes, with admission good all day until 5 p.m.

Bike and Skate Rentals. Dozens of shops and hotels rent skates by the hour and the day; prices average $5 an hour and $20 a day. Gamemaster USA: 23rd Street and Pacific Avenue, (757) 422-5606, rents in-line skates and bikes; Corner 24 Surf Shop, 24th Street and Pacific Avenue, (757) 428-3389, rents skates; Cherie's Bicycle Rentals, four stands at 8th, 22nd, 24th, and 37th Streets, (757) 437-8888, rents bikes and in-line skates and offers skating lessons for novices; RK's Surf Shop: 16th Street and Pacific Avenue, (757) 428-7363; rents skates and bikes.

Beach Adventures

Biking. The Seashore State Park trail system can be readily reached by trail from the boardwalk. It has miles of paved and dirt trails that travel through the wetlands and along Broad Bay. All trails are clearly marked. The main bike path runs south of the boardwalk, following General Booth Boulevard past the Virginia Marine Science Museum and Ocean Breeze Fun Park.

Diving. Virginia Beach waters contain dozens of shipwrecks that can be explored by snorkeling and diving. Contact:

Lynnhaven Dive Center, 1413 North Great Neck Road, (757) 481-7949, a full-service shop offering guided dive trips.

Mid-Atlantic Dive Center, 5350 Kemps River Drive, (757) 420-6179, a complete dive center with a full line of equipment.

Surfing. Eastern surfing began in Virginia Beach. That was about 1912. Today, Virginia Beach annually hosts the East Coast Surfing Championships and is home to many surf shops, many of which rent equipment. Among them:

17th Street Surf Shop, 17th Street and Pacific Avenue, (757) 422-6105, is the longest running show in town.

RK's Surf Shop, 16th Street and Pacific Avenue, (757) 428-7363, rents surf and boogie boards.

Wave Riding Vehicles, 1900 Cypress Avenue, (757) 422-8823, is the area's largest surf board manufacturer.

Beach Food

Zero's Subs, 21st and Pacific Avenue; (757) 491-2355. Hot and cold subs and Philly cheese steaks.

Uncle Harry's Cones & Cream, 37th Street and Pacific Avenue; (757) 425-8195.

Dough Boys California Pizza, three locations on Atlantic Avenue; (757) 422-6111.

Family-Friendly Restaurants

The region offers a plethora of fine family dining. Williamsburg, especially, offers a number of good, basic pancake houses and breakfast places that serve it up quick, hot, and tasty. Virginia Beach presents all the options you'd expect in a major seaside resort town, including chains and many hotel restaurants. In Norfolk, Newport News, and Portsmouth, you'll find more of the same. Among the dozens, here are a few selections.

CARMELA'S BASTA PASTA

207 Bypass Road, Williamsburg; (757) 253-6544

Meals served: Lunch and dinner
Cuisine: Italian
Entree range: $8.95–16.95
Children's menu: Yes
Reservations: Yes
Payment: Major credit cards

Carmela's serves classic Italian fare, from plain spaghetti and wood-fired pizzas to Cannelloni al Forno and Crabby Shrimp Alfredo. It's in a homey, busy atmosphere, where families are expected and kids are welcome. Carmela's also has restaurants in Newport News and Hampton.

ISLAND REPUBLIC

19th Street and the Boardwalk, Virginia Beach; (757) 425-7738

Meals served: Lunch and dinner
Cuisine: Seafood and steaks
Entree range: $6.95–18.95
Children's menu: Yes
Reservations: Yes
Payment: Major credit cards

An oceanfront cafe with entertainment at night. A little funky and very friendly. Just the kind of place you want during a beach vacation.

OLD CHICKAHOMINY HOUSE

1211 Jamestown Road, Williamsburg; (757) 229-4689

Meals served: Breakfast and lunch
Cuisine: Southern
Entree range: $3.95–7.95
Children's menu: No
Reservations: No
Payment: Major credit cards

Authentic Southern fare is served in this Colonial house. "Plantation" breakfasts feature Virginia ham, eggs, biscuits, cured country bacon, sausage, and grits. Lunches lean toward Brunswick stew, Virginia ham biscuits, fruit salad, homemade pie, etc. An antique/gift shop is on site.

Central Virginia

This large, triangular piece of Virginia countryside runs from the Blue Ridge Mountain foothills across to the sea, and from the Charlottesville area down to the North Carolina line, including Richmond, Lynchburg, Madison, and Danville. There's a lot of history to be explored here, plus some beautiful hills, farmlands, and horse country. The Appalachian Trail and the Blue Ridge Parkway can be accessed from the region's western perimeter (see Shenandoah Valley and Southwestern Blue Ridge).

Richmond is the state capital and offers many city sites and facilities. The **Black History Museum & Cultural Center of Virginia** (call (804) 780-9093) is found here, covering the state's African-American history. The **Children's Museum of Richmond** (call (804) 788-4949) keeps two to ten year-olds nicely amused. Everyone loves money, and the **Federal Reserve Bank Money Museum** (call (804) 697-8108) looks at money and its history. The **Virginia Historical Society: The Museum of Virginia History** (call (804) 358-4901) travels through the state's history, and the **Virginia Fire & Police Museum** (call (804) 644-1850), set in a unique National Historic Landmark building, displays firefighting history. The **State Capitol Building** (call (804) 786-4344), designed by Thomas Jefferson, hosts guided tours daily. For a pleasant water outing, **Annabel Lee Riverboat Cruises** (call (800) 752-7093) ply the James River.

Charlottesville is home to the **University of Virginia** (call (804) 924-0311), which houses all the arts and athletic activities expected at a major college. Nearby is Thomas Jefferson's home, **Monticello** (see page 369). Jefferson wasn't the only president to live here. **Ash Lawn-Highland** (call (804) 293-9539), home to James Monroe, is located about 2.5 miles from Monticello and features tours, crafts, and a summer music festival. The **Virginia Discover Museum** (call (804) 977-1-25) is aimed at kids up to age ten. During winter, the **Charlottesville Ice Park** (call (804) 817-2400) entertains skaters of all ages.

South of Richmond, **Petersburg** has many Civil War sites (see Virginia Civil War Sites, page 317). Farther south lies **Appomattox,** site of the Civil War's final episode and of the **Appomattox Historical Museum** (call (804) 352-8106). It's also home to the amiably local **Fred's Car Museum** (call (804) 352-0606). Speaking of amiable, country music buffs should detour through the town of **Crewe,** where **Jim's Country Music and Movie Cowboy Museum** (call (804) 645-7550) not only displays memorabilia for free, but the folks there can give you directions to Roy Clark's birthplace. Way south, **Danville** is home to the **Danville Museum of Fine Arts and History** (call (804) 793-5644), which hosts exhibitions, workshops, and special events, and the **Danville Science Center** (call (804) 791-5160) a hands-on science museum for everyone. **Tobacco Auction Tours** (call (804) 793-5422) may be a tough call if you're discouraging kids from smoking, but it's a fascinating look at an age-old lifestyle and ritual. Nearby, **Martinsville** houses the **Virginia Museum of Natural History** (call (540) 666-8600), the official state museum, and **Martinsville Speedway** (call (540) 956-3151), one of the Southeast's most famous auto-racing facilities.

In historic **Hopewell,** the **City Point Early History Museum at St. Dennis Chapel** (call (800) 863-8687) is an 1887 chapel that serves as the area's historical archive. The **City Point National Historic District** (call (804) 540-2459) has buildings built from 1613–1886; tour it on fort, along with an exhibit on the **City Point Rails & Waterways.** The **Flowerdew Hundred Museum** (call (804) 541-8897) is a restored nineteenth-century home with an eighteenth-century windmill. For more modern history, **Sears Roebuck & Co. Houses by Mail** (call (804) 541-2461) is a 1920s neighborhood of homes bought from the Sears catalog; you can tour the neighborhood by car.

When in **Lynchburg,** near the Blue Ridge foothills, stop at the **Lynchburg Community Market** (call (804) 847-1499) for its local craftspeople, produce, restaurants, and special events. The **Lynchburg Museum** (call (804) 847-1459) covers area history and should be supplemented by a visit to **Old City Cemetery** (call (804) 847-1465), an interesting—if somewhat macabre—site with a medical museum, mourning museum, and antique rose garden.

The city of **Madison** has the **On the Wild Side Zoo** (call (540) 948-4000), a small, interactive zoo, and **The Roaring Twenties Antique Car Museum** (call (540) 948-6290), a family's collection of 1920s cars.

Smith Mountain Lake, a resort area located between Danville and Lynchburg, is home to the **Booker T. Washington National Monument** (call (540) 721-2094), his birthplace.

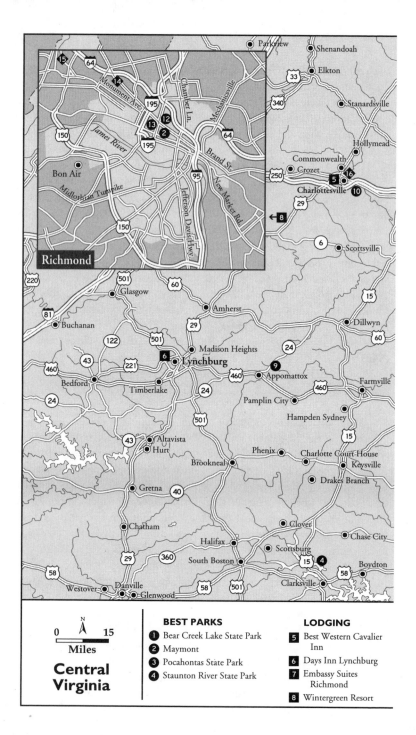

Richmond

Bon Air

Parkview Shenandoah
Elkton
Stanardsville
Hollymead
Commonwealth
Crozet
Charlottesville
Scottsville

Glasgow
Amherst
Dillwyn
Buchanan
Madison Heights
Lynchburg
Bedford
Timberlake
Appomattox
Farmville
Pamplin City
Hampden Sydney
Altavista
Hurt
Phenix
Charlotte Court-House
Brookneal
Keysville
Gretna
Drakes Branch
Chatham
Clover
Chase City
Halifax
Scottsburg
Phenix
Boydton
South Boston
Clarksville
Westover Danville
Glenwood

0   15
Miles

**Central
Virginia**

BEST PARKS

❶ Bear Creek Lake State Park
❷ Maymont
❸ Pocahontas State Park
❹ Staunton River State Park

LODGING

5 Best Western Cavalier
   Inn
6 Days Inn Lynchburg
7 Embassy Suites
   Richmond
8 Wintergreen Resort

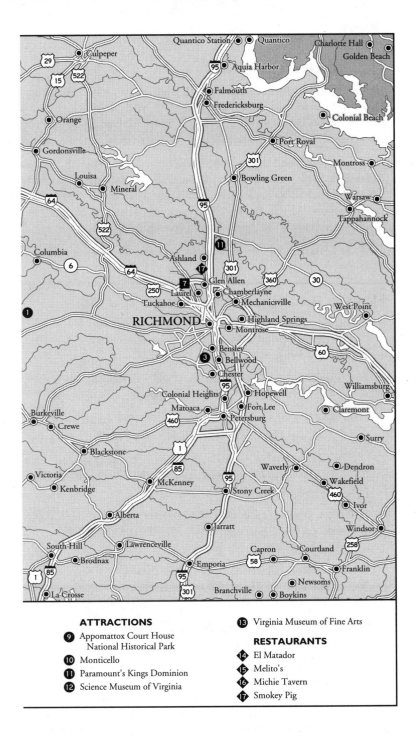

ATTRACTIONS

9 Appomattox Court House
National Historical Park

10 Monticello

11 Paramount's Kings Dominion

12 Science Museum of Virginia

13 Virginia Museum of Fine Arts

RESTAURANTS

14 El Matador

15 Melito's

16 Michie Tavern

17 Smokey Pig

How to Get There

By Car. I-95 runs directly north-south through Richmond, accessing the eastern side of the region. At Petersburg, I-85 heads southwest. I-64 moves east-west across the top of the area, U.S. 29 runs north-south down the western perimeter, and U.S. 58 travels east-west across the southernmost area.

By Plane. Richmond International Airport is served by 18 airlines; 1 Richard E. Byrd Terminal Drive, Richmond International Airport; (804) 226-3000. Lynchburg Regional Airport is served by United Express/Atlantic Coast Airlines, USAir Airways Express, and Delta Connection/Atlantic Southeast Airlines; 4308 Wards Road, Lynchburg; (804) 582-1150.

By Train. Amtrak services both Richmond and Lynchburg; (800) 872-7245.

How to Get Information before You Go

Appomattox County Chamber of Commerce/Visitor Information Center, 5 Main Street, P.O. Box 704, Appomattox, VA 24522; (804) 352-2621; www.appomattox.com.

Ashland/Hanover Visitors Center, 112 North Railroad Avenue, Ashland, VA 23005; (800) 897-1479; www.town.ashland.va.us.

Bedford Area Chamber of Commerce, 305 East Main Street, Bedford, VA 24523; (540) 586-9401; www.bedfordchamber.va-web.com.

The Charlottesville/Albemarle Convention & Visitors Bureau, P.O. Box 178, Charlottesville, VA 22902; (877) 386-1102 or (804) 977-1783; www.charlottesvilletourism.org.

Greater Lynchburg Chamber of Commerce, P.O. Box 2027, 2015 Memorial Avenue, Lynchburg, VA 24501; (804) 845-5966; www.lynchburgchamber.org.

The Richmond Convention and Visitors Bureau, 550 East Marshall Street, Richmond, VA 23219; (800) 370-9004; www.richmondva.org.

The Best Beaches and Parks

Bear Creek Lake State Park. The 40-acre lake is the main attraction. It has a boat launch, swimming beach, lakeside picnicking, camping, and hiking trails. The swimming beach has a bathhouse and concession/snack bar. Bike and boat rentals are available from Memorial Day through Labor Day. Camping is at 53 campsites for both RVs and tents. Hiking includes the 16-mile Willis River Trail and the 14-mile Cumberland Multi-Use Trail, available, too, for bikes and horses. The park is surrounded by the 16,000-

acre Cumberland State Forest, which provides opportunities for a wide range of outdoor activities, especially hiking, mountain biking, and observing nature on a network of forest roads. 929 Oak Hill Road, Cumberland; (804) 492-4410.

George Washington and Jefferson National Forests. (See Shenandoah Valley and Southwest Blue Ridge section, page 382.)

Maymont. This 100-acre park in the heart of Richmond features native Virginia wildlife exhibits, a children's farm, a carriage collection, the Maymont Café, a tram ride, carriage rides, hay rides, and special events like Musical Mondays and Victorian Christmas at Maymont. 1700 Hampton Street, Richmond; (804) 358-7166; main entrance at 2201 Shields Lake Drive.

Pocahontas State Park. Just 20 miles from downtown Richmond, Pocahontas State Park is among the most popular of the state parks. A large swimming pool operates from Memorial Day to Labor Day, outfitted with a large bathhouse and concessions. There are hiking, biking, and bridle trails, including a five-mile trail around Beaver Lake, a five-mile bicycle trail, and a disabled-accessible trail. Numerous other trails for hikers and cyclists wind through the surrounding woodlands. 10301 State Park Road, Chesterfield; (804) 796-4255.

Smith Mountain Lake. A 20,000-acre and set resort area not far from Lynchburg and Roanoke, this is a major retreat offering full facilities and amusements, from boat rentals and lake cruises to golf and water skiing. Contact the Chamber of Commerce, 16430 Booker T. Washington Highway, Unit 2, Moneta; (800) 676-8203.

Staunton River State Park. Covering 1,597 acres and set 18 miles east of South Boston near the North Carolina line, the park harbors the John H. Kerr Reservoir and the Dan and Staunton rivers, a swimming pool, campgrounds, camping cabins, picnic shelters, and nature trails. Total campsites number 48, with seven cabins. The pool complex has a wading pool and a bathhouse and concessions. Hiking is done on six wooded trails along the Dan and Staunton rivers, as well as around Buggs Island Lake. Guided hikes and canoe trips are sometimes offered. 1170 Staunton Trail, Scottsburg; (804) 572-4623.

Family Outdoor Adventures

Hiking. Crabtree Falls Trail in Nelson County features a series of five major cascades and a number of smaller ones that drop some 1,200 feet. The hiking can be strenuous and precipitous, but the views of the falls from the overlooks accent the beauty of the valley, and the first overlook is just 700 feet from the parking lot. Located in the Blue Ridge Mountains off Route 56. Simmons Gap Hiking Trail is a beautiful 1.6-mile round trip along a quiet stream maintained by the Potomac Appalachian Trail Club; 118 Park Street SE, Vienna; (703) 242-0693.

Horseback Riding. Rodes Farm mounts up for one-hour trail rides daily, mid-March through December, as well as kids' pony rides, sunset trail rides, and lessons; Rodes Farm Drive, Nellysford; (804) 325-8260.

Mountain Biking. Wintergreen Resort (see Attractions, page 373) rents bikes and offers instruction and weekend shuttle service. Bear Creek Lake State Park (see The Best Beaches and Parks, above).

Paddling. Adventure Challenge offers guided trips, lessons, and tours in whitewater kayaking, coastal kayaking, river tubing, and river rafting; 8225 Oxer Road, Richmond; (804) 276-7600. James River Runners – A Canoe Livery offers canoeing, innertubing, rafting, and kayaking on the James River; afternoon, day, or overnight river float trips are offered, as well as trips through novice rapids and camping; 10082 Hatton Ferry Road, Scottsville; (804) 286-2338.

Skiing. Wintergreen Resort (see Attractions, page 373), has 19 trails on a full variety of terrain, plus ski school, equipment rentals, and children's programs.

Swimming. Holliday Lake State Park, not far from Appomattox, has a beach area on its 150-acre lake, with a bathhouse and concession operation. Route 2, Appomattox; (804) 248-6308. Swimming can also be fun at Bear Creek Lake State Park and Pocahontas State Park (see The Best Beaches and Parks, above).

Family Lodging

Best Western Cavalier Inn

Adjacent to the University of Virginia, this 116-room property offers a complimentary continental breakfast and has an on-site restaurant and outdoor pool. Pets are allowed. Rates: $60–80. 105 Emmet Street, Charlottesville; (800) 528-1234 or (804) 296-8111.

Days Inn Lynchburg

You get a free hot breakfast when you stay here. Plus, the property sits next to an 85-store shopping mall and is near more than 20 restaurants. It has a pool and a playground. Rates $60–100. 3320 Candlers Mountain Road, Lynchburg; (800) 787-3297 or (804) 847-8655.

Embassy Suites Richmond—The Commerce Center

An all-suite hotel within striking distance of downtown Richmond. It has an indoor pool, exercise facilities, in-room coffee makers, irons, movies, and free breakfast. Rates: $119–139. 2925 Emerywood Parkway, Richmond; (804) 672-8585.

Wintergreen Resort

Wintergreen Resort offers many options, from two-bedroom condominiums to a seven-bedroom house. Many package plans available. See Attractions, page 373. Rates: $205–740. Route 664, Wintergreen; (800) 266-2444.

Attractions

Appomattox Court House National Historical Park

Route 24, Appomattox; (804) 352-8987; www.nps.gov/apco

Hours: Visitor Center: Memorial Day–Labor Day, daily 9 a.m.–5:30 p.m.; Labor Day–Memorial Day, daily 8:30 a.m.–5 p.m.; closed on federal holidays and November–February

Admission: Memorial Day–Labor Day, $4 per person with a $10 maximum per vehicle; Labor Day–Memorial Day, $2 per person with a $5 maximum per vehicle

Appeal by Age Groups:

Pre-school	Grade School	Teens	Young Adults	Over 30	Seniors
★★	★★★★	★★★★	★★★★★	★★★★★	★★★★★

Touring Time: Average 4 hours, minimum 2 hours

Rainy-Day Touring: Yes

Services and Facilities:

Restaurants No	Lockers No
Alcoholic beverages No	Pet kennels No
Disabled access Yes	Rain check No
Wheelchair rental Yes; free	Private tours No
Baby stroller rental No	

Description and Comments   Appomattox is where the Civil War ended. The National Park encompasses 1,700 acres and includes the McLean home (the surrender site) and the village of Appomattox Court House. Take advantage of the full schedule of daily programs offered from Memorial Day to Labor Day. They include living history, ranger talks, and audio-visual programs. After Labor Day, only audio-visual programs are offered, but you can (and should) follow the at least part of the six-mile, self-guided walking tour and spend a couple of hours in the village.

Monticello

931 Thomas Jefferson Parkway, Charlottesville; (804) 984-9822; www.monticello.org

Hours: Monticello: March 1–October 31, daily 8 a.m.–5 p.m.; November 1–February 28, 9 a.m.–4:30 p.m. Monticello Visitors Center: March 1–October 31, daily 9 a.m.–5:30 p.m.; November 1–February 28, 9 a.m.–5 p.m.; closed Christmas Day

Admission: Monticello: $11 adults, $6 children ages 6–11, free for children under 6; Monticello Visitors Center: free

Appeal by Age Groups:

Pre-school	Grade School	Teens	Young Adults	Over 30	Seniors
★★	★★★★	★★★★	★★★★★	★★★★★	★★★★★

Touring Time: Average 3 hours, minimum 2 hours

Rainy-Day Touring: Yes

Services and Facilities:

Restaurants Yes; April–October	Lockers No
Alcoholic beverages No	Pet kennels No
Disabled access Yes	Rain check No
Wheelchair rental Yes	Private tours No
Baby stroller rental No	

Description and Comments   Monticello, located about two miles southeast of Charlottesville, was Thomas Jefferson's home, and clearly he was more house-proud than your average guy. He designed it, then kept redesigning and rebuilding it for more than 40 years. This is no ordinary mansion, however; it's considered a world heritage site and one of the world's architectural wonders. It was also a working farm and a plantation of 5,000 acres, and you can still visit the vegetable garden, fruit garden, and flower gardens, as well as tour the park-like grounds. Be aware: in high season this place is packed, so arrive early. The walk from the parking lot is about a half-mile, and a shuttle bus runs every five minutes or so. A welcome and intelligent Line Release System is implemented when the house-tour wait exceeds 45 minutes, allowing you to wander the grounds while waiting to see the house. House tours run every five minutes in groups of 25 and last about a half-hour. From April 1 through October 31, guided walking tours of the slave sites and of the grounds are also offered. There are also plantation community and garden tours. Best of all, from June 15 through August 15, the site stages daily tours specifically aimed at families with children ages 4 through 12, in which hands-on objects and a child-friendly focus are accented. Monticello Visitors Center is on Route 20 near I-64. It houses a permanent exhibition entitled *Thomas Jefferson at Monticello* that explores Jefferson's domestic life. An award-winning film, *Thomas Jefferson: The Pursuit of Liberty,* is screened hourly in summer and at 11 a.m. and 2 p.m. in the off-season.

Paramount's Kings Dominion

I-95, Exit 98, Doswell; (804) 876-5000;
  www.kingsdominion.com

Hours: Park opens 10:30 a.m.; closing time varies by season and day of
  the week

Admission: $36.99 adults, $30.99 seniors 55 and older, $25.99 children
  ages 3–6, free for children ages 2 and under

Appeal by Age Groups:

Pre- school	Grade School	Teens	Young Adults	Over 30	Seniors
★★★★★	★★★★★	★★★★★	★★★★★	★★★★★	★★★★★

Touring Time: Average 6 hours, minimum 4 hours

Rainy-Day Touring: Yes

Services and Facilities:

Restaurants Yes	Lockers Yes
Alcoholic beverages Yes	Pet kennels Yes
Disabled access Yes	Rain check No
Wheelchair rental Yes	Private tours No
Baby stroller rental Yes	

Description and Comments   Another big-time theme park: we're talking ten
roller coasters. One of them is something called the HyperSonic XLC, pur-
ported to be the world's first compressed-air launch coaster that pulls zero-
gravity airtime and horrifies with free-fall drops. All the other good stuff is
here, including a water park, but what we like are the small, child-friendly
aspects and the throwbacks to simpler times. Richard Scarry's Busytown
Show brings his wonderful books to life, and The Green Slime Zone in
Nickelodeon Central brings that kid-favorite TV show to life. There's a
whole games section, with old-fashioned endeavors like Quarter Toss, Basketball Shoot, and Bushel Basket. Not to worry, there's plenty for thrill-
seekers, like the free-falling Extreme Skyflyer. The park stages plenty of
shows, and walk-around characters are all over the place to meet and greet
your kids. And you. *Note:* The park also operates a commercial campground.

Science Museum of Virginia

2500 West Broad Street, Richmond; (804) 367-6552; www.smv.org

Hours: Museum: Monday–Thursday 9:30 a.m.–5 p.m., Friday and
  Saturday 9:30 a.m.–7 p.m., Sunday 11:30 a.m.–5 p.m.; closed
  Thanksgiving and Christmas days. IMAX and Planetarium:
  Monday–Thursday 10:30 a.m.–5 p.m., Friday and Saturday
  10:30 a.m.–9 p.m., and Sunday noon–5 p.m.

Admission: Exhibits only: $5 adults, $4.50 seniors 60 and older, $4 children ages 4–11, free for children age 3 and under; exhibits and IMAX: $8 adults, $8.50 seniors, $8 children

Appeal by Age Groups:

Pre-school	Grade School	Teens	Young Adults	Over 30	Seniors
★★★★	★★★★★	★★★★★	★★★★★	★★★★★	★★★★★

Touring Time: Average 4 hours, minimum 3 hours

Rainy-Day Touring: Yes

Services and Facilities:

Restaurants Yes	Lockers Yes
Alcoholic beverages No	Pet kennels No
Disabled access Yes	Rain check No
Wheelchair rental Yes; free	Private tours No
Baby stroller rental No	

Description and Comments   One of the things we like here is the live learning entertainment: the Carpenter Science Theatre program. KidStage is aimed at the young ones, while MainStage features full-length plays that challenge older kids' and adults' ideas of what science is all about. OnStage performs short, face-to-face exchanges at random spots in the exhibit galleries. You might be just strolling along when suddenly you're talking to Queen Hatshepsut, Egypt's first female pharaoh. Gotta love it. The *ZOOM* zone is the interactive part of things where, among other things, kids get to do some of the experiments they've seen on the PBS-TV program *ZOOM*. You shouldn't miss the Madagascar Hissing Cockroaches and the puppet shows. The physics exhibits are also always a hit.

Virginia Museum of Fine Arts

2800 Grove Avenue, Richmond; (804) 340-1400; www.vmfa.state.va.us

Hours: Tuesday, Wednesday, and Friday–Sunday 11 a.m.–5 p.m., Thursday 11 a.m.–8 p.m.; closed Monday and New Year's, Independence, Thanksgiving, and Christmas days

Admission: $5 per person suggested donation

Appeal by Age Groups:

Pre-school	Grade School	Teens	Young Adults	Over 30	Seniors
★	★★★	★★★★	★★★★★	★★★★★	★★★★★

Touring Time: Average 3 hours, minimum 2 hours

Rainy-Day Touring: Yes

Services and Facilities:

Restaurants Yes

Alcoholic beverages Yes

Disabled access Yes

Wheelchair rental Yes, free

Baby stroller rental No

Lockers No

Pet kennels No

Rain check No

Private tours No

Description and Comments   This is a major art museum. It's perhaps best known for its priceless Pratt Collection of jeweled Fabergé objects from the court of the Russian czars. The art of the world is represented here: Africa, North America, Ancient America, the Mediterranean, Asia, and Europe. Saturdays are special because the museum offers morning family workshops and children's workshops. These free programs use hands-on experiences to link art and the every day, with an emphasis on fun. The museum also stages family open houses on select Saturdays, in which a full day is spent looking at art, seeing performances, and engaging in storytelling and art activities. And, last, but certainly not least, the museum houses the Children's Art Resource Center, aimed at kids from ages 5 to 15. The center offers studio art programs, special exhibitions, and printed materials that interpret the art in the galleries.

Wintergreen Resort

Route 664, Wintergreen; (800) 266-2444 or (804) 325-2200; www.winergreenresort.com

Hours: Vary by activity

Admission: Varies by activity

Appeal by Age Groups:

Pre-school	Grade School	Teens	Young Adults	Over 30	Seniors
★★★★★	★★★★★	★★★★★	★★★★★	★★★★★	★★★★★

Services and Facilities:

Restaurants Yes

Alcoholic beverages Yes

Disabled access Yes

Wheelchair rental Yes; free

Baby stroller rental No

Lockers Yes

Pet kennels No

Rain check No

Private tours No

Description and Comments   Wintergreen is a four-season destination mountain resort. You can participate in the full gamut of winter and summer sports, as well as attend concerts, hike, and just look at the scenery. Accommodations run from studios to seven-bedroom villas. Among the programming features we like are the summertime Kids In Action, a day camp divided by age groups (ages 2 to 5 and 6 to 12). The day camp includes everything from butterfly hikes and finger painting for the young ones to nature programs, sports clinics, and field trips for the older kids. Junior Explorers, for ages 9 to 14, is an outdoor adventure day camp that encompasses hiking, canoeing, rock climbing, and rappelling. The resort also offers Kids Night Out for ages 6 to 12 and Kids Night Out-Camp Out, giving parents an evening to themselves. Worthwhile summer specialty programs include Junior Golf Camp, Junior Tennis Camp, and special Mountain Bike Dirt Camps for ages 12 to 16. The Wintergreen Summer Music Festival stages summer concerts by the Richmond Symphony Orchestra, as well as country music, bluegrass, and other events.

Come winter, the programs maintain their excellence. Ski Cubs, for ages 3 through 12, combines flexible ski time with indoor activities. Ski Cats/Rider Cats provides basic ski and snowboard lessons for ages 6 through 12, while Mountain Explorers is aimed at more advanced skiers ages 7 through 14. One program we really like is Ski Buddy, in which young expert skiers (ages 6 and up) can just ski their tails off with an older "ski buddy."

Family-Friendly Restaurants

EL MATADOR

1903 Betty Lane, Richmond; (804) 285-3813

Meals served: Lunch and dinner
Cuisine: Mexican
Entree range: $4.25–10.50
Children's menu: Yes ($2.95)
Reservations: No
Payment: Major credit cards

This small, third-generation, family-owned eatery serves all the Mexican classics with high quality and large quantities. The menu nicely describes all selections and provides definitions and pronunciations — a cool way to practice some Spanish with the kids. The so-called "Adventure Combo" lets you configure your own personalized combination plate.

MELITO'S

8815 Three Chopt Road, Richmond; (804) 285-1899

Meals served: Lunch and dinner

Cuisine: American
Entree range: $5.95–9.95
Children's menu: No
Reservations: No
Payment: Major credit cards

This place serves basic American pub food, from soft pretzels and hummus/pita snacks to burgers and sandwiches to baked three-cheese spaghetti and steaks. It has a loyal local following and is famous for its hot dogs. It also has the unfortunate reputation of being a smoky place (if that turns you off, forget about it). But, it's convenient to a movie theater and shopping mall on Richmond's west end.

MICHIE TAVERN

683 Thomas Jefferson Parkway, Charlottesville; (804) 977-1234

Meals served: Lunch
Cuisine: Colonial American
Entree range: $10.95
Children's menu: Children's price $5.50
Reservations: No
Payment: Major credit cards

What you eat at this Southern buffet is fried chicken with the all fixins, circa 1784. That's when this landmark tavern or "ordinary" went into business. It's just a mile or so from Monticello. Costumed hostesses and waitresses serve homemade Southern fare based on period recipes. You can then tour the Tavern-Museum and shop at the General Store. It's a bit touristy, to be sure, but fun.

SMOKEY PIG

212 South Washington Highway, Ashland; (804) 798-4590

Meals served: Lunch and dinner
Cuisine: Southern barbecue
Entree range: $4.95–16.95 (lunch and dinner)
Children's menu: Yes
Reservations: No
Payment: Major credit cards

A Virginia-born pal of ours once said that you have to eat barbecue when you come to the South or else you haven't really been there. So eat. This local landmark tends to get crowded, especially on weekends, but the decor is straight out of pig-mania and kids love it. They also get a pig place mat and crayons. If you don't want barbecue, there are burgers, etc. Oh, and go ahead, have some collard greens with that. Great homemade deserts, too.

Shenandoah Valley and Southwest Blue Ridge

If you're mountain people, this is the place for you. The Blue Ridge Mountains run down the length of this territory, providing incredible scenery, recreation, history, and exploration. Skyline Drive and the Blue Ridge Parkway present one of the most beautiful scenic drives in the country, if not the world, and two huge national forests—George Washington and Jefferson—assure thousands of square miles of unspoiled landscape.

The town of **Winchester** marks the northern end of the Shenandoah Valley. There, **Glen Burnie Historic House** (call (540) 662- 1473), home to the city's founder, has acres of gardens on display. **Dinosaur Land** (call (540) 869-2222) displays nearly 40 life-sized dinos. **Strasburg** has **Crystal Caverns at Hupp's Hill** (call (540) 465-866), said to be Virginia's oldest cave, and the **Museum of American Presidents** (call (540) 465-5999), where more than 60 years of presidential memorabilia are on display.

Front Royal calls itself the gateway to the Blue Ridge, and it's home to a number of outdoor outfitters, as well as **Skyline Caverns** (call (800) 296- 4545 or (540) 635-4545), where you can not only explore the caves, but also ride a miniature train ride. **New Market** offers still more underground tours at **Endless Caverns** (call (540) 896-2283). Moving south, **Harrisonburg** is home to **James Madison University,** where the **JMU Life Science Museum** (call (540) 568-6378) covers natural history. The **Shenandoah Heritage Farmer's Market** (call (540) 433-3929) is a fun collection of antiques, crafts, and homestyle foods purveyors, while the **Virginia Quilt Museum** (call (540) 433-3818) displays quilts and looks at their historical role. Just east, **Shenandoah Caverns of Virginia** (call (888) 422-8376) offers yet another place to explore below ground.

Continuing south, in **Staunton, Grand Caverns Regional Park** (call (888) 430-2283) provides still more underground exploration, and the **Jumbo Antique Fire Engine** (call (540) 332-3884) is said to be the only

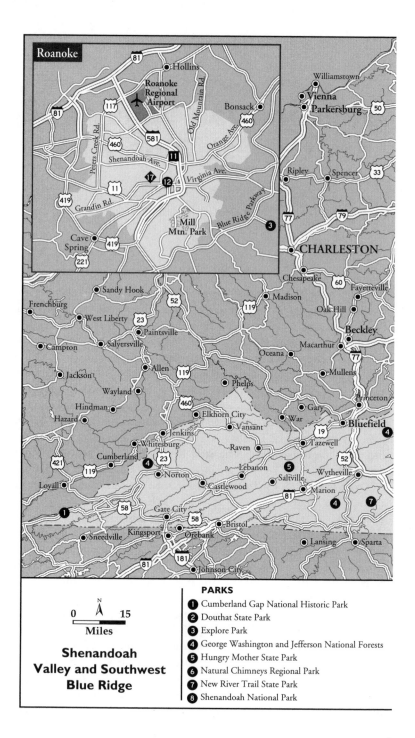

PARKS

1 Cumberland Gap National Historic Park

2 Douthat State Park

3 Explore Park

4 George Washington and Jefferson National Forests

5 Hungry Mother State Park

6 Natural Chimneys Regional Park

7 New River Trail State Park

8 Shenandoah National Park

0   15
Miles

**Shenandoah
Valley and Southwest
Blue Ridge**

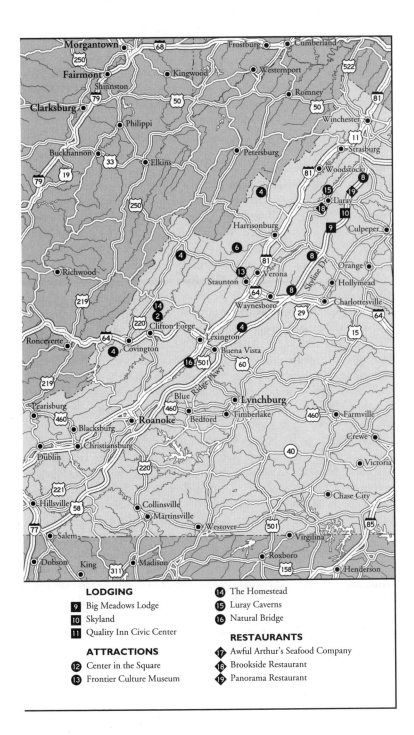

LODGING

9 Big Meadows Lodge
10 Skyland
11 Quality Inn Civic Center

ATTRACTIONS

12 Center in the Square
13 Frontier Culture Museum

14 The Homestead
15 Luray Caverns
16 Natural Bridge

RESTAURANTS

17 Awful Arthur's Seafood Company
18 Brookside Restaurant
19 Panorama Restaurant

remaining 1911 Robinson pumper. **Lexington** has the **Virginia Horse Center** (call (540) 463-2194), a world-class show facility; **The General Store** (call (540) 261-3869), which opened in 1891 and remains much the same; the **George C. Marshall Museum** (call (540) 463-7103), where the famous general's life is the subject; **Stonewall Jackson House** (call (540) 463-4088), his home before the Civil War; and the **Virginia Military Institute Museum** (call (540) 464-7334), which focuses on that college's history and other military memorabilia.

West of Lexington, **Clifton Forge** houses the **Chesapeake and Ohio Historical Society** (call (800) 453-2647 or (540) 862-2210), where railroading history is interpreted. **Warm Spring** is the site of **Jefferson Pools** (call (540) 839-5346), a natural hot springs frequented by folks since the eighteenth century. Moving south again, **Roanoke** is the region's largest city and offers much to do. The **Harrison Museum of African American Culture** (call (540) 345-4818) focuses on regional black art and history. The **Historic Farmers' Market** (call (540) 342-2028) is a bustling marketplace, the longest operating one in Virginia. **To the Rescue Museum** (call (540) 776-0364) presents the story of the National Emergency Medical Services organization and includes many hands-on exhibits. Just outside town, **Virginia's Explore Museum** (call (800) 842-9163 or (540) 427-1800) is a living history installation re-creating Colonial and Native American life. The **Virginia Museum of Transportation** (call (540) 342-5670) features vintage vehicles of all sorts.

The Southwest Blue Ridge region continues the mountainous terrain to the Kentucky and Tennessee state lines. In **Tazewell,** the **Historic Crab Orchard Museum and Pioneer Park** (call (540) 988-9400) looks at regional culture and the pioneer period. **Abingdon** holds the **Morgan McClure Motorsports Museum** (call (540) 628-3683), filled with NASCAR memorabilia. More underground action can be found in **Bristol** at **Bristol Caverns** (call (423) 878-2011), said to be the largest cave in the Smokey Mountains. At **Big Stone Gap,** the **Harry W. Meador Coal Museum** (call (540) 523-4950) depicts the region's mining culture, and the **Southwest Virginia Museum** (call (540) 523-1322) looks at the state during pioneer days. **Pennington Gap** has the **Appalachian African-American Cultural Center** (call (540) 546-5144), where black culture in Appalachia is the subject. **Rose Hill** is home to the **Museum of the Middle Appalachians** (call (540) 496-3633), which preserves the region's history.

HOW TO GET THERE

By Car. From north or south, I-81 runs right down the middle of the valley. I-77 comes north and south from North Carolina and West Virginia, intersecting I-81 at Wytheville, about two-thirds of the way south in the region. I-64 moves east-west at about the region's mid-point. And, of course, the Blue Ridge Parkway, a 35 mph road, meanders down the length of the region's eastern perimeter.

By Plane. Roanoke Regional Airport is serviced by Delta, COMAIR, Northwest Airlink, United Express, and USAirways; 5202 Aviation Drive, NW, Roanoke; (540) 362-1999.

By Train. Amtrak offers passenger service to Lynchburg and Clifton Forge; (800) 872-7245.

HOW TO GET INFORMATION BEFORE YOU GO

Shenandoah Valley Visitors Center & Travel Association, I-81 Exit 264, P.O. Box 1040, New Market, VA 22844; (540) 740-3132; www.svta.org.

Harrisonburg-Rockingham Country Visitors Center, 10 East Gay Street, Harrisonburg, VA 22801; (540) 434-2319; www.hrcvb.org.

Roanoke Valley Visitors Center, 114 Madison Street, Roanoke, VA 24011; (800) 635-5535; www.visitroanoke.com.

Western Highlands Travel Council, 241 West Main Street, Covington, VA 24426; (540) 962-2178.

Southwest Highlands Gateway Visitors Center, Factory Merchants Mall at Fort Chiswell, Drawer B-12, Max Meadows, VA 24360; (800) 446-9670; www.virginiablueridge.org.

Appalachian Mountain Region Visitors Center, 17507 Lee Highway, Suite 2, Abingdon, VA 24210; (888) 827-6867.

The Best Beaches and Parks

Cumberland Gap National Park. Both Native Americans and settlers moving west passed through the Cumberland Gap. Daniel Boone was hired to blaze a trail through the gap—the Wilderness Road—and later Civil War battles were fought over control of the strategic crossroads. Beautiful scenery and Civil War remnants are the highlights. Middlesboro; (606) 248-2817 or (606) 248-7276.

Douthat State Park. The park is located east of Clifton Forge. It contains campgrounds, restored Civilian Conservation Corps log cabins built the 1930s, and a 50-acre lake with good fishing, boating, and a sandy beach with a bathhouse, restaurant, and convenience shop. Maybe most interesting for kids are the fossil sites and self-guided walking trails. In summer, park staff organizes campfires and children's programs. Hiking trails serve all skill levels and lead to waterfalls, wildflower meadows, and scenic overlooks. Route 1, Douthat Road, Millboro; (540) 862-8100.

Explore Park. A 1,100-acre park at Milepost 115 of the Blue Ridge Parkway, Explore Park combines outdoor recreation with environmental and historical education. Three historic areas depict Virginia life from year 1000 to 1850. Costumed staff members interpret the various historical periods. Recreation includes scenic hiking trails along the Roanoke River gorge, mountain biking, canoeing, kayaking, fishing, and picnicking; equipment can be rented for all these activities. Roanoke; (800) 842-9163 or (540) 427-1800; www.explorepark.org.

George Washington and Jefferson National Forests. The George Washington and Jefferson National Forests constitute the largest publicly owned land base for recreation in the eastern United States, encompassing 1.8 million acres in an area of 350 miles, divided among twelve Ranger Districts. Within their boundaries you'll find a place to enjoy just about any type of outdoor recreation—camping, cabin camping, fishing, swimming, hiking, mountain biking, horseback riding, off-road vehicle driving, scenic driving, wildlife watching—the list seems endless. The Appalachian Trail runs through here, as does the Blue Ridge Parkway, one of the most scenic drives anywhere. If you're interested in pursuing some of these recreational opportunities, first determine where geographically you want to go, then contact the park for more information. Their web site is very thorough and contains most of the information you'll need to orient yourself. Headquarters, 5162 Valleypointe Parkway, Roanoke; (888) 265-0019 or (540) 265-5100; www.fs.fed.us/gwjnf.

Hungry Mother State Park. Just another unbelievably beautiful Blue Ridge spot, this one is just off I-81 in the southwestern section. It centers on a 108-acre lake. Swimming takes place on a sandy beach with a bathhouse, plus you'll find boating, a disabled-accessible fishing pier, campgrounds, cabins, a restaurant, a visitor center, hiking paths, and guided horseback trail rides. Route 5, Marion; (540) 783-3422.

Natural Chimneys Regional Park and Campground. The limestone Natural Chimneys rise up to 120 feet above the Shenandoah Valley, looking like massive medieval castle turrets. The park has hiking, camping, and other activities. 94 Natural Chimneys Lane, Mt. Solon; (888) 430-2267 or (540) 350-2510.

New River Trail State Park. A "Rails to Trails" project, this is a linear park that runs 57 miles through four counties from Galax north to Pulaski (just south of Blacksburg), often paralleling the New River. Many access points are available for hiking, biking, horseback riding, and, near the trail, boating. Route 1, Austinville; (540) 699-6778 or (540) 236-8889.

Shenandoah National Park. (See Attractions, page 389.)

Family Outdoor Adventures

Biking. Allegheny Outdoor Center rents mountain bikes and leads tours; 218 West Main Street, Hot Springs, (888) 752-9982 or (304) 536-3596. Adventure Damascus Bicycle Shop & Tour Company provides mountain bike rental, guides, and shuttle service for the Virginia Creeper Trail and area and the Mt. Rogers Recreation Area; 128 West Laurel Avenue, Damascus, (888) 595-2453 or (540) 475-6262. Mountain Empire Outdoor Center offers package southwest Virginia mountain bike tours with or without lodging, plus equipment rentals; c/o Land, Air, & Water, Inc., P.O. Box 1210, St. Paul, VA 24283; (540) 762-7500. For other biking opportunities, also see The Homestead (page 387) and New River Trail State Park (page 382).

Hiking. Chessie Nature Trail follows the Maury River for seven miles from Lexington to Buena Vista along the old railroad bed; Lexington Visitor Center, Lexington; (540) 463-3777. Cascades National Recreation Trail, offers a scenic, four-mile round-trip, of low to moderate difficulty, along a shaded mountain creek from a picnic ground to a 70-foot waterfall; Blacksburg Ranger District, USDA Forest Service, Jefferson National Forest, 110 South Park Drive, Blacksburg; (540) 552-4641. Big Walker Lookout in Bland County is a good trek for kids. It leads to a 100-foot tower at Big Walker Lookout that yields spectacular views. Or you can take a 20-minute hike on a novice trail that goes to Monster Rock Overlook. Trailside facilities include a craft/gift shop and sandwich/ice cream shop; Star Route, US 52, Wytheville; (540) 228-4401. New River Trail State Park (see The Best Beaches and Parks, page 382).

Horseback Riding. Fort Valley Stable/Twin Lakes Cabin offers guided and unguided rides, lasting from an hour to a half-day; overnight wilderness trips are also available; 299 South Fort Valley Road, Fort Valley, (540) 933-6633. Mountain View Trails leads trail rides through the George Washington National Forest and offers beginners' lessons; 2607 Mt. Torrey Road, Lyndhurst, (540) 949-5346. River Ridge Ranch is a bed-and-breakfast ranch that features trail rides and old-fashioned hay wagon rides as well as biking, fishing, and tubing; Route 1, Millboro, (540) 996-4148 or (540) 996-4149. Mallard Cove Stables leads trail rides and overnight camping rides; reservations required; Route 1, Rocky Mount, (540) 721-6333.

Paddling. Allegheny Outdoor Center leads guided canoe tours or combination pedal-and-paddle tours in Bath, Allegheny, and Greenbrier counties' regions of Virginia and West Virginia. They also offer self-guided kayak touring on Lake Moomaw, and family tours of half-day, full-day, or three days; 218 West Main Street, Hot Springs, (888) 752-9982 or (304) 536-3596. Appalachian Adventures offers canoe, kayak, and mountain bike rentals; 1122 Wasena Avenue, Roanoke, (540) 344-8926. Front Royal Canoe Company stages canoe, kayak, raft, and tube trips on the Shenandoah River (including a guided full moon float) on novice- to intermediate- class waters; 8567 Stonewall Jackson Highway, Front Royal, (800) 270-8808 or (540) 635-1574. Shenandoah River Trips specializes in affordable family outings with highly personalized service; Route 613, Bentonville, (540) 635-5050.

Skiing. Massanutten Resort, a full four-season mountain resort with skiing for all abilities, plus extensive kids' programs and night skiing; lodging in 500 condominiums and 140 hotel rooms; Harrisonburg, (800) 207-6277 or (540) 289-4954, www.massresort.com. Bryce Resort is a small area with eight trails, but it offers a complete ski school and on-snow lessons for kids ages five and up; Bayse, (800) 821-1444 or 540-856-2121, www.bryceresort.com. Other skiing opportunities are available at The Homestead (see page 387).

Family Lodging

SHENANDOAH NATIONAL PARK/ BLUE RIDGE PARKWAY LODGES

Two lodges (Big Meadows and Skyland) operate within the park under a concession contract. Reservations are made through Aramark, Virginia Sky-Line Company, P.O. Box, 7727NP, Luray, VA 22835; (800) 999-4714 or (540) 743-5108.

Big Meadows Lodge

Big Meadows' main lodge holds 20 rooms, while 72 rustic cabins, multi-unit lodges, and modern suites are also available. Open mid-May to late-October, the lodge features a playground, ranger programs, TVs only in some rooms, and no in-room phones. Rates: $68–142; children under age 16 stay free. Skyline Drive, milepost 51.

Skyland

Skyland has 177 guest rooms, rustic cabins, multi-unit lodges, and modern suites, with TVs only in some rooms. Bonuses for families are nightly entertainment, a craft shop, ranger programs, horseback activities, and a playground. It's open late March to early December. Rates: $82–170; children under age 16 stay free in parents room. Skyline Drive, mile 41.7.

Quality Inn Civic Center

A mid-priced motel not far from downtown Roanoke attractions, this one has an on-site restaurant, in-room coffee makers and irons and ironing boards, an outdoor pool, and a free breakfast buffet. Rates: $70–90; children age 18 and under stay free in same room as parents. 501 Orange Avenue, Roanoke; (800) 228-5151 or (540) 342-8961.

Attractions

Center in the Square

One Market Square, Roanoke; 540-342-5700; www.centerinthesquare.org

Hours: Vary by time of year and specific attraction; typically, the Science Museum is open seven days a week, and the Art and History Museums are open Tuesday–Sunday; closed New Years, Easter, and Thanksgiving days

Admission: Varies by activity

Appeal by Age Groups:

Pre-school	Grade School	Teens	Young Adults	Over 30	Seniors
★★★★	★★★★★	★★★★★	★★★★★	★★★★★	★★★★★

Touring Time: Varies by activity

Rainy-Day Touring: Yes

Services and Facilities:

Restaurants Yes	Lockers No
Alcoholic beverages Yes	Pet kennels No
Disabled access Yes; mostly	Rain check No
Wheelchair rental No	Private tours No
Baby stroller rental No	

Description and Comments   This is Roanoke's downtown cultural complex. It's made up of the Art Museum of Western Virginia (call (540) 342-5760); the History Museum & Historical Society of Western Virginia (call (540) 342-5770); Science Museum of Western Virginia and Hopkins Planetarium (call (540) 342-5726); Mill Mountain Theatre (call (540) 342-5740 or (800) 317-6455); Opera Roanoke (call (540) 982-2742); and the Roanoke Ballet Theatre (call (540) 345-6099). Bunched together as they are, and set near the Farmer's Market, the various installations can be visited as an all-day outing or in bits and pieces, combined with the market and dining.

The Art Museum exhibits art from diverse cultures around the world, but it keeps a special emphasis on American and regional Virginia art. Children's programs are offered regularly, and guided tours can be arranged by calling (540) 224-1223 in advance. The History Museum's focus is western

Virginia, presented through exhibits about events, industries, people, and cultures that have influenced the region. This History Museum also offers children's programs and special events. The Science Museum's latest feature is its MegaDome Theatre, showing large-format 70-mm films. As would be expected in any modern science installation, interactive exhibits abound, covering such topics as anatomy, light, color, sound, physiology, weather, and animals. It also features a Chesapeake Bay Touch Tank.

The performing arts are well represented at Center in the Square. Mill Mountain Theatre is a year-round, professional theater, counted among the country's better regional theaters. In addition to a repertory of dramas and musicals, children's plays and programs are offered. Opera Roanoke is a professional company. They produce two fully staged productions annually and a Sunday concert series. Finally, Roanoke Ballet Theatre presents several productions each year and also sponsors local performances by nationally and internationally known companies.

Frontier Culture Museum

1250 Richmond Avenue, Staunton; (540) 332-7850;
    www.frontiermuseum.org

Hours: Mid-March–November, daily 9 a.m.–5 p.m.; December–
    mid-March, daily 10 a.m.–4 p.m.; closed on Thanksgiving and
    Christmas days, plus some days in January

Admission: $8 adults, $7.50 seniors 60 and older, $7 students ages
    13–18, $4 children ages 6–12, free for children age 5 and under

Appeal by Age Groups:

Pre-school	Grade School	Teens	Young Adults	Over 30	Seniors
★★★	★★★★★	★★★★	★★★★★	★★★★★	★★★★★

Touring Time: Average 3½ hours, minimum 2 hours

Rainy-Day Touring: Yes

Services and Facilities:

Restaurants No	Lockers No
Alcoholic beverages No	Pet kennels No
Disabled access Yes; mostly	Rain check No
Wheelchair rental No	Private tours No
Baby stroller rental No	

Description and Comments   This impressive collection of period buildings aims to promote an understanding of the European cultures that sent significant numbers of immigrants to this area during the seventeenth and eighteenth centuries, contributing to the country's westward expansion beyond Virginia. Three "farms" have been developed: German, Scotch-Irish, and English, on which are displayed relocated original, period buildings from those countries. The historical representations and interpretations are well done and fascinating, and younger kids will go for the animals. The German farm once stood in the German farming village of Hordt. Its peasant farmhouse dates to 1688. The farm depicts the years 1700–1750, the period of heaviest German emigration from that region. The buildings from Northern Ireland are from Claraghmore, County Tyrone, circa 1830, and life in the early 1700s is depicted. The English exhibits show the years 1675–1700 and includes buildings from West Sussex and the West Midlands regions of England. This is living history with a bit of a different slant, and it's quite enjoyable.

The Homestead

U.S. 220 North, Hot Springs; (800) 838-1766 or (540) 839-1766; www.thehomestead.com

Hours: A four-season resort

Admission: Varies by activity

Appeal by Age Groups:

Pre-school	Grade School	Teens	Young Adults	Over 30	Seniors
★★★★★	★★★★★	★★★★★	★★★★★	★★★★★	★★★★

Rainy-Day Touring: Yes

Services and Facilities:

Restaurants Yes	Lockers No
Alcoholic beverages Yes	Pet kennels No
Disabled access Yes	Rain check No
Wheelchair rental Yes; free	Private tours No
Baby stroller rental No	

Description and Comments   The Homestead is a major, high-end destination resort, with grounds covering some 15,000 acres and offerings that the span the full range of outdoor and other activities. More than 100 miles of hiking, mountain biking, and riding trails are here. There are three self-guided hiking trails plus guided hikes through Cascades Gorge. Mountain biking is available for all ability levels. The stable holds some 50 horses for trail riding, or if you'd rather, you can take a carriage ride in a vehicle dating to the early 1900s. Tennis is played on eight courts plus three KidsClub courts. You can also swim in indoor and outdoor pools, play golf, enjoy a spa treatment, go fly fishing or bowling, or try falconry. In winter, there's a full skiing facility on nine runs, an Olympic-sized ice rink, and a snow-tubing facility.

The resort's KidsClub program offers far more than babysitting or day activities. It has its own clubhouse and includes a Literary Center, an Art & Design Center, and a Science & Biology Center. Half- and full-day programs are available for ages 3 to 12. In winter, Bunny Ski School teaches ages 5 to 11. Accommodations are high-end in a classic resort hotel of Georgian architecture. Rates are $132–635 per person, including breakfast and dinner, in 500-plus guest rooms and suites up to two bedrooms. Family packages are available.

Luray Caverns

970 U.S. 211 West, Luray; (540) 743-6551; www.luraycaverns.com

Hours: March 15–June 14, daily 9 a.m.–6 p.m.; June 15–Labor Day, daily 9 a.m.–7 p.m.; after Labor Day–October 31, daily 9 a.m.–6 p.m.; November 1–March 14, Monday–Friday 9 a.m.–4 p.m., Saturday and Sunday 9 a.m.–5 p.m.

Admission: $14 adults, $12 seniors, $6 children ages 7–13, free for children under age 7

Appeal by Age Groups:

Pre-school	Grade School	Teens	Young Adults	Over 30	Seniors
★★★	★★★★★	★★★★★	★★★★★	★★★★★	★★★★★

Touring Time: Average 2½ hours, minimum 1 hour

Rainy-Day Touring: Yes

Services and Facilities:

Restaurants Yes	Baby stroller rental No
Alcoholic beverages Yes	Lockers No
Disabled access No; but can be done with assistance	Pet kennels No
	Rain check No
Wheelchair rental No	Private tours No

Description and Comments   This is one of the eastern United States' largest and best-known caves, a U.S. Natural Landmark noted for the variety of formations and natural colors. You walk on well-lit, paved paths through chambers as tall as ten stories high, filled with towering stone columns and crystal-clear pools. A bit hokey but of note is the so-called "Stalacpipe" organ, in which stalactites in an area covering 3.5 acres produce tones by being electronically tapped by rubber-tipped mallets. Strict ecologically minded folks might find this a bit of an intrusion, but you can't ignore its uniqueness. One-hour guided tours of the caverns depart every 20 minutes.

Other features at Luray are the Historic Car & Carriage Caravan and the Garden Maze (extra fee). Some 140 items are displayed relating to transportation, including cars, carriages, coaches, and costumes dating from 1725. Highlight vehicles include an 1892 Benz, one of the oldest cars in the country still in operating condition, and a Conestoga wagon. The maze is a one-acre ornamental garden containing a one-mile pathway; if you like mazes, it's worth the extra few bucks.

Natural Bridge

U.S. 11, Natural Bridge; (540) 291-2121

Hours: Vary

Admission: Natural Bridge Drama of Creation only: $10 adults, $5 children, free for children under age 5; cavern only: $7 adults, $3.50 children; Wax Museum only: $7 adults, $3.50 children; two attractions: $14 adults, $7 children; three attractions: $17 adults, $8.50 children

Appeal by Age Groups:

Pre-school	Grade School	Teens	Young Adults	Over 30	Seniors
★★★	★★★★★	★★★★	★★★★	★★★★★	★★★★★

Touring Time: Average 3 hours, minimum 2 hours

Rainy-Day Touring: Yes

Services and Facilities:

Restaurants Yes	Lockers No
Alcoholic beverages Yes	Pet kennels No
Disabled access No	Rain check No
Wheelchair rental No	Private tours No
Baby stroller rental No	

Description and Comments   Originally surveyed by a young George Washington and once owned by Thomas Jefferson, this is a natural wonder that's magnificent, if a bit over-commercialized. With kids, you'll definitely want to see *The Drama of Creation* sound and light show that plays daily at dusk. It uses symphonic music and a colored light show to tell the Biblical story of creation and runs from mid-March until the weather gets too wintry. Guided cave tours feature hanging gardens, flowstone cascades, rock draperies, and water pools. A very touristy wax museum and Factory Tour is also offered, in which you see 125 life-like figures from presidents to trappers to a ten-foot grizzly bear. A lot of sound, light, and animation are utilized to make things entertaining, and you then tour the "factory" to see how the figures are made. A recent addition to the site is the Monacan Indian Village, a living history re-creation, where you meet and talk with Monacan Indians, learning about and assisting with tool-making, gardening, meal preparation, rope-making, weaving, canoe building, hide tanning, and shelter construction. Also, take the short hike beyond the Bridge to Lace Waterfalls.

Shenandoah National Park

3655 U.S. Highway 211, East Swift Run Gap Entrance, Luray; (540) 999-3500 or (540) 298-9625; www.nps.gov/shen/home.htm or www.visitshenandoah.com

Hours: All facilities and services operate mid-May–late October. Most also function during April, early-May, and November. During January and February, food, gas, and lodging must be obtained outside the park. Sections of Skyline Drive may be closed in winter due to hazardous driving conditions; from early November to early January, sections may be closed at night to control wildlife poaching

Admission: $10 per vehicle, valid for seven days

Description and Comments   Mileposts are measured from north to south, milepost zero being located at the north entrance. The park has three visitor centers: Dickey Ridge Visitor Center (mile 4.6), Harry F. Byrd Sr. Visitor Center (milepost 51), and Loft Mountain Information Center (mile 79.5), where general information, Ranger Programs, and other materials can be obtained. The following are popular activities for park visitors:

Driving Tours. A ride along Skyline Drive is something your family will always remember. You must drive slowly (speed limit is 35), and you'll encounter 75 overlooks if you drive the full length (105 miles). Go slowly and ogle.

Hiking. The park contains more than 500 miles of trails, including 101 miles of the Appalachian Trail. Many trails can be accessed from Skyline Drive. Particularly fun with kids are the short trails leading to waterfalls or scenic viewpoints. Several hiking guides are sold at the visitor centers' stores. Good for modest, recreational hikers are: *Frazier Discovery Trail* ($1), a guide to a 1.3-mile loop on Loft Mountain in the South District; *Hikes to Waterfalls in Shenandoah National Park* ($2), which will direct you to all the park's waterfalls; *Short Hikes in Shenandoah National Park* ($1), a booklet describing short hikes from .25 to 2.8 miles long, of varying degrees of difficulty.

Horseback Riding. The park holds more than 150 miles of horse trails. Guided trail rides are offered at Skyland from May through October.

Fishing. The park's streams are home to many fish species, and eastern brook trout are especially abundant. Check at a visitor center for regulations governing fishing, which are strictly enforced, and a list of park streams designated as open for fishing.

Camping. There are four major campgrounds in the park at mileposts 22.1, 51.3, 57.5, and 79.5. All campgrounds have large sites outfitted with picnic tables, grills, showers, laundries, and a store. None have hookups, but Mathews Arm, Big Meadows, and Loft Mountain have dump stations. Two operate on a first-come, first-serve basis; Big Meadows and Dundo do not. And all can be accessed from Skyline Drive.

Special Events. Many, ranging from night-sky observations to concerts in the amphitheater at Skylands (see Family Lodging, page 384), are offered by Aramark, the official park concessionaire; visit www.visitshenandoah.com for a listing of events and dates. The Park Service operates a large variety of Ranger Programs.

Family-Friendly Restaurants

AWFUL ARTHUR'S SEAFOOD COMPANY

108 Campbell Avenue, SE, Roanoke; (540) 344-2997

Meals served: Lunch and dinner
Cuisine: Seafood
Entree range: $8.95–19.95
Children's menu: Yes
Reservations: Yes
Payment: Major credit cards

A small regional chain that's big on atmosphere. This bustling location is right in the heart of the Farmers Market/Center in the Square action in Roanoke and has a raw bar. Steaks and pasta are available if you don't like seafood.

BIG MEADOWS LODGE

Skyline Drive, Mile 51.2; (540) 999-2221

Meals served: Breakfast, lunch, and dinner
Cuisine: American
Entree range: $8.95–18.75 (dinner)
Children's menu: Yes
Reservations: No
Payment: Major credit cards

Both sites serve traditional favorites like fried chicken, trout, country ham, and excellent pie. They also have tap rooms with live nightly entertainment. Both will also prepare box lunches to take on the road.

BROOKSIDE RESTAURANT

2547 U.S. 211, Luray; (540) 743-5698

Meals served: Breakfast, lunch, and dinner
Cuisine: American
Entree range: $4.95–24.95 (lunch and dinner)
Children's menu: Yes

Reservations: Yes
Payment: Major credit cards

A down-home place adjacent to cabin accommodations, this is a local favorite. It offers no surprises but has good stuff, like homemade soups and a salad bar.

PANORAMA RESTAURANT

Skyline Drive, Mile 31.5 at U.S. 211; (540) 999-2265

Meals served: Lunch and dinner
Cuisine: American
Entree range: $7.95–19.85
Children's menu: Yes
Reservations: No
Payment: Major credit cards

This is a dining room with table service and carry-out service. The varied menu includes soup, salads, sandwiches, and pizza.

Part Seven

West Virginia

They don't call West Virginia the "Mountain State" for nothing. From the Blue Ridge in the east to the Ohio River in the west, the state is rippled lengthwise with hills. And it's those hills that have shaped the state's history and character. From hard-driving railroading and coal mining to the state's separation from neighboring Virginia, the mountains have made West Virginia what it is. Today, those same mountains create one of the best places in the region—no, in the country—for outdoor play. It's a Mecca for white-water rafting, hiking, skiing, mountain biking, and more.

We start in the north with the aptly named **Northern Panhandle,** which sticks up defiantly between Ohio and Pennsylvania. We then jump all the way across the state to the **Eastern Panhandle,** a small region filled with Civil War history and healing spa waters. **Mountaineer Country,** the north-central region, follows and is dominated by Morgantown, home to West Virginia University. In the eastern-set **Potomac Highlands** we find myriad ways in which to indulge in high country play, while **Central West Virginia** offers water attractions, both lake and river. We finish in **Southern West Virginia,** where we find the state capital and world-class white-water rafting in a magnificent setting at the New River Gorge National River. "Almost heaven," says the John Denver song. Believe it.

How to Get Information before You Go

West Virginia Division of Tourism, State Capitol Complex, Charleston, WV 23505; (800) 225-5982; www.westvirginia.com.

State Parks Information, West Virginia Division of Natural Resources, State Capitol Complex, Charleston, WV 23505; (304) 558-2771; www.wvparks.com.

West Virginia's Not-to-Be-Missed Attractions

Northern Panhandle   Ogelbay Park
West Virginia Penitentiary Tours

Eastern Panhandle   Harpers Ferry National Historical
Park
Cacapon Resort State Park

Mountaineer Country Pricketts Fort State Park

Potomac Highlands   Snowshoe Mountain
Canaan Valley Resort and
Conference Center
Cass Scenic Railroad State Park/
Historic District

Central West Virginia Stonewall Jackson Lake State Park
Dam Tour
Blennerhassett Historical State Park

Southern West Virginia
New River Gorge National River
White-water Rafting in New River
Gorge Area
Huntington Museum of Art
Beckley Exhibition Coal Mine
The Greenbrier
Pipestem Resort State Park

Calendar of Festivals and Events

March

Eastern Panhandle: George Washington's Bathtub Celebration, Berkeley Springs.
A uniquely named festival to welcome spring; (800) 447-8797 or (304)
258-9147.

Potomac Highlands: West Virginia Maple Syrup Festival, Pickens. The local
historical society celebrates tree tapping with food, square dances, quilting,
and, of course, syrup; (304) 924-5096.

Southern West Virginia: Appalachian Weekend, Pipestem. Authentic crafts, storytelling, music, food, etc.; (304) 466-1800.

April

Potomac Highlands: Spring Mountain Festival, Petersburg. What we like best here is not the fishing derby or train rides but the jousting; (304) 257-2722.

May

Eastern Panhandle: West Virginia Wine and Arts Festival, Martinsburg. Vintners gather from around the state over Memorial Day weekend, while jazz and blues musicians play; (800) 498-2386 or (304) 264-8801.

Mountaineer Country: Three Rivers Festival, Fairmont. Civil War reenactments are the highlight, with various parades, fireworks, food, and a carnival; (304) 363-2625.

Southern West Virginia: Vandalia Gathering, Charleston. A multicultural heritage celebration at the Capitol Complex, including a liar's contest (honest); (304) 558-0220.

June

Mountaineer Country: New Deal Festival, Arthursdale. The 1930s come back to life; (304) 864-3959.

Potomac Highlands: Allegheny Echoes, Snowshoe. The ski resort hosts a week of events and workshops focused on West Virginia music, dance, and poetry; (800) 336-2623.

Central West Virginia: West Virginia State Folk Festival, Glenville. An emphasis on pre-1930s music, with fiddlers, banjo pickers, and lots of square dancing and food; (304) 462-8427.

Central West Virginia: Mid-Ohio Valley Multi-Cultural Festival, Parkersburg. Two days of arts, food, and fun to celebrate ethnic diversity; (304) 428-4405.

Southern West Virginia: Point Pleasant Sternwheel Regatta and River Festival, Point Pleasant. Includes sternwheel boat races and tugboat "shoving" competitions; (304) 675-6897.

July

Northern Panhandle: Jamboree in the Hills, Wheeling. Called the Super Bowl of country music, this festival features the biggest stars in a series of outdoor concerts; (800) 624-5456 or (304) 234-0050.

Potomac Highlands: Pioneer Days in Pocahontas County, Marlinton. Banjos, fiddles, square dances, bluegrass, and all things mountain culture; (304) 336-7009.

August

Northern Panhandle: Wetzel County Town & Country Days, New Martinsville. A week-long bash with entertainment, food, and all that good-time stuff; (304) 386-4444.

Potomac Highlands: Augusta Festival, Elkins. The culmination of five weeks of workshops at the Augusta Heritage Festival, showcasing traditional music, dance, crafts, etc.; (304) 637-1209.

Southern West Virginia: Sternwheel Regatta, Charleston. A ten-day, pre–Labor Day festival with sternwheeler races, a huge car show, rubber ducky races, and more; (304) 348-6419.

Southern West Virginia: State Fair of West Virginia, Lewisburg. The state's big one; (304) 645- 1090.

September

Northern Panhandle: West Virginia Oil & Gas Festival, Sisterville. Celebrate the Gay Nineties with antique engines, Ohio River ferry rides, food, and vendors; (304) 652-2939.

Mountaineer Country: Mason-Dixon Festival, Morgantown. River parades, cruises, and old-fashioned frontier music events; (304) 599-1104.

Potomac Highlands: Autumn Harvest and Roadkill Cook-Off, Marlinton. Don't be alarmed—the roadkill cook-off actually features wild game dishes; (800) 336-1824.

October

Eastern Panhandle: Mountain State Apple Harvest Festival, Martinsburg. Dances, apple pie baking contests, music, and crafts to honor apple pickin' time; (304) 263-2500.

Central West Virginia: Storytelling Festival, Voices of the Mountains, Weston. Tales of Appalachia told by storytellers from around the state and across the country; (304) 269-7328.

Southern West Virginia: West Virginia Pumpkin Festival, Milton. Minimum pumpkin weight—200 pounds; (304) 743-9222.

Southern West Virginia: New River Gorge Bridge Day, Fayetteville. The only day when the bridge is open to pedestrians, so folks come to BASE jump or just walk across and take advantage of the view, food, and music; (800) 927-0263 or (304) 465-5617.

November

Northern Panhandle: Winter Festival of Lights, Wheeling/Oglebay Park. Miles and miles of holiday lights and a parade highlight the season from November 1 until New Year's Day, downtown and in the park; (800) 828-3097 or (304) 243-4066.

Southern West Virginia: Guyandotte Civil War Days, Guyandotte. A massive re-enactment, living history, and music event; (304) 525-5720.

December

Mountaineer Country: The Spirit of Christmas in the Mountains, Salem. A celebration of Scotch-Irish and German holiday cultures at Fort New Salem; (304) 782-5245.

Central West Virginia: Christmas on the Island, Parkersburg. The Blennerhassett Mansion gets all dressed up for Christmas; (304) 420-4800.

WEST VIRGINIA'S STATE PARK RESORTS

Unique in the Mid-Atlantic, West Virginia has created eight resort state parks—reserves that offer hotel-style lodge accommodations and/or cottage lodging, as well as on-site restaurants. Room amenities include color TV, air-conditioning, and telephones. Cottages come with housekeeping essentials and full kitchens. The result—a rare opportunity to explore the beautiful backwoods without sacrificing creature comforts. Lodging rates are generally equal to a moderately priced motel.

Eastern Panhandle

Cacapon Resort State Park. Cacapon offers 30 cabins, some insulated for year-round use and some with stone fireplaces. Cacapon Lodge has 50 rooms and a nifty public lounge paneled in black walnut—a great place to sit in front of the fire. A restaurant, recreation room, and craft shop are also on-site. In addition, the park operates The Old Inn, a classic, 11-room, 1930s Colonial building built by the Civilian Conservation Corps. Check out the hand-hewn log beams. For recreation you'll find hiking and bridle trails, swimming, fishing, rental row and paddle boats for use on Cacapon Lake, tennis, volleyball, basketball, cross-country skiing, and to top it all off a Robert Trent Jones–designed golf course. Nature and recreation programs are offered year-round. Route 1, Box 304, Berkeley Springs, WV 25411; (304) 258-1022; www.cacaponresort.com.

Mountaineer Country

Tygart Lake State Park. As the name implies, the headline feature here is a lake—an 11-mile-long lake, actually. Boating, fishing, waterskiing, scuba diving, and swimming take place there, with boat and equipment rentals available at the park marina. Tygart Lodge offers 20 guest rooms and a restaurant with panoramic waterfront views. Ten vacation cottages and a 40-site camping area round out the lodging options. Non-lake recreational facilities include game courts, playgrounds, hiking, and a nearby golf course, as well as seasonal nature/recreational programs. Route 1, Box 260, Grafton, WV 26354; (304) 265-3383; www.tygartlake.com.

Potomac Highlands

Blackwater Falls State Park. Blackwater Lodge holds 54 guest rooms, a game room, a sitting room with fireplace, an indoor pool, and a restaurant. You'll find 26 cabins here, each fully winterized, and a 65-site tent and RV campground; 30 sites have electric hookups. Recreation includes ten miles of hiking trails, fully equipped riding stables with guided rides, a bicycle center, a nature center, ranger-led nature and recreation programs, swimming and boating (with boat rentals) on Pendleton Lake, and tennis, volleyball, and basketball courts. Oh, yes, and fishing, too—on trout-stocked Blackwater River or on the lake. In winter, a full-service cross-country ski center offering ski lessons and equipment rental and a quarter-mile, rope tow–equipped sledding hill go into action. Route 32, Davis, WV 26260; (304) 259-5216; www.blackwaterfalls.com.

Canaan Valley Resort and Conference Center. Canaan Valley is a major resort. The lodge has 250 guest rooms with amenities like satellite TV and in-room movies, a complete spa and fitness club, an indoor lap pool, and saunas. Twenty-three private cabins and cottages, with two to four bedrooms, are available. Golf is played on a championship course, while hiking and biking range throughout the park's 18 miles of marked trails to the adjacent million-acre Monongahela National Forest. Novice fly-fishers can take lessons here, and guided white-water rafting trips are offered on the Cheat River. Ski chairlift rides yield great views to the sedentary and downhill rides to mountain bikers. The park's Camp Canaan program, available for both half and full days, serves children ages 5–12.

In winter, 34 alpine ski trails excite downhill skiers of all levels; full rental and ski school operations are available. Cross-country skiers and snowshoers get 30 kilometers of marked trails. And, there's a full snow-tubing park and an outdoor, lighted ice skating rink. HC 70, Box 330, Davis, WV 26260; (800) 622-4121 or (304) 866-4121; www.canaanresort.com.

Central Virginia

North Bend State Park. North Bend Lodge offers 29 guest rooms and a wonderful glass-enclosed restaurant with great views. The lodge's solid oak furnishings are impressive, too. Eight vacation cottages sit on a secluded ridge in a pine forest. Two camping areas border a river and feature 78 sites; 26 sites have electric outlets. Recreational options include tennis and volleyball courts; a miniature golf course; a playground; a paved hiking trail with disabled access and written and braille interpretive signs; extensive hiking, bicycling, and horseback riding; easy access to the 72-mile, rails-to-trails North Bend Trail; and a year-round organized recreation program. Route 1, Box 221, Cairo, WV 26337; (304) 643-2931; www.northbendsp.com.

Southern West Virginia: New River/Greenbrier Valley Region

Pipestem Resort State Park. Pipestem's 113-room Mckeever Lodge is complemented by the 30-room Mountain Creek Lodge set at the base of the 1,000-foot-deep Bluestone Canyon; it's accessible by aerial tramway only. The park also has 25 cottages and an 82-site campground. Here, too, you can ride horses, hike, swim, play tennis on lighted courts, and golf on a championship nine-hole par-three or on mini-golf courses. McKeever lodge has an indoor swimming pool, sauna, and exercise and game rooms. In winter, there's rope tow–facilitated sledding, winter horseback riding, and cross-country skiing. Route 20, Box 150, Pipestem, WV 25979; (304) 466-1800; www.pipestemresort.com.

Hawks Nest State Park. Set in the heart of New River Gorge National River white-water rafting country, Hawks Nest offers a 31-room lodge. Paddleboat on Hawks Nest Lake or, to get the adrenaline flowing, hop on a New River jet boat ride. The park also offers a museum, constructed by the Civilian Conservation Corps, where Indian and pioneer artifacts are displayed. P.O. Box 857, Ansted, WV 25813; (304) 658-5212; www.hawksnestsp.com.

Twin Falls Resort State Park. Mountaintop Lodge has 20 guest rooms (all with balconies), a restaurant, a gift shop, and a nature center. Thirteen vacation cottages are set in a thickly wooded area, and the park campground has 50 sites. Unique here is the Pioneer Farm, a living history farm depicting life in the 1830s. Recreation facilities include hiking, game courts, an outdoor pool, and a playground. P.O. Box 1023, Mullens, WV 25882; (304) 294-4000; www.twinfallsresort.com.

WEST VIRGINIA TRAIN RIDES

Railroading is integral to the Mountain State's history, and many tracks meander through incredible scenery. Railroading's heyday can still be enjoyed through various excursions. Among them:

Cass Scenic Railroad, Cass Scenic Railroad State Park. The only steam-powered excursion trains in West Virginia offer three different rides of varying length. You can also visit a refurbished railroad company town. Trains operate May–October. (304) 456-4300.

The Potomac Eagle. Operating out of Romney on the South Branch Valley Railroad, the route follows the South Branch of the Potomac River into a narrow river valley known as "The Trough." The diesel-powered train offers open-window coaches, first-class cars, and an open-air sight-seeing car. Operates weekends May–September, with daily operation the first three weeks in October. (800) 223-2453.

West Virginia Central Railroad. The Durbin & Greenbrier Valley Railroad (D&GV) operates two excursions on this line. The diesel-pulled "Tygart Flyer" has six streamlined passenger cars and runs between the towns of Belington and Elkins on weekends June–October. The second excursion uses a British-built railbus known as the "Cheat Mountain Salamander." It runs a mountainous, 35-mile round trip. A third option is the "Little LeRoi," a 90-minute run operating out of Durbin that follows the Greenbrier River; ride in an open observation car or a wooden caboose April–December. (877) 676-7245.

West Virginia Northern. This excursion departs from Kingwood and takes on steep grades plus a double switchback en route to Tunnelton, where coal trains were once interchanged with the B&O Railroad. (800) 253-1065.

New River Excursions. The Collis P. Huntington Railroad Historical Society operates a series of day-long October foliage trips from Huntington through the New River Gorge, using a mix of Amtrak and private equipment. Other excursions are offered during the year to Greenbrier, Lewisburg, and Pence Springs. (606) 325-8800.

Mountain State Mystery Tours. These tours operate year-round to various events, activities, and destinations within the New River Gorge National River Recreation Area and beyond. (304) 529-6412.

Cool Web Sites for West Virginia–Bound Kids

West Virginia State Parks Kids-Only Page:
www.dnr.state.wv.us/wvwildlife/kids/default.htm

Class VI River Runners Kids Page: www.raftwv.com/kids.htm

Northern Panhandle

This lick of land is West Virginia's birthplace. The Ohio River forms its western boundary, and the river's power and commerce provided the seed for founding the various towns here. **Wellsburg** once rivaled Wheeling as a commercial center, and the **Wellsburg Historic District** presents a good look at buildings from the late 1700s to mid 1800s, including the **Brooke County Historical Society Museum** (call (304) 737-2787), which displays furniture manufactured in the area, clothing of the 1800s, toys, and other artifacts. **Wheeling,** an old river port town, remains the area's largest city, and boasts a vibrant old-town section. **Independence Hall** (call (304) 238-1300) was the seat of the new government after independence from Virginia was declared. **Centre Market** (call (304) 234-3878) is among the oldest market houses in the country—a good place to browse and eat. The **Wheeling Suspension Bridge** was first built in 1849 as the world's longest single-span suspension bridge and remains quite a sight today, especially when lit at night. **Wymer's General Store Museum** (call (304) 232-1810) shows off memorabilia and antiques in the Artisan Center. And, **Jamboree USA** (call (304) 234-0050), a local entertainment icon, has presented live country music as well as other shows in conjunction with WWVA radio since 1933.

Moving south, **Grave Creek Mound State Park** (call (304) 843-1410) in Moundsville has an Adena burial mound dating to 250 B.C., the largest conical earthen mound of its kind (69 feet high and 295 feet in diameter), and the **Delf Norona Museum and Cultural Center. In New Martinsville, Thistle Dew Farm** (call (304) 455-1728) is a working honey farm that sells beeswax and honey.

How to Get There

By Car. I-70 and U.S. 40 run east-west through Wheeling. WV 2, a four-lane, limited access highway runs north-south along the western perimeter of the region.

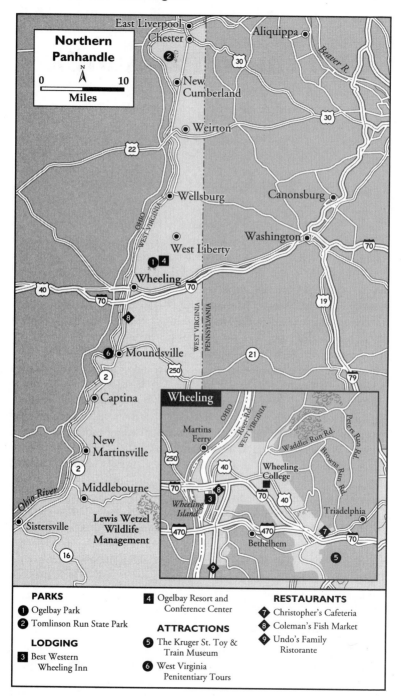

Northern Panhandle

N

0 _____ 10

Miles

East Liverpool

Chester

Aliquippa

New Cumberland

Weirton

Wellsburg

Canonsburg

Washington

West Liberty

Wheeling

Moundsville

Captina

New Martinsville

Middlebourne

Sistersville

Lewis Wetzel Wildlife Management

OHIO RIVER

OHIO / WEST VIRGINIA

WEST VIRGINIA / PENNSYLVANIA

Wheeling

Martins Ferry

Wheeling College

Wheeling Island

Triadelphia

Bethelhem

OHIO

River Rd.

WEST VIRGINIA

Waddles Run Rd.

Browns Run Rd.

Peters Run Rd.

PARKS

❶ Ogelbay Park

❷ Tomlinson Run State Park

LODGING

❸ Best Western Wheeling Inn

❹ Ogelbay Resort and Conference Center

ATTRACTIONS

❺ The Kruger St. Toy & Train Museum

❻ West Virginia Penitentiary Tours

RESTAURANTS

❼ Christopher's Cafeteria

❽ Coleman's Fish Market

❾ Undo's Family Ristorante

By Plane. Wheeling–Ohio County Airport offers limited commercial service; Route 5, Box 5, Wheeling, WV 26003; (304) 234-3864.

HOW TO GET INFORMATION BEFORE YOU GO

Wheeling Convention & Visitors Bureau, 1401 Main Street, Wheeling, WV 26003; (800) 828-3097 or (304) 233-7709; www.wheelingcvb.com.

The Best Parks

Ogelbay Park. Located just north of the U.S. 40/I-70 junction, this 1,500-acre park has a lot to offer: a glass museum, gardens, greenhouses, miniature and par-3 golf, a zoo, a brand new environmental education center with a "discovery trail system," a swimming pool, a restaurant, a miniature train ride, a small ski area, and boating and fishing. Illuminated fountains and a water-and-light show are staged evenings from late spring to early fall; (304) 243-4000.

Tomlinson Run State Park. Located at the extreme tip of the region, this park has a 50-site campground, ponds and lakes with paddle and rowboat rentals, fishing, an Olympic-size swimming pool with a waterslide, tennis, miniature golf, and hiking trails; P.O. Box 97, Route 2, New Manchester, WV 26056; (304) 564-3651.

Family Outdoor Adventures

Biking. Heritage Bike and Jogging Trail, a 17-mile paved path, primarily follows the Ohio River out of Wheeling; (800) 828-3097.

Hiking. Ogelbay Park and Tomlinson Run State Park (see The Best Parks, above).

Family Lodging

Best Western Wheeling Inn

Right in the heart of town, this recently remodeled 80-room hotel includes free continental breakfast Monday–Thursday and has an on-site restaurant and an all-weather terrace overlooking the famous Suspension Bridge. Rates: $75–85; children age 12 and under stay free. 949 Main Street at Tenth Street, Wheeling; (800) 528-1234 or (304) 233-8500.

Ogelbay Resort and Conference Center

Located in Ogelbay Park, the center includes Wilson Lodge, a nicely appointed 212-room hotel with an indoor pool, jacuzzi, sauna, and fitness room. Cottages are also available; they have air-conditioning, an open fire-place, a TV, two to six bedrooms, and a fully equipped kitchen. The resort offers supervised children's programs in summer and ready access to the park's facilities, including the zoo, skiing, miniature golf, etc. Rates: $65–140 for lodge; $180–290 daily, $490 weekly for cottages. Children age 12 and under stay free. Special packages are available. Route 88 North, Wheeling; (800) 624-6988 or (304) 243-4000.

Attractions

The Kruger Street Toy and Train Museum

144 Kruger Street, Wheeling; (877) 242-8133 or (304) 242-8133; www.toyandtrain.com

Hours: June 1–October 31, Wednesday–Monday 10 a.m.–6 p.m.; November 1–December 31, daily 10 a.m.– 6 p.m.; January 2–May 31, Friday–Sunday 10 a.m.–6 p.m.; closed Easter, Thanksgiving, Christmas, and New Year's days

Admission: $8 adults, $7 seniors 65+, $5 students; children age 10 and under free

Appeal by Age Groups:

Pre-school	Grade School	Teens	Young Adults	Over 30	Seniors
★★★★	★★★★★	★★★	★★★★	★★★★	★★★★

Touring Time: Average 2 hours, minimum 1 hour

Rainy-Day Touring: Yes

Services and Facilities:

Restaurants No	Lockers No
Alcoholic beverages No	Pet kennels No
Disabled access Yes	Rain check No
Wheelchair rental No	Private tours No
Baby stroller rental No	

Description and Comments   Housed in a restored Victorian school, this museum holds more than 100,000 items—all toys and trains—including an enormous O-gauge railroad layout and some toys that will take mom, dad, and even grandparents back to good memories.

West Virginia Penitentiary Tours

818 Jefferson Avenue, Moundsville; (304) 845-6200; www.wvpentours.com

Hours: April–December, Tuesday–Sunday 10 a.m.–5 p.m.; January–March by appointment only; closed Easter, Thanksgiving, and Christmas days

Admission: $8 adults, $5 children ages 6–10, children age 5 and under free

Appeal by Age Groups:

Pre-school	Grade School	Teens	Young Adults	Over 30	Seniors
★★	★★★★	★★★★★	★★★★★	★★★★★	★★★★★

Touring Time: 1½ hours

Rainy-Day Touring: Yes

Services and Facilities:

Restaurants No	Lockers No
Alcoholic beverages No	Pet kennels No
Disabled access Yes	Rain check No
Wheelchair rental Yes; free	Private tours No
Baby stroller rental Yes; free	

Description and Comments This place may be too intense for young or sensitive children. But the Gothic, fortresslike setting alone gives most others that exciting creepy-crawly feeling, like something out of old Hollywood. Built to house the worst criminals, it's just eerie. Guided tours last 90 minutes and show such hair-raising sites as the "North Hall" solitary confinement area, a typical five-by-seven-foot cell (they lock you in . . .), and "Old Sparky," the electric chair. This was a maximum security prison, and the guides have many stories to tell.

Family-Friendly Restaurants

CHRISTOPHER'S CAFETERIA

10 Elmgrove Crossing Mall, Wheeling; (304) 242-4100

Meals served: Lunch and dinner
Cuisine: American
Entree range: $4.95–9.95 (lunch and dinner)
Children's menu: Yes
Reservations: No
Payment: Cash only

Set in a mall, this spot is known for hearty, healthy fare and for making things from scratch—like the breads, soups, mashed potatoes, and deserts.

COLEMAN'S FISH MARKET

Centre Wheeling Market, Wheeling; (304) 232-8510

Meals served: Lunch and dinner
Cuisine: Seafood sandwiches
Entree range: $2–5.95
Children's menu: No
Reservations: No
Payment: Cash only

Locals love this place. The deal is to order one of their famous fish sandwiches. You can get other seafood stuff, but the sandwich is the thing, which you then eat out in the Centre Market commons.

UNDO'S FAMILY RISTORANTE

753 Main Street, Benwood; (304) 233-0560

Meals served: Lunch and dinner
Cuisine: Italian
Entree range: $5.95–16.95 (lunch and dinner)
Children's menu: Yes
Reservations: Yes
Payment: Major credit cards

Part of a family-owned mini-chain, this one is the original and is found a few miles south of Wheeling. The food is good, portions are generous, and service is very friendly.

Eastern Panhandle

This region covers just the very northeastern tip of West Virginia and can be reached in an hour from many major metropolitan areas. But, it still presents the state's classic hills and mountain-life setting. **Harpers Ferry** is perhaps the best-known town in the area. In addition to visiting its national historic park, you can take a different look at local history by joining a **Harpers Ferry Ghost Tour** (call (304) 725-8019), lantern-lit walking tours offered May–November. The **John Brown Wax Museum** (call (304) 535-6342) tells the famous antislavery figure's story and depicts scenes from his famous raid on the Harpers Ferry arsenal. You'll find more on John Brown at the **Jefferson County Museum** (call (304) 725-8628) just south in **Charles Town.** The museum also displays Civil War artifacts. Farther south, at the **Summit Point Raceway** (call (304) 725-8444) in **Summit Point,** they race everything from go-carts to international Grand Prix autos. Moving west, the **James Rumsey Steamboat Museum** (call (304) 876-6907) in **Shepherdstown** is dedicated to the steam engine's inventor. In **Martinsburg,** the **Belle Boyd House** (call (304) 267-4713), home to the Civil War spy Belle Boyd, houses six museums and a spectacular rose garden. Reward yourselves afterward with a stop at **Rock Hill Creamery** (call (304) 264-2373) for some homemade ice cream. In **Hedgesville** the **L. Norman Dillon Farm Museum** (call (304) 267-7519) displays antique horse-drawn farm machinery on weekends April–October. North of Martinsburg in nearby **Brunswick, MD,** stands the **C&O Canal Historic Park** (call (301) 739-4200) for excellent paddling, walking, and biking (see Maryland, Capital Region Attractions.) At the region's western edge stands **Berkeley Springs,** an arts-oriented community that is home to famous restorative springs at Berkeley Springs State Park. The **Museum of the Berkeley Springs** (call (304) 258-3743), located above the 1815 Roman Bath House, highlights the history and geology of the springs. **Berkeley Castle** (call (800) 896-4001 or (304) 258-3274) is a half-size replica of England's Lord Berkeley Castle.

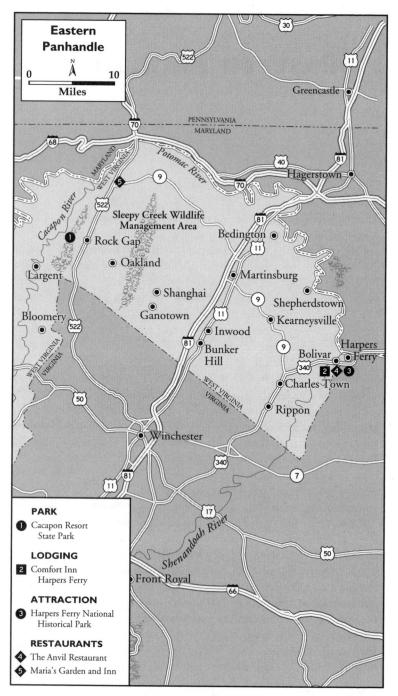

Eastern Panhandle

N

0   10

Miles

Greencastle

PENNSYLVANIA
MARYLAND

Potomac River

Hagerstown

Cacapon River

Sleepy Creek Wildlife Management Area

Bedington

Rock Gap

Oakland

Martinsburg

Largent

Shanghai

Shepherdstown

Ganotown

Kearneysville

Bloomery

Inwood

Harpers Ferry

Bunker Hill

Bolivar

WEST VIRGINIA
VIRGINIA

Charles Town

Rippon

Winchester

Front Royal

Shenandoah River

PARK

❶ Cacapon Resort State Park

LODGING

❷ Comfort Inn Harpers Ferry

ATTRACTION

❸ Harpers Ferry National Historical Park

RESTAURANTS

❹ The Anvil Restaurant

❺ Maria's Garden and Inn

How to Get Information before You Go

Travel Berkeley Springs, Inc., 304 Fairfax Street, Berkeley Springs, WV 25411; (800) 447-8797 or (304) 258-9147; www.berkeleysprings.com.

Jefferson County Convention & Visitor Bureau, P.O. Box A, Harpers Ferry, WV 25425; (800) 848- 8687 or (304) 535-2627; www.jeffersoncountycvb.com/main.htm.

Martinsburg–Berkeley County Convention & Visitors Bureau, 208 South Queen Street, Martinsburg, WV 25401; (800) 498-2386 or (304) 264-8801; www.travelwv.com.

The Best Park

Cacapon Resort State Park. (See also West Virginia's State Park Resorts.) This park has some advanced hiking and bridle trails, plus a road that climbs 1,400 feet to the mountain summit. Spur trails lead to large rock outcrops and nifty valley views. Cacapon Lake beckons swimmers, anglers, and boaters; rowboats and paddle boats can be rented on site. Also, tennis, volleyball, and basketball courts are available, and during summer ranger-led guided hikes, slide shows, movies, and craft workshops are offered. Overnight accommodations include a modern lodge, cottages, and campgrounds; Route 1, Box 304, Berkeley Springs; (304) 258-1022; www.cacaponresort.com.

Family Outdoor Adventures

Cross-Country Skiing. Coolfront Resort offers trails and equipment rentals, as well as snowtubing; 1777 Cold Run Valley Road, Berkeley Springs; (800) 888-8768 or (304) 258-4500; www.coolfront.com.

Hiking. The Appalachian Trail passes near Harpers Ferry; (304) 535-6331.

Horseback Riding. Coolfront Resort's Triple "C" Outfitters stages trail rides aimed at beginner and intermediate riders; 1777 Cold Run Valley Road, Berkeley Springs; (800) 888-8768 or (304) 258-4500; www.coolfront.com. Homestead Farms Riding Stable offers western-style trail rides; Thatcher Road, Martinsburg; (304) 267-6584.

Paddling. Blue Ridge Outfitters leads trips through Class II and III rapids on the Shenandoah River and half-day trips down the Potomac; Route 340, Charles Town; (304) 725-3444 or (304) 725-3445. River Riders runs trips on the Shenandoah by raft, canoe, kayak, ducky, or tube; Alstadts Hill, Harpers Ferry; (800) 326-7238 or (304) 535-2663.

Family Lodging

Cacapon Lodge

(See also West Virginia's State Park Resorts.) 50 rooms and 30 cabins highlight this state park lodge. Rates: $59–70 rooms; cabins $330–660 per week. Route 1, Box 304, Berkeley Springs; (304) 258-1022.

Comfort Inn Harpers Ferry

This AAA-rated three-diamond, 50-unit motel sets just a mile from the national historic park. There's no pool, but swimming isn't far away. Rates: $66–90 with continental breakfast. Route 340 and Union Street, P.O. Box 16, Harpers Ferry; (800) 228-5150 or (304) 535-6391.

Attraction

Harpers Ferry National Historical Park

P.O. Box 65, Harpers Ferry; (304) 535-6298; www.nps.gov/hafe

Hours: Memorial Day–Labor Day, daily 8 a.m.–6 p.m.; Labor
  Day–Memorial Day, daily 8 a.m.–5 p.m.; closed Christmas Day

Admission: $5 per vehicle or $3 per person for cyclists and pedestrians
  for three-day pass

Appeal by Age Groups:

Pre-school	Grade School	Teens	Young Adults	Over 30	Seniors
★★	★★★★	★★★★	★★★★★	★★★★★	★★★★★

Touring Time: Average 4 hours, minimum 2 hours

Rainy-Day Touring: Yes

Services and Facilities:

Restaurants No	Lockers No
Alcoholic beverages No	Pet kennels No
Disabled access Yes	Rain check No
Wheelchair rental Yes; free	Private tours No
Baby stroller rental No	

Description and Comments   The park lies at the confluence of the Potomac and Shenandoah Rivers, and actually sits in three states: West Virginia, Virginia, and Maryland. Although most famous for abolitionist John Brown's raid on the federal arsenal here, the town was the site of much history. The first successful application of interchangeable manufacturing, the completion of the first successful American railroad, the Civil War's largest surrender of Federal troops, and the education of former slaves in one of the earliest integrated schools in the United States all took place here. Start at the visitors center, then take a bus to Lower Town. Among the installations there are: Industry Museum, Restoration Museum, Wetlands Exhibit, John Brown Museum and Fort, Storer College Museum, Black Voices Museum, Civil War Museum, Harper House, and Jefferson Rock. Living History Exhibits open on a seasonal basis.

If your kids are good walkers, climb to Maryland Heights, 1,448 feet above the rivers. You're rewarded with great views and some surprising Civil War fortification ruins. Also, take advantage of the ranger-led tours offered daily Memorial Day–Labor Day. The tours are themed (i.e., John Brown's Raid, It's Civil War, Stories of Camp Hill, etc.) and will greatly enrich your experience here.

Family-Friendly Restaurants

THE ANVIL RESTAURANT

1270 Washington Street, Harpers Ferry; (304) 535-2582

Meals served: Lunch and dinner
Cuisine: Steaks and seafood
Entree range: $4.95–9.95
Children's menu: Yes
Reservations: Yes
Payment: Major credit cards

This pleasant place sports a rustic atmosphere—fireplace, brick walls—and antiques. The food is good, as are the kids' menu choices, which include crab cakes, pizza, burgers, pasta, sandwiches, and Kentucky Derby pie for dessert.

MARIA'S GARDEN AND INN

201 Independence Street, Berkeley Springs; (888) 629-2253 or (304) 258-2021

Meals served: Lunch and dinner
Cuisine: Italian and sandwiches
Entree range: $7.95–14.95
Children's menu: Yes
Reservations: No
Payment: Major credit cards

In the heart of town, this quaint spot offers real homemade American-Italian cuisine: pasta, seafood, salads, soups, subs, pizzas, and desserts. Real local stuff and real friendly folks.

Mountaineer Country

This area, the north-central part of the state, is home to the state university, pioneer forts, covered bridges, and some excellent trails and paddling opportunities. In **Morgantown** take a ride on the **PRT—Personal Rapid Transit** (call (304) 293-5011), a driver-less monorail that connects West Virginia University's three campuses and downtown; behind-the-scenes tours are offered. The **Cook-Hayman Pharmacy Museum** (call (304) 293-5101) at the WVU School of Pharmacy displays a typical nineteenth-century drugstore. West of Morgantown, the **Henry Clay Iron Furnace** (call (304) 594-1561), a 30-foot stone pyramid circa 1834, is found in **Bruceton Mills,** within Coopers Rock State Forest; it's the last vestige of the state's smelting industry. In the **Fairmont** area, the **West Augusta Historical Society Round Barn** (call (304) 986-2636 or (304) 986-1089) is not only a unique structure but also exhibits old-fashioned tools and farming equipment. South of Fairmont in **Salem, Fort New Salem** (call (304) 782-5245) presents a reconstructed frontier settlement with living history programs. The **West Virginia Northern Railroad** (call (800) 253-1065) runs scenic and historic excursions out of **Kingwood.** And **Terra Alta,** in the east-central part of the region, is home to the **Americana Museum** (call (304) 789-2361), which features an old-fashioned doctor's office, country store, carriage house, and blacksmith shop. In the northeastern corner of the region stands **Arthurdale,** the first "New Deal" town; the **Arthurdale Historic District** (call (304) 864-3959 or (304) 864-6659) includes a museum dedicated to that federal homesteading project. South of Clarksburg, the **Simpson Phillippi Creek Covered Bridge** can be found in **Barrackville** at the junction of U.S. 250 and WV 32.

How to Get There

By Car. North-south bound I-79 and east-west bound I-68 meet in Morgantown at the north central part of the region. I-79 continues south

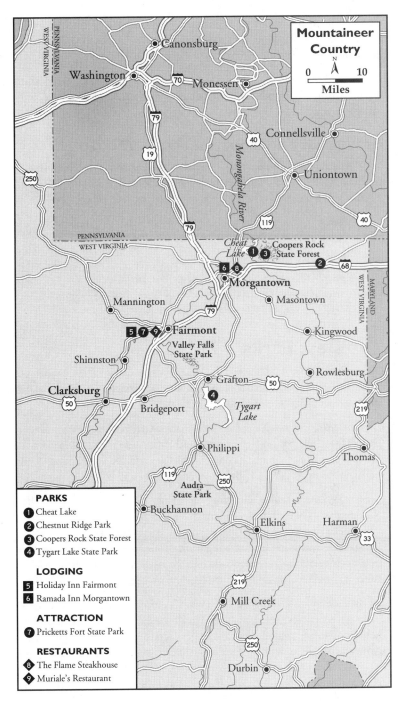

Mountaineer Country

N

0 ——— 10

Miles

PENNSYLVANIA
WEST VIRGINIA

Canonsburg

Washington

70

Monessen

79

19

250

40

Connellsville

Uniontown

40

PENNSYLVANIA
WEST VIRGINIA

79

119

Monongahela River

Cheat Lake ❶ ❸ Coopers Rock State Forest

❻ ❽ ❷ 68

Morgantown

Mannington

Masontown

WEST VIRGINIA
MARYLAND

79

❺ ❼ ❾ Fairmont

Kingwood

Valley Falls State Park

Shinnston

Clarksburg

50

Bridgeport

Grafton

50

❹ *Tygart Lake*

Rowlesburg

219

Philippi

Thomas

119

Audra State Park

250

Buckhannon

Elkins

Harman

33

219

Mill Creek

250

Durbin

PARKS

❶ Cheat Lake
❷ Chestnut Ridge Park
❸ Coopers Rock State Forest
❹ Tygart Lake State Park

LODGING

❺ Holiday Inn Fairmont
❻ Ramada Inn Morgantown

ATTRACTION

❼ Pricketts Fort State Park

RESTAURANTS

❽ The Flame Steakhouse
❾ Muriale's Restaurant

through the region's heart past Fairmont, Clarksburg, and Bridgeport. U.S. 50 runs east-west along the southern part of the region, also passing through Clarksburg and Bridgeport.

By Plane. Morgantown Municipal Airport offers daily USAirways shuttle service from Pittsburgh and Washington National; 389 Spruce Street, Morgantown; (304) 291-7461.

How to Get Information before You Go

Bridgeport-Clarksburg Convention & Visitors Bureau, Eastpointe Business Park, 109 Platinum Drive, Bridgeport, WV 26330; (800) 368-4324 or (304) 842-7272; www.bridgeport-clarksburg.com.

Marion County Convention & Visitors Bureau, 110 Adams Street, Fairmont, WV 26555; (800) 834-7365 or (304)368-1123; www.marioncvb.com.

Greater Morgantown Convention & Visitors Bureau, 709 Beechurst Avenue, Seneca Center, Morgantown, WV 26505; (800) 458-7373 or (304) 292-5081; www.mgtn.com.

The Best Parks

Cheat Lake. This 1,730-acre lake near Morgantown offers canoe, pontoon, power boat, and ski boat rentals and food service; Edgewater Marina, Morgantown; (304) 594-2630.

Chestnut Ridge Park. Near Cooper's Rock State Forest, Cheat Lake, and Cheat River, this park offers wooded and streamside trails, cabins, a nature center, recreation programs, fishing, swimming, and the Sand Springs Camping Area; Route 1, Box 267, Bruceton Mills; (304) 594-1773.

Coopers Rock State Forest. Covering more than 12,700 acres, this park holds a campground for both tents and trailers, a playground, and a "trading post" with snack bar. Recreational offerings include fishing, hiking, cross-country skiing, and swimming and boating at the Buffalo Lake Recreational Area. Trolling motorboats, paddleboats, and aqua cycles are available for rent; Route 1, Box 270, Bruceton Mills; (304) 594-1561 or (304) 745-4000.

Tygart Lake State Park. (See also West Virginia's State Park Resorts.) A 2,134-acre park centered on an 11-mile lake. Extensive water activities include boating, fishing, water skiing, scuba diving, and swimming; the marina offers boat rentals. Extensive hiking trails are complemented by other recreational activities—game courts, playgrounds, and a nearby golf course, as well as summer nature programs and guided hikes; Route 1, Box 260, Grafton; (304) 265-3383.

Family Outdoor Adventures

Biking. Caperton and Decker's Creek Trail extends through three counties with 51 miles of easily accessible trails for excellent biking; trails are paved in Morgantown and crushed limestone or packed sand beyond; (304) 292-5081. McTrail, a 2.5-mile path running from Pricketts Fort State Park to downtown Fairmont, is highlighted by a lighted tunnel; (304) 363-7037. North Bend Rail Trail runs 72 miles to North Bend State Park and passes through ten tunnels along the way; Harrisville; (304)643-2931.

Camping. Tygart Lake State Park (see The Best Parks, above) has a 40-site campground open late April–late October.

Hiking. Core Arboretum, part of WVU, offers annotated hiking trails with varied species of trees, shrubs, and wildflowers; WVU Department of Biology, Morgantown; (304) 293-5201. West Fork River Rail Trail runs 16 miles from Fairmont to Shinnston beside the West Fork River; (304) 363-7037 or (304) 592-0177.

Paddling. Adventures on Magic River operates guided kayak tours that emphasize local ecology and history, telling tales about the storied past of the Monongahela River; children age 12 and under paddle for half price; 200 Wagner Road, Morgantown; (877) 338-9003 or (304) 276-8306; www.magicriverwv.com. Appalachian Wildwaters, operating from multiple locations, is one of the largest white-water outfitters in the East; here they run trips on the Cheat and Tygart Rivers in Class III and IV whitewater in rafts or duckies; special kids' rates are available, and their Cheat River Outdoor Center in Rowlesburg offers dormitory-style lodging and tent camping sites; P.O. Box 100-CH, Rowlesburg; (800) 624-8060 or (304) 454-2476; www.awrafts.com.

Family Lodging

Holiday Inn Fairmont

This pleasant 106-room facility is located halfway between Morgantown and Clarksburg, allowing a relatively short drive to a number of state parks. The motel has a pool; in-room coffee, refrigerators, and movies; and an on-site family restaurant. Rates: $69–109. 930 East Grafton Road, Fairmont; (304) 366-5500.

Ramada Inn Morgantown

A 153-room hotel with full amenities—heated pool, cable TV, on-site restaurant—plus some nice kid-friendly touches like basketball and horseshoes courts. It's conveniently located just outside town with easy access to I-68. Rates: $75–115. U.S. 119, P.O. Box 1242, Morgantown; (304) 296-3431.

Tygart Lake State Park

See West Virginia's State Park Resorts. Twenty rooms plus cabins, a restaurant, and supervised children's programs in the summer. Rates: rooms $55–65; cabins $420–550 per week; children age 13 and under stay free. Route 1, Box 260, Grafton; (304) 265-3383; www.tygartlake.com.

Attraction

Pricketts Fort State Park

Pricketts Fort Memorial Foundation, Route 3, Box 407, Fairmont; (304) 363-3030; www.wvparks.com/prickettsfort

Hours: Historical attractions: mid-April–October, Monday–Saturday 10 a.m.–5 p.m., Sunday noon–5 p.m.; other park facilities open year-round

Admission: Historical attractions: $5 adults, $4.50 seniors 54+, $2.50 children ages 6–12; state park facilities: free

Appeal by Age Groups:

Pre-school	Grade School	Teens	Young Adults	Over 30	Seniors
★★	★★★★	★★★★	★★★★★	★★★★★	★★★★★

Touring Time: Average 3 hours, minimum 2 hours

Rainy-Day Touring: Yes

Services and Facilities:

Restaurants No	Lockers No
Alcoholic beverages No	Pet kennels No
Disabled access Yes	Rain check No
Wheelchair rental No	Private tours No
Baby stroller rental No	

Description and Comments   This rustic log fort is a re-creation of the original 1774 Pricketts Fort, which served as a refuge from Indian war parties on the western frontier of Colonial Virginia. Living history is the main attraction here. Costumed interpreters relate late-eighteenth-century life and demonstrate colonial crafts. Start in the visitors center with the introductory video, then take in the exhibits of pioneer and Native American artifacts. When you head out to the fort and the Prickett House, you'll encounter the guide interpreters who will fill you in on what you're seeing and what activities you can see that day. Among the craftspeople at work at any given time: basket makers, musicians, cloth dyers, militiamen, blacksmiths, spinners, and weavers. There's also a gun shop that features public demonstrations of eighteenth-century firearms. Also of note: in

June and July, the West Virginia Shakespeare Festival is in residence here, performing free in the park's amphitheater.

Family-Friendly Restaurants

THE FLAME STEAKHOUSE

76 High Street, Morgantown; (304) 296-2976

Meals served: Dinner
Cuisine: Steaks, seafood, and Italian
Entree range: $6.95–24.95
Children's menu: Yes
Reservations: Yes
Payment: Major credit cards

This local favorite in a historic house with separate and differently themed dining rooms serves excellent steaks and superb lamb chops.

MURIALE'S RESTAURANT

1742 Fairmont Avenue Extension, Fairmont; (304) 363-3190

Meals served: Lunch and dinner
Cuisine: Italian
Entree range: $6.95–16.95 (lunch and dinner)
Children's menu: Yes
Reservations: No
Payment: Major credit cards

Homemade pasta and sauces are the thing here, but you can get a steak if you must. In summer, dine on the deck overlooking the Tiger River.

Potomac Highlands

This region comprises the back side of Virginia's Blue Ridge and is equally an outdoors paradise. Huge tracts of preserved wilderness, the state's highest elevations, some of its largest caverns, and mile upon mile of hiking, equestrian, and ski trails pervade the area. There are history and mountain arts here, too, of course—and some fine four-season resorts at which to enjoy it all.

Starting in **Romney,** a town in the north-central part of the region, the **Potomac Eagle Excursion Train** (call (800) 223-2453 or (304) 822-7464), rides through the remote South Branch Valley on weekends April–September and daily during the October foliage season. **The Bottling Works** (call (304) 822-4783), open on a similar schedule, shows an unusual collection of Coca-Cola and soda pop memorabilia. Moving south, the **Country Store Opry** (call (304) 257-1743) in **Petersburg** showcases country music and touts itself as the "Country Music Capital of the Potomac Highlands," offering shows on alternate Saturdays April–December. In **Lost River,** the **Lost River General Store** (call (304) 897-6169) is an arts and crafts cooperative that displays and sells the work of top regional artisans, and in **Elkins** the **Augusta Heritage Center** (call (304) 637-1209) at Davis & Elkins College features **USA Folk Arts for Kids,** public performances in all the arts aimed at children ages 8–12. **Artists at Work** (call (304) 637-6309), another co-op, offers more crafts and fine art. Down in **Durbin,** toward the region's south-central section, another train—the **Durbin and Greenbrier Valley Railroad** (call (304) 456-4935)—offers scenic looks at the Greenbrier Valley April–November. In addition, the **West Virginia Central Railroad** (call (877) 676-7245) travels through mountain wilderness to Big Cut May–late October. The **National Radio Astronomy Observatory** (call (304) 456-2011), found a few miles away in **Green Bank,** has a set of huge radio telescopes that can be visited on a narrated bus tour mid-June–October. And, a more earthly anomaly is found at **Ice**

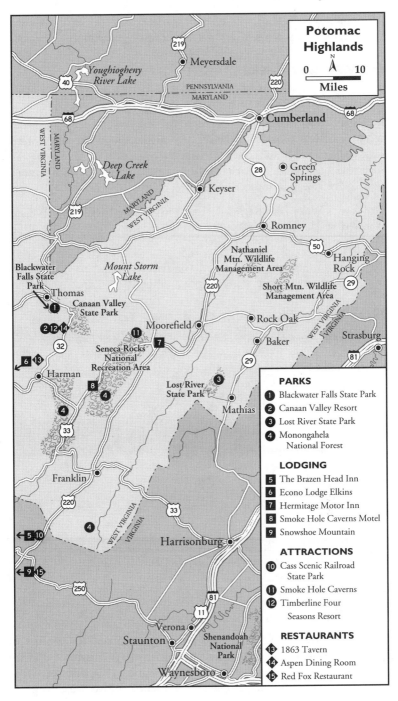

Potomac Highlands

N

0   10

Miles

PARKS

① Blackwater Falls State Park
② Canaan Valley Resort
③ Lost River State Park
④ Monongahela National Forest

LODGING

5 The Brazen Head Inn
6 Econo Lodge Elkins
7 Hermitage Motor Inn
8 Smoke Hole Caverns Motel
9 Snowshoe Mountain

ATTRACTIONS

⑩ Cass Scenic Railroad State Park
⑪ Smoke Hole Caverns
⑫ Timberline Four Seasons Resort

RESTAURANTS

⑬ 1863 Tavern
⑭ Aspen Dining Room
⑮ Red Fox Restaurant

Mountain (call (304) 345-4350) in **Slanesville,** where the terrain keeps ice on the mountain year-round and spawns unusual vegetation.

How to Get There

By Car. No interstate highways here. You can access Romney and the northern sections from I-81 in Virginia by taking U.S. 50 west; U.S. 33 meanders east-west through the center of the region. Traveling north-south, U.S. 220 runs down the region's middle about two-thirds of the way, while U.S. 219 runs down the western edge, drifting toward the center at the area's southern reaches. WV 28 runs north-south from centrally located Petersburg to southern Marlinton.

By Plane. Cumberland Regional Airport in the Keyser/Ridgley, MD, area is served by US Air Express and Crown Airways; Route 1, Box 99, Wiley Ford, WV 26767; (304) 738-0002.

By Train. To the north, Amtrak offers service into Harpers Ferry; to the south, trains serve White Sulphur Springs; (800) 872-7245.

How to Get Information before You Go

Elkins-Randolph County Chamber of Commerce & Convention & Visitors Bureau, 200 Executive Plaza, Elkins, WV 26241; (800) 422-3304 or (304) 636-2717; www.randolphcountywv.com.

Tucker County Convention & Visitors Bureau, William Avenue, P.O. Box 565, Davis, WV 26260; (800) 782-2775 or (304) 259-5315.

Mineral County Convention & Visitors Bureau, Route 220 South, Polish Pine Business Complex, Suite 24, Keyser, WV 26726; (304) 788-2513.

Pocahontas County Tourism Commission, 700 4th Avenue, P.O. Box 275, Marlinton, WV 24945; (800) 336-7009 or (304) 799-4636.

West Virginia Mountain Highlands Travel Council, 1200 Harrison Avenue, Lower Level, Suite A, Elkins, WV 26241; (304) 636-8400; www.mountainhighlands.com.

The Best Parks

Blackwater Falls State Park. (See also West Virginia's State Park Resorts.) Set in a west-central locale, this park offers a bit of everything: more than ten miles of hiking trails, a riding stable that is open May–October for guided rides, a nature center, fishing on the stocked Blackwater River, a bicycling center with rental bikes, swimming and boating at Pendleton Lake (including rental boats), and tennis, volleyball, and basketball (equipment can be supplied); P.O. Drawer 490, Davis; (304) 259-5216; www.blackwaterfalls.com.

Canaan Valley Resort & Conference Center. (See also West Virginia's State Park Resorts.) Another place that has it all, also in the west-central area: 18 miles of hiking and/or mountain biking trails linked with hundreds of miles of trails in the Monongahela National Forest, a fly-fishing school, guided white-water rafting on the Cheat River, scenic summer chairlift rides, and an organized children's day camp program. In winter, full alpine and Nordic ski centers, ice skating, and snow-tubing are offered. Plus, the place has a complete spa and fitness club, an indoor lap pool, sauna, and a championship golf course; HC 70, Box 330, Davis; (800) 622-4121 or (304) 866-4121; www.canaanresort.com.

Lost River State Park. On the east-central side of the region, this park has hiking trails, a swimming pool, tennis courts, volleyball courts, an archery range, badminton and horseshoe facilities, and riding stables. Equipment can be rented for a nominal fee. Cabins are available for overnight stays; Route 2, Box 24, Mathias; (304) 897-5372; www.lostriversp.com.

Monongahela National Forest. Spreading over more than 900,000 acres in the region's center, the Forest contains the Spruce Knob–Seneca Rocks National Recreation Area. Altogether, there are untold miles of hiking trails, plenty of camping, boat rentals, fishing, swimming, rock climbing, picnicking, and cross-country skiing; 200 Sycamore Street, Elkins; (304) 636-1800.

Family Outdoor Adventures

Cross-Country Skiing. White Grass has 45 trails covering 50 kilometers— some groomed, some not—plus equipment rentals; HC 70, Box 299, Davis; (304) 866-4114. Elk River Touring Center grooms 10 kilometers of trails and offers access to 35 kilometers of ungroomed terrain, plus equipment rentals and instruction; HC 69, Box 7, Slatyfork; (304) 572-3771; www.ertc.com.

Hiking. Greenbrier River Trail is a 76-mile former railroad bed that meanders through small towns, over some 35 bridges, and into 2 tunnels, connecting Greenbrier and Seneca State Forests and the Watoga and Cass Scenic Railroad State Parks; North Caldwell and Cass; (304)799-4087.

Seneca Rocks is a 900-foot-tall strata of Tuscarora sandstone dating to the Silurian Age set within the Monongahela National Forest; considered by many climbers to be the best climb in the East, there's also a visitors center that shows an audiovisual presentation with instructions for hiking to the top of the rocks; Seneca Rocks; (304) 567-2827 or (304) 257-4488.

Horseback Riding. Mountain View Stables offers guided outings; (304) 335-4793. Yokum's Seneca Rocks Stables mounts rides to the top of Seneca Rocks; Route 28 North, Seneca Rocks; (304) 567-2466. Lost River State Park and Blackwater Falls State Park (see The Best Parks, above).

Mountain Biking. Elk River Touring Center offers multiday tours and local riding maps to plan your own ride; HC 69, Box 7, Slatyfork; (304) 572-3771; www.ertc.com. Snowshoe Resort, Canaan Valley Resort, and Timberline Mountain Resort (see Attractions).

Paddling. Eagle's Nest Outfitters stages guided day or overnight canoe and fishing trips with shuttle service; P.O. Box 731, Route 220, Petersburg; (304) 257-2393. Trough General Store rents canoes for use on the South Branch of the Potomac River; River Road, Romney; (304) 822-7601.

Family Lodging

The Brazen Head Inn

Located six miles from Snowshoe Resort, this new 20-room, log cabin–style guesthouse sets on 6.5 acres and offers 8 doubles and 12 quads, all with private baths. Second-floor rooms have kid-friendly sleeping lofts. It's furnished with antiques, and handmade quilts adorn the beds (some are four-posters). The gift shop sells West Virginia–made crafts. You'll also enjoy a public sitting room with a TV and surrounding outdoor deck. The dining room/restaurant serves breakfast, Friday and Saturday night buffets, and Sunday brunch for guests. Rates: $75–90 summer, $100–125; two-night minimum on weekends; breakfast is extra. Route 219, HC 69, Box 28A, Mingo; (304) 339-6917.

Canaan Valley Resort and Conference Center

(See also West Virginia's State Park Resorts.) Lodge in cottages or the modern lodge—273 rooms in all. Full services are available, plus a plethora of activities and unbeatable scenery. Rates: $64–104; suites from $119; cabins from $565–879 weekly; family packages available. Canaan Valley State Park, HC 70, Box 330, Davis; (800) 622-4121 or (304) 866-4121.

Econo Lodge Elkins

This basic but clean and pleasant motel has an indoor pool. Rates: $45–70. 4533 U.S. 33 East, Elkins; (304) 636-5311.

Hermitage Motor Inn

This small (39 rooms), converted 1840s inn has a pool and is a pleasant and different alternative to your typical motel. Rates: $50. 203 Virginia Avenue, P.O. Box 1077, Petersburg; (304) 257-1711.

Smoke Hole Caverns Motel

A full-service motel and cabins at the caverns. The motel rooms and cabins have air-conditioning; free HBO, ESPN, and Disney Channel; fully equipped kitchens; and fireplaces or wood-burning stoves. Kids will love swimming in the Olympic-size pool. Rates: $49–79, motel rooms; $149–249, cabins that sleep six; children age 12 and under stay free; weekly rates available. HC 59, Box 39, Seneca Rocks; (800) 828-8478 or (304) 257-4442.

Snowshoe Mountain

A full range of condominiums, plus the 148-room Inn at Snowshoe, with all the expected resort facilities. Rates: $130–217 condos; $70–140 Inn at Snowshoe rooms. Various winter and summer package plans available. P.O. Box 10, 10 Snowshoe Road, Snowshoe; (877) 441-4FUN or (304) 572-1000; www.snowshoemtn.net.

Attractions

Cass Scenic Railroad State Park/Historic District

WV 28/92, Cass; (304) 456-4300

Hours: Train departs Cass to Whittaker (1½-hour trip): Memorial Day–Labor Day and October 1–mid-October, daily 10:50 a.m., 1 p.m., and 3 p.m.; September and mid-October–end of October, Friday–Sunday, 10:50 a.m., 1 p.m., and 3 p.m. Train departs Cass to Bald Knob (4½-hour trip): Memorial Day–Labor Day, daily noon; October 1–mid-October, Tuesday–Sunday noon; September and mid-October–end of October, Friday–Sunday noon

Admission: Cass to Whittaker: $12 weekdays and $14 weekends adults; $7 weekdays and $9 weekends children ages 5–12; Cass to Bald Knob: $16/$18 adults, $9/$11 children

Appeal by Age Groups:

Pre-school	Grade School	Teens	Young Adults	Over 30	Seniors
★★★	★★★★	★★★★	★★★★	★★★★★	★★★★★

Touring Time: Average 3 hours, minimum 2 hours

Rainy-Day Touring: Yes

Services and Facilities:

Restaurants Yes	Lockers No
Alcoholic beverages No	Pet kennels No
Disabled access Yes	Rain check No
Wheelchair rental No	Private tours No
Baby stroller rental No	

Description and Comments This is for anyone who harbors the least bit of interest in classic steam trains and beautiful scenery. Antique lumber trains adapted to carry passengers are pulled by massive Shay steam locomotives to the summit of Bald Knob, the state's second-highest peak. At Cass stands a turn-of-the-century town, one of the country's best preserved lumber company towns, where the local museum tells the town's history, and the country store fills souvenir and shopping needs. Then, at Whittaker Station, four miles up the track, you tour a recreated logging camp. Check out the Lidgerwood tower skidder—one of only two left in the world—a machine that carried logs on high-flung aerial cables.

Smoke Hole Caverns

HC 59, Box 39, Seneca Rocks; (800) 828-8478 or (304) 257-4442; www.smokehole.com

Hours: Memorial Day–Labor Day, daily 8:30 a.m.–7:30 p.m.; Labor Day–Memorial Day, daily 9 a.m.–5 p.m.

Admission: $7.50 adults, $5 children ages 5–12

Appeal by Age Groups:

Pre-school	Grade School	Teens	Young Adults	Over 30	Seniors
★★★	★★★★	★★★★★	★★★★★	★★★★★	★★★★★

Touring Time: Average 2½ hours, minimum 1 hour

Rainy-Day Touring: Yes

Services and Facilities:

Restaurants Yes	Lockers No
Alcoholic beverages No	Pet kennels Yes
Disabled access No	Rain check No
Wheelchair rental No	Private tours No
Baby stroller rental No	

Description and Comments 45-minute guided cavern tours leave every half hour and explore some unique formations. The Crystal Cave Coral Pool is reputed to be found in only one other cavern worldwide, and the Sparkling Room of a Million Stalactites stands 274 feet high. But probably the kids will best remember the six-ton World's Largest Ribbon Stalactite—it's big, very big.

Snowshoe Mountain

10 Snowshoe Road, P.O. Box 10, Snowshoe; (877) 441-4386 or (304) 572-1000; www.snowshoemtn.net

Hours: Vary by season and activity

Admission: Varies by season and activity

Appeal by Age Groups:

Pre-school	Grade School	Teens	Young Adults	Over 30	Seniors
★★★★★	★★★★★	★★★★★	★★★★★	★★★★★	★★★★★

Rainy-Day Touring: Yes

Services and Facilities:

Restaurants Yes

Alcoholic beverages Yes

Disabled access Yes

Wheelchair rental No

Baby stroller rental No

Lockers Yes

Pet kennels No

Rain check No

Private tours No

Description and Comments   Snowshoe refers to itself as "an upside-down mountain" because its "base" facilities are actually at the top. Unusual, true, but this resort is operated by the same company that operates such international giants as Whistler-Blackcomb in British Columbia and Mont Tremblant in Quebec. It's a first-class operation in every sense. In summer, activities cover the full gamut, from the expected—mountain biking, hiking, horseback riding, scenic chairlift rides, and full water activities at Shavers Lake, located at the bottom of the hill—to the unusual—the Outpost Adventure Park, which includes a skate park for in-liners or skateboarders, a BMX bike race track, and a rock climbing facility; Snowshoe's Sporting Clays, a shooting sport with instruction for all ages; fly-fishing instruction; and, perhaps most unique, something called Amphibious ATV Tours, in which six folks climb into a Hydro Traxx Amphibious ATV and not only tour the mountain but also head onto the lake. And if that isn't thrilling enough, there's bungy jumping, too. A Kids' Night Out program is offered on Saturday evenings for children ages 6–12; activities include natural history hikes, scavenger hunts, stream exploration, a cookout, campfires, and storytelling.

In winter, the resort offers skiing and snowboarding on 56 trails with 11 lifts. A nice adjunct for families is Ruckus Ridge Adventure Park, where you'll find snow-tubing, night skiing, an elaborate terrain park, and the winter version of Kids' Night Out. "Kids' World" is a separate facility for younger children that offers its own ticket sales, rentals, and lessons. Another cool program is "Night Moves," an evening program in which any first-time rider age seven and up can try snowboarding for two hours. A full childcare facility is also offered.

Timberline Four Seasons Resort

488 Timberline Road, Canaan Valley; (800) 766-9464;
   www.timberlineresort.com

Hours: Vary by season and activity

Admission: Varies by season and activity

Appeal by Age Groups:

Pre-school	Grade School	Teens	Young Adults	Over 30	Seniors
★★★★★	★★★★★	★★★★★	★★★★★	★★★★★	★★★★★

Rainy-Day Touring: Yes

Services and Facilities:

Restaurants Yes	Lockers Yes
Alcoholic beverages Yes	Pet kennels No
Disabled access Yes	Rain check No
Wheelchair rental No	Private tours No
Baby stroller rental No	

Description and Comments   Somewhat smaller than Snowshoe, Timber-line still offers all the four-season resort facilities and programs we've come to expect from a top ski resort. Their Mountain Biking Center is particularly active, offering programs for novices to experts, including scenic trails that beginners can handle. There is horseback riding, too, plus scenic chairlift rides, white-water rafting, hiking, and camping. The resort also houses Noah's Ark Petting Zoo.

Winter facilities include almost 100 acres of skiable terrain on 35 slopes. For kids, it's "Timber's Adventure Klub" (TAK), a full-day program for children ages four to seven with coaching, lunch, equipment rental, and indoor activities. The Mountain Safari program serves ages 8–12, and there's also a licensed day care on site for infants and young children. Lodging here comprises fully equipped condominiums and homes.

Family-Friendly Restaurants

1863 TAVERN

U.S. Route 33, Elkins; (304) 636-1400

Meals served: Dinner
Cuisine: American
Entree range: $9.95–19.95
Children's menu: Yes
Reservations: Yes
Payment: Major credit cards

The early American theme is perfect for presenting classic American food. The cinnamon rolls are special.

ASPEN DINING ROOM

Canaan Valley Resort & Conference Center, Canaan Valley State Park, HC 70, Box 330, Davis; (800) 622-4121 or (304) 866-4121

Meals served: Breakfast, lunch, and dinner
Cuisine: Continental and New American
Entree range: $8.95–19.95 (lunch and dinner)
Children's menu: Yes
Reservations: Yes
Payment: Major credit cards

The food here, like everything else at this terrific resort, is excellent— almost as good as the mountain views. The resort also has a coffee shop, if you're looking for something a little less formal. The large buffet is always a popular choice with all ages.

RED FOX RESTAURANT

Snowshoe Road, Snowshoe Resort, Snowshoe; (304) 572-1111

Meals served: Lunch and dinner
Cuisine: Continental
Entree range: $4.95–29 (lunch and dinner)
Children's menu: Yes
Reservations: Yes
Payment: Major credit cards

A long-time Snowshoe favorite that showcases some nifty mountain views. If you're feeling West Virginian, try one of the wild game dishes. If not, the steaks are good, too.

Central West Virginia

The Mountain Lakes region sits smack in the middle of the state, offering the expected mountain terrain plus a handful of lakes for excellent water play. History, of course, is an important ingredient, and it's often combined here with the scenery by way of a train ride. In the northern reaches the **Jackson's Mill Historic Area Historic District** (call (304) 269-5100) in **Weston** encompasses the Jackson Family Mill Museum (Stonewall Jackson's family, that is), a historic grist mill, and cabins. The **Central West Virginia Farmers Market** (call (304) 269-2667) is a fun shopping experience year-round. At the **Bulltown Historic District** (call (304) 452-8170 or (304) 853-2371) in **Burnsville,** a mile-long interpretive trail spans the Civil War—remnants of Union trenches and Bulltown Battlefield—with a restored turn-of-the-century farm, log cabins, and a church, including displays of early 1800s memorabilia and battle artifacts. Another of the state's covered bridges is found in **Walkersville,** this one just 39 feet long, but built in 1903.

The Mid-Ohio Valley occupies the west-central section of the state and is bordered on its western edge by the Ohio River. **Parkersburg,** the region's largest town, is a place to hop a paddleboat for an old-time river ride. **Ruble's Sternwheelers** (call (740) 423-7268) operates out of Belpre, Ohio, and from Parkersburg's Point Park, also offering service to Blennerhassett Island (see Attractions). The **Cultural Center of Fine Arts** (call (304) 485-3859) displays art of national and international stature and offers guided tours. The **Oil & Gas Museum** (call (304) 485-5446 or (304) 428-8015) chronicles Parkersburg's industrial heritage, showcasing equipment, photos, and video from the city's early days. Nearby, historic **Smoot Theatre** (call (304) 422-7529) was constructed in 1926 as a vaudeville house; today it stages family entertainment and special events. Although the **Lee Middleton Doll Factory** (call (800) 233-7479 or (740)

423-1481) lies across the river/state border in Belpre, Ohio, it's worth the side trip to watch vinyl transformed into collectible dolls.

Moving west, **Berdine's 5 & Dime** (call (304) 643-2217) in **Harrisville** purports to be the nation's oldest five-and-dime; true or not, the oak bins overflowing with toys and bulk candy are eye-catching. In **Boaz,** the **Early Americana Museum** (call (304) 375-7842) depicts early American life, and **Mountain State Muzzleloading Supplies** (call (304) 375-7482) offers a combination store and museum filled with early American firearms, clothing, and things like tomahawks and powder horns. Another unique shopping experience is found at **R.C. Marshall Hardware** (call (304) 628-3321) in **Cairo,** a spot that specializes in supplies for turn-of-the-last-century homesteaders and oil drillers, as well as modern-day travelers and campers. Heading south, the **Cedar Lakes Crafts Center** (call (304) 372-7860) in **Ripley** invites folks to participate in weekend and week-long workshops in everything from basketry and blacksmithing to painting and pottery making. It's also the site of the annual Mountain State Arts and Crafts Fair. And, in **Ravenswood, Washington's Lands Museum and Park** (call (304) 372-5343) looks at regional pioneer and river history.

HOW TO GET THERE

By Car. I-79 serves as the main north-south thoroughfare, running from the top of the Mountain Lakes about two-thirds of the way down from Jane Lew and Weston through Sutton. South of Sutton, U.S. 19 travels south to Summersville. U.S. 33 runs east-west at the top of Mountain Lakes, with WV 39 running the same at the southern end. U.S. 50 crosses east-west at the northern end of the Mid-Ohio Valley, while U.S. 33 crosses the south-central area, and I-77 runs north-south along the western edge of the region.

By Plane. Charleston/Yeager Airport is the nearest facility. It's served by Continental, USAirways, US Air Express, United Express, Atlantic Southeast, Comair, and Northwest Airlink. From there, rent a car and take I-77 and I-79 into the regions. 100 Airport Road, Charleston; (304) 344-8033.

By Train. Amtrak serves Charleston; (800) 872-7245.

HOW TO GET INFORMATION BEFORE YOU GO

Lewis County CVB, P.O. Box 379, 345 Center Avenue, Weston, WV 26452; (304) 269-7328; www.stonewallcountry.com.

Summersville Convention & Visitors Bureau, 411 Old Main Drive, Summersville, WV 26651; (304) 872-3722.

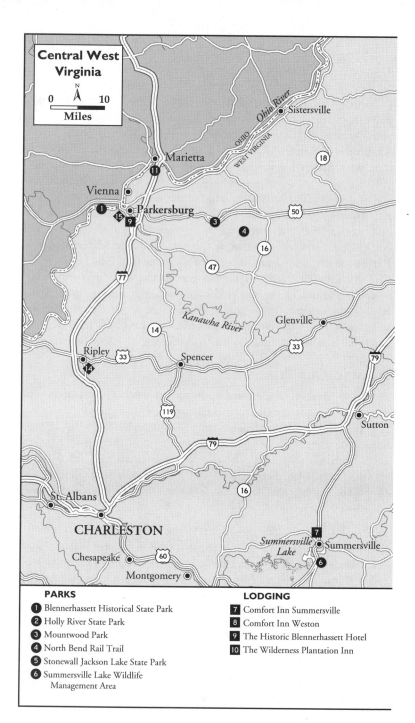

Central West Virginia

0 N 10
Miles

Sistersville

Ohio River

OHIO

WEST VIRGINIA

Marietta

11

Vienna

1

15

9

Parkersburg

3

50

4

18

16

47

77

Kanawha River

Glenville

14

33

33

Ripley

33

14

Spencer

79

119

Sutton

79

16

St. Albans

CHARLESTON

Chesapeake

60

Montgomery

Summersville Lake

7

Summersville

6

PARKS

1 Blennerhassett Historical State Park
2 Holly River State Park
3 Mountwood Park
4 North Bend Rail Trail
5 Stonewall Jackson Lake State Park
6 Summersville Lake Wildlife
Management Area

LODGING

7 Comfort Inn Summersville
8 Comfort Inn Weston
9 The Historic Blennerhassett Hotel
10 The Wilderness Plantation Inn

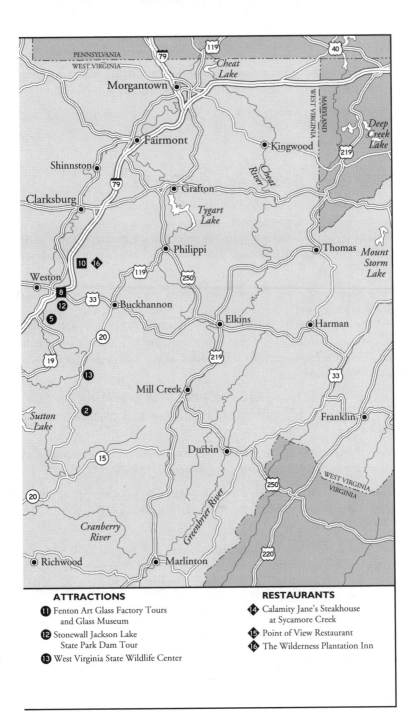

ATTRACTIONS

11 Fenton Art Glass Factory Tours
and Glass Museum

12 Stonewall Jackson Lake
State Park Dam Tour

13 West Virginia State Wildlife Center

RESTAURANTS

14 Calamity Jane's Steakhouse
at Sycamore Creek

15 Point of View Restaurant

16 The Wilderness Plantation Inn

Buckhannon/Upshur Convention & Visitors Bureau, 16 South Kanawha Street, Buckhannon, WV 26201; (304) 472-1722.

Parkersburg County CVB, 350 Seventh Street, Parkersburg, WV 26101; (800) 752-4982 or (304) 428-1130; www.parkersburgcvb.org.

The Best Beaches and Parks

Blennerhassett Historical State Park. (See Attractions.) This island park features a reconstructed eighteenth-century mansion and offers bike rentals, picnicking, guided mansion tours, horse-drawn wagon rides, and a traditional crafts village with demonstrations; 137 Juliana Street, Parkersburg; (304) 420-4800.

Holly River State Park. Encompassing more than 8,000 acres, this park offers a swimming pool; basketball, volleyball, and tennis courts; an archery range; and badminton, croquet, and horseshoe facilities. Camping, hiking, a trout-rearing pond, and a variety of ranger-led programs round out the experience; P.O. Box 70, Hacker Valley; (304) 493-6353; www.hollyriver.com.

Mountwood Park. Located about 12 miles east of Parkersburg, this 2,600-acre county park offers camping, hiking, boating, fishing, game courts, and a playground. Route 50 East, Parkersburg; (304) 679-3611.

North Bend Rail Trail. A scenic 71-mile hiking/biking/horseback riding trail that passes through ten tunnels; Cairo; (304) 643-2931.

Stonewall Jackson Lake State Park. (See Attractions.) Occupying 20,451 acres, this park is highlighted by a 26-mile lake; Route 1, Box 0, Roanoke; (304) 269-4588.

Summersville Lake Wildlife Management Area. Covering nearly 6,000 acres in the southern reaches of the Mountain Lakes Region, this heavily forested reserve offers fishing, picnicking, camping, and hiking. RR 2, Box 470, Summersville; (304) 872-5809.

Family Outdoor Adventures

Camping. Cedar Creek State Park has a 48-unit, brookside campground for tents and RVs, with a pool, playground, miniature golf course, and staff-run recreational educational programs; Route 1, Box 9, Glenville; (304) 462-7158. Holly River State Park has an 88-site campground with electric hookups, picnic tables, and cooking grills at each site, plus nine cabins; Route 20, Hacker Valley; (304) 493-6353.

Hiking. Mountwood Park, Holly River State Park, Summersville Lake Wildlife Management Area, and North Bend Rail Trail (see The Best Beaches and Parks, above).

Mountain Biking. Charles Fork Lake, near the town of Spencer, features mountain biking trails on 2,000 acres of lakeside land; Roane County Chamber of Commerce, 273 East Main Street, Spencer; (304) 927-1780.

Water Sports. Sarge's Dive Shop at Summersville Lake offers diving and snorkeling lessons and jet ski rentals; Summersville Lake, Summersville; (304) 872-1782 or (304) 872-0015.

Family Lodging

Comfort Inn Summersville

One of several chains in this resort area, this one offers a pool, wading pool, and free breakfast. Rates: $51–119. 903 Industrial Drive, Summersville; (304) 872-6500.

Note: In Summersville, other acceptable chain motels equipped with swimming pools are the Hampton Inn (phone (304) 872-7100) and the Sleep Inn (phone (304) 872-4500).

Comfort Inn Weston

A comfortable motel with a pool and on-site restaurant. Rates: $59–69. Route 33 East, P.O. Box 666, Weston; (304) 269-7000.

The Historic Blennerhassett Hotel

A beautifully restored, 104-room hotel in the heart of town. Although it has no pool, it does offer nearby health club privileges and a complimentary full breakfast. Rates: $69–95; children age 18 and under stay free. 4th and Market Streets, Parkersburg; (800) 262-2536 or (304) 422-3131.

North Bend Lodge

This 29-room lodge in North Bend State Park (see West Virginia's State Park Resorts) is accompanied by eight deluxe vacation cottages. Located about 35 miles east of Parkersburg, the property has, in addition to the state park trails and facilities, a swimming pool, a playground, tennis and volleyball courts, and an on-site restaurant. Rates: lodge $53–59, cabins $520–595 per week; children age 12 and under stay free. North Bend State Park, Route 1, Box 221, Cairo; (304) 643-2931.

The Wilderness Plantation Inn

This 39-room roadside motel has a convenience store, a heated pool, and a restaurant (see Family-Friendly Restaurants, below). Some rooms have water beds and whirlpool baths. Rates: $52–63. Off I-79, Exit 105, P.O. Box 1278, Jane Lew; (800) 716-6835 or (304) 884-7806.

Attractions

Blennerhassett Historical State Park

137 Juliana Street, Parkersburg; (304) 420-4800

Hours: May–Labor Day, Tuesday–Saturday 10 a.m.–5 p.m., Sunday noon–5 p.m.; Labor Day–October, Thursday–Saturday 10 a.m.–4:30 p.m., Sunday noon–4:30 p.m.; downtown museum open year-round with the same hours

Admission: Free

Appeal by Age Groups:

Pre-school	Grade School	Teens	Young Adults	Over 30	Seniors
★★★	★★★★	★★★★	★★★★★	★★★★★	★★★★★

Touring Time: Average 3 hours, minimum 2 hours

Rainy-Day Touring: Yes

Services and Facilities:

Restaurants Yes	Baby stroller rental No
Alcoholic beverages No	Lockers No
Disabled access Yes; except man-	Pet kennels No
sion second floor	Rain check No
Wheelchair rental Yes; free	Private tours No

Description and Comments Aaron Burr, although some find it hard to believe, was a U.S. vice president who plotted to turn the Southwest into his own personal independent empire. He allegedly did the planning right here with his cohort Harman Blennerhassett. The Blennerhassett mansion is this island park's centerpiece. Guided tours of the mansion are offered, but there's much else to do here. First, you arrive on sternwheeler boats that depart from Parkersburg's Point Park. The island is a great spot to rent a bike for an easy ride. Horse-drawn wagon rides are also offered, and crafts demonstrations are presented in the crafts village. You should couple an island visit with a stop at the Blennerhassett Museum (in town at Second and Juliana Streets), after which you'll have a pretty good handle on local history.

Fenton Art Glass Factory Tours and Glass Museum

700 Elizabeth Street, Williamstown; (304) 375-7772; www.fenton-glass.com

Hours: Monday–Friday 8 a.m.–4:50 p.m.; closed on national holidays and during the annual two-week factory vacation from late June to early July

Admission: Free

Appeal by Age Groups:

Pre-school	Grade School	Teens	Young Adults	Over 30	Seniors
★	★★★	★★★★	★★★★★	★★★★★	★★★★★

Touring Time: Average 2 hours, minimum 1 hour

Rainy-Day Touring: Yes

Services and Facilities:

Restaurants No	Baby stroller rental No
Alcoholic beverages No	Lockers No
Disabled access Yes; except hand decorating section	Pet kennels No
	Rain check No
Wheelchair rental Yes; free	Private tours No

Description and Comments Glass was first produced here in 1905, and over the years the product has gained an international reputation for quality and beauty. This is the country's largest factory producing handmade glass, and the 45-minute tour shows how master craftsmen have been creating glass for centuries. As with most glass production demonstrations, it's simply fascinating to watch. What you see on any given tour depends on what's being produced at the time. The wide variety of work produced since 1880 by the company and other regional glass artisans is displayed at the adjacent museum. An introductory film sets the scene nicely. *Note:* Children age 2 and under are not permitted on the tour.

Stonewall Jackson Lake State Park Dam Tour

Route 1, Box 0, Roanoke; park, (304) 269-0523; dam tour, (304) 269-4588

Hours: By appointment

Admission: Free

Appeal by Age Groups:

Pre-school	Grade School	Teens	Young Adults	Over 30	Seniors
★	★★★★★	★★★★★	★★★★★	★★★★★	★★★★★

Touring Time: 1 hour

Rainy-Day Touring: Yes

Services and Facilities:

Restaurants No	Baby stroller rental No
Alcoholic beverages No	Lockers No
Disabled access Yes, park; no, dam tour	Pet kennels No
	Rain check No
Wheelchair rental No	Private tours Yes

Description and Comments   The state's newest park boasts its lake as the central attraction. The dam, however, is what causes the lake to be here, and the tour is a fascinating chance to explore the dam's innards. Offered year-round, tours start at the bottom—some 75 feet under water—and range all the way to the top service bridge where you can view the lake on one side and the out-flowing water on the other. The ranger/guide explains the dam's history, its benefits (largely recreational), and how it works. Call at least a week ahead to book your tour.

As for the lake formed by the dam, it offers an array of water activities. The park operates a large marina where you can rent boats—pontoon, v-bottom, and even houseboats—and obtain bait. A disabled accessible fishing pier is also available. Other facilities include a fitness trail, picnic areas, hiking trails, and a new campground. An 18,000-acre wildlife management area abuts the park, so animal-watching can be terrific. Cabins, a 200-room lodge, a golf course, and a swimming pool are scheduled to open here in spring 2002.

West Virginia State Wildlife Center

Route 20, P.O. Box 38, French Creek; (304) 924-6211 or
   (304) 924-5370

Hours: May–September, daily 9 a.m.–6 p.m.; October–April, daily 9 a.m.–4:30 p.m.

Admission: $2 adults, $1 children ages 3–15; children age 3 and under, free

Appeal by Age Groups:

Pre-school	Grade School	Teens	Young Adults	Over 30	Seniors
★★★	★★★★★	★★★★	★★★★	★★★★★	★★★★★

Touring Time: Average 3 hours, minimum 2 hours

Rainy-Day Touring: Yes

Services and Facilities:

Restaurants Yes	Lockers No
Alcoholic beverages No	Pet kennels No
Disabled access Yes	Rain check No
Wheelchair rental Yes; free	Private tours No
Baby stroller rental Yes; free	

Description and Comments   A nifty little place that offers exhibits and a chance to see deer, elk, bears, buffaloes, mountain lions, bobcats, foxes, bald eagles, wild boars, and river otters in a natural woodland habitat. A great place for a picnic, too.

Family-Friendly Restaurants

CALAMITY JANE'S STEAKHOUSE AT SYCAMORE CREEK

Route 1, Box 427, Ripley; (304) 372-1800

Meals served: Lunch and dinner
Cuisine: American
Entree range: $4–19.95 (lunch and dinner)
Children's menu: No
Reservations: Yes
Payment: Major credit cards

Casual dining in a golf course setting not far from Cedar Lakes Crafts Center.

POINT OF VIEW RESTAURANT

Blennerhassett Heights Road, Parkersburg; (304) 863-3366

Meals served: Lunch and dinner
Cuisine: Prime rib, steak, and seafood
Entree range: $4–22 (lunch and dinner)
Children's menu: Yes
Reservations: Yes
Payment: Major credit cards

An excellent, family-owned restaurant in a wonderful setting—overlooking Blennerhassett Island and the Ohio River. The food is good, the service excellent, the baked goods homemade, and the folks friendly.

THE WILDERNESS PLANTATION INN

Off I-79, Exit 105, Jane Lew; (304) 884-7095

Meals served: Breakfast, lunch, and dinner
Cuisine: American
Entree range: $7.99–15.99 (dinner)
Children's menu: Yes
Reservations: No
Payment: Major credit cards

Part of the motel complex (see Family Lodging, above), this eatery serves all-American food at reasonable prices, including around-the-clock breakfast.

THE WOODLAND STATION AT NORTH BEND STATE PARK

Route 1, Box 221, Cairo; (304) 643-2931

Meals served: Breakfast, lunch, and dinner
Cuisine: American
Entree range: $3.95–10.95
Children's menu: Yes
Reservations: Yes
Payment: V, MC, AE, DC

Dine in a country atmosphere with oak furniture. Three sides of the restaurant are glass, and it's always a kick to watch the wildlife wander by. They prepare an excellent West Virginia trout, plus steaks, pasta, and burgers. The all-you-can-eat Sunday buffet is very popular.

Southern West Virginia

If the Potomac Highlands features West Virginia's mountains at their finest, the southern reaches of the state showcase its most beautiful river setting. The New River Gorge is nothing short of spectacular, and the recreation it spawns—white-water rafting, hiking, mountain biking, rock climbing, fishing—is as good as it gets. And the Metro Valley is home to two vibrant cities. Moving west to east, **Huntington** is a college town (Marshall University) with a long history as a glassmaking center. The **Heritage Farm and Village Museum** (call (304) 697-8764) offers a look at early American life through restored log buildings and its collection of antique machines, cars, and tools, plus a nifty general store. The **Jewel City Sternwheeler** (call (304) 453-5544) hearkens back to paddlewheel days for cruises on the Ohio River. The **Museum of Radio and Technology** (call (304) 525-8890) displays thousands of artifacts covering the history of radio. Moving east, the town of **Barboursville** offers a vibrant **Historic District Walking Tour** comprised of 36 nineteenth-century buildings and an old cemetery. The **Blenko Glass Visitor Center and Factory Outlet** (call (304) 743-9081), famous for hand-blown glassware and stained glass, is found in Milton and features glassblowers in action. The **Blenko Historical Museum** is also on premises. In **Hurricane,** more history is revealed through **Hurricane's Historic Homes** (call (304) 562-5896) and historic murals displayed on Main Street. The **Museum in the Community** (call (304) 562-0484) features innovative, hands-on exhibitions. In **Dunbar, Dunbar Wine Cellar Park** (call (304) 766-0223) features wine cellars built in the 1850s.

Charleston is the state capital, and the **Capitol Building** (call (304) 558-3809) itself is quite remarkable (see Attractions), its dome standing taller than the U.S. Capitol. The complex also includes the Governor's Mansion, the Cultural Center, the West Virginia State Museum, and **Mountain Stage** (call (304) 558-3000), a National Public Radio show

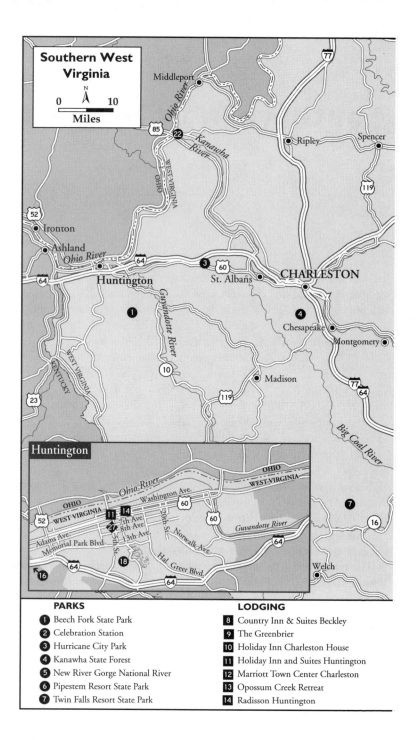

Southern West Virginia

0 — 10 Miles

N

Middleport

Ohio River

Kanawha River

Ripley

Spencer

Ironton

Ashland

Ohio River

Huntington

St. Albans

CHARLESTON

Guyandotte River

Chesapeake

Montgomery

Madison

Big Coal River

KENTUCKY

WEST VIRGINIA

Huntington

Ohio River

OHIO

WEST VIRGINIA

Washington Ave.

7th Ave.
8th Ave.
13th Ave.

Adams Ave.

Memorial Park Blvd.

Norwalk Ave.

Hal Greer Blvd.

Guyandotte River

Welch

PARKS

1 Beech Fork State Park
2 Celebration Station
3 Hurricane City Park
4 Kanawha State Forest
5 New River Gorge National River
6 Pipestem Resort State Park
7 Twin Falls Resort State Park

LODGING

8 Country Inn & Suites Beckley
9 The Greenbrier
10 Holiday Inn Charleston House
11 Holiday Inn and Suites Huntington
12 Marriott Town Center Charleston
13 Opossum Creek Retreat
14 Radisson Huntington

440

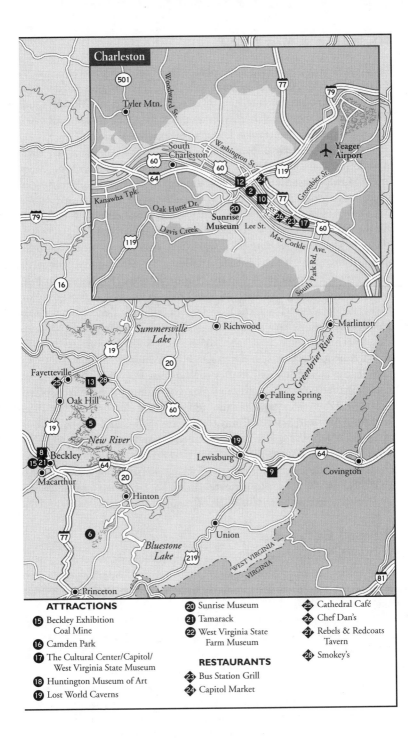

ATTRACTIONS

15 Beckley Exhibition
Coal Mine

16 Camden Park

17 The Cultural Center/Capitol/
West Virginia State Museum

18 Huntington Museum of Art

19 Lost World Caverns

20 Sunrise Museum

21 Tamarack

22 West Virginia State
Farm Museum

RESTAURANTS

23 Bus Station Grill

24 Capitol Market

25 Cathedral Café

26 Chef Dan's

27 Rebels & Redcoats
Tavern

28 Smokey's

heard nationwide, featuring jazz, folk, blues, rock, and classical music. Be sure to stop at the **Capitol Market** (call (304) 344-1905), a huge indoor-outdoor bazaar with much to look at and, of course, to eat. Moving south, **Williamson,** along the Kentucky border, has the **Coal House** (call (304) 235-5240), which is constructed entirely of locally mined coal.

The **New River–Greenbrier Valley** region features some of the state's most scenic spots. Following U.S. 60 east out of Charleston soon brings you to **Hawks Nest State Park Museum** (call (304) 658-5212) in **Ansted,** where early pioneer days, the Civil War, and Native Americans are featured, as is a spectacular view of the New River Gorge. **Grandview,** near **Beckley,** has the **Outdoor Dramas at Grandview** (call (800) 666-9142 or (304) 256-6800), where *The Hatfields and McCoys, Honey in the Rock,* and other offerings are staged at the Cliffside Amphitheater. Moving south along the New River to **Hinton,** you'll find the **Hinton Railroad Museum and John Henry Woodcarving Exhibit** (call (304) 466-5420), which displays rolling stock, railroad artifacts, and the tools used to build Big Bend Tunnel, site of the legendary John Henry's race with a steam drill. The **Bluestone Museum** (call (304) 466-1454 or (304) 466-3596) exhibits mounted wildlife, Native American artifacts, and rocks and fossils from the region. Southern-most in the area, **Bluefield** houses the **Eastern Regional Coal Archives** (call (304) 325-3943), where the state's coal mining history is displayed through exhibits, photographs, mining implements, and films. The **Bluefield Area Arts and Science Center** (call (304) 325-8000) displays a visual arts gallery and houses a science center, restaurant, and theater, while the **Science Center of West Virginia** (call (304) 325-8855) is the state's first hands-on science museum. At the region's far western side is **Organ Cave** (call (304) 645-7600) in **Ronceverte,** said to be among the longest caves in the United States with 40-plus miles of mapped passageways.

How to Get There

By Car. The Metro Valley, on the state's southeastern side, is cut east-west by I-64, which runs from Huntington in the west to Charleston, about two-thirds of the way to the east. From there, I-64/77 (the West Virginia Turn-pike) moves southeast to Montgomery, while I-79 travels northeast and I-77 due north. Also from the Charleston area, U.S. 35 wanders to the northwest part of the region, and U.S. 119 travels southwest. U.S. 52 follows the Kentucky border on the southwestern side of the region. I-64/77 continues south through the center of the New River–Greenbrier Valley region; at about the midpoint, just south of Beckley, I-64 turns due east, bisecting the region en route to White Sulphur Springs at the Virginia line. U.S. 52 continues south along the area's western edge. In the north, access to the New River Gorge National River is found along U.S. 60, which parallels the river and I-64/77.

By Plane. Charleston/Yeager Airport is served by USAirways, US Air Express, United Express, Atlantic Southeast, Comair, Northwest Airlink, and Continental airlines; 100 Airport Road, Charleston, WV 25311; (304) 344-8033.

Beckley/Raleigh County Memorial Airport, a small facility, is served by US Air Express Commuter and offers rental car services; 469 Airport Circle, Beaver, WV 25813; (304) 255-4076.

Lewisburg/Greenbrier Valley Airport is served by US Air Express Commuter and, in summer, by USAirways, with major rental car companies available; U.S. 219 North, P.O. Box 329, Lewisburg, WV 24901; (304) 645-2211.

By Train. Amtrak operates regular service through Huntington, Charleston, and White Sulphur Springs; (800) 872-7245.

How to Get Information before You Go

Southern West Virginia Convention and Visitors Bureau,   P.O. Box 1799, Beckley, WV 25802; (800) 847-4898 or (304) 252-2244; www.visitwv.com or www.visitwv.org.

Charleston Convention & Visitors Bureau,   200 Civic Center Drive, Charleston, WV 25301; (800) 733-5469 or (304) 344-5075; www.charlestonwv.com.

Cabell-Huntington Convention & Visitor Bureau,   739 Third Avenue, P.O. Box 347, Huntington, WV 25708; (800) 635-6329 or (304) 525-7333.

The Best Parks

Beech Fork State Park. Camping and fishing are the prime attractions at this 3,981-acre park just south of Huntington. The park features 275 campsites, hiking trails, picnicking, game courts, and a seasonal naturalist program. Some 10,000 acres of public land are adjacent. 5601 Long Branch Road, Barboursville; (304) 522-0303.

Celebration Station. A Robert Leathers public playground at Piedmont Elementary School, all constructed of fabricated wood, with forts, tire swings, tunnels, and a blacktop map of the world; Quarrier Street, Charleston; (304) 348-1910.

Hurricane City Park. A perfect place to take a break and picnic, this nifty town park has a super playground, a fitness trail, sports fields and courts, and fishing from disabled accessible docks. Route 34, Hurricane; (304) 562-5896.

Kanawha State Forest. Its proximity to Charleston makes this 9,302-acre forest one of the state's busiest. Camping, swimming, hiking, cross-country skiing, horseback riding, picnicking, playgrounds, fishing, and hunting are featured. Route 2, Box 285, Charleston; (304) 558-3500.

Pipestem Resort State Park. (See also West Virginia's State Park Resorts.) Set in the south-central part of the New River–Greenbrier Valley region, the park is 14 miles north of Princeton on WV 20. Hiking and equestrian trails, swimming, lighted tennis courts, mini-golf, fishing, paddle boating, and 18-hole and 9-hole golf courses are offered. Box 150, Pipestem; (304)466-1800.

Twin Falls Resort State Park. (See also West Virginia's State Park Resorts.) Located southwest of Beckley off WV 16, this park has hiking trails, picnic grounds, a 50-site campground, a nature center, and a swimming pool/playground/game court complex. P.O. Box 1023, Mullens; (304) 294-4000.

New River Gorge National River

Visitors Centers   The New River, contrary to its name, is one of the world's oldest waterways. Here it passes through a gorge to create truly magnificent scenery. The National River, a unique national park, presents myriad opportunities to see and experience the gorge and surrounding landscape. A man-made highlight is the New River Gorge Bridge, a remarkable and beautiful span touted to be the world's longest steel arch. Four park visitors centers offer exhibits, audio-visual presentations, and printed materials to interpret the area's history and attractions. From north to south, they are: Canyon Rim Visitors Center, Thurmond Depot Visitors Center, Grandview Visitors Center, and Hinton Visitors Center.

At Canyon Rim Visitors Center, you can immediately admire the scenery from the adjoining boardwalk. Two videos are shown—one covers the construction of the New River Gorge Bridge, and the second tells how the gorge was formed. From the center's rear deck, a two-mile view of the gorge and bridge is revealed. A boardwalk descends into the gorge, yielding unobstructed views of the mile-wide canyon and bridge. The center offers organized programs year-round, including ranger-guided bus tours in summer, slide shows, and a variety of guided walks and hikes. All the visitors centers are open Labor Day–Memorial Day, daily 9 a.m.–5 p.m.; and Memorial Day–Labor Day, daily 9 a.m.–8 p.m. The Canyon Rim Visitors Center is on US 19, just north of Fayetteville; (304) 574-2115.

Hiking   While you can mountain bike and rock climb in the park, the two most popular activities are hiking and white-water rafting. Hiking trails are found throughout the park, ranging from a quarter mile to seven miles long, with all degrees of difficulty. Some trails link to others to create long treks. Trail maps can be obtained at all visitors centers. Some good walks for casual hiking families include:

Canyon Rim Boardwalk at Canyon Rim Visitors Center; a 20-minute round trip descends into the gorge, with overlooks for great views.

Canyon Rim Trail from Grandview Visitors Center; this 3.2-mile round-trip hike offers marvelous viewpoints.

Grandview Trails; a series of five trails from Grandview Visitors Center that ranges from three-eighths of a mile to two miles, offering terrific views and some fascinating geology.

Commercial White-Water Rafting This is counted among North America's most active and best white-water rafting sites, and anyone who comes here really ought to experience at least a day's outing. Trips on the New River are available almost year-round, some of which are limited to gentle ripples in Class II rapids. The Gauley River features "big water" that may intimidate some, but it yields thrills so fine you'll come back for more. The main season is early September–mid-October. A number of licensed outfitters offer guided trips. We recommend these three:

Class VI River Runners. Class VI is the rating for the biggest white-water, and these guys earn the highest ratings for running a tight, safe ship with trips for everyone. They say that 80 percent of the National River section of the New River is perfect for families and those desiring a mild introduction to white-water. One-day and unique multiday family trips are offered, the latter with riverside overnight camping and amazingly wonderful food prepared by the guides. Lodging packages with Opossum Creek Retreat and the Country Inn & Suites (see Family Lodging) are available. Box 78, Lansing; (800) 252-7784 or (304) 574-0704; www.raftwv.com.

North American River Runners. Another top-notch outfitter who runs what they call "Family Class" trips, five- to seven-hour runs through Class I and II rapids with a stop for a gourmet riverside lunch; for ages five and older. They offer on-site camping and cabin tents; the latter are outfitted with bedding and linen service and built-in decks with grills. U.S. 60, Hico; (800) 950-2585; www.narr.com.

Appalachian Wild Waters. They offer three- to five-day "Mini Family Vacations," a complete package of lodging, adventure, and evening activities. Included are sight-seeing at Beckley Exhibition Coal Mine Tour and other sites, plus rafting and various activities. They offer regular on-site camping and platform tent camping with continental breakfast. Route 19, Rowlesburg; 800.624.8060; www.awrafts.com.

Other Activities   Mountain State Rails to Rivers and Trails Train travels the river one-way by train, then brings the river up-close and personal, accompanied by outfitters, in the mode of your choice—skiing, white-water rafting, hiking, mountain biking, or horseback riding. Huntington and Charleston; (800) 347-1231 or (304) 529-6412. New River Jet Boats offers a chance to travel the river in a fast, furious, and fun way without paddling. Hawks Nest State Park, P.O. Box 857, Ansted; (304) 469-2525 or (304) 658-5212.

Family Outdoor Adventures

Camping. 8,123-acre southwestern Cabwaylingo State Forest offers rental cabins, camping, and a group camp. Recreational facilities include swimming, hunting, hiking, picnicking, and a play area. Route 1, Box 85, Dunlow; (304) 385-4255.

Hiking. The Kanawha Trace is a 32-mile foot trail stretching from Barboursville at the confluence of the Mud and Guyandotte Rivers to Fraziers Bottom on the Kanawha River; a guidebook is available; Huntington; (304) 523-3408. Sandstone Falls sets nine miles north of Hinton on New River Road and is accessible by a river walk. It is the largest waterfall on the New River Gorge National River, spanning the river at 1,500 feet wide with a 25-foot drop. Huntington; (304) 523-3408.

Horseback Riding. Glade Springs Resort, located six miles south of Beckley on Route 19, houses a full-service equestrian center and offers trail rides and lessons on 4,100 acres of land; 200 Lake Drive, Daniels; (800) 634-5233 or (304) 763-2000; www.gladesprings.com.

Paddling. Coal River Livery leads day and overnight trips for fishing, camping, and canoeing; Route 119, Alum Creek; (800) 226-6311 or (304) 756-9608.

Skiing. Winterplace Ski Resort offers skiing and snowboarding on 27 trails served by nine lifts with full snow-making, rentals, a ski school, and a snow-tubing park; slope-side restaurants and lodging are available; Route 19, Flat Top; (800) 977-3754 or (304) 787-3221; www.winterplace.com.

Family Lodging

Country Inn & Suites Beckley

A new and pleasant 157-suite hotel with a heated pool, in-room coffee, free breakfast, and a video game room. It's conveniently located within easy driving distance of the New River Gorge National River and all its activities. Rates: $75–85. 2120 Harper Road, Beckley; (800) 456-4000 or (304) 252-5100.

The Greenbrier

This first-class, upscale resort hotel is ranked among the best in the country by major travel magazines. 650 accommodations include 121 guesthouses and 33 suites. All stays include a full breakfast and dinner daily. It's not cheap, but it's terrific. (See also Attractions.) Rates: $192–298 per person; children age 17 and under stay, eat, and enroll in programs free. 340 West Main Street, White Sulphur Springs; (304) 536-1110 or (800) 624-6070; www.greenbrier.com.

Holiday Inn Charleston House

A 256-room high-rise hotel with a pool, exercise facilities, a restaurant, and great river views. This provides an excellent base for the annual Sternwheel Regatta. Rates: $99–109 with weekend packages available; children age 18 and under stay free. 600 Kanawha Boulevard East, Charleston; (304) 344-4092.

Holiday Inn Hotel and Suites Huntington

A major hotel right in the heart of town with all amenities. Rates: $89–95. 800 Third Avenue, Huntington; (304) 523-8880.

Marriott Town Center Charleston

This full-service downtown hotel features a heated pool, a fitness center, a game room, and an on-site restaurant. It's convenient to in-town attractions. Rates: $89–140; children age 18 and under stay free. 200 Lee Street East, Charleston; (304) 344-4092.

Opossum Creek Retreat

Located just five minutes from the National River and Class VI River Rafters and other outfitters, these delightful, secluded cottages enjoy a wooded setting and offer hot tubs, fully equipped kitchens, and air-conditioning. The two newest cabins have a unique soft wall between the cabin and the screened porch that can be raised one panel at a time to let in as much or as little light and air as desired. Rates: $90–120 for two people for cottages sleeping four to six; $180 for four people for houses sleeping up to 20; $25 per night per extra person; children age 12 and under (one per adult) stay free. Route 219, P.O. Box 221, Lansing; (888) 488-4836 or (304) 574-4836; www.opossumcreek.com.

Radisson Huntington

A comfortable hotel with a full health club, outdoor pool, on-site restaurant, and complimentary transportation to city attractions. Rates: $88–119. 1001 Third Avenue, Huntington; (304) 525-1001.

Attractions

Beckley Exhibition Coal Mine

New River Park, Drawer AJ, Beckley; (304) 256-1747;
   www.vweb.com/www/exhibition_coal_mine

Hours: April 1–November 1, daily 10 a.m.–5:30 p.m.

Admission: $8 adults, $7 seniors 55+, $5 children ages 4–12

Appeal by Age Groups:

Pre-school	Grade School	Teens	Young Adults	Over 30	Seniors
★★★★	★★★★★	★★★★★	★★★★★	★★★★★	★★★★★

Touring Time: Average 2 hours, minimum 1 hour

Rainy-Day Touring: Yes

Services and Facilities:

Restaurants No	Lockers No
Alcoholic beverages No	Pet kennels No
Disabled access Yes	Rain check No
Wheelchair rental No	Private tours No
Baby stroller rental No	

Description and Comments   Set in Beckley's New River Park, the highlight here is a guided, 35-minute underground tour. Veteran coal miners take you through and show you how mining was—and is—done, from the early, labor-intensive, manual techniques to modern machinery. Above ground, the three-room coal miner's house and coal camp beautifully illustrate life in a company town circa 1925 or so, when the camps supplied all life's necessities from goods at the company store to doctors and churches. You'll also see a three-story structure that was constructed for the mine superintendent and his family that, oddly, resembles a small English mansion. The Coal Life Exhibit further illustrates life in the mines. This is one of the Mid-Atlantic's better coal mining tourist sites.

Camden Park

Route 60 East, Huntington; (304) 429-4321;
   www.camdenpark.com

Hours: Open early May to mid-October; days and hours vary by date

Admission: $12.95 adults, $8.95 seniors and children 48 inches and
   shorter; children age 2 or under, free; on Fridays, $6 after 6 p.m.

Appeal by Age Groups:

Pre-school	Grade School	Teens	Young Adults	Over 30	Seniors
★★★★★	★★★★★	★★★★★	★★★★★	★★★★★	★★★★★

Touring Time: Average 6 hours, minimum 4 hours
Rainy-Day Touring: Yes
Services and Facilities:

Restaurants Yes	Lockers No
Alcoholic beverages No	Pet kennels No
Disabled access Yes	Rain check No
Wheelchair rental No	Private tours No
Baby stroller rental Yes; free	

Description and Comments This good-old-fashioned amusement park opened in 1903. Today it features some of the old and some of the new, and an altogether pleasant day for those who go for this sort of thing. The park holds 25 rides, including 3 roller coasters. There's a kiddieland, haunted house, games, food stands, a cafeteria, miniature golf, picnic grounds, and an authentic Native American burial mound. Take your kids on the old reliables you remember from childhood—Dodge 'Em Cars, The Whip, and The Big Dipper, a classic wooden coaster. For the less daring, stick to the frontier train ride.

The Jewel City Sternwheeler, a 149-passenger vessel, leaves from the park for hour-long narrated tours on the Ohio River. Admission: $4 adults, $3 children.

The Cultural Center/Capitol Complex/ West Virginia State Museum

Greenbrier Street, Charleston; (304) 558-0220

Hours: Monday–Friday 9 a.m.–5 p.m., Sunday 1–5 p.m.

Admission: Free

Appeal by Age Groups:

Pre-school	Grade School	Teens	Young Adults	Over 30	Seniors
★★	★★★	★★★★	★★★★★	★★★★★	★★★★★

Touring Time: Average 2 hours, minimum 1 hour
Rainy-Day Touring: Yes
Services and Facilities:

Restaurants Yes	Lockers No
Alcoholic beverages Yes	Pet kennels No
Disabled access Yes	Rain check No
Wheelchair rental No	Private tours No
Baby stroller rental No	

Description and Comments The West Virginia State Capitol was built in the Italian Renaissance style, and it has an incredible 293-foot, gold leaf dome that boasts, within the rotunda, an even more incredible two-ton chandelier comprised of 10,080 pieces of Czechoslovakian crystal. Gawking is permitted. Twenty-minute tours are offered, highlighting the building's basic features—rotunda, house and senate chambers, etc. Also housed in the complex are the State Museum, a craft shop, and a theater at which West Virginia Public Radio's nationally known Sunday program *Mountain Stage* is performed. If you're timing's right, make it a point to attend. How often do you get to see national radio done live? The museum focuses on state history, as well as changing exhibits of West Virginian artists in the Museum Gallery.

The Greenbrier

340 West Main Street, White Sulphur Springs; (800) 624-6070 or
  (304) 536-1110; www.greenbrier.com

Hours: Vary by activity and season

Admission: Varies by activity and season

Appeal by Age Groups:

Pre-school	Grade School	Teens	Young Adults	Over 30	Seniors
★★★★★	★★★★★	★★★★★	★★★★★	★★★★★	★★★★★

Touring Time: Average 2–3 days, minimum 1 day

Rainy-Day Touring: Yes

Services and Facilities:

Restaurants Yes	Lockers Yes
Alcoholic beverages Yes	Pet kennels No
Disabled access Yes	Rain check No
Wheelchair rental Yes; free	Private tours No
Baby stroller rental No	

Description and Comments   This is, plain and simple, one of the country's premier resorts. It's self-contained and simply world-class. It all began when folks came to town for the healing sulphur springs, starting back in 1778. Today, of course, the Greenbrier's spa (still utilizing the sulphur water) is a feature attraction. But, you can play golf or tennis, shop, swim, or indulge in myriad activities of every stripe. The kids programs are top-notch. "Brier Bunch" offers supervised activities for ages three to five; "T'Weeners" caters to ages six to nine; "Clubbers" serves ages ten to twelve; and for those ornery teens, special sports schools are offered in golf or tennis. In summer, the resort also runs children's cooking classes on Wednesdays, Fridays, and Saturdays, for an extra fee. And babysitting is always available for parents who prefer it. There are multiple restaurants in which to dine, and all stays are predicated on a Modified American Plan basis with breakfast and dinner included (see Family Lodging). The Greenbrier is not inexpensive, but for quality its value is unmatched.

Huntington Museum of Art

2033 McCoy Road, Huntington; (304) 529-2701

Hours: Wednesday–Saturday 10 a.m.–5 p.m., Tuesday 10 a.m.–9 p.m., and Sunday noon–5 p.m.; closed Monday

Admission: Donation

Appeal by Age Groups:

Pre-school	Grade School	Teens	Young Adults	Over 30	Seniors
★★★	★★★★	★★★★	★★★★★	★★★★★	★★★★★

Touring Time: Average 2 hours, minimum 1 hour

Rainy-Day Touring: Yes

Services and Facilities:

Restaurants Yes	Lockers No
Alcoholic beverages No	Pet kennels No
Disabled access Yes	Rain check No
Wheelchair rental Yes; free	Private tours Yes; call ahead
Baby stroller rental No	

Description and Comments   This is West Virginia's largest professionally accredited art museum. It features both permanent and changing exhibits, plus an Education Gallery. Performances and concerts are offered in its theater and amphitheater. The outdoor features comprise really welcome highlights: the sculpture garden offers kids a chance to see art in a less austere setting; the 2.5-mile annotated nature trail encourages exploration; and the state's only plant conservatory exhibits Ma Nature's own artwork. The museum offers a free "KidsArt" program on summer Saturday afternoons for kindergartners to fifth graders in which working artists and teachers engage the kids in various forms of expression, using the works in the museum to stimulate the kids' own art. Very cool for those whose timing is right for the occasion.

Lost World Caverns

Route 6 Box 308, Lewisburg; (304) 645-6677

Hours: Memorial Day–Labor Day, daily 9 a.m.–7 p.m.; Labor Day–Halloween, 9 a.m.–5 p.m.; Halloween–Memorial Day, 10 a.m.–4 p.m.

Admission: $8 adults, $4 children ages 6–12; children 5 and under, free

Appeal by Age Groups:

Pre-school	Grade School	Teens	Young Adults	Over 30	Seniors
★★★	★★★★★	★★★★★	★★★★★	★★★★★	★★★★★

Touring Time: Average 1½ hours, minimum 1 hour

Rainy-Day Touring: Yes

Services and Facilities:

Restaurants No	Lockers No
Alcoholic beverages No	Pet kennels No
Disabled access No	Rain check No
Wheelchair rental No	Private tours No
Baby stroller rental No	

Description and Comments   Another of West Virginia's worthwhile underground experiences. The self-guided walking tour requires about 35 minutes. The primary features are the pedestal-like stalagmites, waterfalls, hex stone formations, and a main chamber that measures 1,000 feet long and 75 feet wide. Check out the column they call Goliath, which stands 40 feet tall and measures 25 feet around. The waterfalls are most active in spring due to snowmelt and spring rains. And the Snowy Chandelier, a compound stalactite, is thought to be one of the world's best displays of pure white calcite. Caves are endlessly fascinating, and this one's certainly worth a look. "Wild tours," requiring hard hats, knee pads, gloves, and flashlights (all provided), are offered to the hearty who would like to explore beyond the tourist area; they require four hours and are recommended for guests age nine and up; cost is $45 per person for groups of two to ten.

Sunrise Museum

746 Myrtle Road, Charleston; (304) 344-8035;
   www.sunrisemuseum.org

Hours: Wednesday–Saturday 11 a.m.–5 p.m., Sunday noon–5 p.m.

Admission: $3.50 adults, $2.50 seniors 54+ and students; children under age 3, free

Appeal by Age Groups:

Pre-school	Grade School	Teens	Young Adults	Over 30	Seniors
★★★	★★★★	★★★★	★★★★★	★★★★★	★★★★★

Touring Time: Average 2 hours, minimum 1 hour

Rainy-Day Touring: Yes

Services and Facilities:

Restaurants No	Baby stroller rental No
Alcoholic beverages No	Lockers No
Disabled access Yes; partial in science hall	Pet kennels No
	Rain check No
Wheelchair rental Yes; free	Private tours No

Description and Comments   Another museum that combines indoor and outdoor activities. Set in two historic mansions, the indoor facilities include art galleries, a science museum, and a planetarium. Outside, you should explore the 16-acre gardens and nature trails.

Tamarack

I-77 Exit 45, Beckley; (888) 262-7225 or (304) 256-6843; www.tamarackwv.com

Hours: January–March, daily 8 a.m.–7 p.m.; April–December, daily 8 a.m.–8 p.m.; closed Christmas Day

Admission: Free

Appeal by Age Groups:

Pre-school	Grade School	Teens	Young Adults	Over 30	Seniors
★★★	★★★★	★★★★	★★★★★	★★★★★	★★★★★

Touring Time: Average 2 hours, minimum 1 hour

Rainy-Day Touring: Yes

Services and Facilities:

Restaurants Yes	Lockers No
Alcoholic beverages Yes	Pet kennels No
Disabled access Yes	Rain check No
Wheelchair rental No	Private tours No
Baby stroller rental No	

Description and Comments   In truth, what we have here is a kind of shopping mall. But, it has been created to showcase the state's culture, history, and cuisine. You can look at and buy a boatload of West Virginia–made crafts, arts, and agricultural products. Or you can drop into the restaurant and eat some of the goods. Watching the working artisans demonstrate their skills is always fun, and outside kids can let off steam in the sculpture garden, on the nature trail, or in the playground. Performances, films, and readings are often offered in the small indoor theater and outdoors at the festival park stage.

West Virginia State Farm Museum

Route 1, Box 479, Point Pleasant; (304) 675-5737

Hours: April 1 through the day before Thanksgiving, Tuesday–Saturday 9 a.m.–5 p.m. and Sunday 1–5 p.m.

Admission: Free

Appeal by Age Groups:

Pre-school	Grade School	Teens	Young Adults	Over 30	Seniors
★★★	★★★★★	★★★★	★★★★	★★★★★	★★★★★

Touring Time: Average 2 hours, minimum 1½ hours

Rainy-Day Touring: Yes

Services and Facilities:

Restaurants No	Lockers No
Alcoholic beverages No	Pet kennels No
Disabled access Yes	Rain check No
Wheelchair rental Yes; free	Private tours Yes
Baby stroller rental No	

Description and Comments This living history farm museum encompasses 31 reconstructed buildings, including a log cabin, church, country store, blacksmith shop, and schoolhouse. We like the antique farm implements (which include a tractor collection), the working blacksmith shop, and the old railroad cars. Guided tours are offered, and this is also a good place to bring a picnic.

Family-Friendly Restaurants

BLUESTONE DINING ROOM/MOUNTAIN CREEK DINING ROOM

Pipestem Resort State Park, Box 150, Pipestem; (304) 466-1800

Meals served: Breakfast, lunch, and dinner
Cuisine: American (plus theme nights)
Entree range: $3.95–11.95 (lunch and dinner)
Children's menu: Yes
Reservations: Yes
Payment: Major credit cards

This good state park resort dining hall combines home cooking and buffets with incredible canyon views. Theme nights can include seafood, Italian, and western. The Mountain Creek Dining Room is open only in summer and is reached only by aerial tram, adding a bit of adventure to the dining experience.

BUS STATION GRILL

1579 Quarrier Street, Charleston; (304) 343-2870

Meals served: Lunch and dinner
Cuisine: Seafood, pastas, steaks, chicken, salads, soups
Entree range: $12.95–22.50
Children's menu: Yes
Reservations: Yes; for eight or more
Payment: V, MC, AE

Dine in a pair of authentic London double-decker buses, on the outdoor patio, or indoors in the main dining area. They serve good food here— superb Maryland crab cakes, for example, and excellent soups and salads. But it's the buses that will tickle the kids' fancy.

CATHEDRAL CAFE

134 South Court Street, Fayetteville; (304) 574-0202

Meals served: Breakfast, lunch, and dinner
Cuisine: American
Entree range: $5–17
Children's menu: Yes
Reservations: No
Payment: Major credit cards except AE

Set in a converted church, this coffeehouse/cafe serves good, solid basic food. Before or after dining, browse at the adjacent bookstore or upstairs crafts shop.

CHEF DAN'S

222 Broad Street, Charleston; (304) 344-2433

Meals served: Lunch and dinner
Cuisine: Seafood and pasta
Entree range: $8–15.95 (dinner)
Children's menu: Yes
Reservations: Yes
Payment: Major credit cards

You'll find good seafood and pasta dishes done with a continental flair, plus a nice salad bar. A good value.

REBELS & REDCOATS TAVERN

412 Seventh Avenue, Huntington; (304) 523-8829

Meals served: Lunch and dinner
Cuisine: American
Entree range: $4.95–19.95 (lunch and dinner)
Children's menu: Yes
Reservations: Yes
Payment: Major credit cards

Good steaks, seafood, and pasta served in a colonial atmosphere. There's a bowling alley next door, but please dress neatly or, as they say, "dressy casual."

SMOKEY'S

Class VI River Runners, Box 78, Lansing; (800) 252-7784 or (304) 574-0704

Meals served: Breakfast and dinner
Cuisine: American
Entree range: Buffet: $16.95 adults; $8.95 kids
Children's menu: Yes
Reservations: Yes
Payment: Major credit cards

Smokey's is set in a timber frame structure with breathtaking views of the surrounding mountains and New River Gorge, but you don't have to be a Class VI white-water customer to dine here. The menu takes on something of an Appalachian twist with entrees of native game and a wild greens salad bar.

TWIN FALLS RESTAURANT

Twin Falls State Park, Bear Hole Road, Mullens; (304) 294-4000

Meals served: Breakfast, lunch, and dinner
Cuisine: American and regional
Entree range: $3.95–11.95 (lunch and dinner)
Children's menu: Yes
Reservations: Yes
Payment: Major credit cards

In the Twin Falls Lodge, this restaurant serves a full range of entrees and desserts. It's one of the good state park facilities.

Capitol Market

We love these old-fashioned markets, and particularly grazing our way through the various eating spots and food stands. Here, stop in for a sandwich at the Roasted Pepper, follow it up with desert at Ellen's Homemade Ice Cream, or grab a snack at the Pretzel Place. 800 Smith Street, Charleston; (304) 344-1905.

Index